HOW NEWARK
BECAME NEWARK

HOW NEWARK BECAME NEWARK

The Rise, Fall, and Rebirth of an American City

BRAD R. TUTTLE

RIVERGATE BOOKS

AN IMPRINT OF
RUTGERS UNIVERSITY PRESS
NEW BRUNSWICK, NEW JERSEY, AND LONDON

Second printing, 2011

Library of Congress Cataloging-in-Publication Data

Tuttle, Brad R.
How Newark became Newark : the rise, fall, and rebirth of an American city /
   Brad R. Tuttle.
        p.   cm.
   Includes bibliographical references and index.
   ISBN 978–0-8135–4490–8 (hardcover : alk. paper)
   1. Newark (N.J.)—History. 2. Newark (N.J.)—Social conditions. 3. Newark (N.J.)—
      Economic conditions. 4. Industrialization—New Jersey—Newark—History.
      5. Social change—New Jersey—Newark—History. 6. Urban renewal—
      New Jersey—Newark—History. I. Title.
   F144.N657T88 2009
   974.9 32—dc22

                                                                      2008026186

A British Cataloging-in-Publication record for this book is available from the British
   Library.

Visit our Web site: http://rutgerspress.rutgers.edu

Manufactured in the United States of America

Typesetting: Jack Donner, BookType

For Jessica

CONTENTS

PART III
Rebirth   209

ACKNOWLEDGMENTS

I would first like to thank Samuel G. Freedman, the book-writing guru at the Columbia School of Journalism. If it were not for Sam, this book—and dozens of others from former students like me—would never have happened. Sam has been a mentor, long after my days in his intense classroom. The more I write, the more his lessons are invaluable. I've also found his influence somewhat inescapable. Periodically throughout the researching and writing of this book, I happened upon one of Sam's *Times* articles about Sharpe James or the binder of one of his books staring at me from a library shelf. He is, and probably always will be, the editor in the back of my head, and my work is better for it.

Sam Freedman also holds the responsibility for introducing me to the editor of this book, Marlie Wasserman. I owe Marlie my gratitude for her wonderful observations and suggestions, for her level-headed, no-nonsense approach, and most importantly, for the fact that she never stopped believing in this project. I would also like to thank my agent, Sam Stoloff, of the Frances Goldin Literary Agency, for his support, as well as guidance, insight, and advice on book writing and the publishing world.

To all the people I bored for three-plus years with discussions on all sorts of Newark-related topics—Puritanism, canals, the Industrial Revolution, prohibition, organized crime, public housing, race relations, and so on—I apologize. Thanks to the folks who were not only interested in what I was babbling about, but who discussed these matters with me in-depth and informed the text greatly, notably Rutgers-Newark professor Dr. Clement Price, Monsignor Joseph Granato of Saint Lucy's Church, Linda Caldwell Epps, president and CEO of the New Jersey Historical Society, and Arthur Stern, CEO of Cogswell Realty.

Research can be a lonely, frustrating occupation. Piecing together characters and events to create a narrative can also be thrilling, almost in a private-eye sort of way. I owe a huge debt to all of the folks who joined me in my sleuthing, especially the librarians pulling reams of microfilm and unearthing dusty manuscripts at the Newark Public Library, Rutgers-Newark's Dana Library, and the New Jersey Historical Society. I would like to single out two library staffers to thank in particular: Brad Small, formerly of the Newark Public Library, who offered dozens of suggestions and research tips (and once showed me mug shots of Depression-era gangsters he'd just discovered in a filing cabinet that had been locked for years); and Maureen O'Rourke, the New Jersey Historical Society's remarkably knowledgeable, friendly, and witty librarian.

Thanks to my friends and family who I've leaned on for the duration of this project—firstly, to my mother and father, who read drafts and offered helpful critiques from the time this book was in proposal stage, and who more importantly have given me unending support and love my entire life. To my sons, William and Owen: thanks for not banging on the door of daddy's office too often, and thanks also for the times when you did. Sometimes turning off the computer and playing with trains or Star Wars guys was the best thing for me, and for the book. You two (and your sibling yet to be born as I'm writing this) are the best distractions a writer could ever hope for. Thanks also to my very large extended family and to assorted cronies and colleagues whose friendship and support I'm lucky to have.

Finally, I must thank my wife, Jessica, to whom this book is dedicated. She encouraged me to take this project on, and then had to handle even more than her usual share of parenting responsibilities as her husband was off digging through archives on weekends and plopped in front of a computer until well after midnight on countless weeknights. She had to endure God-knows-how-many stories about the quirks, dead-ends, and conundrums I encountered at the Newark Public Library and other facilities that became my pseudo office. For months, the conversations I had with my wife consisted mostly of my latest paper cut (the tally was six by the time the manuscript was done) and the types of coins accepted by various library copy machines. If that's not love, I don't know what is. (FYI, Newark Public's microfilm copiers only take nickels and dimes, though some staffers are nice enough to make change for patrons.) During the moments I felt overwhelmed swimming in research or frustrated with life in general, Jessica always listened and responded with the calm, eminently sensible words, "Go write a book." Well, we did it.

HOW NEWARK
BECAME NEWARK

PRIDE IN NEWARK

A 300TH ANNIVERSARY AND A CITY ON THE BRINK

The story of Newark is America's story. It is the story of colonization, independence, growth, and maturity. It is the story of a brave people.

—Lyndon B. Johnson

With those words of congratulations and warm wishes, issued by President Lyndon B. Johnson on the first day of 1966, a festive year began in which Newark celebrated its 300th anniversary. It seemed as if every one of the city's community groups, businesses, schools, and houses of worship got in on the birthday festivities, which were spread over a full twelve months. Social calendars were filled with concerts and banquets, from a health services dinner dance, to a sports awards dinner for local legends holding records in track, basketball, and gymnastics, to an evening honoring Old First Presbyterian, the church founded by Newark's original Puritan settlers.[1]

Founder's Day activities on Wednesday, May 18, marked the year's highlight. Church bells and factory whistles rang at noon, kicking off a three-hour parade of bagpipers, historic steam engines, marching bands, soldier brigades, and floats sponsored by corporations and city agencies. Some four hundred banners emblazoned with the circular "Pride in Newark" logo lined Broad Street, the exceptionally wide road that had served as the grand main drag for three centuries. From Lincoln Park, the parade crept north past dignitaries and everyday citizens lined up in front of the elegant granite façade of City Hall. Farther up, just after the Four Corners of Broad and Market streets, once acclaimed as the world's busiest intersection, the Prudential Insurance Company's glowing-white corporate headquarters rose twenty-four stories into the sky, where "300" was visible in red hundred-foot-high numerals. Skyscrapers built during the city's early 1900s heyday sat across Broad Street, followed by Military Park and quaint Trinity Church, whose classic columns and white spire wouldn't have seemed out of place in a New England village.[2]

The Newark Museum joined the anniversary-year celebration with a series of special exhibits, including a display showcasing the works of Adolf

Konrad. A classically trained painter born in Bremen, Germany, Konrad lived in downtown Newark from Prohibition times through the post–World War II era. As other artists had found endless inspiration in Paris or Venice, Konrad spent his days painting the streetscapes and riverside factories of Newark. "Instead of a Doge's Palace I created my fantasies around the deserted Java Bread Company building," Konrad explained. "In place of the Lions of St. Mark I introduced the statue of that unique and creative genius, Seth Boyden."[3]

The museum ended its anniversary series with a look at "Newark: Present and Future." Scale models revealed high-rise offices and college buildings that were either under construction or planned. Photos showed off the recently expanded operations of the city's two daily newspapers, the *Newark Evening News* and the *Star-Ledger. This Is Newark, 1966,* a short film funded by the Port Authority, which ran the city's airport and seaport, ran on a loop starting every fifteen minutes. The film consisted mostly of aerial shots viewing the likes of Military Park, Broad Street skyscrapers, and high-rise public-housing buildings and other urban-renewal projects. "In our time, one-fifth of the city will have been rebuilt with projects like these," the narrator said. Particular attention was paid to the city's largest green space, Branch Brook Park, and its surroundings, notably the Cathedral of the Sacred Heart. Adorned with dazzling gargoyles and stained glass, Sacred Heart had opened in 1954 as a vision reminiscent of Europe's great cathedrals.[4]

The anniversary was a natural time for newspapers, academics, and others observers to take the long view with assessments of the current state of affairs and projections for what the future might hold. Everyone admitted Newark had problems. But, it was often stressed, issues such as the disappearance of manufacturing, increase in crime, rising tax rates, and inadequate housing were not unique to Newark in the 1960s.

A drastic population shift was another of the challenges faced by Newark and many older cities. Well over one hundred thousand white Newark residents left the city in the two decades after World War II. A corresponding influx of African Americans placed people of color in the majority by the mid-1960s. Despite the wild population turnover and widespread racial tensions during the era, Newark's still overwhelmingly white power structure maintained that the city's race relations were nothing short of exemplary. Hugh Addonizio won the mayoralty in 1962 through a coalition of Italian, black, and liberal Jewish supporters. Once in City Hall, Addonizio was Newark's first mayor to appoint African Americans to top government positions. With a reputation as a progressive, Addonizio cruised to another term with an easy 1966 election triumph. Many supporters cited the leadership of Mayor Addonizio and others as the reason violent racial outbreaks hadn't surfaced as they had in Harlem and Watts.

"Newark through the summer of 1966 had not been rocked by the riots and disorder that had swept other cities," wrote John T. Cunningham, New Jersey's leading popular historian, in his thick illustrated history of Newark, published for the tercentenary. "It certainly is not a matter of luck. For one thing, there has long been sincere dialogue between volunteer Negro and white leaders. City-appointed racially mixed commissions have worked hard at settling racial tensions before the point of explosion."[5]

———

Newark's main problem, it would soon be glaringly apparent, was that leaders had grown accustomed to systematically whitewashing its problems. A deeply troubled city lay beneath the 300th anniversary façade. The truth was visible to anyone who cared to look. Filthy, crime-ridden streets crisscrossed poverty-stricken, all-black neighborhoods where white business owners locked iron gates over their stores nightly before departing for home in the suburbs. Children attended worn-out, feebly equipped schools that were de facto segregated. Merely a decade after welcoming their first hopeful tenants, Newark's high-rise public-housing projects were dreary and dilapidated, plagued with violence and sullied with graffiti.

The truth was also on display at the Newark Museum in the form of artist Adolf Konrad's canvases. Newark may have been Konrad's inspiration, but the city he painted in oils was something of an urban nightmare. Grim, tired old factories belched gray smoke. Windows of shops and apartment buildings were dark and foreboding. In Konrad's Seth Boyden series, the statue of Newark's acclaimed nineteenth-century inventor appears in silhouette amid weed-choked Washington Park, his chin lowered as if in dejection. Most of Konrad's scenes were completely bereft of human life. The few people he did paint were generally faceless wraiths haunting the city—hunched-over workers leaving a factory after the day's grind, a disheveled junk man placing garbage into a cart, a crudely rendered figure cradling his head while slumped on a park bench.[6]

As might be expected, the positive image projected by Newark boosters told only a portion of the city's story. Sacred Heart, the soaring cathedral on the edge of Branch Brook Park, was symptomatic of the city's overstretched ambitions and economic struggles during the early twentieth century. The cornerstone had been laid in 1898 when Newark was flush with industrial riches. Yet as the years passed, the project periodically ran out of funds as manufacturing wealth shrunk and more and more of the church's patrons debarked for the suburbs. Work wasn't completed until 1954.

Much about the city's projected future as exhibited by the Newark Museum would never be reached. Several projects shown in scale models did not proceed beyond the blueprint stage. The excitement around the expanded *Newark Evening News* building would be shattered in 1972 when the publication generally regarded as New Jersey's newspaper of record went out of business.

The state of race relations and ghetto life was so atrocious in mid-1960s Newark that national activists targeted their efforts on the city. The newcomers included charismatic young leaders such as Students for a Democratic Society founder Tom Hayden, as well as a colorful militant character who called himself Colonel Hassan and protested through the streets with Black Liberation Army soldiers. They and others chose to come to Newark often with the idealistic—perhaps also naïve and opportunistic—concept of tackling inner city problems head-on in the place they deemed the worst of the worst.

Despite the omnipresent signs, Newark politicians and the chamber of commerce generally glossed over just how deep-rooted its troubles were. Disaster came as a consequence, most obviously during the summer after the 300th anniversary year when frustrations spilled over into five days of riots that left behind more than two dozen dead, $10 million in damages, and a foul legacy of distrust and hate.

City leaders could not honestly say that they'd been completely caught off guard by the riots. Observers had been saying for years that Newark was on the brink of economic ruin and widespread upheaval. The criticisms reached a peak during the mayoral election of 1966. Kenneth Gibson, an African-American engineer who came in a strong third place, harped on the need to end police brutality by hiring more people of color in the department and creating an independent civilian review board. Leo Carlin, the reformist former mayor who'd been ousted in the 1962 election, decried the Addonizio administration's ties to organized crime, as well as its failures to build a single school, stem crime rates, or remedy the city's rapidly escalating property tax situation. "Newark is a city in trouble, a city that is running out of time," Carlin warned.[7]

The claims of impending doom could not be cast off as mere political rhetoric. During the summer of 1966, leaflets circulated through Newark's slums detailing how to make Molotov cocktails for firebombing, the latest form of protest among angry radicals. "Light rag and throw at some white person or white person's property," the leaflet suggested in its final step.[8]

In the spring of 1967, months before riots burned through the Central Ward, the Addonizio administration itself flatly owned up to the desperate state of affairs confronting Newark. "The most uncommon characteristic of the city may well be the extent and severity of its problems," stated Newark's application for federal urban-renewal funding via the recently created Model Cities program. "There is no other major city in the nation where these common urban problems range so widely and cut so deeply." The application cited the city's poor, unstable population and the highest per capita tax rate in the nation, among its many troubles. "Boasting about progress is unthinkable," the proposal said. "Times are too volatile and to ignore that fact in a welter of self-praise would be fatal."[9]

Local leaders pointed the finger at larger forces as the causes of many problems enveloping the city. As industrial bases shifted in the mid-twentieth century, all the Northeast's rusted older cities suffered, none more so than Newark. The white-flight phenomenon hit Newark particularly hard because of its small size: just twenty-four square miles. Newark residents with the means could easily skip out on the city's oppressive taxes by moving to nearby suburban towns. Newark's tax burden was passed along to the folks remaining, who were increasingly too poor to own homes. By 1967, about 75 percent of whites and 87 percent of black residents were renters, who felt the exorbitant tax rises with regular bumps in monthly checks to landlords—who typically lived outside the city.[10] Within a shockingly brief period of time, the situation snowballed so that Newark became a lopsided, bottom-heavy city, with poor people stacked on top of each other in densely populated slum areas and middle-class and affluent residents left only in a few pockets.

Still, much of the blame for Newark's troubles rested squarely in the hands of city leadership. Decades of mismanagement, bloated government agencies rampant with patronage jobs, and overwhelming corruption caught up with the city in the form of outrageous tax rates and inevitable political scandals. An ad purchased in 1966 by the city for the *Star-Ledger*'s special 300th anniversary section listed the names of the mayor and the eight councilmen running for reelection.[11] In late 1969, Mayor Addonizio and six of those councilmen were indicted alongside a handful of organized crime members for involvement in a racket that had awarded city contracts in exchange for hundreds of thousands of dollars in kickbacks.

Corruption has evolved into something of a tradition in Newark, dating back at least to the late 1800s. It has survived in Darwinian fashion, adapting and taking new shape in response to reformers' efforts and swings in voter populations. For most of the nineteenth century, government power sat in the hands of rich manufacturers and bankers who established policies aimed mainly at safeguarding their wealth. Later, as groups of Irish, Jews, and Italians crept to prominence, they came to see politics not simply as a way to maintain wealth, but as a means to produce it for their working-class compatriots, and for themselves personally. Ethnic politicians drew support based on the promise of doling out patronage jobs. Patronage led to inefficiency and graft, which in turn led to unbridled corruption.

Officials running Newark during the 1930s gangster era might be thought of as the grandfathers of the city's modern comprehensive system of corruption. Meyer Ellenstein, a handsome, charismatic dentist and lawyer, guided the city as mayor. Some people said that Abner "Longy" Zwillman, Newark's unquestioned king of organized crime, had handpicked his old friend Ellenstein to serve as the mob's official henchman. Tales circulated during the Ellenstein years of rampant election fraud and regular looting of the city treasury. Prosecutors often failed to get convictions related to such accusations, typically because both jurors and evidence were tampered with during criminal trials.

Newark installed a new mayor-council form of government in 1954 in the hopes of restoring some semblance of honesty and efficiency. Even after the switchover, however, power remained in the hands of relatively few people, and corruption thrived at the expense of citizens and the city's overall well-being.

Between 1954 and 2006, Newark had only four mayors. Three of those four faced indictments on corruption charges either while in office or shortly afterward. The nine-member city council similarly experienced few turnovers during the first half-century of the mayor-council system; eight council members were elected to four or more four-year terms. And in the city where an old joke goes, "Newark politicians leave office in only one of two ways: death or conviction," the council has likewise been plagued with scandals. No fewer than eighteen council members have been indicted over the years, typically for accepting kickbacks or some other misuse of power.[12]

————

Neither great cities nor slums are created overnight. Newark's epic downfall was decades in the making, rooted in forces from outside and within the city. As post–World War II public policy neglected urban centers and fostered the blossoming of suburbs and the nation's highway system, cities across the United States found themselves in predicaments similar to Newark. Yet Newark was an exceptional case. It stood out for the extraordinary speed, depth, and viciousness of its decline, and for the monumental difficulties the city faced while attempting to dig itself out from the hole.

In the post-riot years, Donald Malafronte, a top aide of Mayor Addonizio and his successor, Kenneth Gibson, voiced a much-repeated observation often attributed to Gibson. "Wherever our cities are going, I'll bet Newark gets there first," Malafronte said.[13] Unfortunately, after the bloodletting of the 1960s riots, Newark was not heading toward racial healing or a newfound vibrancy in urban life. Instead, Newark led the pack as cities approached hopelessness. Once, our cities were regarded as places of opportunity and glamour, places where ethnic groups could carve out niches for themselves and live the American dream. By the mid-1970s, cities were more often viewed as economic black holes dependent on outside subsidies to stay afloat. They were filthy dens of crime where poor people of color lived because they had no other choice. Cities were places to be avoided, if possible.

Newark didn't hit rock bottom during the riots but years later in the desperate 1970s when the economy floundered to new lows and militant, hate-spewing demagogues provoked racial standoffs that were arguably uglier than the looting, arson, and violence of the late 1960s. Crime soared to unparalleled levels in the 1970s. Whereas rates for violent crime (murder, rape, robbery, and assault) rose 25 percent across the United States during that tumultuous decade, they skyrocketed 91 percent in Newark.[14] Residents and good-intentioned officials caught in the crossfire—literally, or in the form of a tense, racially polarized atmosphere—often simply gave up. They abandoned their old neighborhoods for safer, more pleasant surroundings. Between 1960 and 1990, Newark lost nearly one-third of its population, a drop of more than 125,000 people.

Journalists invented new superlatives to sum up the extent of Newark's 1970s freefall. The city was "a classic example of urban disaster," according to *Newsweek*, and "a study in the evils, tensions, and frustrations that beset the central cities of America," in the words of a *New York Times Magazine* writer. Most infamously, a 1975 feature story in *Harper's* named Newark far and away "The Worst American City."[15]

Joke-tellers found an easy target in Newark. "It's such a disaster area it don't deserve no organized crime," a character says in a 1980 Off Off Broadway play.[16] "Have you heard?" quipped talk-show host Johnny Carson. "The city of Newark is under arrest."

Philip Roth, the famous author who set many of his novels in his home-town of Newark, offered an extremely brutal assessment of the post-riot city in his 1981 book *Zuckerman Unbound*. In one scene, the renowned novelist Nathan Zuckerman (Roth's alter ego) is accosted by a man who feels it is his duty to set Zuckerman straight about the city he writes of so often with a semblance of nostalgia. "What do you know about Newark, Mama's Boy!" the man says. "Moron! Moron! Newark is a nigger with a knife! Newark is a whore with the syph! Newark is junkies shitting in your hallway and everything burned to the ground! Newark is dago vigilantes hunting jigs with tire irons! Newark is bankruptcy! Newark is ashes! Newark is rubble and filth!"[17]

Newark's grim reputation persisted even as the city mounted its much-heralded recovery. Years after the New Jersey Performing Arts Center opened downtown to much acclaim, after the city's population finally stabilized and the real estate market rebounded, surrounding towns sought to dissociate themselves from Newark. Tired of paying Essex County taxes—which people believed disappeared in the county seat of Newark to the benefit of very few—Cedar Grove, Verona, Montclair, and other suburban towns voted in 2004 to secede from the county. The votes were mostly symbolic; secession requires approval from the governor and state legislature, which is highly unlikely. Yet the point was made that taxpayers wanted to rid themselves of the city they viewed as a burden.[18]

Destroying ties among communities is probably not in anyone's best interest. New Jersey has a long history of towns splitting up into smaller municipalities for the sake of home rule, and the result is pervasive duplication of services and one of the most inefficient, heavily taxed states in the country. On the contrary, if Newark had retained the land once within its borders—nearly all of Essex County—the city certainly wouldn't have struggled as desperately as it did during the latter twentieth century. If Newark encompassed all of Essex County today, it would be home to about eight hundred thousand people, making it one of the nation's leading cities, the twelfth biggest overall (rather than the sixty-fifth). The taxes paid by Verona, Montclair, and other towns probably would never have reached their current oppressive levels had they been joined all along in the larger city of Newark. Some people may argue that these towns have been better off distanced from the city's corruption. Yet Newark might not have been quite as corrupt had more voters been deciding who ran the city. It's hard to believe, for instance, that Sharpe James would have been elected mayor five times if all of Essex County had a say in the matter.

All of these points are of course moot. The fact is that all of Essex County—and all of New Jersey—has vested interests in Newark, the state's largest city. As far back as 1968, the groundbreaking *Report for Action*, commissioned after the riots by the governor, plainly made the case that still holds today: "Suburban residents must understand that the future of their communities is inextricably linked to the fate of the city, instead of harboring the illusion that they can maintain invisible walls or continue to run away. Such change is possible only when the people in our more fortunate communities understand that what is required of them is not an act of generosity toward the people in the ghettoes, but a decision of direct and deep self-interest."[19] In other words, Newark's failure affects us all. And if Newark succeeds, we all do.

Another reason for taking an interest in the city is that, to paraphrase President Lyndon Johnson's 1966 sentiments, Newark's story *is* America's story. Newark was born as a direct descendant of the Puritan New England village, the unyielding, strictly controlled institution that played such a key role in establishing an early sense of American character. After the Revolution, Newark's story is that of urban America in extremis. No community hopped aboard the runaway train that was the Industrial Revolution as wholeheartedly as Newark. In its embrace of manufacturing, Newark grew as quickly as any city. When the United States rode to prominence as a world power, it did so on the backs of cities like Newark. Then, to use a modern cliché, Newark experienced the perfect storm of twentieth-century urban troubles: deeply entrenched corruption, industrial abandonment, white flight, racial conflict, soaring crime rates, fiscal insolvency, dire poverty. Newark's saga reflects the rollercoaster ride of Everycity, U.S.A., only with a steeper rise, sharper turns, and a much more dramatic plunge.

To understand the tragedy of urban America in the post–World War II years, one must understand the unvarnished truth of the city walloped the hardest. With that in mind, this book aims to take a fresh, honest, and critical look at Newark, in all its grit and glory.

———

Writing a history that is both comprehensive and of readable length is simply impossible; there's just too much ground to cover. Rather than a broad, likely bland era-by-era lecture, this book instead tells detailed stories focused on people and events that either contributed directly or otherwise embodied the overall rise, fall, and rebirth of Newark. This approach, while hopefully producing a more interesting read, meant that certain stories could not be told, and certain individuals and groups would have to be largely excluded. Most obviously, there's an underrepresentation of women, who through much of Newark's history have played roles that were important but unfortunately too behind-the-scenes to figure prominently into the narrative. Mea culpa.

Although the centerpiece of this book is Newark's precipitous decline, this is also a tale of survival and of redemption. The city was too much of a commodity, with too prime a location, to remain mired in despair. Though the idea of a renaissance in Newark has been promoted starting as early as the 1970s, the city has indisputably hit a streak of prosperity in recent years. The upswing parallels the rebound seen in cities all over the United States.

Besides Newark's booming real estate market, perhaps the best sign for the city is a population that, at long last, is growing.

With the renaissance has come a renewed sense of interest and—indeed—pride in Newark. It's obviously felt by entrepreneurs, business owners, community groups, and new and longtime residents reinvigorating city streets. Former Newarkers are also demonstrating newfound pride in the place they deserted long ago. Nostalgic Web sites like VirtualNewarkNJ.com are flooded with people sharing stories and photos from the old neighborhoods. Grassroots efforts celebrate the city's history through institutions like the Jewish Museum of New Jersey and the Newark First Ward Heritage & Cultural Society.

While Newark still has far to go before it can be categorized as an unabashed success story, the city is certainly not the terminal case critics have made it out to be. And if the consensus of opinion is correct, Newark is destined for much brighter days ahead.

PART I

RISE

For a century after its 1666 founding, Newark existed largely as a quiet, deeply religious, but otherwise unexceptional village. As the network of roads expanded in the pre-Revolution era, Newark found itself on the main path between the Hudson and Delaware rivers—the most important route in American colonial history. Once bridges were built in the late 1700s to efficiently connect Newark to Jersey City, and onward to Manhattan via ferry, the tiny town fulfilled its destiny and emerged as a key transportation and trade hub.

It is here, just after the colonies won their independence and Newark started its swift transformation from minor village to powerful city, that our narrative begins in full. Newark grew at an extraordinary pace in the early 1800s, from forty-five hundred at the turn of the century to just under twenty thousand when it incorporated as a city in 1836, up to 71,941 on the eve of the Civil War. Newark's standing as an industrial power and important hub—connected to roads, rails, and canals—blossomed during this boom time period, covered in chapter 1.

Much of the growth during the early 1800s came due to the runaway success of manufacturers producing leather and other goods sold primarily to the South, lending Newark a reputation as a "Southern workshop." Men such as William Wright, a Newark mayor, U.S. senator, and preeminent saddle manufacturer with long-established trading partners throughout the South, openly sympathized with the Confederate cause, creating an especially tense and bitter atmosphere in Newark during the Civil War years, described in chapter 2.

After peace between the North and South was declared, Newark again experienced brisk growth as businesses expanded in both output and scope and immigrants eagerly flooded into the city to sign on for abundant factory jobs. Newark reached a quarter-million residents by 1900, and in the course of the next decade, the city welcomed another one hundred thousand newcomers, representing its largest-ever population influx. Chapter 3 spans this era, roughly from the end of the Civil War to 1910.

Growing pains accompanied the wild population spurts during Newark's nineteenth-century rise to power and prominence. Efforts to build sewers, pave roads, and otherwise improve the city's infrastructure and health lagged behind the needs of the public. Political bosses rose to power and retained influence through the dispensing of patronage jobs and control of the ballot box. Businessmen and politicians—who were often one and the same—decided public-policy issues despite blatant conflicts of interest. As residents filled out the city's borders, foresighted leaders realized they faced a problem potentially even more worrisome than corruption: those borders would likely be too constricting to accommodate Newark's ambition to become one of the country's leading metropolises.

CHAPTER 1

CORPORATION

SHELTERED PURITAN VILLAGE
TO TEEMING INDUSTRIAL HUB

The people who founded Newark might be thought of as the purest of New England's Puritans. Many of the families had moved from place to place for decades, always on the quest to establish a theocratic outpost where they could live quiet lives ruled strictly by God and the Bible. Their journeys had taken them from England to the Netherlands, Massachusetts, Long Island, and, eventually, to a trio of villages in New Haven Colony: Milford, Branford, and Guilford. Each settlement along the way failed to prove satisfactory largely because outside authorities—typically colonial governments or the king of England himself—prevented the rigid, uncompromising Puritans from forming the entirely God-focused community they desired.

Frustrated but not ready to give up on their theocratic ambitions, in the early 1660s, the Puritans sent Robert Treat, a leading citizen of Milford, and a small party of envoys to inquire about settling Dutch-controlled land west of Staten Island. Treat's party landed in New Amsterdam, boarded the private barge of Peter Stuyvesant, the gruff, peg-legged director general of New Netherland, and sailed onward through the narrow strait called Kill Van Kull ("water channel" in old Dutch) beyond a large bay to a place known as Achter Col ("behind the bay").[1] The Dutch sometimes referred to all the territory that became northern New Jersey as Achter Col.

The area toured by Treat and his colleagues seemed ideal. Above the banks of a wide river were well-drained, fairly level lands that would suit farms, roads, and homes. A Dutch document written about the time of their visit described the region as having "the best climate in the whole world," including abundant deer and other game, rivers and bays filled with "excellent fat and wholesome fish," and fertile land that produced apples, pears, peaches, and melons of a quality that "far surpasseth" any in Europe.[2] The site also seemed remote and protected, which were assets to a band of Puritans hoping to establish a community free of outside influence.

During land negotiations, Stuyvesant and his council agreed to let the Puritans practice their religion freely. New Netherland officials, however, wanted to reserve limited oversight, including the rights to confirm (or deny) the appointment of officials and approve (or deny) local laws and ordinances.[3] The Puritans, seeking absolute autonomy, balked.

Robert Treat again returned to this same area in early 1666, which by then had fallen under British control alongside New Amsterdam, immediately renamed New York. The territory west of Staten Island christened as New Jersey suddenly had new owners—John Berkeley and George Carteret, both wealthy friends of the royals—who were so eager to attract settlers (and begin collecting taxes) that they were willing to allow communities to pick their own ministers. The landmark Concessions and Agreements document, which served as both an advertisement and contract for early New Jersey settlers, also promised that so long as inhabitants didn't "disturbe the civill peace," they would not be punished "for any difference of opinion or practice in matters of Religion."

Treat and approximately three hundred people from Milford, Branford, and Guilford seized the opportunity and moved to New Jersey, banding together to try once more to establish the stable theocratic community that for decades had seemed just out of reach.[4] The settlers were an extremely close-knit bunch, many with ties stretching back to England. Of the sixty-nine adult male settlers, nine were related to at least three other men by blood or marriage.[5]

While early records simply called the community something along the lines of "our Town on Passaick River," people often referred to it as Milford. A map from 1700 in fact labeled the area west of the river as both its tentative early name, Milford, and the one which survived, Newark.[6] Within a year of the initial settlement, the community had officially renamed itself in honor of the place where Abraham Pierson, its first minister, was ordained, Newark-on-Trent, England.

For much of the colonial era, Newarkers largely remained an inward-looking community, where lives revolved around farm work and God. The sheltered Puritan town grew slowly. There were 86 families in 1673, increasing to 100 families by 1680.[7] Alexander MacWhorter, Newark's leading minister in the late 1700s, said it best when describing the town's early settlers as "a remarkably plain, simple, sober, praying, orderly, and religious people."[8]

As the decades passed, however, it became increasingly clear that, because of inevitable outside influences and simple human nature, Newark could not live up to its lofty theocratic ambitions. Conflicts over land rights, religion, and business practices split the populace along class, wealth, and spiritual lines, bringing to an end Newark's era as a one-church community.

Newark's settlers never intended for their community to become a trade hub, let alone a teeming city. Through the late 1700s, both Elizabethtown, where New Jersey's first governors established their center of power, and Perth Amboy, a prized port at the mouth of the Raritan River, were regarded as far more important towns than Newark. Elizabethtown, now known simply as Elizabeth, held the title of most populous New Jersey community at least through the Revolution. Perth Amboy, with its magnificent harbor, seemed destined to become New Jersey's great metropolis, perhaps even rivaling Manhattan.

Ironically, Newark, which was founded partly because its location seemed isolated in the 1660s, transformed into a trade center due to that same location, which wasn't nearly as remote a century later. Its role as a hub evolved with northern New Jersey's growing system of roads. At first, crude dirt paths connected Newark to copper mines north and west of town, to villages that fell within its borders, including the modern-day Oranges, Bloomfield, and Montclair, and of course to neighboring Elizabethtown.

As the road network expanded, surveyors came to the obvious realization that Newark lay a short distance directly west of lower Manhattan. New Jersey authorities saw the potential of connecting the city to Newark, as well as villages and farms farther west. Bridging the two rivers on the route, the Hackensack and Passaic, was out of the question in colonial times. Construction would have been too costly and time-consuming. In 1765, officials authorized the establishment of ferries to cross the rivers and a new road between Newark and Powles Hook (Jersey City), where ferries already passed back and forth to Manhattan. A news account described the system—a model of efficiency in the era—as "very commodious for Travellers," offering "short and easy Access of a large Country to the Markets of the City of New-York."[9]

Newark suddenly became a stopover on the main route connecting the Hudson and Delaware rivers. The thoroughfare was the most important in all of America, and "as fine a road as ever trod," in the words of founding father John Adams.[10] The village of Newark, with perhaps a thousand residents and 150 homes at the time, would never feel remote or sheltered again.

Newark's Matthias Ward began charging for passage on the new road aboard his stage wagon at least as early as 1767. By the following year, Ward was advertising two daily round trips (Sundays excepted), most likely in open-air, flat-bed carts rolling on four wheels pulled by horses.[11]

By no little coincidence, Newark began hosting an annual autumn market for buying and selling livestock and farm equipment. "Newark, from its Vicinity to New-York, and other Circumstances attending its Situation, is by many, esteemed a most proper Place for such a Cattle Market," a notice read.[12]

Entrepreneurs in the pre-revolutionary period opened businesses in Newark at a steady pace, which in turn led to further commercial opportunities. For all the growth, however, as the conflict between the colonies and mother England loomed, the town's status was still merely that of a tiny cog in an expanding transportation network. In 1776, an English traveler passing through described Newark in a few terse words: "Nothing more than a Village."[13]

———

New Jersey, poised between two cities with opposite sympathies during the Revolutionary War—New York, a Tory haven, and patriots' stronghold Philadelphia—saw more than its share of bloodshed and horror during the war. Newark, on the main land route linking the Hudson and Delaware rivers, was a particularly unstable, strife-ridden place through much of the struggle. Alternating forces came through one after another, retreating, attacking, encamping, foraging for supplies, and plundering in every way imaginable.

Once the volatile, destructive war years had finally ended, Newark recouped, rebuilt, and looked forward to a new century, one full of potential. In many ways, by the mid-1790s Newark appeared to be a completely different town than it had been a few decades earlier. Upon visiting in 1795, a French duke complimented Newark as "one of the finest villages in America."[14]

East of Broad Street, around modern-day Kinney Street, sat the grand six-acre estate of William Burnet, a patriot doctor, officer, and confidante of George Washington who had been appointed as a judge after the war. Farther north on Broad, past freshly repaired houses and shops selling shoes, clothing, cabinets, hats, and other goods, the Presbyterian reverend Alexander MacWhorter presided over his spacious parsonage. Across the street, Samuel Sayres, a major in the Continental cause, served as proprietor of the Eagle Tavern—one of no fewer than four inns then lining Broad Street.[15]

Half a block farther north was where the real changes had taken place. The old county courthouse had been converted into a jail, seeing as the old Presbyterian meeting house had been transformed into a courthouse. Tombstones jutting up behind the former meeting house revealed that the burying ground still remained, however. Next door, Jabez Parkhurst, a town clerk for several years, operated a tavern in his fourteen-room home. After dismounting horses and tying them up at a trough in the yard, Parkhurst's guests could enjoy a drink in the barroom with a view of the graveyard. Directly opposite on Broad Street was the handsome stone New Presbyterian Church, opened in 1791 with ornate Venetian windows behind the pulpit. From atop the church's 204-foot-high steeple, one could look eastward over treetops, the Passaic, and vast marshlands for glimpses of Staten Island, the Hudson River, and Manhattan.[16]

A thirty-second walk later, one would arrive at the town crossroads, Broad and Market. Clusters of taverns, stores, government offices, and neat, two-story homes with backyard gardens extended in each direction. Many of the buildings were owned by Continental officers, including John Cummings, a colonel and later a president of Newark's first bank, and William Pennington, a poor orphan who enlisted and was promoted successively, ending the war as brevet captain. Apprenticed to a hatter before the war, Pennington operated a successful hat store next door to a blacksmith and a barbershop. He later became New Jersey governor, as did his son, also named William Pennington. A few doors away from the hat store, Aaron Pennington, William Sr.'s brother, ran one of Newark's first newspapers, the *Centinel of Freedom*.[17]

It was during this era that Market Street was named, for its function. Previously, the road had been referred to simply as "the East and West street." Leading from the Passaic River ferry landing, past Broad Street, westward to villages and farms, the street naturally evolved into an area where merchants met with farmers and purchased butter, grain, meat, and produce. In May of 1795, a new two-story stone building opened its doors on Market Street as the official spot to conduct such business. In between Broad Street and what became Halsey Street, the tiny twenty-square-foot building had a public school upstairs and two ground-floor stalls serving as the town's first market. With its opening, proper city life was feasible. Families at last had a convenient place to buy the fruits, vegetables, chickens, and most everything else they formerly had to barter for or raise themselves.

Swinging from a post at the northeast corner of Broad and Market, a large sign depicting a foxhunt announced the entrance to the hub of all town activity, the Hounds and Horn tavern. Run by a beefy, affable, unapologetic gossip named Archer Griffon, the inn was the town's finest and most popular spot to take tea, toss back grog, feast on quail, and hobnob with wealthy travelers and local power brokers. For spells, all the mail riders and stage coaches bypassed all other stops when entering Newark and pulled directly to the tavern's stables. President John Adams would be a Hounds and Horn visitor more than once.

Continuing up Broad Street, across from the Military Training common, Newark Academy's latest building had been completed in 1792. The town's finest private school, established in 1774 and currently run by President (and Presbyterian minister) Alexander MacWhorter, was now housed in a stately three-story building near the corner of what appropriately became Academy Street. Another tavern, a carpenter's shop, a saddlery business, the office of the town's other newspaper, the *Newark Gazette*, and several homes filled surrounding blocks. Immediately north of the training ground, the landmark Trinity Church stood where it always had, but it too had experienced recent change. The Church of England understandably couldn't survive in America after the Revolution. So, like other Anglican affiliates in America, Trinity Church became an Episcopal affiliate.

Just after Broad Street bends to the northwest, a street extended eastward to the river and remarkably continued up and over a bridge crossing it. State legislators had realized that the system of roads and ferries organized in 1765 was outdated, and in 1790 approved building bridges for both the Passaic and Hackensack rivers. Both were completed by the summer of 1795. The Passaic's nearly 500-foot-long expanse, "neatly framed of wood, with a draw bridge, to let the schooners and other vehicles pass," in the words of an English traveler, was composed of several layers of logs covered with sod and gravel.[18] An even more impressive bridge, double the length of the Passaic's, stretched the Hackensack.

More than any other advancement, the introduction of these two bridges placed Newark unmistakably on the path to growth and urbanity. America, then a fledgling nation in which more than 90 percent of men still farmed for a living, stood poised for enormous change. No town would transform more, or more rapidly, than Newark.

The new bridges established Newark as *the* hub of northern New Jersey, where manufacturing and industry were already taking root. Up the Passaic River, the Great Falls proved to be an irresistible power source. The visionary Alexander Hamilton and a group of land speculators had recently chosen the spot for an ambitious, experimental new town—designed in part by Washington, D.C., architect Charles L'Enfant—that was expressly created for industry, textiles in particular. The town was named in honor of then-governor William Paterson, who allowed the businessmen to operate for ten years tax free. After a slow start, in which L'Enfant's beautiful but impractical plans had to be jettisoned, the Great Falls district's mills and factories attained fame for churning out silk, locomotives, and Colt revolvers, among other goods. Paterson, sometimes pointed to as the spot where America's industrial revolution was born, eventually became New Jersey's third biggest city.[19]

Even before the Passaic and Hackensack bridges opened, Newark had developed steadily as a country town. Besides its reputation as a meeting place for trading farm goods, Newark's prime location and natural resources attracted small-time merchants and craftsmen to set up businesses. In the early days of the new nation, being productive wasn't only a means to make money, it was the duty of every patriotic citizen. With "the increase of Wool being of the highest importance to the interest and prosperity of this Country," Newark duly sponsored a contest. "The Person who shall shear off of his own Sheep in the Spring of 1789, the greatest quantity of good clean Wool," won £10, with runners-up receiving £2 to £8.[20]

During the decade after the war ended, the town's population roughly doubled, to two thousand. One Newark visitor reported that during the same time period land values tripled, from £10 to £30 per acre.[21] Once the bridges expedited travel to and from Newark, the population mushroomed, more than doubling again in the last five years of the eighteenth century.

In terms of number of residents and overall importance, Newark quickly leapfrogged neighboring Elizabethtown, which for a century had been the region's leading town. From an estimated forty-five hundred people at the beginning of the century, Newark grew to six thousand in 1810, a year when surveys showed that Elizabethtown and Trenton were each home to about half that number. (The Quaker town of Trenton became the state's permanent capital in 1790 largely due to its proximity to Philadelphia and what was then a sizeable population; in the years just after the Revolution, the state legislature had moved about, meeting in Perth Amboy, Elizabethtown, Princeton, and other towns. Newark was never considered a contender.) Over the next two decades, while Elizabethtown and Trenton experienced little or no growth, Newark's population sailed to nearly eleven thousand in 1830, and to just under twenty thousand when it officially became a city in 1836. On the eve of the Civil War, the shift to city life was well under way. One-quarter of New Jerseyans then lived in one of the state's six biggest cities. Newark's 1860 population, by far the largest in the state, stood at 71,941, representing one out of every ten people in New Jersey.[22]

Newark's traditional, religious-minded community worried about how the growth spurts were irrevocably changing their once-quiet spiritual haven. Reverend Alexander MacWhorter and other town ministers had overwhelmingly supported the bridges' construction, but the faithful were uneasy that the bridges provided physical and figurative links to all sorts of new and strange people, commercial interests, and ideas. As the end of the eighteenth century neared, all of the outside influences apparently had resulted in a distressing trend: the sacredness of the Sabbath was clearly in jeopardy.

Sunday was no longer being treated with proper respect, many Newarkers believed. Certain people were going about their lives as if the Sabbath was just another day, conducting business, socializing with friends, and skipping religious services. A group calling itself the Voluntary Association of the People of Newark to Observe the Sabbath signed an oath on July 10, 1798, agreeing to "reflect upon their ways and reform whatever they think is contrary to the word of God." Because "vice, like a flood, deluges a land," members pledged that on the Sabbath they would "neither give nor partake of parties or pleasure or entertainments," "neither ride out nor travel," "attend divine worship on that day, and compel our children, apprentices and servants to do the same," and "exert ourselves to suppress all manner of employment and worldly business." Alexander MacWhorter's name topped a list of signatures of eighty-five townsmen.[23]

The actions of some fanatical members of the association were at odds with its "voluntary" status. They stopped the federal mail coach from running on Sunday, and on several occasions threatened to tar and feather parties traveling through town or otherwise engaged in unapproved activities on the Sabbath. The era when Newark was run strictly according to religion had long since passed, however. Officials in Washington warned that anyone who interfered with the mail would be arrested, and judges ordered that travelers must be allowed to proceed through town on any day of the week.

Attempts by the association to halt the consumption of liquor on Sundays also failed. A few men erected stocks on the plot where the original Congregational meeting house once stood, with the hope of intimidating those disrespectful of the Sabbath. The stocks were torn down within twenty-four hours, however. After one last gasp at strictly upholding the community's original Puritanical principles, the old systems for enforcing behavior and morality disappeared forever.

———

One of Newark's most enduring anecdotes from the postwar era concerns an eccentric fellow named Moses Combs, who in various incarnations was a Presbyterian preacher, tanner, shoemaker, founder of his own church and school, zealous abolitionist and temperance advocate, and town "pound master," in charge of rounding up stray cows, sheep, pigs, and other animals. One day around the year 1790, a gentleman from Georgia walked into the Hounds and Horn and began a conversation with the tavern's garrulous owner, Archer Griffon. In his earlier wanderings about the streets of Newark, the traveler had noticed the abundance of shoemakers and leather goods. Griffon suggested that the traveler visit Moses Combs, a superb shoemaker whose shop could be found on the south side of Market Street.

Combs, "a little black-eyed man," as the traveler described him, had begun tanning leather and making shoes and boots around 1780. Shoes were arguably the most important product then made in America—not surprising considering how much people walked during the era. Farmers often busied themselves during the slow winter months by making shoes, for sale or personal use, and some men eventually dedicated themselves to the craft as a year-round profession. By the time the traveler from Georgia popped into Combs's workshop, he found a master craftsman. Combs's work was so outstanding that orders for shoes were coming in from far outside New Jersey, even from the South. A handful of other Newark shoemakers also shipped shoes, no more than a few pairs at a time, down the Atlantic coast. No one had taken on an order like the one requested by the obviously impressed Savannah businessman: two hundred sealskin shoes.

Within a few years, shoe orders flooded into Newark, primarily from the South. One particularly large sale supposedly netted Combs $9,000. Combs had always been an exacting, argumentative stickler of a man, which was fine—perhaps even helpful—when it came to making shoes. He easily became frustrated with Alexander MacWhorter's preachings and his church's arbitrary rules, however, and traveled to Orange on the Sabbath to worship at the Presbyterian church there instead. After his runaway business success, Combs could indulge his whims. He had a two-story wooden house put up on Market Street with a school on the upper floor. Downstairs was a small church, where Combs installed himself at the pulpit. Explaining his actions in third person, curious as ever, Combs said, "Silver showered on him so plentifully that he did not know what else to do with it."[24]

Following Combs's lead, apprentices and journeymen flocked to Newark. In 1806, the inscription on the first-ever published map of downtown Newark stated that the town "is noted for its Cider, the making of Carriages of all sorts, Coach-lace, Men's and women's Shoes. In the manufactures of the last article one third of the Inhabitants are constantly employ'd." For a town symbol, the map's creator combined traditional American motifs—the eagle, symbol of liberty, and a shield adorned with three plows to represent agriculture—with the figure of a hunched-over shoemaker busily crafting the product for which Newark would become renowned.[25]

Combs's success also marked the beginning of trade on a grand scale between Newark and the South. Throughout the early 1800s, Newark developed a reputation for innovation and high-quality manufacturing, often due to the work of quirky, obsessive entrepreneurs like Combs. As the years passed, Newark's range of products expanded, and so did its business relationship with the South. In the 1820s, five vessels regularly carried passengers and freight between Newark and Savannah, and eight ships sailed twice a week back and forth between Newark and Charleston.[26] By Civil War times, Newark was plainly referred to as a "Southern workshop." Somewhere between two-thirds and three-quarters of all products made in town—notably, shoes, carriages, harnesses, saddles, and clothing—were shipped for sale below the Mason-Dixon Line.

Newark's rise in manufacturing was part of a larger trend, in which riverside towns all over New England and the Middle Atlantic states rapidly grew and industrialized after the Revolution. One added impetus to the rise of manufacturing occurred during the War of 1812, when the British blockaded ships from reaching Atlantic coast ports. Forced to become self-sufficient, the United States began producing goods it had formerly imported. As a temporary war tactic, the blockade may have had success. But the lasting impact was that England unknowingly fostered a rival to challenge its long-running manufacturing dominance. In the decades after the war, towns in Massachusetts, Connecticut, New York, New Jersey, and elsewhere would match and surpass the output of Birmingham and other industrial centers in England.

One requirement for successful manufacturing was a concentrated pool of workers, which is why industrial growth during the antebellum years took place nearly exclusively in the densely populated Northeast. People in the South, on the other hand, tended to live on plantations scattered about the vast countryside, miles from anything resembling a town. As it was, the South couldn't compete with northern states in terms of manufacturing. Southern businessmen instead focused on exploiting the plantation system to maximize profits. That generally meant using slave labor and growing proven moneymakers like cotton and tobacco.

A certain codependence arose. Towns like Newark thrived because Georgia, Alabama, and the Carolinas basically conceded shoemaking and other industries to the Northeast. In the early 1800s, the North-South division of production was a mostly balanced and mutually beneficial relationship. However, as the power and influence of industrial northern states soared, and the abolitionist movement gained momentum, the South rightly felt threatened. Newark and other towns with strong economic ties to the South were bound to be conflicted—even hostile, as would be seen—concerning any situations that jeopardized their key trading partners.

———

Newark's early success in shoes attracted more and more shoemakers to set up shop in town. All the competition led to better, cheaper products, which in turn led to more shoes sold, as well as an upswing in related industries like tanning, the gruesome, foul-smelling process of turning animal hides into leather. Businesses making saddles and harnesses naturally moved in or sprang from the ground up to take advantage of a sizeable labor force skilled in leather working. The quality, range, and overall output of products increased dramatically. Newark evolved into something of a breeding ground for innovation, and a magnet for entrepreneurs.

Amid this creative ferment, a brilliant, restless young man named Seth Boyden entered the scene. A gentle, inquisitive character who conducted experiments at all hours of night and day and was known to bathe fully clothed in a pond outside his house, Boyden was easily a match for Moses Combs in terms of eccentricity. Boyden was an odd-looking man with deep-set eyes and extraordinarily large ears. He rarely bothered with grooming. Even in formal portraits, errant clumps of hair point off into the air or curl across his forehead, as if the man just rolled out of bed or, more likely, out of the workshop. Were it not for his kindly eyes and quiet demeanor, Boyden would have been the very picture of a mad scientist. After a career in which he advanced by leaps and bounds the manufacture and production of industries as disparate as leather, iron, steam engines, and cameras, Boyden would be called "one of America's greatest inventors" by someone who should know: Thomas Edison.[27]

Born in 1788 in Foxborough, Massachusetts, Boyden was one of ten siblings. A talent for invention and mechanics was in the family blood. His maternal grandfather, Uriah Atherton, operated a foundry and reportedly cast the first cannon in America, which was used to attack the British during the Revolution. Boyden's father, also named Seth, was a farmer and forge owner who invented a machine for splitting animal hides at any specified thickness—obviously something of interest to those in leather production.

Seth Jr. came of age in a world in transition. While most Americans remained rooted in agriculture, inventions and new business theories were quickly changing both the way people earned their living and how they lived. Eli Whitney, also a Massachusetts native, patented the cotton gin in 1793, thereby making it possible to remove seeds from cotton fifty times faster than the traditional method of plucking them by hand. If cotton wasn't already the South's king crop, it was crowned as such soon thereafter. The power of steam was being harnessed by men such as John Fitch, John Stevens, and Robert Fulton, whose innovations revolutionized transportation on water and rail. A textile worker named Samuel Slater smuggled out of England designs for a mechanized mill and set up a state-of-the-art, water-powered factory for spinning and weaving cloth in 1793 in Pawtucket, Rhode Island. In 1807, Slater expanded the idea and built Slatersville, an entire town dedicated to textiles, with a handful of factories, along with churches, schools, and stores for the workers.

Seth Boyden received little formal education, but absorbed everything he saw in his family's foundry, farm, and workshops, as well as what he observed in the forests, meadows, and rivers of Massachusetts. To Boyden, there was no reason to distinguish one sphere of knowledge from another. They all existed to inform him, and to inspire his creations. Though Boyden always took notice of the latest inventions and products, the largely self-taught man tended to base his own work more on what he witnessed in nature. Some men later complained to Boyden that the fire engine they commissioned him to build contained cylindrical piping, not the rectangular sort more commonly used at the time. "Gentlemen, you read your Bibles, no doubt, more than I do," Boyden replied. "You go to church, no doubt, more than I do. But I observe the laws of God as well as you do. God, in all His works, never made a right angle."

While still a teenager in Massachusetts, Boyden built a telescope and microscope and earned a reputation for a remarkable ability to repair clocks and guns. An obsessive tinker, by the time he turned twenty-one Boyden had designed machines for making nails, brads, tacks, and cutting files. In 1813, Boyden left Massachusetts with an improved version of his father's hide-splitting machine in tow. He relocated to Newark, as good a place as any for an entrepreneur involved in the leather business to make a living.

Boyden's success in Newark came almost immediately. He and his wife, Abigail, bought a house that doubled as a workplace on Broad Street, near Bridge Street. Boyden initially used his machine to cut thin layers of sheepskin and leather for sale to bookbinders. The machine also proved handy in crafting harnesses, a widely needed product in an age when carts, carriages, and plows were pulled by horses and oxen. Always a perfectionist, Boyden was unsatisfied with the buckles and other metal parts then sold to go along with leather harnesses. So, naturally, Boyden tapped into what he had learned in his grandfather's foundry and created a side business making all the harness peripherals in addition to the harnesses themselves.

Word traveled slowly during the era, especially among inventors and businessmen eager to keep trade secrets away from competitors. Even so, reports drifted over from Europe praising a new kind of glazed ornamental leather invented in France. One day in 1818, on a trip to New York City, Boyden came across a German military helmet. The helmet's visor, covered in what looked like thick lacquer, gave Boyden his first glimpse of the new leather. Though the visor was exceptionally stiff and brittle, Boyden was inspired enough to create his own version of glazed leather.

A series of experiments eventually yielded a product far more flexible, and therefore more useful, than the one sold in Europe. Boyden's leather came as a result of applying successive coats of varnish to a hide stretched over a wooden frame. The hide was dried after each coat and finally baked in an oven. The baking process became known as patenting, hence the name of Boyden's invention: patent leather.

In 1819, Boyden opened America's first factory for making patent leather, which was used immediately and widely in the production of shoes, harnesses, and carriages, all staples in Newark's manufacturing world. Boyden grew rich, at least temporarily, though he never reaped the fortune he might have. Local tanners copied the new leather—ironically, Boyden never patented it or many of his other inventions. Newark's leather industry flourished. As of 1837, the city was home to 155 patent-leather manufacturers. By 1860, Newark was responsible for 90 percent of all patent leather made in the United States.

Never one for enjoying success or resting on his laurels, Seth Boyden seemed to tire of the leather business soon after changing it for good. He feverishly moved on to experiments with iron. Boyden slept in his work clothes—boots and all—so that he was ready to jump back into the latest trial the moment he woke. He paused occasionally to bathe, usually in a pond near his home. Even on chilly mornings, he leaped into the water with his clothes on and rarely bothered to change or dry off before quickly returning to the workshop.

The iron experiments stretched into the summer of 1826. Boyden was a committee member for Newark's celebration of the fiftieth anniversary of the Declaration of Independence, but he was notably absent for the Fourth of July parade and all-day party. Earlier that year, Boyden had observed how a piece of cast iron reacted when it fell into the furnace. He furiously conducted test after test, heating and treating iron in the hope of creating a material that was cheaper than wrought iron, less brittle than cast iron, and more malleable than both. His work required that a fire be kept running for days at a time. To ensure that he wouldn't sleep through the night (and risk the fire dying out), Boyden rigged an alarm clock of sorts, nailing a lit candle to the wall. When the candle burned down, it fell loudly into a pan, alerting Boyden it was time to tend the furnace.

Sometime after the parade of July 4, 1826, a few of Boyden's friends came looking for him. Sure enough, he was in the workshop near Bridge Street, oblivious to the festivities under way. Late in the afternoon, Boyden reached the goal he had been pursuing day and night for months, as he pounded away on the first piece of malleable iron ever produced in the country. Two year later, Boyden sold off his patent leather interests for far less than they were worth in order to open a malleable iron foundry—the nation's first—on Orange Street, near the Passaic. That same year (1828), Philadelphia's Franklin

Institute held an exhibition on the latest iron creations, and Boyden was awarded one of the top prizes for his castings. Boyden's malleable iron particularly suited the buckles, bits, harnesses, and other parts used in the carriage and blacksmithing industries.

In 1835, Boyden's attentions shifted yet again—this time to steam engines—and he sold his iron foundry for $25,000. Again, it was a handsome sum in the era, but far less than the business was ultimately worth. Boyden's operation eventually landed in the hands of the Sacks-Barlow company, which by the mid-1950s operated 113 foundries around the country, with forty thousand employees producing nearly one million tons of castings annually. The parts it made were used in automobiles, appliances, railroad and farm equipment, and all sorts of other products.

Boyden would continue on industriously until the day he died in 1870 at age eighty-two. He built locomotives for northern New Jersey's emerging railroad system, and periodically invented whatever interested him—steam engine valves, a hat-forming machine, an alloy used in imitation gold jewelry. Boyden consulted with his friend, fellow Massachusetts native Samuel Morse, and helped him perfect one of the century's monumental creations, the telegraph. Impulsively, Boyden left Newark for San Francisco during the Gold Rush of 1849, only to return two years later, broke. He was never much of a businessman. In his latter years, Boyden lived in a rural area west of Newark which became Maplewood. He spent his days patrolling his garden barefoot, experimenting with strawberries that grew larger and more delicious with every passing season.

It was Boyden's two early inventions—patent leather and malleable iron—that would be his greatest, most lasting achievements. Their impact in Newark was especially immediate and tangible, inspiring industries to sprout, flourish, and multiply.

———

According to the 1826 census, conducted in honor of the Declaration of Independence's fiftieth anniversary, Newark's population stood at 8,017. Though shoemakers employed 35 percent of the workforce, significant numbers were also making carriages, chairs, hats, saddles, cabinets, and jewelry. The census listed thirty-four individual crafts represented in town, as well as major employers including three distilleries; three iron and brass foundries; two breweries; two grist mills; and seventeen factories producing items such as tin, sheet iron, chocolate, mustard, soap, candles, pottery, glass, and tobacco. All told, 80 percent of Newark workers were involved in some form of manufacturing. For the most part, work in these "factories" continued to be done by hand. Different artisans often handled separate tasks in the production process, but there was nothing yet resembling a mechanized assembly line, which wouldn't fully come of age until the early twentieth century.[28]

Though Newark's growth and economic expansion in the early 1800s was extraordinary, the pace would only quicken in the years to come. The population more than doubled between 1826 and 1836. By 1860, it had more than doubled again, reaching 72,000, roughly the same number of people then living in Washington, D.C. The nation's leading cities similarly grew by leaps and bounds. Between 1830 and 1860, Boston nearly tripled its population, from 61,000 to 178,000, and Philadelphia and New York City quadrupled, up to over 550,000 and 800,000 respectively. Newark, while much smaller than those cities, increased sevenfold between the 1830 and 1860 censuses. The only U.S. city surpassing Newark's growth rate was Buffalo, a boomtown that owed its population explosion to the monumental 363-mile-long Erie Canal. Once the canal connected Albany to Buffalo in 1825, the population of the town on Lake Erie soared, from around 8,500 in 1830 to over 80,000 in 1860.[29]

Some of Newark's growth can also be attributed to a canal, though not nearly to the extent as in Buffalo. The idea of creating a water route between New York Harbor and the Delaware River via New Jersey's "waist" had been around at least since 1676, when William Penn sent surveyors out to explore the possibility. A canal didn't seem feasible. The land simply rose too high and too quickly in New Jersey's interior. Great Pond, otherwise known as Lake Hopatcong, was the largest body of water between the Hudson and Delaware rivers. The lake was an obvious link should a canal ever be built, yet it rested at a bit over nine hundred feet above sea level.[30]

Roads in the early 1800s tended to be poorly maintained and slow-going, so that sending iron and agricultural products across New Jersey was formidably expensive. During a fishing trip at Lake Hopatcong in 1820—three years after ground had been broken on the Erie Canal—a Morristown businessman named George Macculloch dreamed up an alternative to New Jersey roads. Damming the lake could double its capacity. That, combined with locks and some creative engineering techniques, meant that a canal could at last cross the state, Macculloch believed. While vague on details, Macculloch's plan received hearty support from the beginning among Morris County's farmers and ironworkers, who stood to benefit most from the canal's construction.

The New Jersey legislature was less enthusiastic. In 1822, it authorized a preliminary survey of the proposed route, from the Passaic River at Newark to the Delaware River at Phillipsburg. Ultimately, the legislature passed on funding the project—despite the conclusion drawn by Macculloch's group that the canal would contribute to "good morals" in the community, in that "apples and cider would be exported instead of being converted into ardent spirits."[31]

Without state funding, the Morris Canal & Banking Company, a private enterprise chartered at the end of 1824, sold shares of stock to raise money to pay for the canal. Though the distance covered was about sixty miles as the crow flies, the canal's route zigzagged more than a hundred miles through the mountainous countryside. In the final plan, the canal skirted through northern New Jersey's two emerging industrial centers, Paterson and Newark; Elizabethtown, which also hoped to land on the path, lost out. On October 15, 1825, ground was broken at Lake Hopatcong amid the celebratory roar of cannons.

Throughout 1826, eleven hundred carpenters, stonemasons, engineers, and laborers toiled along different sections of the canal route. Axmen came in first and cleared dense forests. Men or mules dragged away the fallen trees. Unskilled laborers—often, immigrants from Ireland and England—who slaved away with shovels and picks earned a dollar per day. Originally, the canal they dug measured thirty-two feet wide at the water line, tapering off to twenty feet wide at the bottom, four feet down. (All dimensions would later be enlarged.) When payday came, on Sunday, workmen's wages were paid partly in whiskey, ensuring a lively evening of brawls.[32]

The digging was just one task to build the canal, and far from the most complicated. When completed, the Morris Canal would rise 760 feet from the Delaware River to Lake Hopatcong, and from there descend 914 feet to the tidewaters near the Hudson. Not only was the 1,674-foot overall elevation change then the largest of any U.S. canal, slopes on the route were exceptionally steep. The Morris Canal averaged eighteen feet per mile of vertical movement, compared to only one foot per mile on the Erie Canal. Quite simply, the engineers in New Jersey had to design a canal that climbed mountains.[33]

A Columbia College professor named James Renwick accepted the challenge and created a design that strategically combined twenty-four locks and twenty-three inclined planes. Basically short-track railways, the planes were used in the steepest sections. As a canal boat approached an inclined plane, the boat settled into a U-shaped plane car, or "cradle," on the inclined plane's track. A massive rope pulled the cradle (and boat) up the track with the assistance of an underground water turbine. At the other end of the rope, another cradle and boat counterbalanced the up-going cradle and boat. While the boats rested in the cradles, captains strapped feedbags onto the mules that pulled boats from towpaths on shore. Designers ingeniously crafted both cradles and boats in two sections with a hinge in the middle, so that they could bend at the hump of each inclined plane.[34]

The Morris Canal opened for navigation between Phillipsburg and Newark in the spring of 1832. The canal path approached downtown Newark from the north and turned east at a street named in the era, Lock. From there the canal stretched along modern-day Raymond Boulevard, including an inclined plane between what were then called Plane and Bellevue streets. (Today, they're University Avenue and Martin Luther King Boulevard, respectively, and the plane sat at about the dividing line between Rutgers-Newark and Essex County College campuses.) The canal finally cut through an underground tunnel around Mulberry Street before reaching the Passaic.[35]

Amid much excitement, as many as twenty canal boats full of coal, iron ore, bricks, lumber, and other goods began arriving daily in Newark. Almost immediately, however, it was apparent that if the canal had a prayer of turning a profit, it would have to be extended to New York Harbor. The entire length of the canal would also have to be widened to accommodate barges large enough for safe towing across open waters to New York.[36]

When Thomas Gordon published his *Gazeteer of the State of New Jersey* in 1834, $2 million had already been spent on the canal, more than double the original estimate. Though the canal's "use has been most beneficial upon the business of the country through which it passes," Gordon wrote, the canal company "is deeply in debt, and pays no dividends to the stockholders."[37]

With no funds available to pay for improvements, company directors resorted to questionable, if not fraudulent, tactics to keep their businesses and their canal boats afloat. "They embarked on financial ventures which were nothing short of criminal," one early-twentieth-century historian wrote. "They participated in fake promotion schemes, floated loans on spurious collateral, perpetrated swindles through dummy organizations, and divided illegal gains with crooked agents and brokers."[38] Jacob Little, a New York City trader, made a fortune by manipulating stock in the Morris Canal & Banking Company, driving the price from $10 to $185 per share in 1834.[39]

No one was ever prosecuted for involvement with the canal, and in 1836 an eight-mile extension to Jersey City was completed. Nonetheless, the canal company filed for bankruptcy five years later, only to reform as a new Morris Canal & Banking Company in 1844. The new owners then widened the canal to forty feet. Over the next decade, they repaired and rebuilt the original wobbly inclined planes and lined areas prone to seepage with clay. By the mid-1850s the canal was in as sound condition as ever and transporting over 500,000 tons annually. For the year 1860, the canal's tonnage topped 700,000. The canal peaked in 1866, transporting just under 890,000 tons, more than half of which was coal.[40]

Unfortunately for Morris Canal backers, the waterway reached its prime around the same time railroads were rendering canals obsolete. There were only twenty-three miles of railroad in the United States in 1830, the same year that workers furiously hacked through the earth, building both the Morris Canal and the Delaware & Raritan Canal—a shorter, similarly financially troubled waterway connecting New Brunswick to Trenton and other towns along the Delaware. By 1840, nearly three thousand miles of railroad track had been laid in the United States. As of 1860, while the United States represented only about 5 percent of the world's population, it was home to more than thirty thousand miles of railroads—roughly the same amount that existed in the rest of the world combined.[41]

In New Jersey, forever defined as an in-between place, railroads held enormous possibility. Private corporations raised money from speculators and laid tracks early and often across the state. After the Camden and Amboy line opened a section of track between Perth Amboy and Bordentown in 1832, passengers and freight could zip between New York City and Philadelphia in seven hours, including time on the ferries. The Morris & Essex Railroad began operation between Newark and Morristown in 1837 with the help of Seth Boyden's six-ton locomotive *Orange*, named for the hilly region it chugged over on the route. Railroad connections expanded all over northern New Jersey in the mid-1800s, with branches reaching Boonton, Paterson, Scotch Plains, Bound Brook, Princeton, Jersey City, Hoboken, Phillipsburg, Rahway, Trenton, and New Brunswick, among other towns. Commuting was born.[42]

Railroads held obvious advantages over canals. Trains ran year-round, while canals were forced to shut down after the first winter freeze. By around 1870 a trip via rail between the Hudson and the Delaware rivers took roughly six hours; the same journey on the Morris Canal lasted four or five days. Trains could move passengers and freight, while canals handled the latter almost exclusively. One canal barge accommodated about the same amount of coal that could fit in just two railroad cars. Moving coal on and off a canal boat was arduous and time-consuming, whereas an overhead chute quickly and efficiently could dump a load of coal into a train car. There really was no competition between the two modes of transportation. Just as quickly as the canal had replaced the wagon for hauling goods, the train supplanted the canal boat.[43]

In 1871, the Lehigh Valley Railroad signed a ninety-nine-year lease for use of the Morris Canal, but the waterway would never show a profit again. Each year, the company moved more and more coal via train rather than boat. Shipping on the Morris Canal declined precipitously, down to under four hundred thousand tons in 1880—less than half of what it had been in the mid-1860s—and only thirty thousand tons per year around the turn of the century.[44]

Massive infrastructure projects from the pre–Civil War era left lasting marks all over increasingly urban northern New Jersey. In addition to the new canals, roads, and railroads crisscrossing the landscapes, the people brought in to toil away on the developments often stayed behind long after construction had ended. Naturally, they flocked to where they could find employment. For many, that meant the factories of flourishing industrial hubs such as Newark, which had undeniably become a city.

———

Though Newark was technically still only a township in the early 1830s, "city" problems—crime, poverty, housing shortages, general filth—had already surfaced alongside the extraordinary population growth. According to an 1836 report from the State Temperance Society, in the preceding eighteen months 517 people had been committed to the Newark Jail. Not surprisingly given its authors, the report pointed to alcohol as the cause of people's problems. Whatever the case, Newark was obviously home to a substantial number of troubled families: a little over 20 percent of the men arrested were charged with "beating and abusing their wives and children."[45]

In the early days, Newark appointed one or two citizens to tend the town's scant few poor. Each year, men interested in taking the poor into their homes placed bids, and the town handed over caretaking responsibilities for poor families to the lowest bidder. By 1805, this archaic welfare system didn't seem adequate, so town officials approved a poorhouse to be built. A decade passed before Newark actually had its own poorhouse, however. In 1815, the township purchased a farmhouse to shelter the poor and educate their children. This arrangement too quickly proved inadequate, and in 1823 the poorhouse was expanded.[46]

The State Temperance Society's 1836 report said that during a recent eighteen-month period, 252 paupers were admitted to Newark's poorhouse. Again, the report blamed alcohol abuse, with more than half the cases "distinctly traceable to intemperance alone."[47]

While typical urban problems plagued Newark, signs of its farming-village roots were slow to fade. Through at least 1831, the township found it necessary to pass laws fining the owners of pigs running at large.[48] Newark lacked street lamps, street maintenance, and other basic services that English towns half its size had. "The condition of the roads is bad, the public houses are not of that class which might be expected, and numerous other matters of a public nature are not satisfactorily attended to," one Newark native listed only as S. F. wrote in the *Newark Daily Advertiser*. The writer had been away from town since 1819 and was shocked at the transformation upon his return in 1834. He applauded "splendid rows of brick stores and dwellings" and the overall "march of improvements," yet grieved the loss of "that innocence and simple beauty" of the Newark of his youth.[49]

Newark had also recently experienced a series of other losses that seemed negligible at the time but would be viewed as missed opportunities, even blunders, a century afterward. For nearly all of its existence, and even for two decades after the Revolutionary War had ended, Newark encompassed most of modern-day Essex County. In the early 1800s, however, interests among the downtown manufacturers were increasingly at odds with the farms and villages to the north and west. In 1806, the township divided itself into three wards—Newark, Orange, and Bloomfield. Each ward measured roughly the same size (twenty square miles), and each had its own representatives and handled certain affairs independently. The arrangement didn't satisfy Orange residents, however, who created their own township the same year. Bloomfield followed suit in 1812. Clinton Township was the next to break off, created in 1834 out of parts of Newark, Orange, and Elizabethtown.[50]

Thus, in three short decades, while Newark reveled in its runaway growth and manufacturing riches, it lost at least two-thirds of the acreage once within its borders—land that would later be some of New Jersey's wealthiest suburbs. The parcels themselves split into tinier towns, with slices of Bloomfield becoming Belleville, Montclair, Nutley, and Glen Ridge. Orange divided into West, South, East, and plain Orange sections, as well as much of Maplewood. Clinton transformed into Irvington and parts of Maplewood, and a small portion returned to Newark. Had Newark maintained its earlier borders, many of its twentieth-century problems—notably, the disappearance of its tax base to the suburbs and a stagnant economy that couldn't grow partly due to Newark's small size—wouldn't have had nearly as severe an impact.

While prosperity in business and manufacturing had reached Newark, the town desperately needed wise, visionary leadership to match. "Some men of influence," the anonymous S. F. wrote in 1834, "may yet arise who will sacrifice themselves a little for the general welfare."

A change in the way Newark was governed seemed appropriate. The town meeting form of government could no longer cope with the needs of Newark's businesses and people, many citizens believed. They proposed officially incorporating Newark as a city. If power was concentrated in the hands of a mayor and a small group of officials, action could be taken promptly and efficiently on behalf of Newarkers. Roads could be paved, cleaned, and kept in order, and professional firemen and policemen could be hired, supporters argued. "Do you wish to have an efficient watch to protect your wives and daughters from insults in the streets?" an editorial rallying for incorporation asked. "Do you wish to have disturbers of the peace, riotous houses, and all others offending against good order brought to speedy justice?"[51]

Voters overwhelmingly answered yes on March 18, 1836, selecting "Corporation" over "No Corporation" in the ballot by a count of 1,870 to 325. That spring, Whig lawyer William Halsey was elected as Newark's first mayor. Progress followed, at least initially. Within weeks of the election, oil lamps lit a few street corners for the first time, and a team of watchmen, or policemen, began patrolling after dark. Newark's waterfront received a boost by being designated one of the country's official ports of entry. In July, Newark and Essex County officials agreed to jointly build a gorgeous Egyptian-style structure to house both the county courthouse and city administration. (Previously, Newark town meetings rotated among various churches and taverns.) Workers laid the new building's cornerstone just a month after the agreement was signed.[52]

As an ominous sign of larger trouble ahead, however, a fire that autumn tore through an entire block of buildings around Market and Mechanic streets. The following spring, years of rampant inflation and speculative real estate and money-lending schemes—often involving canals and railroads—finally caught up with investors in a severe depression, the Panic of 1837. Within a few months, nearly half the banks in the United States went out of business. The aggregate loss in New York City was estimated at $100 million. Manufacturing cities suffered particularly badly. Banks and businesses throughout Newark closed. A factory reportedly worth $30,000 sold at auction for $1,800. Dozens of families left their newly built Newark homes, unable to pay the mortgages. Street lamps went dark in 1838 in a cost-saving move. Despite its prime downtown location, the block burned out by fire the previous fall remained an empty, undeveloped heap of ashes for years.[53]

Newark's population, which crested around twenty thousand in 1836, dropped to just over sixteen thousand in 1838. The first men to lose their jobs, and most likely leave the city, were the Irish immigrants who had come to labor on the canals and stayed in the United States to work in booming factories. The number of immigrants living in Newark, estimated at 7,300 in 1835, fell to just 3,624 after the Panic.[54]

The city finally rebounded in the early 1840s, and another furious growth spurt ensued. The Irish still in Newark from the 1820s were joined by newly arrived Irish fleeing the mid-1840s potato famine. Germans also flooded into town after the failed revolutions of 1848 in central Europe. Thousands of new homes and tenements were built. Dozens of freshly erected smokestacks and church steeples filled the skyline. Manufacturing remained the city's lifeblood, employing nearly three-quarters of the workforce. Between 1845 and 1860, the number of jewelry makers, leather workers, saddle makers, and trunk makers employed in the city increased at least twofold.

The factory setting itself began to evolve, with workers using sewing machines, for example, instead of stitching by hand. From 1840 to 1846, the number of factories driven by steam power in Newark went from none to more than a hundred. A Scottish immigrant named Peter Ballantine built one of the city's first massive industrial plants—a brewery—in 1847 on the Passaic River near Rector Street. New white-collar businesses also made inroads, notably the Mutual Benefit life insurance (founded in 1845) and Howard Savings Institution (1857).[55]

The promise that a city government would clean up the streets and deliver better services was never realized, however, at least not as quickly as citizens hoped. Throughout the mid-1800s, Newark straddled a messy line between prosperous metropolis and unkempt industrial backwater. Mansions and brand-new factories sat blocks away from overcrowded, poorly built homes and gutters clogged with rubbish, manure, and occasionally, dead animals. Not a single Newark road was paved until the 1850s, when round stones were used sparingly. One Newarker recalled riding through the streets on his pony to do errands for his father—picking up tobacco at William A. Brintzinghoffer's, groceries at Whitty's on the corner of Bank and Broad streets, and candles, soap, and other household goods at Marcus L. Ward's store on Market Street. "The distances were not great," he wrote, "the traffic was not dense, but the pavement, where there was any, was bad and treacherous, if not exceedingly dangerous for a small horse."[56]

With feeble drainage systems in place, a decent rainfall turned the streets into rivers of impassable brown muck that swallowed wagon wheels and mule hooves. Flooding was worst, and the risk of malaria highest, in the marshy Down Neck (later, Ironbound) area inhabited mostly by poor Irish immigrants. The smoke and chemicals emanating from factories and tanneries were inescapable, and the stench of coal dust, animal dung, and raw sewage was everywhere.[57]

Several Newarkers died each year of rabies, prompting laws to be passed allowing citizens to kill any dog on sight that didn't have a muzzle and a collar stating its name and residence. Even with the restrictions, packs of wild dogs bedeviled Newark neighborhoods. A group of Newarkers took matters into their own hands in April of 1857, when some 150 dogs mysteriously died. After reports of the deaths surfaced, an anonymous letter arrived at the *Newark Daily Mercury*. For "the greatest good to the greatest number," a group calling itself the Newark Dog Poisoners Association had lived up to its name, leaving poisoned meat in various parts of the city. (They hadn't planned on a young boy eating some of the meat and getting seriously ill.) The writer stated that he himself had been viciously bitten by a dog the previous month, and that "nine-tenths of the community bid us God speed" in their resolve to rid the city of dangerous mutts. In July of 1857, after a pound had opened near Canal Street, a bounty of fifty cents per dog was offered. One boy alone brought in 24 unmuzzled dogs, and in just two days a total of 170 dogs were impounded. By summer's end nearly 2,500 dogs had been captured and killed, either via pistol or drowning.[58]

In some ways, Newark's problems were no different from those of other cities. New York and Boston were arguably dirtier, more dangerous, and less healthy than Newark in the mid-1800s. Still, there was no denying that public services lagged behind in Newark. If the city compared itself to Providence, Troy, Rochester, or other towns of similar size, "we shall find how far we are behind them in municipal improvements," one Newark alderman said in 1851. He estimated that nine out ten Newarkers believed "that our Fire Department needs many facilities which it does not now possess, that our city should be lighted, that a Market should be provided of a suitable character, that greater Common School accommodations are necessary."[59]

The main reason progressive measures came slowly, if at all, during the era was that business and industry led the city in every sense, including politically. With few exceptions, the mayors in the years preceding the Civil War were rich men directly tied to the city's financial and manufacturing industries. First and foremost, their priorities in office revolved around promoting business in the city.[60]

Like good businessmen everywhere, Newark's elected officials were reluctant to part with a dollar. A low tax rate would continue attracting manufacturing interests. To the detriment of the poor and working classes, and the city's overall health, safety, and appearance, Newark spent money on professional fire and police departments, street lighting and paving, and other public services only when there seemed to be no other alternatives. Stingy policies continued even as Newark emerged in 1860 as the largest industrial-based city in the United States—ranking eleventh overall in population at the time.[61]

One especially pound-foolish decision from the era was the failure to preserve land for public parks. Other than the small triangular commons established by Newark settlers in the late 1600s, almost no lots were restricted from development. Buildings had even been erected on the colonial-era South Common, though in 1850 the city officially preserved and expanded the lot for four acres. It was renamed South Park and after the Civil War renamed again as Lincoln Park.

Around the same time New York City was setting aside 843 acres for Central Park, the *Newark Daily Mercury* needled Newark officials to take similarly far-sighted steps, if not downtown than somewhere nearby. "In a few years, our population will have doubled, crowding our mechanics and laboring men into these outer wards," an 1853 editorial stated. "It is therefore more necessary that immediate steps should be taken to secure the great advantages resulting from public parks to the health and welfare of those who most require them."[62]

Real estate was too valuable to be cordoned off for such frivolous purposes, Newark's leadership believed at the time. Decades would pass before any significant acreage in Newark was reserved for parkland. By then, it was too late to follow the advice of another *Mercury* editorial from the 1850s. After praising the city's economic triumphs, the paper asked "our merchants and business men" to "understand their high and responsible duties" and seek "progress in all things calculated to improve the character of our people." A phrase of warning, printed ominously in boldface, ended the call to action: "**The future is purchased by the present.**"[63]

CHAPTER 2

POLITICS TO THE DOGS

SOUTHERN SYMPATHY DURING THE CIVIL WAR

Among the small clique of businessmen-politicians leading Newark through its dramatic mid-1800s rise, few could boast of more wealth or better connections than William Wright. Shown in a portrait with a dignified, stern gaze, thin lips pursed smugly, almost in a frown, and dark hair curling over his ears with flair, Wright was best known as the owner of Newark's preeminent saddle manufacturing company—the largest in the city, if not in the entire country. The Whig Party, which ruled local politics and held the mayoralty through Newark's first two decades as a city, tapped William Wright to run for his first-ever political seat in 1841. He was elected without opposition as Newark's fifth mayor. Serving three consecutive one-year terms, Wright began a meandering, opportunistic political career that stretched through the heart of the nation's bloodiest years.[1]

During the Civil War, New Jersey earned a reputation as the most traitorous state in the North because of men like William Wright. Perhaps the most obvious reason Wright and other Newark manufacturers opposed "Lincoln's war," as they often called it, was that the conflict jeopardized their lucrative business ties with the South. Many "Copperheads," as anti-Lincoln men were called, also clung to a prevalent stance that argued, quite plainly, nothing was wrong with slavery. The institution represented the natural state of race relations, they claimed, and it was the South's prerogative to keep slavery legal if it so chose. The life of William Wright provides a window into the mindset of Civil War-era Newark, when the city, and New Jersey as a whole, may have officially adhered to the Union, but citizens were hardly united behind President Abraham Lincoln. In William Wright, one can also witness the changing state of politics, namely, in the increasingly blatant use of money to gain power and influence.

Born around 1790, Wright was the son of Dr. William Wright, a physician with a respected practice just over the New Jersey border, in New York's

Rockland County. Dr. Wright was a Yale man, earning a bachelor's degree in 1774 and a medical degree three years later. While at boarding school in Poughkeepsie in 1808, the younger William Wright received the unexpected news that his father had died on a visit to the South, and William Wright Jr. never had the chance to follow his father's footsteps in college.

An uncle arranged for William to be apprenticed to Anson Phelps, a Connecticut saddle maker who had much in common with the young man. After Phelps's parents had died in the early 1790s, a preteen Anson became the apprentice of a saddle maker, like William Wright would be one day. Phelps would be remembered much more for his phenomenal talents as a businessman than as a mere craftsman, however. A mercantile business he established in Hartford traded saddles for cotton from Charleston, South Carolina, which Phelps then sold in New York City or directly to England. With his son-in-law William Earl Dodge, Phelps opened the New York–based firm Phelps-Dodge, which traded in brass, copper, and cotton, among other goods, and still exists to this day as a mining and mineral-processing company. Phelps also founded Ansonia, a Connecticut copper-producing industrial village named in his honor, and held considerable investments in railroads, banking, and real estate. When he died in 1853, Phelps's estate was worth more than $2 million.[2]

Certainly, as a young apprentice under the brilliant Anson Phelps, William Wright learned much more than the art of making saddles and harnesses. Sometime after volunteering as a soldier in the War of 1812, Wright had the chance to sail to Charleston, South Carolina, with a load of saddles to sell for Phelps. Wright also brought an eye open for opportunity on the trip. Upon his return to the North, Wright gathered the $300 he'd saved over the years and convinced two wealthy Connecticut industrialists, Sheldon Smith and William Peet, to partner with him in a new venture manufacturing and trading saddles. In 1815, they opened a small store in Bridgeport, Connecticut, as well as a branch in Charleston, under the name Peet, Smith & Company. Early on, customers assumed Wright, the most visible member of the operation, was "Peet Smith," sometimes asking why he didn't spell his first name "Peter." By 1816, with the company blooming, William Peet retired from an active role. Still in his twenties, William Wright became an equal partner in the prosperous, expanding firm Smith & Wright. No one would call him "Peet" again.

After marrying William Peet's daughter Minerva in 1819, the ambitious Wright turned his attentions to New Jersey. Facing increased competition and limited growth potential in Bridgeport, Wright and his partner, Sheldon Smith, quickly saw that Newark, then a growing industrial force of about seven thousand people, had two key assets for a saddle manufacturer: a flourishing leather industry, thanks in part to Seth Boyden's innovations, and established trade connections with the South. Smith & Wright moved its northern operations in the early 1820s to Newark's city center, opening a factory at the southeast corner of Broad and Fair streets. (Fair later became Lafayette Street; the factory stood at about the spot of the Prudential Center arena.) The company soon attained the status as one of the country's top saddle and harness manufacturers, with branches in Charleston, Augusta, Mobile, and New Orleans.[3]

Wright immediately took an interest beyond saddles in his new state. Over the years, he networked relentlessly and sat on the board or held some other official position at the Newark Mechanics' Bank, the Mechanics Insurance Company, the Newark Savings Institution, and northern New Jersey's two leading transportation corporations, the Morris & Essex Railroad and the Morris Canal & Banking Company. Wright also donated liberally to the Episcopal Church and dutifully maintained a presence in society, serving as president of the New Jersey Horticulture Society, among other organizations.[4]

In due time, William and Minerva Wright owned a handsome mansion on Park Place with white pillars at the front door and a view, beyond their yard's tall trees and wrought-iron fence, of the greenery of Military Park. The setting was more reminiscent of Charleston or Savannah than a typical northern city, especially considering that the house was staffed with black maids and cooks.[5]

In contrast to her always-busy husband, Minerva Wright was "averse to taking exercise" and most comfortable at home, according to their son, Edward Henry Wright. In a letter to his sister, Catherine, Edward blamed their mother's lonesome, "sedentary mode of life [as] the cause of those fearful attacks of headache." Minerva Wright spent her time making "a clatter with those dishes in the morning," keeping a close watch on the house's troublesome servants, or "darkies," as Edward wrote. By the early 1850s, Minerva Wright managed to convince William, a notorious penny-pincher known for saying he refused "to pay another cent," to allow her and Catherine to close their Park Place household each winter for a cozy stint at the Clarendon, one of New York City's finest hotels.[6]

Though William Wright occasionally cut back on his son's allowance in college, and was reluctant to pay for his daughter to travel abroad, the Wright children were raised in an undeniably privileged world. Catherine Maria Wright socialized in the most elite circles and in 1855 married a Dutch ambassador. Edward Henry Wright attended the College of New Jersey and studied law under Alexander Hamilton before attending Harvard Law School.[7] Edward traveled extensively in Europe and in the early 1850s became an ambassador in St. Petersburg. While in Russia, he socialized with royalty, attended dozens of balls, and generally lived in splendor, complete with an African American servant kept in his place by Edward's condescending manner. "George, my ebony servant, popped his head in my bedroom this morning, and wished me a happy New Year with the genuine African grin," Edward wrote to his mother from Russia on January 1, 1851. "There was no resisting the appeal of his pearly teeth, so I asked for my purse and made over to him the usual present."[8]

Edward and his sister Catherine—or Kit, as he called her—rarely dared to disagree with their authoritarian father. In letters, they referred to him simply as "the Member." Like most men at the forefront of business and politics in Newark's early days as a city, William Wright was active in the Whig Party. During the course of his political rise, William Wright often came into conflict with another powerful Newark Whig, one-time New Jersey governor William Pennington. The families engaged in what became the bitterest of rivalries. When Minerva Wright was concerned her son might be interested in marrying his old friend Mary Pennington, Edward reassured his mother there was no need to worry. "The family is if anything more odious to me than you," he wrote.[9]

Despite their wealth, travels, and society status, William, Minerva, and their children all shared a glum, antisocial streak. "All the Wrights," Edward wrote, "shut themselves out from the world, even if they have the best advantages. Whether from modesty or pride I know not."[10]

William Wright's fallout with William Pennington began around Wright's final year as Newark mayor, when the Whigs snubbed his quest to run for a House of Representatives seat. Wright decided to run anyway without the endorsement of any political party. He attracted a coalition that included Democrats and defeated William B. Kinney, grandson of doctor, judge, and Revolution-era leader William Burnet. (The "B" in Kinney's name is Burnet.) Kinney was the regular Whig nominee for the district in question, and also a nephew of William Pennington, so Wright's election obviously created friction between the two families.[11]

Two years after Wright won the House seat, voters reelected him for another term. In 1847, the Whigs settled on William Wright as their best chance to win the governorship, despite his infidelity to the party. Wright's nomination outraged the most conservative Whigs, who distributed a pamphlet citing seventeen points why the man should not be elected. "The successive elevation of Mr. Wright to high places of honor, by the votes of the Whig party," point number fifteen stated, "is virtually to declare that it values political expediency above true principle." Among the criticisms were Wright's record of "relying on money—*money*—as the chief element of success" in elections, "placing large sums in the hands of irresponsible persons." With Wright at the helm of the state, point number sixteen charged, he would "set up the office of Governor to the highest bidder, to make it an object of traffic for unprincipled political managers, and to demoralize and corrupt the people." Under the subheading "The Artful Dodger," the paper listed fifteen issues in the legislature—during a single summer—that Wright never bothered to cast a vote upon. "Never before did a man receive, month in and month out, eight dollars a day, for dodging his duty." When he actually did address a topic, Wright managed to be "on both sides of every important question," donating "money freely to Romanists and to Protestants" and waffling on the always testy issue of temperance. "He gives water freely to temperance men, presides in the Big Tent, and gives them a big dinner," the pamphlet claimed, "yet as freely affords something stronger than water to anti-temperance men, and sets the example of drinking it himself."[12]

His campaign sabotaged, Wright lost the election to Daniel Haines, a Democrat who had served as governor a few years earlier. Wright attended the Whig national convention of 1848 as a delegate from New Jersey. By the early 1850s, however, even though Whig Millard Fillmore presided at the White House, it was becoming clear that the Whig Party was nearing its demise in the United States. Edward Wright attributed the Whigs' troubles in New Jersey to "deserting their principles and fighting for *men*. It was no longer a question to be asked as to a candidate, whether he was a Whig, but was he a Wright man, or did he side with the Penningtons."[13]

Many antislavery Whigs turned their allegiance to the emerging Republican Party. William Pennington, for one, became a Republican. Wright, whose saddle business had been partly based in the South for more than three decades, sympathized in the opposite direction. In 1851 he officially defected to the Democratic Party. "I know Father is too honorable a man to have deserted his party for mere personal motives," a hopeful Edward Wright wrote.[14] The timing of Wright's shift seems uncanny in retrospect; the Democrats would win the next two presidential contests and triumph far more often than fail in New Jersey elections over the next two decades.

Though the public never again voted Wright into office, New Jersey Democrats managed to "meet their pledges, and display their gratitude," in the words of the *New York Times*, by appointing the rich, influential Wright to the U.S. Senate twice, in 1853 and 1863. (Before the Seventeenth Amendment passed in 1913, senators were selected by state legislatures, not directly by the people.) "New-Jersey may be said to have touched the lowest deep of degradation," the *Times* reflected upon Wright's first appointment. In pitying tones, the paper declared that Wright "is neither a very strong nor very wicked man. He is simply a weak and excessively vain one."[15]

Wright, however, was merely a "tool for designing men to use for their own shrewd purposes, and mercenary ones to bleed without compunction," little more than "the proxy of the clique whose power placed him there." The *Times* was more concerned about an earlier Democratic appointee, Robert F. Stockton, grandson of Richard Stockton, colonial New Jersey Supreme Court justice and signer of the Declaration of Independence. A naval officer and ruthless businessman, the younger Stockton and his partner, Newark's John Stevens, had combined the Delaware & Raritan Canal and the Camden & Amboy Railroad into the Joint Companies; for years the organization, known as one of the first in New Jersey for blatantly buying off legislators, enjoyed a monopoly on transportation between Philadelphia and New York City. "The election of Stockton was the sale of the State to a great private corporation," the *Times* stated, "and each succeeding fact is nothing more than a transfer of possession, in devout compliance with the terms of the bill of sale."[16]

Wright retired from an active role in Smith & Wright in 1854, devoting himself to public affairs and the Democratic Party. Soon after Wright's Senate term ran out, New Jersey Democrats selected him to represent the party as a delegate at the April 1860 national convention in a city Wright knew well: Charleston, South Carolina.

The convention wound up a bust. Delegates were deeply split on which direction the party should take regarding slavery. Compromise seemed impossible. The meeting adjourned without a presidential nomination after fifty delegates from the South walked out in protest when the party failed to adopt a vehemently pro-slavery platform. In June, Democrats reconvened in Baltimore to try to work out their differences, but this time, 110 Southern delegates walked out. Those remaining selected Stephen Douglas, a moderate who had beaten Abraham Lincoln in an Illinois Senate contest two years prior, after their famous series of debates. The protesting Southern faction nominated its own candidate, John Breckinridge. Formerly a senator from Kentucky and currently vice president under James Buchanan, Breckinridge would go on to lead Confederate troops as a general.[17]

Though Abraham Lincoln received slightly less than 40 percent of the popular vote in the 1860 election, he faced a diluted opposition and carried nearly all of the northern and western states—enough for a victory. New Jersey stood out as the lone northern state that failed to give all of its electoral votes to Honest Abe. Douglas received 52 percent of the popular vote in the state, including majority support in Newark, Trenton, Jersey City, and Camden. The way the system then worked in New Jersey, however, meant that its seven electoral votes would be split, with four going to Lincoln and three to Douglas.[18]

Though the Democrats lost the national election, the party in New Jersey clearly remained formidable. One of the party's 1860 candidates for Congress was a peer of William Wright's named Nehemiah Perry. Insulted as "Knee-High-Miah," the short-of-stature, balding Perry wore bushy pork-chop sideburns extending below his chin. He owned a Newark clothing manufacturing company which, up until the Civil War, exported most of its goods to the South. With the help of strong anti-Lincoln sentiment, Perry beat Wright's nemesis, William Pennington, in his reelection bid as a Republican. A well-respected former New Jersey governor, Pennington was then the Speaker of the House. Many viewed his defeat in an acrimonious campaign as a national embarrassment. Pennington's supporters squarely blamed the episode on "that band of mercenary and unprincipled men, engaged in the Southern trade"—presumably William Wright and his cohorts—"who have been foremost in producing this result," the *Newark Daily Mercury* wrote. "If they had been slaves themselves, and every morning had been lashed into humility, they could not have worked more heartily to carry out the wishes of their Southern masters."[19]

As for Wright, he would have to wait until 1863—when the Democrats had another opportunity to appoint him to the Senate—before he again held political office. During the interim, Abraham Lincoln came into the presidency, and the South seceded from the Union. New Jersey began building its reputation as a haven for antiwar Democrats, or "Copperheads," and William Wright managed to play a role in the loudest, angriest, most influential voice to consistently portray the war as an illegal, misguided abolitionist quest. One of Wright's many investments, a newspaper called the *Newark Daily Journal*, would handle the dirty work.

———

The *Journal* was the child of two failed newspapers—the *Jacksonian* and the *Newark Daily Eagle*—that had both fallen into the possession of William Wright. Edward Fuller, who for five years had been editor of the Portsmouth-based Democratic mouthpiece, the *New Hampshire Gazette*, was imported to take charge of the *Journal*, first published on November 2, 1857. From his second-floor office at 138 Market Street, Fuller tirelessly attacked all opponents of conservatives, states' rights, and the Democratic Party. With the Democrats split in 1860 over who was the party's legitimate presidential nominee,

Fuller sided with the South's candidate, John Breckinridge. A month after Lincoln's win at the national polls—and his loss in New Jersey—the *Journal* proudly claimed that "New Jersey alone breasts the storm of fanaticism," and suggested that the state openly side with the South to "place us in a position of unexampled prosperity." In time, readers would get to know more of the views of Wright's editor: that the abolishment of slavery would be a "worse calamity than disunion," that the draft was nothing short of tyranny, and that President Lincoln was both a "monstrous despot" and a "perjured traitor."[20]

New Jersey, and big cities like Newark in particular, would suffer tremendously in a war with the South, the logic went. With Charleston, Savannah, Mobile, New Orleans, and other southern cities no longer buying carriages, saddles, shoes, clothing, and jewelry from the North, Newark and other manufacturing cities were bound to spiral into depression. Factories would shut, and thousands of workers would be laid off. "What would this place be if it were not for the South?" a Newark newspaper asked as early as 1854. "What would become of the millions of manufactured goods annually exported from this city?"[21] In the 1860 presidential campaign, a broadside addressed to the "mechanics and working-men of Newark" called the Republicans "that party which will be the instrument of taking bread from the mouths of your wives and children." The author of the screed, listed only as "TRUTH," was most likely *Daily Journal* editor Edward Fuller.[22]

The prospect of a Lincoln White House stirred other fears as well—namely, a change in the "peculiar institution." Though New Jersey legislation freed all black children born after 1846 within its borders, there were eighteen elderly human beings still enslaved in the Garden State as of 1860. New Jersey was then the only northern state to have any slaves. It was also the only northern state that allowed runaway slaves to be captured within its borders and sent back to the South.

Abraham Lincoln always presented the Civil War first and foremost as a means to save the Union, not end slavery. Yet, most people assumed that the institution was in jeopardy with Lincoln as president. If the slaves were freed, it was believed, they would naturally head north. Thousands would flood into New Jersey, part of which extended farther south than Baltimore, as often pointed out at the time. Worried about the prospect of competing for factory jobs with newly freed blacks, or motivated by ignorance or sheer racism, some New Jerseyans actively fought to maintain the status quo. Still others were ambivalent about slavery, yet opposed the federal government overstepping its bounds. They might have personally thought slavery was wrong, but genuinely believed in states' rights—that each state, and the state alone, could come to its own conclusions and pass its own laws.

By the time Abraham Lincoln said "the Union of these States is perpetual" and "the central idea of secession is the essence of anarchy" in his inaugural address on March 4, 1861, seven states had already seceded, led by South Carolina. In mid-April, Southern forces seized Fort Sumter in Charleston Harbor. Within two months, four more states joined the Confederacy.

The anti-Lincoln Democrats were known as Copperheads because at first they distinguished themselves by wearing copper Liberty-head coins clipped onto their coats. The name caught on, however, because Copperheads were viewed by many as treacherous snakes. Among New Jersey's Copperheads, Edward Fuller and David Naar, of Trenton's *Daily True American*, ranked as the most influential newspapermen, while William Wright and Congressman Nehemiah Perry stood out as a couple of the highest profile politicians. It's impossible to say exactly how many New Jerseyans were Copperheads. They were not a political organization per se, but a loosely associated group of extremists within the Democratic Party. Rodman Price, New Jersey governor in the mid-1850s, was assuredly one. After the 1860 election, he encouraged not only New Jersey, but also New York and Pennsylvania to "cast their lot with the South" for "every wise, prudential and patriotic reason." After all, "slavery is no sin," Rodman reflected. "Slavery—subordination to the superior race—is his natural and normal condition."[23]

William Wright maintained a fairly low profile for the duration of the war, though the way he spent his money and the company he kept spoke volumes. In 1861, Wright thought it prudent to sell his interest in the controversial *Daily Journal*. He and other Democrats continued to finance operations, however.[24]

As the war commenced, Copperheads witnessed their doomsday prophecies coming true. In the words of Newark Mayor (and Democrat) Moses Bigelow, "the first effect" of the struggle had been "a general prostration" of industrial interests, which "unless soon adjusted, will cause unprecedented deprivation and suffering."[25] An economic malaise settled upon Newark, and what had been a rapidly growing population dropped from seventy-three thousand in 1861 to sixty-eight thousand in 1863.

Despite the bleak outlook, and feelings for Lincoln that were mixed at best, thousands of Newarkers rallied behind their commander-in-chief. "Strong men ground their teeth in rage," in reaction to the Southern secession, wrote one New Jersey Republican. "The Union of our fathers, cemented by so much patriotic blood, was crumbling to pieces, and anarchy alone could follow."[26]

For stalwart Unionists inside and outside New Jersey, Lincoln's inauguration couldn't come quickly enough. In the course of a twelve-day journey by rail from Illinois to Washington, D.C., in February 1861, the president-elect was met by enthusiastic crowds throughout New Jersey. Lincoln's visit to Newark occurred just a few weeks after Mayor Bigelow congratulated New Jersey as "faithful to the Constitution and loyal to the rights and institutions of all her sisters in the Confederacy."[27] Still, thousands of Newarkers gave Lincoln a warm welcome as the train, decorated in flags, streamers, and flowers, rolled in from Jersey City.[28]

"On both sides of the streets was one dense mass of people," a *Philadelphia Inquirer* reporter wrote of the stop in Newark. "Ladies waved their handkerchiefs, and men uncovered their heads. Stalwart mechanics cheered as though their lungs were made of bell metal." Compared to other cities welcoming Lincoln, however, the official reception in Newark was subdued. There was no band, military display, or much of any formal arrangement planned for the visit, which only lasted half an hour. The crowd in the streets, however, had done a little decorating. An effigy inscribed with the words "THE TRAITOR'S DOOM" hung from a lamppost.[29]

Within two weeks of Fort Sumter's fall, Lincoln asked for seventy-five thousand volunteers to enroll in the armed services, and ten thousand New Jersey men had answered the call—more than three times the state's quota. "Friends, our country is in danger," one Newarker cried. "Throw politics to the dogs for the present."[30] Beyond patriotism and the feverish excitement war can inspire in the uninitiated, the decent pay—$15 per month combined from the federal and state governments—and a struggling New Jersey economy with few job prospects led to a surplus wanting to enlist.[31] New Jersey Governor Charles Olden named Newark's Theodore Runyon, a Democrat who had cast one of New Jersey's electoral votes for Stephen Douglas, as brigadier general in charge of the state's first brigade.

As New Jerseyans prepared for war, "An Old Soldier" passed along helpful tips via the *Newark Daily Advertiser* to inexperienced volunteers. "Remember that in a campaign more men die from sickness than by the bullet," he counseled. It was therefore essential to "keep your entire person clean" to prevent "fevers and bowel complaints in warm climates." A small blanket would come in handy "to lay on the ground or throw over your shoulders when on guard duty during a rain storm," while "the best military hat in use is the light colored soft felt, the crown being sufficiently high to allow space for air over the brain." Also, the writer suggested, "let your beard grow, so as to protect the throat and lungs."[32]

Toward the end of April of 1861, a mix of national guardsmen and enlistees could regularly be seen parading the streets of Newark, clad in new shoes and blue coats issued courtesy of the local militia. At 10 AM on April 29, the full regiment of 780 troops gathered at Military Park in full uniform. Throughout the day, the stars and stripes flew in front of nearly every building. An outspoken group had even goaded the *Newark Daily Journal* into displaying a Union flag in its Market Street window. Every few feet, family, friends, and random well-wishers clustered around a man bound to leave that day for Trenton, and, soon thereafter, the war. A young girl said goodbye to her brother. A teary wife adjusted her husband's uniform. A father shook his son's hand and left him holding a revolver.[33]

By noon, crowds estimated between ten thousand and fifteen thousand filled Military Park. A band led a procession from the green, followed by Newark's Fire Department, dressed in red shirts and helmets adorned with Union badges. The soldiers followed the march up Broad Street, turned left on Washington Place, and then moved down Washington Street. Women waved handkerchiefs from windows and balconies of three-story row homes lining the route. Thousands cheering from the sidewalks joined the parade as it passed. Their destination was the city's lone high school, a wide three-story stone building, opened in 1839, with three small towers and neat rows of colonial grille windows. In front, dozens of flags decorated a platform, where city superintendent, George Sears, gave a brief speech and presented the gift of a flag. Made of heavy silk, golden tassels, and lace, and measuring six feet six inches long and six feet wide, the flag was the handiwork of a Broad Street craftswoman. "Take it," Sears said, "and let no traitor ever find shelter under its folds." The crowd applauded and cheered jubilantly. "If this Regiment should ever fall, never let the flag be dishonored," Sears continued. "Let it never return till you have done your all to sustain the 34 stars represented on it."[34]

———

Theodore Runyon's raw New Jersey troops saw action that summer in the war's first major engagement, the First Battle of Bull Run (or Manassas, as it is also known). The mixed results foreshadowed a long struggle ahead. On July 21, 1861, after initial signs of success, Union forces retreated from the northern Virginia battlefields back to Washington, D.C. In the aftermath of the lackluster performance, General George B. McClellan assumed command of the newly formed Army of the Potomac. The brilliant thirty-four-year-old "Little Mac" had been heralded as a prodigy since his days at West Point, where he graduated second in the class of 1846 at the age of just nineteen. Of McClellan's fifty-eight former classmates, forty-four would fight for one side or the other during the Civil War.

Soon enough, however, McClellan proved to be an ineffective leader on the battlefield, often slow to engage the enemy—or to make any decision for that matter. Frequently questioning orders and keeping information away from the president, McClellan, a longtime Democrat, had also proven contentious and pompous. "Again I have been called upon to save the country," he wrote to his wife in typical fashion.[35]

Despite having a significant advantage in troop numbers—and the battle plan of his opponent, General Robert E. Lee, placed in his hand in advance—McClellan failed to register a decisive victory at the Battle of Antietam. The conflict, on September 17, 1862, would be remembered as "the bloodiest day of the war," with some twelve thousand Union men and eleven thousand Confederates killed. Ignoring his orders, McClellan stalled in pursuit of desperate Army of Virginia troops, arguably prolonging the war. Understandably frustrated, Lincoln dismissed McClellan in November, after the commander again dawdled upon receiving orders to push troops southward.[36]

A golden opportunity had been squandered at Antietam. Still, the marginal victory boosted morale somewhat in the North, giving President Lincoln the chance to make a momentous announcement. Within a week of the battle, Union newspapers published a preliminary version of the Emancipation Proclamation. As of January 1, 1863, "all persons held as slaves within" the Confederacy "shall be then, thenceforth and forever free," the document read.

After Lincoln's announcement, McClellan, who was not remotely an abolitionist, felt he had been used. He immediately wrote a draft protesting the doctrine, before a friend convinced him that it was unwise to send it to the president.[37]

Again, Copperhead predictions seemed to be becoming reality. The *Newark Daily Journal's* Edward Fuller called the Emancipation Proclamation "as absurd as it is fanatical." The war, originally envisioned solely to preserve the country, had been co-opted by zealots, they maintained. The rights of white men everywhere were in jeopardy. "If you love your country better than the Negro, the Union better than party, drop these diverting, ruinous measures," Newark's Nehemiah Perry urged his peers in Congress. "Millions for the Union, not one cent for abolition."[38]

As the fall elections of 1862 neared, the New Jersey Democratic Party increased criticisms of the war's handlers. The platform adopted at its convention included a "solemn protest against the reckless extravagance, infamous speculation and political outrages of the party in power," while still advocating "the suppression of the rebellion." As for abolition, the Democrats declared, "That we do entirely reject and abhor the idea that, as an object of the present civil war, any purpose of emancipation of the slaves shall be thereby promoted or at all regarded."[39] The state Democratic Committee took

Lincoln's doctrine to task on the grounds that the government was unlaw-fully seizing private property—slaves—from their owners. In the committee's words, the Emancipation Proclamation represented "an unconstitutional use of power to blot out of existence the institutions of whole states, and destroy the private property of the innocent people of those states."[40]

Running on a campaign that demonized the Republicans and called for "the Constitution as it is and the Union as it was," New Jersey Democrats crushed their opponents on November 4, 1862. Joel Parker, facing off in the governor's race versus Republican Marcus Ward, a popular advocate of servicemen known as "The Soldier's Friend," received nearly 57 percent of the votes. Parker's margin of victory was a record high. He lost only seven counties, all in the southern part of the state. Even in Ward's hometown of Newark, Parker carried eleven of the thirteen wards.

Overall, Democrats increased what was a slight majority into a strangle-hold of the state legislature. They now held a forty-five to seventeen advantage over the Republicans in the assembly, and controlled twelve of the twenty seats in the state Senate. "Uncle Abraham," a giddy Edward Fuller wrote in the *Daily Journal*, "will hear the thunder at the White House and make a note of the fact that the Jersey blues are aroused in defense of their own rights and liberties."[41] The Democrats triumphed nationally as well in 1862, gaining thirty-four seats in Congress.[42]

Now more firmly in control of the New Jersey legislature than ever, the Democrats chose a vehement Copperhead named James Wall for appointment in the Senate. A lawyer from Burlington, Wall attended the 1860 Democratic convention in Charleston alongside William Wright and supported the Southern candidate Breckinridge. Wall wrote regularly for conservative Democratic newspapers including the *New York Daily News* and Wright's *Daily Journal*. Wall became somewhat of a martyr in 1861 after the federal government threw him in jail for two weeks. Officially, his crime was protesting the seizure of antiwar newspapers, though some Republican newspapers reported that Wall had been actively encouraging Maryland to secede. Authorities released Wall after he took an oath of allegiance, but to Democrats the arbitrary arrest remained a sign that with the Republicans in power the rights of citizens everywhere were in danger.[43]

Not all Democrats were pleased with the selection of an extremist such as Wall. "I would be lacking in my duty to my constituents, did I permit this opportunity to pass without entering my solemn protest against the election to the U.S. Senate of such a man as Mr. Wall," one Camden congressman said, addressing the Democratic chairman. "It is my belief, sir, that if he had lived in the days of the revolution he would have been a British patriot . . .

and in this second revolution, that he is a Union patriot with Confederate principles."[44]

Nonetheless, the congressman ultimately cast his support behind Wall, as did all but one of the Democratic legislators voting. Two weeks after the Emancipation Proclamation had gone into effect, the man called the "most implacable anti-administration, anti-war, anti-Union man in the state" was officially named a member of the U.S. Senate.[45]

Wall made it to the Senate only as a short-term replacement. His term was due to end in late February, so New Jersey legislators still needed to vote someone into the Senate for a full term. Wall lobbied for the position, but Democrats instead selected William Wright. The elderly saddle manufacturer had apparently bribed his way to the post, throwing money around to woo support like never before. "Nothing but his wealth enabled him to be elected," was a typical refrain in newspapers.[46]

To Republicans and pro-war Democrats, Wright's appointment was somewhat of a blessing. Compared to a feisty, outspoken Copperhead such as Wall, Wright was a harmless nonentity. He had done the bare minimum during his earlier time in the Senate. Now older and in poor health, he would repeat the performance in his second stint. While Wright would surely go along with whatever Democratic Party leaders decided, and he was believed to sympathize with the most extreme Copperheads, he had kept his personal views largely private of late. Perhaps he was not as antiwar as his friends at the *Daily Journal*, some speculated. Wright's son Edward, after all, served as an officer in the war; he had recently returned to New Jersey with the general he had served under, George McClellan.[47]

With a compliant William Wright and the rest of the new, overwhelmingly Democratic state government in place, the Copperheads "not only brought political, but social and business influences to bear," one New Jersey Republican contemporary wrote. "The anticipated arrival of Lee's army, at the time of the advance upon Gettysburg, was the occasion of undisguised joy among disloyalists, and they would have gladly welcomed him to our state."[48]

Times seemed especially bleak to New Jersey's Republicans. One of their highest-profile publications, the *Newark Daily Mercury*, went out of business that year (1863) because of a lack of support.

Early in that same year, *Daily Journal* editor Edward Fuller and others invited Ohio Congressman Clement L. Vallandigham to give an address at a Union Democratic Club rally in Newark. Vallandigham was the country's best-known, outspoken Copperhead. By May of 1863, he would be sentenced to two years in jail for treason, which Lincoln later commuted to banishment.[49] The February 14, 1863, event at Newark's Concert Hall drew a huge crowd that included Mayor Bigelow, William Wright, and Nehemiah Perry, who introduced the evening's featured lecturer. Congressman Vallandigham, who the *Daily Journal* called a "fearless champion of the people's liberties," spoke for two hours to the cheering masses. He demanded resistance to the expected draft, the ousting of Lincoln from the White House in the 1864 election, and an immediate stop to "this miserable crusade against African slavery."[50]

Emboldened, some New Jersey Democrats pushed a bill on March 18 called "An Act to Prevent the Immigration of Negroes and Mullatoes." The bill, which aimed to deport to Liberia "or some island in the West Indies" all people of color who "shall hereafter come in this state and remain therein for ten days or more," passed in the assembly before dying in the state senate. Another bill considered that day succeeded in being passed into law. In it, the legislature lodged an official protest "against a war waged with the insurgent States for the accomplishment of unconstitutional or partisan purposes . . . against all arrests without warrant . . . against the expenditures of the public moneys for the emancipation of slaves or their support at any time," among other measures.[51]

Upon hearing of the so-called Peace Resolutions passed by their home-state representatives, many New Jersey soldiers were disgusted. One regiment sent its own letter of resolution to the legislature, calling the protest "wicked, weak and cowardly."[52]

The federal Conscription Act, passed on March 3, 1863, had been one of the prime reasons New Jersey's borderline-treasonous Peace Resolutions had been written. Until then, there hadn't been a national draft; each state was responsible for meeting its soldier quota however it saw fit, and Union forces consisted mostly of volunteers and national guardsmen. Now, any man aged eighteen to forty-five was subject to induction into the service—and forced to fight for the black race, anti-abolitionists claimed. Copperheads unsurprisingly reacted with outrage. "If the people have one tithe of virtue and manliness of their fathers," Edward Fuller wrote, "they will steadily refuse to be offered up as victims to the infernal destructive policy of the abolitionists."[53] For that matter, the stipulation that any draftee paying $300 was free from service drew widespread ire from pro-war Republicans and Democrats alike.

Foreseeing trouble ahead, Governor Parker contacted the War Department to arrange an alternative to the draft. He lobbied successfully for an enlistment period to allow New Jersey to meet its quota voluntarily. On June 28, 1863, Parker called for six thousand volunteers and promised bonuses of up to $300 for enlistees.[54]

New Jersey had bought itself some time, and perhaps avoided major incidents such as the riots that took place in mid-July as the draft got under way in New York City. Mobs consisting mostly of working-class Irish roamed Manhattan armed with torches, clubs, rocks, and pistols. They set fires, plundered and looted, and unleashed their anger and frustration especially upon African Americans, eighteen of whom were lynched. Five more were shoved into the river, where they drowned. When order was restored after four days, hundreds of buildings had been burned down, and around a hundred black people, fifty soldiers, and as many as two thousand rioters had been killed.[55]

Smaller riots occurred around the same time in Massachusetts, Vermont, Ohio, and New Jersey. On July 13, the first night of New York's draft riots, groups of men gathered at bulletin boards in Newark looking for updates. Discussions grew rowdy, and an elderly gentleman who apparently sympathized with Lincoln was punched in the face and sent running for safety. An angry crowd moved on to the office of the Republican *Daily Mercury* at around 10 PM, screaming, "We won't be drafted!" The mob broke the *Mercury*'s front door and lobbed rocks through the windows, though no one was inside. The evening's total damage amounted to only about $250—trifling compared to New York City's $5 million of losses.[56]

Still, the potential for serious violence loomed in New Jersey, especially with a draft expected to take place on August 1 if the state's quota wasn't met. Martin Ryerson, a lawyer and Democrat-turned-Republican from Newton, wrote to Secretary of State William Seward in the hopes of sparing New Jersey "the horrors of the New York City riots," as Ryerson put it. "In many parts of the State, especially in the cities and towns along the railroads and in the mining districts, there are large numbers of Irish, and I am convinced that they are organized in every part of the State to resist the draft, many of them armed," Ryerson wrote. "The minds of the poor, even the Republicans, are terribly inflamed by the $300 clause." Because some local police forces and militias "are mainly composed of Copperheads," and Governor Parker "lacks the nerve and decision necessary for such a crisis," Ryerson requested that the draft be postponed.[57] The powers in Washington, D.C., agreed, if only for practical reasons. "The draft will not be ordered in New Jersey," one federal official wrote, "until we are prepared to enforce it."[58]

As it turned out, enough volunteers came through so that no draft occurred in New Jersey in 1863. By the following spring, however, the state struggled to meet its quotas and began conducting drafts. Crowds packed halls in various Newark wards to listen to the names being called. Men hooted, laughed, and jeered whenever a prominent politician or businessman's name was heard. The audience in the fourth ward rose and gave three cheers when the name of Mr. Frazee, an ardent pro-war Democrat, was proclaimed. Frazee leaped to his feet, cheering and swinging his hat. "Being a most ferocious 'war' man," the *Daily Journal* wrote, chiding Frazee, he would no doubt rush "to the gory field, instead of compromising the matter by legal tender greenbacks." Writing under his well-known alias "GEP," Frazee responded, "I will do so, providing" that Edward Fuller, Nehemiah Perry, and other Copperheads "accompany me as a high private and go immediately to the front and fight during the war, as I consider one good union man's life worth ten Copperheads—otherwise I shall stay at home." Weakly attempting to justify his actions, Frazee wrote, "I think by so doing I can be of more service to my country than with the army, as it requires a few honest war Democrats at home to attend to the so-called peace Democrats."[59] In fact, of the thirty-two thousand New Jerseyans drafted in 1864 and 1865, fewer than a thousand would actually serve in the war.[60]

On Tuesday, July 19, 1864, Edward Fuller responded to President Lincoln's latest request for men to be drafted. This time, the president called for an additional five hundred thousand names. "Those who desire to be butchered will please step forward at once," Fuller wrote.

All others will stay at home and defy Old Abe and his minions to drag them from their families. We hope that the people of New Jersey will at once put their feet down and insist that not a man shall be forced out of the State to engage in the abolition butchery, and swear to die at their own doors rather than march one step to fulfill the dictates of that mad revolutionary fanaticism, which has destroyed the best government the world ever saw, and would now butcher its remaining inhabitants to carry out a mere fanatical sentiment. This has gone far enough, and must be stopped. Let the people rise as one man and demand that his wholesale murder shall cease.[61]

While Fuller's words were somewhat stronger than his usual vitriol, they were hardly atypical. Several New Jersey newspapers printed Fuller's editorial, and at least two—the Somerset *Messenger* and the *Bergen Democrat*—endorsed the sentiment.[62] Even so, on the morning of Friday, July 22, Fuller was arrested and charged with violating several federal laws—notably the Conscription Act, which made it illegal to encourage resistance to the draft. The *Journal* reported the news solemnly, steadfastly proclaiming that citizens "can never be made slaves of Abraham Lincoln, and will oppose to the death every attempt to establish a military despotism over the State of New Jersey."[63]

Another Copperhead martyr had been created. "If this be treason, let it be treason," a widely quoted, defiant Fuller said, seemingly prepared to defend himself to the gallows. A week after Fuller's arrest, a group of men from New York and New Jersey met with the editor, out on bail, and presented him with the gift of a gold-headed sword cane. "It is presented to you because you have proved yourself to be a brave man, who has never cowered before the scowling ministers of illegal and despotic power," said C. Chauncey Burr, former editor of the Copperhead *Hackensack Democrat.* "The people know that you are neither a traitor nor the friend of traitors. They know that you love your country, and that you have been doing all that a brave and true man could. . . . Your cause is theirs."[64]

———

By the summer of 1864, nearly four years of war had passed and there was no end in sight. Around the nation, people seemed more anxious than ever for peace. President Lincoln himself believed it unlikely he would win the upcoming election, if an election occurred at all. (Selecting a national leader in the midst of a civil war was unprecedented, and many people predicted the election would be called off.) To attract wider support, particularly among border states, Andrew Johnson, Tennessee governor and a Democrat, was installed as vice president on the Republican ticket with Lincoln.

The Democratic National Convention in Chicago, attended among others by Clement Vallandigham, who had sneaked in from banishment in Canada, selected a nemesis from Lincoln's past as the party's candidate. General George McClellan, dismissed by the president after faltering at Antietam, ran on a platform promising to take every possible measure to end the war quickly. Though a political novice, McClellan was a charismatic, well-known figure, popular inside and outside the military. He had been brave and principled enough to stand up and criticize the president, supporters said, and he was still regarded as brilliant in certain circles. Moreover, with a military man as their nominee, the Democrats believed they could not be called disloyal or antiwar. A resident of West Orange since 1863, McClellan was particularly well liked in New Jersey. Most Copperheads had only lukewarm feelings for McClellan, though. To appease the most anti-Lincoln Democrats, McClellan's running mate would be George Pendleton, an Ohio congressman, and nearly as vehement a peace man as his home-state colleague Clement Vallandigham.[65]

As a campaigner, the egotistical, inexperienced McClellan was mediocre at best. Crucial Union army victories in late summer and early fall—notably, General William T. Sherman's seizure of Atlanta and Admiral David Farragut's famous "Damn the torpedoes! Full speed ahead!" triumph in Mobile Bay—didn't bode well for McClellan's chances either. Lincoln claimed a second term in a landslide. The official Electoral College votes counted 212 to 21. The incumbent even won four out of every five soldiers' votes, despite McClellan's military background.[66]

The election of 1864 marked the first time that soldiers in the field could vote for the president. It was up to each state to decide whether to allow their servicemen to vote, however, and New Jersey was one of the few that declined. The state's Democrats had voted against a measure allowing for absentee balloting, effectively cutting out of the political process tens of thousands of New Jersey soldiers. *Harper's Weekly* had described the state's absentee balloting vote as "31 Copperhead Nays to 19 Union Yeas."[67]

The presidential election gave a strong vote of confidence to President Lincoln. Yet, New Jersey again stood out notoriously from its peers. It would be remembered as the lone northern state to give its electoral votes to George McClellan. (McClellan also won border states Delaware and Kentucky.) Little Mac carried nearly all of the populous north Jersey cities, though surprisingly Lincoln took Essex and Passaic counties. The 53 percent majority McClellan received from the state seemed more than anything an indictment of the war by voters. As the *Daily Journal* wrote in the buildup to the election, "To vote for Lincoln is to vote for further drafts."[68]

———

On February 15, 1865, Edward Fuller entered the U.S. District Court in Trenton to defend himself against charges he had encouraged resistance to the draft the previous summer. Fuller's defense attorneys were as prominent and powerful as any in the state: General Theodore Runyon, the mayor of Newark, and John P. Stockton, a U.S. senator, future New Jersey attorney general, and member of the wealthy Princeton family.[69]

Fuller held a document in his hand and read the carefully worded statement. "I have never been moved by seditious intentions; I have never designed to favor mob law, or to incite insurrection, and I have at all times supposed that in my utterances and publications I was strictly within the just limits of liberty of speech," he affirmed. Nonetheless, Fuller thought it best "to take the advice of my counsel, and retract my plea, and plead guilty." Given Fuller's promise to never "interfere with the action of the military authorities" again, the judge decided against imposing a severe penalty. After paying a $100 fine, Fuller was freed.

That April, within a week of General Lee at last flying the flag of truce, and on the very same day that President Lincoln's assassination made news,

Edward Fuller resigned from the *Newark Daily Journal*. Fuller offered no excuses or apologies. "What we have written and published has been dictated in an independent spirit by an honest and patriotic desire for the welfare of our beloved country," he wrote, as obliviously confident as ever. The publication's only fault, perhaps, was to "have carried the old standard of Democracy too high," and to have maintained opinions that were "too unflinching and straightforward and unbending to secure the highest temporary success and the largest degree of popular favor."[70]

By early June, soldiers in blue appeared again in large numbers on the streets of Trenton, Newark, and other New Jersey cities. Their arrival was unannounced, and they initially received no hero's welcome. That wasn't the only reason the "Jersey Blue" men felt bitter. Because of New Jersey's Copperhead reputation, many soldiers had been pestered incessantly by servicemen from other states. Jokes about New Jersey soldiers needing to take an oath of allegiance before being released from the army were common. The perception was that New Jersey's troops were among the last regiments to be sent home as punishment for their state's traitorous conduct. "Jersey seems to be left out in the cold entirely," one soldier said. "We are snubbed on every side."[71]

For all of the grief they received, the approximately eighty thousand New Jersey men who served in the Union army and navy—including nearly three thousand African Americans—had ample reason to hold their heads high. By war's end, some sixty-four hundred New Jersey soldiers had been killed. New Jersey's troops had fought as admirably and suffered as greatly as any. A corporal from Newark named Edgar Trelease, for example, was among the thirty-three thousand Union soldiers held at the infamous Anderson-ville prison camp, where nearly one-third died. Scurvy and other diseases flourished, maggots filled men's unattended wounds, and food was in such short supply that soldiers dug through the sun-scorched Georgia dirt looking for roots to eat. Prisoners were occasionally shot by guards for approaching a row of stakes called the "dead line." Amid such a desperate atmosphere, Trelease and his fellow POWs consoled each other in conversation. "We talked of home, of wives, mothers, and sisters, upon whose faces we did not expect, many of us, ever to look again," he wrote. "What are they thinking and doing at home? Do they miss us, and long for our coming? Are they still among the living?"[72]

For the soldiers who survived and made it home to Newark during the summer of 1865, the city they returned to served as proof that at least one Copperhead prediction was dead wrong. Business had not suffered due to the war. Quite the opposite occurred, with factories pumping out weapons, knapsacks, clothing, boots, and other supplies for the Union cause. Even Copperheads profited greatly. Congressman and clothing manufacturer Nehemiah Perry, for example, raked in a fortune selling army uniforms. Newcomers had arrived on Newark's manufacturing scene as well. In 1864, William and George Clark, brothers in a Scottish family with a long history of making cotton thread, decided that Newark was the ideal city for them to found a business. Their operations proved so successful that by 1866, the immense, newly built $800,000 Clark Thread Company factory employed more than a thousand workers.[73]

After the initial population drop in Newark at the war's outbreak, the city swelled with workers through the mid-1860s to keep up with the increased productivity. As of 1865, the city was home to over eighty-seven thousand people, a rise of nearly twenty thousand in two years.

As a testament to the city's unparalleled importance in the state, two Newarkers squared off in the contest for governor in the fall of 1865. Mayor Theodore Runyon represented the Democrats. With most of the state's soldiers home—and therefore, finally able to vote—Republicans chose a candidate every returning serviceman would know and like: Marcus Ward. "The Soldier's Friend" had recently secured pensions for those wounded (or for the families of those killed), visited field hospitals, and transformed an old Newark warehouse into a military hospital with volunteer doctors and borrowed beds. Thousands of letters were mailed to Ward during the war because of his reputation for giving soldiers and their families all sorts of assistance. He helped them navigate the maddening bureaucracies involved with sending money, arranged for wounded soldiers to be moved, or simply get paid by the federal government. "Dear Sir," one man from Paterson wrote on behalf of his neighbor, a private wounded at Fredericksburg, "He has received no pay since he joined the Regiment and his finances are very low at present. When you visited us in Paterson you told me you were the soldiers' friend, and as such I would recommend him to you." In another letter, a minister from Elizabeth contacted Ward for a woman whose husband was killed outside of Richmond, asking who to contact regarding the deceased's pension. "Will you please give her a few words writing to the said office for the pension?" the minister asked. "She is a poor woman with her children."[74]

References to the war filled the governor's campaign. A pamphlet, satirically titled "Copperhead Love for the Soldier," criticized the Democrats, particularly their refusal to allow servicemen to vote by absentee ballot. "They were not Democrats—they were Copperheads—rightly named for this cold-blooded, slimy reptile that comes unaware, and strikes with his deadly fangs without warning," the pamphlet stated. "Copperheads they are, and as Copperheads will they be known in all history, taking rank next after the Tories and Refugees of the Revolution!"[75]

Republican campaign songs appealed to returning servicemen who "fought a valiant fight" and should now "defeat the trait'rous Copperheads" who had been "fighting in our rear."[76] Theodore Runyon had actually served in the Union army early on in the war, but his extremely brief, unsuccessful stint had earned him more criticism than accolades. One song roasted Runyon's military performance as downright cowardly: "The Copperhead Candidate/ Runyon, we know/ Was noted for running/ Some four years ago."[77]

Serving as a preamble to the statewide contest, on October 10, 1865, Newark overwhelmingly elected a trunk manufacturer named Thomas Peddie—who incidentally worked for Smith & Wright early in his career—as the city's first Republican mayor in nearly a decade. A month later, the city gave its endorsement to another Republican for governor. Marcus Ward beat Theodore Runyon by nearly sixteen hundred votes in Newark, the home city of both candidates. With 51 percent of the votes statewide, "The Soldier's Friend" became governor. Statistics weren't kept regarding the vote of returning soldiers, but it is assumed the vast majority threw their support to Ward. One soldier was quoted as saying he'd "rather lose my right arm than not vote for Ward."[78]

In the same election, Republicans gained majorities in both branches of the New Jersey state legislature. Voters had their say regarding the most outspoken war critics; the number who could be called full-fledged Copperheads fell from twelve to four in the assembly.[79]

On December 18, 1865, the Thirteenth Amendment was ratified, abolishing slavery throughout the land. While most state legislatures had approved the amendment the previous February, Democrat-dominated New Jersey had postponed a vote until March, whereupon there was a stalemate. That is how the issue stood through the rest of 1865. Once in office in early 1866, Marcus Ward asked the legislature to ratify the amendment, even though it had already become U.S. law. Legislators consented, and New Jersey redeemed itself somewhat at the national level, voicing a symbolic, if inconsequential, message: it too approved of the abolition of slavery.[80]

That November, William Wright, U.S. senator from New Jersey, passed away. For months before his death, Wright had been in exceptionally poor health and had all but disappeared from society and the political scene. On November 3, the day of the funeral, Wright's family, friends, business associates, and colleagues in politics gathered for prayers at his Park Place mansion. It was an assembly of Newark's most powerful and influential politicians, lawyers, and businessmen seeing one of their own off with dignity.

In the afternoon, a procession left the Wright property, streamed past Military Park and up Broad Street, just past the Lackawanna Railroad tracks to a brownstone church with a sharp A-frame roof and a tall steeple. William Wright had been a member and benefactor of the Episcopalian church known as the House of Prayer since it had been built in 1850. William Maybin, the House of Prayer rector, performed the ceremony with the assistance of reverends from four other churches, including one who came in especially for the service from New York City.

Afterward, family and friends proceeded a few miles north. They walked along shaded paths to a soaring rectangular column at the center of the fenced-off Wright family burial plot, which was perched on a bluff overlooking the Passaic River in Mount Pleasant Cemetery. Opened in 1844, the forty-acre oasis was filled with huge monuments, elegantly crafted statues, and marble mausoleums popular among the wealthy in the nineteenth century. William Wright's old rival, William Pennington, had been interred there in 1862. It would also be the final resting place for luminaries such as Copperhead politician Nehemiah Perry, inventor Seth Boyden, and one of Wright's pall-bearers, current New Jersey governor Marcus Ward. White flowers and a cross sat atop the black coffin as it was lowered into the ground.[81]

A simple stone memorial tablet at the House of Prayer honors William Wright as "The loving husband and father, the faithful friend, the prudent counsellor, the benefactor of this, his parish church, from the laying of its corner stone to his last hour." Just above a line from Deuteronomy—"The eternal God is thy refuge, and underneath are the everlasting arms"—is the inscription that "charity was the rule of his life." The *Dictionary of American Biography*, by contrast, memorialized Wright this way: "He is said never to have debated in either house, and his chairmanship of the Senate committee on manufactures alone saves him from virtual oblivion in the records."[82]

A week after the funeral, Governor Ward named Frederick Frelinghuysen as interim replacement for Wright in the Senate. The Wrights and the Frelinghuysens knew each other well. Years earlier in his Whig days, William Wright had been a great supporter of the political career of Theodore Frelinghuysen, Frederick's uncle (and adopted father after the boy's father died). Theodore Frelinghuysen had been Newark's second mayor; he also ran as vice president on the 1844 Whig ticket with Henry Clay in a campaign loudly supported by William Wright. Whereas Wright eventually fell in with the Democratic Party, however, the Frelinghuysens joined the Republicans. In 1860, Frederick Frelinghuysen and William Wright had both been delegates at national political conventions, but they represented opposing parties.

Signs of the changing times—and changing power structure—continued to surface in Newark in early 1867. After Lincoln's assassination, a city alderman proposed to rename South Park in the president's honor. Democrats rejected the motion in 1865, and did so again when it was presented the following year. One bitter alderman opposed to the motion claimed that Henry Clay, Daniel Webster, and others were far greater figures than President Lincoln, and they didn't have parks named for them. Finally, on March 1, 1867, the suggested name change came up again, and Newark's aldermen passed it by a vote of eighteen to three. The Republican mayor, Thomas Peddie, approved the resolution in early April, rechristening the colonial-era South Common as Lincoln Park.[83]

CHAPTER 3

GREATER NEWARK

A METROPOLIS BLOOMS WITH THE DAWN
OF THE TWENTIETH CENTURY

At 7 PM on Tuesday, August 20, 1872, the doors opened at downtown Newark's old skating rink, a long, thirty-five thousand-square-foot building with an arched roof at the corner of Washington and Court streets. Coming by train, on foot, and in horse-drawn streetcars and carriages, crowds streamed into Newark past belching smokestacks, neat row homes, a few ornate, four-story office buildings, and church steeples that would have fit the scenery in small New England towns. It was opening night at the Newark Industrial Exhibition, the first event of its kind in the United States, and spectators were curious about what kind of show New Jersey's biggest city could muster.[1]

In England, booming industrial towns such as Sheffield and Birmingham had recently begun hosting exhibitions of goods made in their respective cities as a way to stir up business and investment. A similar showcase of the best products of Newark, a city colloquially known as the "Birmingham of America," had been discussed but regularly dismissed by skeptics for years. In January of 1872, with Newark in the midst of yet another wild growth spurt—approximately 30,000 residents had been added since the end of the Civil War, bringing the population to about 115,000—government and business leaders agreed that the time for the city's own exhibit was ripe.

Arguably no other U.S. city was so closely associated with industry and manufacturing. Newark ranked third in terms of overall industrial output, despite its comparatively small population, ranked thirteenth in the country. The transitions from selling goods to the South prior to the Civil War, to selling goods to the U.S. government during the war, to selling goods postwar to all sorts of U.S. and foreign cities, had occurred fairly smoothly, thanks to Newark's diversity of goods and quick reaction to the marketplace. Nearly everything then manufactured, bought, and sold in the United States could be found in Newark, probably within a fifteen-minute walk of the Passaic River. "We not only manufacture," the *Newark Daily Advertiser* proclaimed in April 1872, "but we make the things to manufacture with."[2] Even so, some Newark factories still stamped their goods MADE IN NEW YORK to help them sell. A magazine published in Newark after the Civil War pointed out: "The average American citizen knows less about Newark than he does about any other point of equal interest in the United States."[3]

To gain a new level of prominence for the city, a committee led by Mayor Frederick Ricord and Marcus Ward—then out of office as governor and running for Congress—organized the 1872 exhibition, an early progenitor of the business convention. For maximum exposure, the committee invited all local businesses to participate for a reasonable $25 fee. Admission charges for the public were kept low, and the exhibition would last nearly two months. Early on in the planning stages, it became apparent that Newark's old roller-skating rink, which everyone simply called "the Rink," was the best facility to host the event. As more and more firms signed on to participate, even the Rink seemed too small to accommodate all the merchandise to be displayed. Local companies quickly put up the money to build two new wings onto the main building, bringing the total exhibition space up to fifty thousand square feet.

The weather during opening week was awful, with sweltering days in the upper nineties, as well as storms violent enough to uproot trees and take the roofs off a few buildings. Even so, the exhibition's inaugural festivities drew a large crowd; estimates ranged as high as four thousand attendees.

Inside the Rink's front entrance, a marble fountain decorated with flowers and filled with goldfish sprayed water twenty-five feet high, cooling the air a bit on the steamy opening night. Hundreds of gas jets shaded by opal globes spread a rainbow of light through the hall. Funhouse-style mirrors added to the festive atmosphere, distorting the images of patrons as they walked by. Colored streamers and bunting draped the rooms, and flags from France, Germany, England, and other nations hung next to the Stars and Stripes.

Under the Rink's three-story-high ceiling, artisans, laborers, and their families, as well as rich men in three-piece suits and society ladies wearing long, poofy skirts, inched past displays. "The wealthiest and lowliest mingled together with good democratic freedom," wrote the *Newark Daily Journal*. "The silk robed wives and daughters of the prosperous manufacturer examined with as much interest the elegant wares from his establishments as did the plain but neatly dressed wives and daughters of the hard working mechanic."[4] The people of Newark all came "for a common purpose—to see what they had made; to hear about themselves and what most nearly concerned them," in the words of the *Daily Advertiser*. "It was the story of their lives, told not only in words but in a sort of picture writing, in which the characters had substance as well as shapes of glowing beauty."

What exactly had Newark made? Without knowing it, people around the country probably owned dozens of articles that originated in the city. "The trunk you travel with is, nine times out of ten, of Newark manufacture," the *New York Times* explained. "The hat you wear was made there, the buttons on your coat, the shirt on your back, your brush, the tinware you use in your kitchen, the oil-cloth you walk on, the harness and bit you drive with, all owe to Newark their origin." The *Times'* partial list of goods represented at the exhibition included "agricultural implements, machinery and castings, all kinds of plain and fancy lamps, upholstery, gold smelting, cutlery that looks as fine as Sheffield work, gas-fittings, paints and colors, brushes, cabinetwork, pottery, fancy metal work, piano-fortes, oil-cloths, silverware, and very many other articles too numerous to mention." Also, "as to your wife's chain, bracelets, ear rings and pendants, they have been fashioned by some cunning Newark goldsmith."

One of the most prominent items at the exhibition was a huge fifty-horsepower engine from Passaic Machine-works. Women gathered around a marvelous, state-of-the-art "baby-jumping machine," with the designer's own child happily bouncing away in demonstration. Another favorite among the ladies was a trunk that, after a quick conversion, doubled as both a cradle and bathtub. Baseball bats and models of steamships and schooners drew attention from boys. There were also countless innovative new goods for the home—burglar and fire alarms, door locks, wax flowers, decorative collections of butterflies and leaves.

Two wide, newly constructed staircases in the Rink led visitors to a spacious gallery, where patrons viewed statues and paintings of local artists, most notably Thomas Moran. Born in 1837 in Langshire, England, Moran lived in Baltimore and Philadelphia and apprenticed with a wood-engraver as a teen. After studying in Europe, he became enamored with landscape paint-ings, particularly that of Englishman J.M.W. Turner. Moran lived in Newark in the days after the Civil War, and in 1871 he joined a geological expedition to the Yellowstone Territory. Critics instantly praised his work from the trip, particularly *Grand Canyon of the Yellowstone*. In it, two dark, tiny figures in the foreground stand on the edge of an immense canyon that's speckled with evergreens and glowing in shades of orange, yellow, and white.

Newark Exhibition leaders originally planned on showing Moran's *Grand Canyon*, but the federal government, which sponsored the Yellowstone expedition, claimed the painting three weeks before opening night. Instead, Moran contributed with similarly romantic, warmly colored landscapes in *Dreamland, Hemlock Forest,* and *Children of the Mountain.* The *Newark Morning Register* declared the last, featuring a waterfall crashing over craggy rocks at the center and soft, low-lying clouds with hints of purple and yellow above, "undoubtedly the finest work of art in the gallery."[5]

For many, Moran's powerful, idealized natural landscapes depicted a great big world waiting to be explored, one of nearly endless possibility. Considering how rapidly industry was changing how people lived, with advances in trains, electricity, lighting, and farm equipment making age-old toils disappear, Moran's paintings struck a chord—particularly with the people of Newark, a city that prided itself on being at the forefront of such advances. From another perspective, however, the romantic works of Moran and the popular Hudson River School artists were a direct reaction to the urbanization of the era when people moved en masse to cities and lost their connection to nature. The crowds loved the scenes because they were beautiful and pure, without a grimy factory, polluted river, or filthy street in sight.

At 8 PM on opening night, Reinhard's Band, a well-known brass outfit that played at Newark picnics and balls, kicked off the festivities with the elegant Grand March from the opera *Bellisario.* The band also performed a theme song written expressly for the event, which would be heard regularly for the duration of the exhibition. The song began with the lyrics, "Now glory to the workingmen, whose cunning hands to-day/ Have wrought the wondrous things we see spread out in grand array."

After music and an opening prayer came the introduction of Marcus Ward, the Newark native and prominent city merchant, Civil War-era "Soldier's Friend," and former governor. Ward was enough of a local celebrity to be the subject of one of the paintings in the exhibition gallery. As president of the Industrial Exhibition committee, the sixty-year-old Ward approached the podium with his distinct shaggy, mustache-less beard to give the opening address. "The city in which we live is emphatically a manufacturing one," Ward said. "Its growth, its prosperity, its wealth are inseparably connected with these mechanic arts which are here developed in a thousand forms of beauty and taste."

By all accounts, opening night, as well as the rest of the Newark Industrial Exhibition, was a runaway success. The city received what it hoped for in terms of widespread press coverage, especially due to prominent visitors like New Jersey–born General Thomas B. Van Buren, the U.S. commissioner to Vienna. "If the people of Europe could go through the hall, and view the samples of work here shown, they would be amazed at the perfection of American mechanism," Van Buren said during a September visit to Newark. "They would be astounded at the extent of the productions of one single city of this country."

Horace Greeley, the most influential newspaperman in the country and then the Democratic Party's candidate for president, also made an appearance. Two nights after Greeley's visit, his opponent in the election, President Ulysses S. Grant, likewise stopped at Newark for a tour of the exhibition, during which the Rink was "crowded to such an extent that neither the President nor anybody else could see, hear, or move," according to the *Morning Register*.[6] Standing in front of the gallery, Grant bowed to cheers from the crowd below. "This far-famed city of Newark has done well," said President Grant. "The excellency of your manufactures is working a large influence on the importation of foreign manufacture. I heartily thank you for this great pleasure."

By the end of the exhibition's fifty-two-day run, the event had attracted an estimated 130,000 visitors, including many manufacturers and wholesalers from Philadelphia and New York City. More than a thousand exhibitors participated in the show, with presenters periodically altering displays and bringing in new merchandise. Many local visitors opted for the $3 season ticket rather than the one-time 30¢ admission, to view the changing roster of items, as well as to take in the lively social scene. A brass band from Bavaria performed in late August, and other musicians and entertainers played in rotation. "The Rink during the Exposition has become quite a fashionable evening rendezvous for our young people," a social column in the *Morning Register* read. "The music is so fine, you know."[7]

Just as at the opening, Reinhard's band played and Marcus Ward spoke on the exhibition's final night, October 11. "All the good expected from it has been realized," said Ward. "The value and character of our manufacturing interests have been clearly shown." Newspapers uniformly agreed, with the *Sunday Call* describing the exhibition as "the grandest enterprise ever undertaken by the people of Newark." The *New Jersey Freie Zeitung* wrote that "Newark has achieved an enviable prominence among her sister cities. She has thus demonstrated that the name of a 'great manufacturing city,' which she has already borne, was no empty title." "All those from abroad who have honored the city by their attendance have spoken of the Exhibition in terms of the highest praise," said the *Newark Evening Courier*. "The fame of Newark has therefore spread over the land."

Toward the end of the year, a lengthy *New York Times* article proclaimed that "Newark has grown, as the old ladies say, beyond all knowledge, and with a rapidity of late years which throws the growth of New-York and Brooklyn into the shade."[8] All indications pointed to continued success in the days ahead. As written in the *Morning Register*, "No city of its size in the Union has a more prosperous present manufacturing status, and none of any size a brighter future."

———

Newark hosted an industrial exhibition in each of the next three years, though none matched the success of the original; the Panic of 1873 dampened the spirits in the follow-up year in particular. In 1876, with Philadelphia poised to attract hundreds of thousands for its monumental Centennial Exhibition, Newark dropped its industrial fair indefinitely.

However much attention the events brought to manufacturers, the exhibitions also revealed Newark for what it was: a largely one-dimensional city. The variety and sheer amount of items it made had grown exponentially, but simply put, Newark was a producer that sent goods elsewhere to be sold. Newark had built itself up as such, and seemed rather content in its status. "We are only a workshop, a community of manufacturers rather than merchants," the *Daily Advertiser* counseled in 1870. "The transfer of trade must be made mainly in New York, which is our national exchange. Our streets will never be 'crowded with buyers,' but will be with hurrying wagons of goods already sold."[9] The local board of trade held that since "there is a manifest unfitness of our city for a great commercial centre," Newark should focus its energies toward its role as "a monster workshop."[10]

By defining itself, Newark had limited itself. And unfortunately, even as the city was heralding its strength in manufacturing, other industrial-based cities were challenging its dominance. Newark may have been growing as the end of the century neared, but not as rapidly as emerging manufacturing cities such as Detroit and Cleveland. They would both surpass Newark's population by the 1890 census.

While the Industrial Exhibition of 1872 helped to firmly establish Newark as a manufacturing power, many Newarkers grasped that it was unwise to place all of the city's eggs in the lone basket of industry. In the decades ahead, the city needed to expand what defined Newark. New endeavors, particularly in banking, insurance, retail, electricity, entertainment, and education, would be introduced, as would new transportation systems and, at last, beautiful green spaces with fresh air for residents to enjoy. Many of the issues brought to light in the 1850s—unpaved roads, the absence of a public-sewer system or a safe, ample water supply, the proliferation of disease—would need to be addressed. Attempts would also be made to annex significant neighboring lands so that the city might expand physically.

As had already become tradition in Newark, entrepreneurs, inventors, and businessmen took the lead in the city's next stage. Moving well beyond the city's manufacturing staples involving leather, wood, and jewelry, innovators created products for the modernizing world.

While still only in his twenties, Thomas Alva Edison used some of the $40,000 given to him by Western Union for his latest telegraph machine to hire more than a hundred workers and operate as many as five shops simultaneously in Newark in the early 1870s. To Edison and so many other inventors and entrepreneurs, Newark was a quieter, more affordable alternative to New York, with a skilled labor force and ample businesses that produced iron and brass castings, tools, chemicals, and other supplies necessary for endless experiments. Newark was exactly what the young genius needed before moving in 1876 to his famous "invention factory" at Menlo Park. While in Newark, Edison worked on various sewing machines and a new quadraplex telegraph that relayed four messages at once. He also built an electric pen, which, in the era before photocopy machines, proved useful. A tiny needle in the "pen" created stencils for drawings, maps, pamphlets, circulars, and legal briefs.[11]

John Wesley Hyatt, another inventor from the era, came to prominence for creating a plastic material he called celluloid. With the backing of New York financiers, Hyatt built a five-story plant on Newark's Mechanic Street. Throughout his half century in the city, Hyatt received dozens of patents while perfecting his plastics, which were molded into knife handles, dental plates, buttons, combs, novelty gifts, and, with the advent of the automobile, axle bearings.[12]

A doctor and chemist named Edward Weston created dynamos and generators for a New York City company before settling in Newark in 1875 and opening factories for the production of motors, batteries, fuses, magnets, and nearly everything else involved in the exciting new field of electricity. Weston's especially bright arc lights, which could glow in any color desired, impressed city leaders enough to give him a contract to illuminate Military Park in 1881. Two years later, Weston's lights glowed atop the era's most spectacular new marvel, the Brooklyn Bridge. In 1884, Weston helped found a much-needed institution in his adopted city, the Newark Technical School, which would evolve into the New Jersey Institute of Technology.[13]

John Fairfield Dryden, a Yale College dropout from Maine who had failed in several insurance ventures, introduced a concept in Newark in 1873 that was arguably more life-altering than electricity. Insurance at the time was aimed almost exclusively at wealthy customers, with expensive premiums that were paid monthly or quarterly by mail. The middle and lower classes, which constituted the vast majority of Newarkers, could finally afford insurance through Dryden's new Widows and Orphans Friendly Society. Agents visited customers once a week to collect premiums on policies that cost as little as three cents a week (and paid off benefits as meager as $10).[14]

Dryden's outfit renamed itself the Prudential Friendly Society in 1875, before settling two years later on the Prudential Insurance Company. The business expanded extraordinarily quickly, opening new branches in similarly working-class Paterson, Jersey City, Elizabeth, and Camden. Customers bought more than a million Prudential policies by 1890, and three million more by the turn of the century. As a testament to the company's success, an opulent, turret-topped castle of an office building rose on Broad Street in 1892 to serve as Prudential's home office for some four thousand employees. Ornate murals, gargoyles, stained glass, rich wood paneling, and marble decorated the building's every corner. Perhaps most surprising of all, every room was equipped with telephones and electric lights. As a friendly touch—and an unusual one for the era—a drinking fountain was installed for the public. Within a decade, four additional buildings were completed to form a downtown headquarters complex. In the twentieth century, Prudential would expand into a multibillion dollar insurance and financial firm, one more closely identified with Newark than any other company.[15]

———

In retrospect, Dryden's insurance pitch filled an obvious need. Life among turn-of-the-century factories and tenements was unstable and dangerous. Perhaps Dryden's smartest concept was the guarantee that benefits, however minimal, would be paid off within twenty-four hours of a death certificate—of particular appeal to the working classes living paycheck to paycheck.

Immigrants, of course, were well represented in that category, and in Newark in general. From the Civil War well into the new century, the number of Newark's foreign-born residents hovered at around one-third the population. Together with their American-born children, the newcomers constituted the majority in the city.[16]

By the late 1800s, the "early" immigrants from Ireland and Germany were firmly entrenched in the city. Though the Germans still received grief for their insistence on keeping beer gardens open on the Sabbath and the Irish were occasionally excluded from certain lines of work, the two groups had made inroads in politics and business, vastly improving their status since arriving in the United States.

While Newark's biggest ale house was run by Scotsman Peter Ballantine, Germans were responsible for producing most of the lager in the city's enormous brewery industry. In 1876, a writer touring Newark's German quarter, a two-square-mile hilly section of middle-class immigrants just northwest of downtown, encountered no fewer than eight breweries, where customers walked into arched cellars stacked with barrels. "German habits and German customs appear on every side" of the neighborhood, where most families owned their homes and raised vegetables in backyard gardens, she wrote in *Harper's*. "At noon you will see women and children running across the streets and up and down with pitchers in their hands. They are going for lager-beer to drink with their dinners, which is as indispensable as the dinner itself."[17]

Germans also had a large hand in the jewelry industry, one of the city's top-three moneymakers. Just two years after leaving Germany for Newark, Edward Balbach Sr. saw a niche in the city's expanding jewelry business. In 1850 he opened a silver and gold refining plant. The company focused on handling the sweepings from other jewelry factories; previously, particles too tiny for use had to be sent off to refiners in Europe. Edward Balbach Jr. patented a new desilvering process in 1864 that rapidly separated silver and gold from base metals. At the time, only U.S. mints and the Balbach factory were capable of such work. Business boomed as jewelry companies from around the United States, Mexico, and other countries sent their metals to Newark for processing.[18]

It was factories such as Balbach's that provided work for the tens of thousands of newcomers, primarily from southern and eastern Europe, who arrived during turn-of-the-century immigration waves. Most were motivated to emigrate due to the dire, oppressive lives they endured in Italy, Poland, Lithuania, Greece, or Russia. One Italian immigrant, as a fairly typical example, was born in 1872 into a large family in Oratina, a farming village north of Naples. His father grew corn, wheat, and other grains to provide for his family, but did not own the farm. The children worked the fields with their father and were paid only with food and the occasional new pair of pants or shoes, "providing crops had been good and Father could manage to sell part of our share of the crops, which didn't happen every year, you may be sure," the man later recalled. "Work on the farm was hard and I didn't care for it much." When an uncle wrote from Newark and offered to pay for his passage to America, the fifteen-year-old said goodbye to his parents and never saw them again.[19]

Immigrants came to Newark for unromantic reasons. They heard work was available. Often, there were already at least a few of an immigrant's countrymen living in the city, providing some degree of comfort. The newcomers charmed and muscled their way into whatever job they could get, digging ditches for trolleys and sewers, selling vegetables from pushcarts, rolling cigars in factories, or sewing corsets in mills. They usually worked ten hours a day, six days a week. One of the few niches available to young Greeks with limited English skills was the shoeshine parlor, where the workday often lasted sixteen hours. "At night, all the boys slept in the back room," the daughter of one such Greek bootblack said. "My father slept under the sink. There was no heat, the water dripped on his head, and it was freezing."[20]

Immigrants were happy to find work, however monotonous and dangerous it may have been. At the Balbach factory, employees breathed in the smell of gas and acid constantly. Heavy machinery put workers at risk of being burned or maimed. Men scalded by molten metal were occasionally seen bounding frenziedly from factories into the cool waters of the Passaic River.

Workers at hat factories inhaled volatilized mercury, which brought on muscular tremors, or the "shakes," giving rise to the expression "mad as a hatter." In fact, hat workers breathed in all sorts of unhealthy materials; even two weeks after quitting, they continued sneezing and hacking up black dust. The clothing of hat workers often got soaked in the course of the day, either from sweat or regular chores, and a study of Newark factories from 1878 to 1883 showed hatters correspondingly suffered from an unusually high rate of respiratory tract diseases, tuberculosis in particular. With all of the risks, a hatter's life expectancy at the time was less than forty-one years.[21]

When the workday ended in Newark, immigrants could expect to walk through foul-smelling, garbage-strewn streets to overcrowded, poorly ventilated tenements without running water. The grim conditions were similar or worse than the slums of New York City, which the public learned about in the 1890s due to publication of works such as Jacob Riis's photos and essays in *How the Other Half Lives* and Newark native Stephen Crane's novel *Maggie: A Girl of the Streets*.

While all bustling industrial cities faced struggles similar to Newark's, the city's especially rapid, haphazard, and unplanned growth reached a peak—or perhaps, a low point—around 1890. Based on death and disease rates, water supply, and other factors, Newark was statistically America's most unhealthy big city. It ranked highest in mortality of infants and children under five, and had one of the nation's highest percentages of typhoid, malaria, tuberculosis, and other diseases.[22]

Newark's wealthy, conservative citizens had long been reluctant to use tax money for widespread health reforms and infrastructure advancements. Yet the squalid conditions of the city could no longer be ignored. Beyond the obvious concerns, being labeled as the country's most unhealthy city was bad for business. Besides, as working-class groups rose to prominence, a shift in city leadership became inevitable. More and more, power was being taken away from the old-money aristocrats and placed in the hands of popular champions of the people.

———

In the fall of 1883, Newark's working classes elected as mayor a man they saw as one of their own: a burly, sociable, silver-bearded Democrat with a common touch named Joseph E. Haynes. Before entering politics, "Honest

Joe" was a school principal. "There should be no privileged classes in this country," Haynes said in a typical appeal to constituents. Addressing the state of Newark schools, Haynes said they were all "good enough for the rich, and none too good for the poor." With obvious disdain, the *Daily Advertiser* stated that "the undesirable elements"—immigrants and political bosses, in other words—were responsible for putting Haynes into office.[23]

During the ten years Haynes ran the city, the headstrong mayor battled with Republicans and the press, often over the patronage positions he liberally handed out to supporters. Shortly after Haynes entered office, for example, the *New York Times* reported the mayor was replacing forty Republican police officers with forty Democrats. The Newark Board of Health, which was stacked with Haynes's friends, was referred to as the "Board of Junket" by the *Newark Evening News*. Haynes in turn called the paper the "Evening Nuisance."[24]

Nonetheless, Haynes remained popular with a large section of voters, at least partially because he managed to force through a few improvements in street paving, sewer supply, and other services. His most noteworthy achievement was attaining a new water source for the city. Utilizing the Passaic River was clearly not a healthy option. Sewage and factory waste flowed freely into the river in Newark and upstream communities like Paterson, Passaic, and Belleville. "You stop to ask if all the people of these places drink out of the Passaic River," one visitor to the area wondered. "Then you cast your eye up and down and recall to memory what you have seen along its banks, and wonder if you shall ever be thirsty again."[25]

A noted lover of the outdoors who rarely turned down an excursion into the country or a sail out on the water, Haynes accompanied some businessmen into the bucolic hills west of the city one day and became infatuated with the idea of tapping into water from the Pequannock River, twenty miles from Newark. In early 1892, after three years of building pipeline and reservoirs, the Pequannock water reached Newark's reservoir in Belleville. Haynes kept the first jugful as a souvenir. Though critics panned the project's $6 million cost as outrageous, typhoid deaths in the city dropped 70 percent after the water supply changed.[26] "Today," Haynes said, upon the water reaching the city, "the number of the opponents of the new water supply in Newark bears about the same relative proportion to our entire city's population that the number of the inmates of the County Jail holds to the entire population of Essex County."[27]

As a whole, however, Haynes wasn't nearly the honest reformer that supporters liked to portray. He earned a reputation as "Picnic Joe" for "his bacchanalian fraternization with every target company that has been able to buy a keg of beer" at countless outings, according to the *New York Times*. Haynes notoriously accepted gifts in exchange for city contracts. In one instance, an asphalt firm made a presentation to city officials regarding a possible paving contract while Haynes was in Trinidad on a junket arranged by the company. Among Haynes's backers were men who had all but perfected the arts of dishing out patronage positions and stuffing ballot boxes—including Leon Abbett, New Jersey's two-time governor and boss of the state's Democratic machine, as well as members of Jersey City's infamous political ring. Haynes "gathered about him a municipal ring that, if it were exposed, would probably be found to be as much more venal and corrupt than the Jersey City ring as Newark is richer than Jersey City," the *Times* charged. "Water and pavement jobs and street railroad franchises have covered his administration with scandal. Heelers and barroom rowdies are growing rich under the fostering shield of his machine, while self-respecting men are relegated to the rear."[28]

Even though Haynes held the mayoralty for a decade, he often squeaked out electoral victories by the smallest of margins. In the 1887 contest, he received 10,630 out of 25,333 total votes—just over 40 percent—yet the opposition was split among a Republican and a Prohibition candidate. Four years later, at least three Newark banks reported Democratic henchmen placing orders to pick up $10,000 apiece on election day, stipulating that the money come in one- and two-dollar bills—which could be used to pay voters checking Haynes's name. "The air is rife with rumors that the Lehigh Valley Railroad Company," which had a vested interest in the Pequannock water project, "has sent a big check for the use of the bosses," the *Times* said. Nearly a thousand immigrants—mostly poor and Italian—were quickly granted citizenship (and the right to vote) days before the election. Haynes again edged out a political victory, perhaps related to the fact that some precincts curiously reported their results in envelopes that had been used in previous elections. In the precinct with the most old envelopes, Haynes received more than double the votes of his opponent.[29]

Two years later, Haynes declined to run for mayor, taking the comfortable position as Newark postmaster instead. Republican Julius Lebkuecher defeated Democrat James Seymour by nearly five thousand votes. The *Times* surmised Seymour had been crushed because he'd been "burdened with the record of the ring which has controlled the city for the last ten years," and which was as "low-lived a gang of political thieves and gamblers as ever disgraced a State."[30]

Republicans had long pleaded with the brilliant, meticulous Julius Lebkuecher to run for office. Born in Baden, Germany, Lebkuecher emigrated at the age of four with his family in 1848 to live briefly in Jersey City, before settling in Newark. Lebkuecher apprenticed with a Newark jewelry manufacturer and at a New York City mercantile company, and for a time worked as a traveling salesman. In 1869, he and his cousin, George Krementz, founded a jewelry manufacturing firm at 49 Chestnut Street in Newark. Within five years, Krementz & Co. sold a range of fine gold jewelry and employed more than a hundred workers. The tight-fisted, obsessively organized immigrant owners grew wealthy. Thanks to the success of their unique one-piece collar button, patented in 1884 and for years the only such model on the market, the company became one of the country's largest gold manufacturers.[31]

Lebkuecher wore a thick, jet-black mustache that extended over his upper lip and curled out past his smooth, flat cheeks. Wireless spectacles covered his dark eyes, which sat under a high forehead and closely-cropped black hair. While always keeping tabs on his jewelry business, Lebkuecher dabbled in finance and banking. He became an officer in the Union National Bank, the Franklin Savings Institution, and the Fourteenth Ward Building & Loan Association. Always an active Republican, Lebkuecher must have been disgusted by his party's losing streak versus the patronage king Joseph Haynes. Lebkuecher, as a German and a member of a Newark singing society, was also probably doubly offended in 1891 by Haynes's dismissal of the German Saengerfest—a huge choral festival hosted by Newark—as nothing more than an ordinary picnic. Haynes was reportedly angry because he wasn't named an honorary vice president in the celebration. He refused to name the festival an official city holiday. Perhaps the death of Lebkuecher's first wife in 1893 also played a role in prodding Lebkuecher into running for public office.[32]

Despite Haynes's claims of progress and reform, the city turned over to Julius Lebkuecher desperately needed discipline and guidance. Unqualified, incompetent workers remained on the payroll. As late as 1890, two-thirds of the streets—in a city of more than 180,000 people—had yet to be paved. Mayor Haynes steadfastly maintained that a comprehensive sewer system was simply too expensive for the city, and thus two-thirds of downtown and a higher percentage of outlying area had no sewers at all.[33]

Mayor Lebkuecher sought solutions to city problems methodically and immediately. One of his early steps was obvious: collecting the $89,000 in outstanding claims owed to the city by various corporations. The mayor wrangled with state lawmakers to pass a bill allowing cities to pay for street paving over several installments at low interest rates; previously cities had to cover the expenses up front or expect hefty interest penalties. Over sixty years, Newark had paved only about sixty miles of streets; as a result of the new law, Lebkuecher's administration was able to pave thirty additional miles in just two years. With the pace set, by 1910 all but 85 of the city's 620 miles of streets would be covered in cobblestone, brick, or asphalt.[34]

What few sewers Newark did have had been constructed piecemeal over five decades, and they often clogged and emitted horrendous odors because they were too small or poorly graded. Mayor Lebkuecher, in a report to the board of health, said the sewers, "built in the main without regard to general utility or future requirements, fall far short of our needs, and the lack of them, in many instances, is a menace to public health." In 1893, 112 miles of sewers flowed under Newark streets. Thanks to the course the city began under Lebkuecher, there would be nearly three times that many miles of sewers—310 miles in total—as of 1910.[35]

According to an 1885 study, Newark contained but eleven small parks—18.36 preserved acres in total. By contrast, two cities with similar populations—Buffalo and Washington, D.C.—had 620 acres and 1,000 acres of parkland, respectively. In Lebkuecher's second year of office, Newark signed over 60 acres of swampy reservoir and hilly land northwest of downtown to the newly created Essex County Parks Commission. Studies had been conducted as early as 1867 about creating a park 700 acres in size around the reservoir. Decades passed before any action was taken, however, and when it was, in 1895, only one-third of the originally proposed site was still undeveloped. The Ballantines and other families donated land to the long, narrow Branch Brook Park, as it became known, which eventually expanded to 360 beautifully cultivated acres.[36]

————

It didn't take a cunning business mind like Julius Lebkuecher's to grasp that the massive projects under way in Newark cost a lot of money. The mayor's streamlining of operations and cutbacks on Haynes-era extravagances and inefficiencies meant tax increases had been minimal. But, as the city pushed further improvements along involving roads, public transportation, electricity, and other conveniences, the tax rate was bound to rise.

One way to minimize the impact on city taxpayers was the idea of dispersing costs over a wider area and larger number of people. At the end of the nineteenth century, Bloomfield, the Oranges, Montclair, and other neighboring towns that had once been a part of Newark faced similarly steep costs for sewers and other municipal projects. For half a century after the Civil War, many people believed it inevitable that Newark would engulf the land around the city and thereby create a "Greater Newark." "Perhaps Newark," one writer speculated in 1876, "with her aspiring tendencies, will yet spread forth her arms and embrace the whole of Essex and Hudson counties."[37]

All over the country, consolidation was a trend. Chicago, for example, had been founded in 1837 with only ten square miles of territory. In 1889, neighboring towns voted to be annexed by the city in order to share costs and receive better public services. As a result, Chicago expanded to 185 square miles by century's end. With a couple hundred thousand more people counted as new city residents in the 1890 census, Chicago passed Philadelphia as the United States' second most populous city. New Year's Day of 1898 marked the merging of the nation's first and fourth largest cities, when Manhattan and Brooklyn combined into a new New York City, which also encompassed the Bronx, Staten Island, and Queens.

Newark recouped most of Clinton Township in parcels acquired in 1869, 1897, and 1902, and annexed Woodside in 1871 after agreeing to cover some of the woodsy northerly area's debt. In the late 1880s, two towns on the other side of the Passaic River—Kearny and Harrison, also known as East Newark—openly sought to join Newark and break from ties with their corrupt, distant county seat, Jersey City. Newark leaders stalled and an agreement was never reached.

As the years passed, suburban towns not only lost interest in consolidating with Newark, they steadfastly opposed such a measure. In the fall of 1894, with rumors spreading that Newark had its sights on acquiring several adjoining Essex County towns, a movement began to consolidate the Oranges and thereby present a united front against Newark's overtures. "Advocates are coming forward on all sides and declaring that it is simply a fight for self-preservation," the *Times* reported. "They say that if the project is not successfully carried through it will not be many moons before the City of Newark will have absorbed all four of these delightful suburbs and their identity and individual attractions will have been lost." It was believed that Newark would also target Bloomfield, Montclair, Belleville, Irvington, Vailsburg, Millburn, Short Hills, Caldwell, Roseland, Livingston, and Verona.[38]

The following March, news broke that Mayor Lebkuecher and a handful of other leading Newarkers had stealthily asked former city attorney Joseph Coult to ready a bill for the legislature. A composed man with a neatly trimmed white beard and small, oval-shaped spectacles, Coult was a dedicated Republican, regarded as a genius in surreptitiously getting bills signed into law. He had just recently written a bill, which many legislators heard about only after its passage, in which Glen Ridge separated from Bloomfield and incorporated as an independent borough. Supporters of the so-called Greater Newark bill were hoping to get it passed quickly and quietly just before the legislature adjourned. In the bill, the consolidation of Newark with the Oranges, Vailsburg, Clinton, Montclair, Bloomfield, Belleville, and Irvington would be put to a vote. "As Newark has three-fourths of the entire population of the county, a good majority in favor of the project there would settle the matter," the *Times* wrote, "The other places, which would bitterly oppose the measure, would practically have no voice in the deciding the question."[39]

The *Times* reported that Lebkuecher's goal was to push through his ambitious plan before his two-year mayoral term expired. Always a man of decisive action, Lebkuecher was more motivated than usual to seize the moment. Republican bosses, upset the independent-minded Lebkuecher had made appointments that didn't tow the party line, had already begun lining up against him in his quest for a second term as mayor.[40]

The consolidation issue stirred debates throughout the region. Some people agreed with Mayor Lebkuecher that a Greater Newark made economic sense. The majority of suburban residents, however, were wary of joining forces with a city—especially one known for unhealthy conditions and, in the recent past, corruption. To avoid being annexed by Newark, most residents in the Oranges seemed to be leaning toward consolidating themselves into a mid-sized city that would rival Newark. "There is no other course to be pursued," said Dr. Francis J. E. Tetrault, the city physician of Orange. Like many suburbanites, Tetrault feared that if their towns became part of Newark, "the New-York business men who now live here would forsake us for the more rural communities of Summit, Morristown, and Madison, further up the road."[41]

Joseph Coult and Julius Lebkuecher distanced themselves from the Greater Newark bill as soon as news of it surfaced. At first they said the bill did not exist, then they assured the public that if any vote did occur, each community would get to decide its own fate, regardless of what Newarkers supported. Coult spoke at length with reporters about the benefits of a Greater Newark, including enormous region-wide savings on sewer, water, and electrical systems. "The new public park scheme, too, offers a powerful argument for consolidation," said Coult. "As one city Newark and the suburbs would work together harmoniously to have parks placed where they would do the greatest good to the greatest number."[42]

After months of discussions, however, a Greater Newark bill never materialized. The Oranges never rejoined with each other either. Talk of consolidation didn't entirely disappear, however. A group of real estate owners in the Oranges organized a petition in 1898 to join Newark. In 1899, East Orange, then a wealthy Republican stronghold of about fifteen thousand residents, incorporated as a city, presumably ending the conversation about consolidation. Yet a year later, as the expiration of East Orange's contract for water loomed, and leaders in all of the Oranges anticipated millions of dollars to pay for sewers, discussions revived concerning a Greater Newark.[43]

By then, the issue had long been taken out of the hands of Julius Lebkue-cher. After two brief, remarkably productive years in office, Lebkuecher lost in the campaign for a second term to James Seymour, the same man he had faced off against in 1894. Apparently too many people in the city had grown weary of Lebkuecher's unyielding, businesslike rule. Without the unanimous backing of the Republican Party, Lebkuecher lost by over four thousand votes, roughly the same margin by which he had won in the previous election.[44]

Lebkuecher returned his focus to the jewelry business, though he still managed to follow through on a long-desired public-health initiative. As commissioner and chairman of the Passaic Valley Sewer Commission from 1902 to 1912, he helped put an end to the polluting of the river by building sewers in communities from the Great Falls in Paterson all the way to Newark.

————

The steady flow of U.S.-bound immigrants turned into a tidal wave after the turn of the century. "The invasions of the Goths and the Vandals destroyed the Roman empire," read an article printed by the *Newark Sunday Call* in 1906. "Will the invasion of the hordes of ignorant Europeans destroy our republic?" The news column voiced what was a widespread concern at the time. More than a million immigrants had entered the United States over a recent twelve-month period. "Don't you think Uncle Sam is biting off more than he can chew?" the writer wondered. "A million in the raw is a big mouthful. Can the country masticate and digest it?"[45]

Worries over the newcomers centered on cities such as Newark, where two-thirds of the city's 350,000 population (circa 1910) were either foreign-born or the children of immigrants. Well over one hundred thousand Newarkers were Jews, Italians, and Slavs—the "ignorant Europeans" referred to by the writer.

At first, Newark's immigrants lived wherever rent was minimal, work was nearby, and the landlords would have them. Other than the sections where the middle-class Germans or Irish were dominant or on High Street and other areas where the wealthy industrialists built their mansions, most neighborhoods had a mix of ethnicities, perhaps with Italian, Greek, Jewish, and African American families living in tenements on the same street. As time passed, however, to create power in numbers, for personal comfort, a sense of connection to the old country, or simply because they had no other viable places to live, those of similar background gravitated to certain areas. A map issued to Newark social agencies in 1912 pinpointed nearly thirty distinct neighborhoods where one ethnic group dominated, including a small section of Chinese around Lafayette and Mulberry Street.

According to the map, a particularly rich mix of different ethnic neighborhoods stretched the length of Springfield Avenue. Beginning at Market Street and walking southwest along Springfield in the early 1900s, one would first pass a thin Greek enclave, where Greek men played cards and talked of politics, work, and women at the local *kefeneion* (coffeehouse), followed by a larger section of Negroes, as the map then labeled African Americans. (The influx of African Americans into Newark will be handled in a later chapter.) High Street, later to become Martin Luther King Boulevard, marked the beginning of a German neighborhood, which around Howard Street gave way to a large Jewish section that included Prince Street, the cobbled shopping thoroughfare where people ran errands on mule-drawn carts and vendors selling vegetables, clothing, and other wares called out to mothers pushing strollers. Farther along Springfield, one would have encountered areas carved out by Slavs, Jews, and Germans, and, within a few blocks, Greek, Italian, and Irish residents.

Neighborhoods were often in flux in terms of ethnic demographics, and the takeover of an area by an emerging group could be ugly. Street brawls and racial epithets were common, for example, as more Italians moved into what had been a mostly Irish area north of the Lackawanna Railroad Depot. Eventually, Italians primarily from Avellino and other southern provinces ruled the section known as the First Ward (later, North Ward). Immigrants from other parts of Italy—including Nocera, San Gregorio, Buccia, and Calabria—settled in Newark's Down Neck section along Ferry Street. A group of mostly Sicilians established themselves around Fourteenth Avenue. In each of these neighborhoods, Italian bakeries, restaurants, and social clubs sprouted. Vegetables and grapes grew in the tiny backyards of tenement homes. By 1901, Newark held four Italian churches, including Saint Lucy's, established in 1891 in the First Ward, and Our Lady of Mount Carmel in a Down Neck building that was converted from a former Protestant church around the turn of the century.[46]

Likewise, Newark Jews lived and worshipped not simply with other Jews, but with those from as similar a background as possible, sometimes former neighbors in the old country. Polish Jews attended Temple B'nai Abraham, which moved locations several times before building a gorgeous synagogue on Clinton Avenue in 1924. Russian Jews instead tended to join Anshe Russia, which was founded in 1885 and headquartered on Prince Street.

In lieu of government-run welfare programs, which were nearly nonexistent, Newark's temples, churches, and ethnic-based social groups helped provide for their people, finding them jobs and giving financial and other assistance to families in need. Anshe Russia dues of $6 annually paid for a place to worship and socialize, as well as burial plots and sick and death benefits. Various Jewish groups created organizations for health, welfare, and social needs, including the Friendly Sisters and the Young Men's Welfare Society. One group, the Young Men's Hebrew Association, leased a three-story building in 1881 on Pine Street—renamed Hebrew Hall—that included a library, bowling alley, gymnasium, and dance hall. In response to anti-Semitism, Beth Israel Hospital was founded in 1901.[47]

With the wheels of reform already set in motion thanks to Julius Lebkuecher and other progressives, and with newcomers in Newark holding clout if only due to their sheer numbers, life slowly improved for everyone in the city. Newark's schools, overwhelmed by the influx of immigrant children, hired about a hundred more teachers in 1898, bringing the average number of pupils per classroom down from sixty to forty-eight—a progressive change by that era's standards.[48]

The Newark Public Library, built of granite and marble, opened in 1901 facing Washington Park. John Cotton Dana, a fierce-looking Vermonter with a bald head, bushy white mustache, and furrowed brow, ruled the institution with a fervent belief in the power of books from 1902 until his death in 1929. "To attend a movie is to be primitive; to attend a lecture is to be a cave man," Dana wrote. "To read is civil." The head librarian emphasized serious works in his collection, which he expanded to include books in Polish, Italian, Yiddish, and Russian, among other languages, in order to cater to Newark's newcomers. He set rigid standards for his staff, including "Buy of recent novels only a few," "Spend less money on fiction," and "Spend the money saved on duplicate copies of other good books." Viewing the culture in his adopted city as severely lacking, Dana led the way in fostering museums, music performances, and literary associations, as well as improvements to Newark's schools, parks, and overall appearance. In 1905, Dana took matters into his own hands and opened a science museum on the library's fourth floor; its descendant, the Newark Museum, was officially founded inside the library in 1909. In 1926, thanks to a generous donation from department store tycoon Louis Bamberger, the museum moved into a restored mansion on Washington Street, a few buildings away from the library.[49]

The replacement of horse-drawn trolleys with electrified models in the 1890s was met with mixed emotions. People loved the convenience and deplored the traffic and danger. "Life is not as safe as it was before 'Rapid Transit' came," Mayor Haynes related in his 1891 city council message. "Mothers who formerly allowed their children to play in the streets, find it necessary to call the roll frequently to ascertain if any are missing." Sadly, "the Coronor has been called in a number of cases, but the electric cars are here to stay," he wrote. "I do not like the overhead wires, neither do I like the reeking horses, and the overloaded cars, that are to be seen upon the recurrence of every storm."[50]

By around 1900, more than 300 trolleys crossed the corner of Broad and Market each hour during peak times; a decade later, more than 550 trolleys per hour passed the intersection. The city installed trolley islands down streets as a safety measure, but without a comprehensive system to regulate all the trains, trolleys, pedestrians, horse-drawn carriages, and a growing number of automobiles, accidents inevitably occurred. In 1903, a grisly collision between a train and a trolley killed nine and injured thirty.[51]

Hazardous and frustrating as it was, Newark's widely expanded public-transportation systems and an emerging class of citizens with newly discovered disposable income made a vibrant, welcoming, cleaner, and more modern downtown possible. Newark became more than simply a solid place to live and work. It evolved into a regional destination, an exciting, convenient magnet for people in outlying towns seeking big-city diversions, with shopping at the top of the list.

———

The early winter of 1906—one of the best holiday shopping seasons ever, store managers then said—is as good a time as any to take a close look at Newark's thriving downtown. Nowhere was prosperity more apparent than in the city's wondrous department stores, including Bamberger's, Plaut's, and Hahne's.

Originally a seller of birdcages, Hahne & Co. transformed into a general merchandise store in the 1870s. By 1900 the company filled a grandiose building bounded by Broad, New, and Halsey streets, becoming one of Newark's "mammoth establishments rivaling the great stores of New York," in the words of the *Sunday Call*.[52] Around Thanksgiving of 1906, Hahne's advertised that "the store never held such gigantic stocks, never displayed such a multitude of gift things, never showed such a variety, never had such splendid facilities for transacting the enormous business sure to come to us this season." Among the long list of recommended gift ideas offered by Hahne's were tool chests, mirrors, sewing machines, music cabinets, soup ladles, butler's trays, dress patterns, perfumeries, and writing desks. A twenty-five-foot-high Santa Claus with a six-foot head decorated a three-story-high aisle in the heart of the store. Santa pointed the way to the vast toy section on the second floor. Children were encouraged to send letters for Santa directly to Hahne & Co. "Mail them in or hand them in to the store," an ad suggested. "Mamma will tell you which is best to do."[53]

Plaut's, the city's oldest department store, likewise invited children to address their Santa letters "care of L. S. Plaut & Co." Nicknamed the "Bee Hive" for the unique shape of its building, Plaut's had been founded in 1870 by a Jewish man from Connecticut. Louis Bamberger represented an even greater Jewish success story. Bamberger had bought the bankrupt stock of a Market Street dry goods store in 1892, and by 1898 Bamberger's occupied all six of the building's floors. (An even bigger store opened in 1912 at the corner of Market and Washington streets.) Bamberger's ads for the 1906 season heralded its state-of-the-art "moving stairways" that zipped patrons among the first four floors.[54]

Bamberger's and its competitors ushered in a new era for shoppers. With set prices listed on every item sold, Old World-style haggling all but disappeared. Not only did they offer an astonishing mass of goods for sale, the department stores ushered in a previously unheard-of "customer is always right" policy. Conscious of their image on every level, the enormous stores also presented a beautiful appearance inside and out. Streets in shopping areas correspondingly became cleaner, more welcoming, and better for business.

Big and small stores alike in downtown Newark were generally busiest from nine in the morning until noon. Women from the suburbs and every Newark neighborhood came by trolley and train or the family's horse-drawn carriage. "Up to four years ago it was the practice of wealthy Newark and New Jersey women to do all their shopping in New York," one department store manager said in 1906. "But they have learned from experience that they can do better in Newark stores." Department stores hired hundreds of extra workers solely to deliver purchases via carriage to shoppers' homes, as was the custom for all but the smallest items.[55]

Before the turn of the century, Newark had been described by various visitors as "a prosperous but uninteresting city," in which because "New York is too conveniently near," there was little "encouragement for artists and actors."[56] Now, however, the city had transformed into a haven for shoppers as well as a growing entertainment hub. The theater section of the *Newark Sunday Call* previewed the 1906 holiday season's shows at the city's six main theaters, including *Brigadier Girard*, the latest comedy from Sherlock Holmes creator Arthur Conan Doyle, at the Newark Theatre; singing comedian George Mack's performance as a jockey in *Ruled off the Turf* at Blaney's Theatre; and *The Golden Crook Spectacular and Extravaganza Company*, a forty-person variety show at Waldmann's Opera House. Proctor's Theatre was hosting a musical quartet that had been scheduled to play in San Francisco but had to cancel due to the catastrophic earthquake that killed at least three thousand earlier in the year.[57]

As the peak of this prosperous, festive holiday season neared, Newark held the opening of the magnificent new City Hall on December 19. The elegant, imposing building rose from Broad Street as a powerful symbol that the city had evolved from its role as a mere industrial workshop and fully arrived as a cultured, cosmopolitan metropolis. "Newark, queen city of New Jersey, came into her own today," the *Newark Evening News* proclaimed, proudly noting that the building had been designed and constructed by Newarkers. It was truly "a triumph of local genius and civic enterprise."[58]

From the sidewalk on the east edge of Broad Street, a grand stairway led up to the Renaissance Revival-styled building's five-story granite façade, topped with an enormous dome. Inside, the centerpiece was a glorious rotunda nearly eighty feet high and encircled with balconies and soaring pillars. Speakers addressed the masses below from a large platform reached by a pair of winding marble staircases. With all the municipal offices housed in the new building, better communication and a more efficient government were expected. "The dignity of dignified and cleanly surroundings can not but sooner or later impress itself upon the individual," the *Sunday Call* reflected.[59]

The previous City Hall, as many men recalled during the opening ceremonies, was a converted hotel across the street that Newark purchased for $120,000 during the Civil War, when the population stood at around seventy thousand. The new facility, supposedly large enough to house all city offices for a century, had been constructed at a cost of $2 million. It was a luxury that many of Newark's three hundred thousand residents believed the rising star of a city deserved. The handsome building was the crowning achievement for a hard-working people made good. A *Sunday Call* illustration showed the brand-new city headquarters atop a sturdy tree, along with a tiny, acorn-shaped Puritan meeting house, all under the headline "A Mighty Oak from an Humble Acorn."[60]

While the city seemed eminently pleased with itself, decision makers could not have been entirely happy with the way money was raised for City Hall's construction. Newark had sold off several parcels of land, most notably the Old Burying Ground downtown. The cemetery, which held Puritan settlers' remains, had fallen into disrepair at least by the pre–Civil War era. Headstones slumped over or sat atop each other amid overgrown grass and shrubs. Part of the two-acre plot was even converted into a public urinal. In 1858, a law passed forbidding the burying of more bodies there. To much dismay, in the late 1880s the remains in the cemetery were dug up, dropped into pine boxes, and carted off to make way for development. The desecration was unforgiveable to many Newarkers, no matter how valuable the piece of land may have been. Former mayor Theodore Runyon reflected on Newark's shameful treatment of the dead during an 1872 speech rallying the city to build a monument to one of its great citizens, the recently deceased Seth Boyden. "We pile their tombstones in a great heap together," Runyon said, "and long for the opportunity to run a street through the old Burying Ground where their ashes rest."[61]

When Jacob Haussling, the mayor-elect soon to begin the first of his four terms, spoke at City Hall's opening, he addressed another issue of which the city could not be proud. "We have not, I fear, been as careful of outward appearances as we might be," Haussling said. "Much of our time is spent in the streets, and when we fail to do things that make them attractive, we are depriving ourselves of part, and a very important part, too, of the pleasure of life." He stated his dreams of a new era accompanying Newark's new City Hall, a period when every part of the city would became more attractive and healthier, and when the quality of life would improve for all Newarkers. "Is it too wild a hope," Haussling asked, for an era to follow in which "the gloomy, forbidding factory shall disappear and in which the ugly tenement shall be abolished?"[62]

———

The following autumn, the keys to another $2 million edifice in downtown Newark were handed over to the freeholders in a ceremony opening the new Essex County Courthouse at the corner of Market Street and Springfield Avenue. "There was no graft in this building," the commissioner in charge of construction said, somewhat defensively. "It is a structure built with clean hands."[63] Behind the courthouse's double Corinthian columns, huge murals and sculptures of bronze and marble decorated the various halls inside.

As Jacob Haussling envisioned, efforts to further beautify the city and counter the foul-smelling factories were well under way in his first years as mayor. "A city that lacks beauty is a city behind the time," stated an appeal from Newark's Shade Tree Commission, which by the end of 1907 planted more than three thousand trees along twenty-five miles of streets. "Trees are among the first things which impress a stranger in forming a judgment as to whether a city is, or is not, a good place to live in." By 1910, the popular movement had shaded 290 miles of streets with trees.[64]

Other attempts to provide for Newark's current and future needs weren't quite as successful. Although Vailsburg, a small suburban neighborhood surrounded by the Oranges and Irvington, had been annexed by Newark in 1905, efforts for comprehensive consolidation into a Greater Newark had been met with strong resistance. Irvington residents debated the possibility of being annexed by Newark before putting the issue to a vote in 1903. Pro-annexation leaders argued that Irvington citizens would receive "Technical School privileges for young men; better fire protection; better police protection; increased property valuations; equal taxation of property; City Hospital rights, and all that implies, and better trolley service," according to the *Newark Evening News*. Voters overwhelmingly defeated the motion, however, 614 against to only 273 in favor.[65]

After Vailsburg approved consolidation with Newark in 1905, Irvington stood out as an independent wedge surrounded by the bigger city on two sides. Momentum built toward another vote, which was scheduled for November of 1908. At a large meeting of anti-annexation forces, one judge warned, "If we go into Newark, we simply go into it blindly and take what we can get, which to my mind will be very little but promises." Another speaker said, "The city of Newark is bonded to its limit," and would only use Irvington to increase its tax base. Still another cautioned, if Irvington were to be annexed, "They will do with us as they did with Vailsburg—just what they please."[66]

Again, Irvington voters rejected Newark's advances. Through the years, the Newark Board of Trade and other groups occasionally gave lip service to the dream of a Greater Newark. As late as 1936, when twenty-five hundred people gathered at Newark's Mosque Theater to kick off the city's centennial, speakers proclaimed the wisdom of large-scale consolidation.[67]

Well into the twentieth century, older U.S. cities in particular continued attempts to engulf surrounding lands. While some efforts were successful— Baltimore, for example, annexed fifty square miles around World War I—most failed. Typically, outlying areas didn't want their fates tied to metropolises that they viewed as unwieldy, inefficient, and corrupt. Ambitious consolidation efforts planned for Boston, St. Louis, Pittsburgh, Cleveland, Birmingham, Louisville, and other cities never came to fruition. Suburban towns often preferred to go it alone.[68] As for Newark, Vailsburg would be the last suburb it successfully annexed.

As of the 1910 census, Newark ranked fourteenth in population of all U.S. cities with a count of 347,469 people. The city had experienced its largest-ever population expansion, adding approximately a hundred thousand residents in just a decade. Yet Newark measured only about twenty-four square miles—tiny compared to Philadelphia, Chicago, and New York, which each had well over a hundred square miles of land. Of those in the 1910 census's twenty most populous cities, only Jersey City and Milwaukee occupied less territory than Newark.

Newark would remain stuck at its 1905 size, which was sufficient to allow for relative prosperity over the next few decades, especially due to war-related industrial booms. But as Sun Belt cities such as Phoenix and Jacksonville— roughly four hundred and eight hundred square miles, respectively—came of age, Newark's twenty-four square miles seemed ridiculously small. In certain ways, Newark's fate had already been sealed.

PART II

FALL

Newark largely appeared to be a booming city through the first decades of the twentieth century. The population continued to swell in the 1910s and 1920s, and even with a Depression-related loss of thirteen thousand people during the 1930s, the number of residents nearly doubled between 1900 and the end of World War II, an overall increase of about two hundred thousand people. Still, as early as the 1920s, a shift in the populace was notable as working-class immigrants and African Americans replaced wealthy citizens heading for the suburbs. Even more worrisome than the disappearing tax base, the advent of Prohibition fostered an ever-deepening relationship between organized crime and Newark's business and political leaders. Chapter 4 covers this period around the world wars, bookended by two major reform-minded changes in the city's form of government. While the early twentieth century is often remembered as a golden era, it was also a time in which corruption proved an unseemly, toxic influence, and swarms of rich citizens and manufacturing interests left the city, marking the start of Newark's long decline.

After World War II, the federal government passed legislation that encouraged both the blossoming of suburbs and a face-lifting of dilapidated city neighborhoods. Under the leadership of the powerful Newark Housing Authority executive director, Louis Danzig, Newark immediately embraced the federal urban-renewal programs. Before too long, Newark had attracted more federal money per capita, and used the funds to flatten entire neighborhoods and build more public-housing units per capita than any city in the country. Chapter 5 describes the postwar remaking of Newark through the lens of the Christopher Columbus Homes public-housing projects, which were erected in the heavily Italian First Ward.

Urban-renewal initiatives, as well as policies making it easy for middle-class whites to own homes in the suburbs, quickened the pace of Newark's ethnic transformation. By the mid-1960s, African Americans held the majority, yet whites still had a stranglehold on virtually all power in the city. The frustrations over police brutality, discrimination, and appalling housing conditions were "bound to explode," the title of chapter 6, which details the evolution of Newark's black community and the inevitability of the deadly civic disturbances of 1967.

In the wake of the riots, the sharp population turnover, and kickback scandals that sent Mayor Hugh Addonizio to prison, Newark elected Kenneth Gibson as its first African American mayor in 1970. The city Gibson inherited was a fiscal disaster, having steadily lost its tax base for decades. It was also tainted with a reputation for corruption, crime, and racial disharmony. Despite the trying state of affairs, Gibson remained a competent administrator who managed to hold the city together, even during the bitter, divisive 1970s, described in chapter 7.

CHAPTER 4

DEAD WEIGHT

PROHIBITION, POLITICS, AND THE GROWTH
OF ORGANIZED CRIME

In the early 1900s, as progressives around the country ambitiously sought to rid their cities of partisan politics, corruption, wasteful spending, and all manner of vice and immorality, a thought occurred to reformers: perhaps the systems of municipal government themselves were part of the problem. Efforts to simply vote political bosses and their lackeys out of office had yielded few lasting improvements. Something more drastic seemed necessary, and a new form of city government, born out of a turn-of-the-century tragedy, was heralded as the cure.

The 140-miles-per-hour hurricane that ripped through Galveston, Texas, in the fall of 1900 destroyed over three thousand buildings and killed an estimated eight thousand people, nearly a quarter of the city's population. The storm still ranks as the nation's worst-ever natural disaster. Galveston's government, often criticized in preceding years as paralyzed by corrupt political machines and quarrelsome bureaucrats, was not up to the critical task of rebuilding, many believed. A group of Galveston businessmen suggested creating an orderly, corporate board-style commission to oversee the monumental work ahead. The suggested commission would be run in a businesslike fashion, with each of five commissioners responsible for a separate sphere of government. The Texas legislature approved the motion, and initial reactions to Galveston's new commission government were overwhelmingly positive locally and around the country.[1]

Commission government soon became thought of as a solution not only to a hurricane's aftereffects, but also to the ills of cities in general. By 1915, 350 U.S. cities were run by modern, streamlined commissions similar to the one created in Galveston. Most commissions consisted of five officials who collectively held all the city's executive and legislative powers. One member served as mayor, though he basically had no more power than any other commissioner. In the hopes of limiting the influence of political party bosses, officials were typically elected in at-large nonpartisan contests.

One early in-depth study, by an Indiana state attorney named Oswald Ryan in 1915, pronounced commission government "the most promising" system in existence. Already, "large floating debts have been wiped out, sinking funds created, and the public credit restored," the *New York Times* said, paraphrasing Ryan's book, *Municipal Freedom*. "The observer finds that an improvement—an unmistakable improvement—has occurred in the various public services, there being a purer water supply, better streets, more efficient fire and police services." What's more, "current expenses have been curtailed; taxes have been decreased," and "as far as the moral tone of the commission cities is concerned, here, too, is much improvement, in the opinion of Mr. Ryan. Gambling and the red lights are no more."[2]

Cities were clearly eager for all sorts of reforms in the early 1900s. The newfound anonymity of city living had brought with it drastic shifts from the days when village elders closely enforced societal standards. Old-fashioned watchdog groups were not ready to concede their governments, or the morality of their communities at large, to the corruptions of the modern world, however.

In Newark, about the same time hundreds of U.S. cities were adopting the progressive new commission form of government, a group called the Citizens Committee sponsored a series of late-night undercover investigations to study the extent to which vice had infiltrated the city's downtown neighborhoods. The group, which included clergymen and leading figures like Louis Bamberger, published a 1914 report in the hopes of ridding Newark of its rampant "social evil conditions," as stated in the report's headline.[3]

At least four hundred prostitutes worked Newark's streets, the study said. Prostitutes solicited clients in back rooms of two-thirds of the ninety-three city saloons investigated, often with the encouragement of bartenders and waiters. Among the other findings in the report, which did not claim to be comprehensive, 750 cases of gonorrhea were treated in Newark in a single week. Investigators quickly and easily purchased morphine and cocaine, and one stumbled onto the scene of a white man and a black woman in a saloon hallway "performing an indecent and degenerate act."[4]

"An even graver menace" than the prostitute, according to the committee, was the "Charity Girl." Professional call girls created the term of derision for women "who sin sexually in return only for the pleasures given or the company of the men with whom they consort," in the study's words. The industrial era had brought with it the possibility that large numbers of women could support themselves and live independently for the first time ever. An estimated ten thousand young, unattached (and unsupervised) women then lived in Newark. They worked in department stores or factories, lived in furnished boarding houses, and spent their evenings as they pleased, flirting at cafes or hopping into automobiles with men they'd just met—scandalous behavior for the era. "Their lack of knowledge of the effects of contact with men renders them infinitely more liable than the professional prostitute to spread venereal disease," the committee report stated. Most worrisome of all, according to the report, "they contaminate other girls."[5]

One investigator ventured into a largely African American section of the city. "This is the toughest place in Newark, and in the country, I guess," a seventeen-year veteran police officer said. While white prostitutes charged an average of $3 for their services, their "colored" counterparts asked only fifty cents "to do the lowest acts of perversion," the investigator reported. Once a customer followed the woman, the police said, he was often robbed. "They offer to go with a man for a few cents," one officer said. "Then they get him in a lot or room and steal every cent he has got." In a fairly typical scene in one saloon, a bartender approached the investigator as he watched several women dance provocatively. "Say, brother," the bartender said, "I'll fix you up with a nice black girl. You needn't be afraid; I'll see that you're taken care of."[6]

Another report aimed at reform, written by social worker Willard Price in 1912, focused on the Ironbound, where there were three well-known gambling houses and 122 saloons—one for every seven residential buildings. The Ironbound at the time was "a district of industrial uproar, drifting smoke, heavy atmosphere, dangerous acid fumes and unforgettable odors," Price wrote. "Its people are a hodgepodge of nationalities, speaking many old-world tongues, and making pathetic efforts to adjust to their new and unwholesome American surroundings."[7]

The findings from these reports—prostitution, casual sex, gambling, drug use, intermingling of races—shocked Newark's traditional moral code. Reformers blamed the conditions on a number of factors, including the lack of supervision for young women, the influx of immigrants, and corrupt or lazy policemen who refused to enforce the law. (Oddly, poverty was rarely named a cause.) Whatever the reasons, vice was present to varying degrees in every city, and clergy-led crusades such as Newark's Citizen Committee's spread all over the country in pre–World War I days. Reformers targeted everything from smoking to jazz music. Dancing was often viewed as a sign of loose morals. The risqué Charleston was worst of all, but various women's clubs also banned the tango, the fox trot, and the waltz.[8] The granddaddy of all vices, however, which reformers almost universally pointed the finger at as a cause for so many societal ills, was alcohol.

Temperance societies had been asking men and women in America to "take the pledge" and swear off alcohol at least since the colonial era. The Prohibitionist movement gained new traction amid the reform-minded early 1900s, and the Volstead Act, which rendered the manufacture or sale of liquor illegal, officially went into effect on January 17, 1920.

A loud minority of Newark's clergy and reformist business leaders zealously welcomed Prohibition and pushed city officials to enforce the law throughout the era. Overall, however, the immigrant-heavy city never gave the movement anything close to majority support. Working-class Germans, Irish, and Italians, in particular, opposed limitations on their right to have a drink. As many on the "wet" side asked: how could such a basic right be denied to soldiers returning from fighting for freedom in Europe during World War I?

Another of the era's major reforms, on the other hand, did receive the overwhelming backing of Newarkers. Prior to the war, Newark's municipal government consisted of a mayor elected by all voters, as well as a legislative body of thirty-two aldermen divided among sixteen wards. The responsibility for streets, sewers, and water lay in the hands of a separate board of elected officials. Other services, such as health, police, and fire departments, were run by appointees named by the mayor or aldermen. With power scattered among a "weak mayor" and so many officials and boards—many of whom were in the pocket of political machines—city government was incapable of responding efficiently to the needs of the people. Improvements to streets, parks, and other services occurred far more slowly and haphazardly than frustrated citizens hoped.[9]

Following the national trend, in 1917 Newark voters considered adopting a commission government in which five commissioners would be elected in nonpartisan, at-large contests. Each voter could cast as many votes as there were openings (five), and the candidates receiving the most votes were named commissioners, serving four-year terms. The five winners would divvy up various domains of responsibility, with one director of public safety, in charge of fire and police departments, for example, and another commissioner placed in control of streets and public improvements.[10]

Thomas Raymond, Newark's mayor since 1914, was one of the few city leaders opposing the commission. Among other reasons, Raymond worried that the new system would not root out corruption or partisan control. A commission government, Raymond argued, instead seemed "certainly made for [political] bosses."[11]

Essex County's most powerful political boss, Democrat James R. Nugent, in fact supported the change to a commission. Newark's Board of Trade and voters in general did as well. The motion passed by a count of 19,069 to only 6,053. "What the city has accomplished," a *Newark Evening News* editorial cheered, "has been to cast off the outworn system which has been a dead weight to its progress."[12]

————

If reformers believed the switch to commission government would bring with it bold new leadership, they must have been somewhat disappointed in the election held five weeks after the referendum passed. The nonpartisan, at-large structure opened up the election to anyone and everyone, resulting in a disorganized, chaotic campaign. More than eighty candidates vied for five seats. The top vote-getters wound up being familiar faces, including two Irish Democrats: Charles Gillen, a high-profile realty man with ties to Newark's financial institutions, and William J. Brennan, the police commissioner appointed by Mayor Raymond in 1917. Raymond himself, despite his opposition to the commission system, also secured enough votes for a spot. Gillen, however, received the most votes, and he was named to the mostly nominal position of mayor.[13]

The back-to-back votes in Newark seemed to relay a mixed message, with the first calling for a complete overhaul of the government, the next giving a pat on the back to the men running the government. Voters were essentially indicting their outdated form of government, not the men in charge, who seemed to be doing a decent job. In fact, by most indications, Newark in the precommission era was a flourishing city. "One cannot come in contact with a live business man in Newark," the *Times* wrote in 1913, "without being influenced by [a] spirit of optimism."[14]

Physical signs of progress were everywhere. As of 1911, a train line connected Newark to Hoboken, Jersey City, and then on to New York City via "the tubes," which became the PATH (Port Authority Trans-Hudson) train system. Work began in 1914 to dig a channel in Newark's swampy Meadowlands and deepen its port to accommodate huge ships loaded with cargo. According to a 1915 count, 280,000 pedestrians crossed through the Four Corners in a thirteen-hour period, making it arguably the nation's busiest intersection. The first skyscrapers arose downtown, notably the twelve-story Kinney Building and, a few doors down, the slim sixteen-story Fireman's Insurance Company headquarters, built in 1916 at the northeast corner of Broad and Market. Also in 1916, in coordination with Newark's 250th anniversary, a three hundred-room hotel with an extravagant, second-floor ballroom opened overlooking

Military Park. The city's first luxury hotel, it was named in honor of Newark founder Robert Treat. A few months after Newark elected its inaugural board of commissioners, with the city in the midst of a war-related economic boom, the port's Submarine Boat Corporation laid the keel for the first steel ship built in the country.[15]

Early on, Newark's commissioners seemed eager to make the idea a reality that government could be more efficient and truly work for the people. Mayor Gillen staged battles versus various train and trolley companies every time they tried to raise prices. At one point in 1919, a trolley raised prices from six to seven cents a trip, prompting Gillen to board and refuse to pay the extra penny. In another instance, Gillen managed to get the cost of passage from Newark to New York on the tubes reduced from fifty-four cents to thirty-three cents for a round trip.[16]

Those initial years of commission government were remarkable because, rather than being bogged down with internal squabbles, city officials seemed to work together. At least on the surface, Newark's commissioners were almost always cordial, cooperative, and supportive of each other. The public seemed content as well, favoring incumbents for more than a decade. Four of the five original commissioners were reelected in 1921. Voters kept Gillen in office through 1933. Raymond remained a commissioner until his death in 1928; he even became mayor again for the last three years of his life.[17]

Of all the long-serving 1920s commissioners, none was more beloved by voters, his peers, or the press than Irishman William Brennan. Bill, as everyone called him, was witty and blunt-spoken, known as a principled, strict but fair administrator and disciplinarian. Through circle-rimmed glasses, Brennan's fierce stare was dreaded by underlings who had somehow disappointed the commissioner. Brennan was also a family man, raising eight children in his home near Vailsburg Park. One of his sons, William J. Brennan Jr., would go on to serve for thirty-four years in the U.S. Supreme Court as one of the most liberal, distinguished justices ever.

Bill Brennan Sr. was born with light eyes and curly red hair in 1872 in County Roscommon, northeast of Galway. In his late teens and desperate to earn a decent wage, he left his homeland, heading first to England, then on to the United States in 1892. Brennan found employment as a fireman in Trenton before settling in 1894 in Newark, where he also joined the fire department. His work with the fireman's union evolved into stints as president of the Essex Trades Council and executive board member of the New Jersey Federation of Labor. Republican Mayor Thomas Raymond was impressed enough with Brennan to name him police commissioner in 1917, even though Brennan was a Democrat. Nine months after the appointment, voters gave one of the five commission seats to Brennan, where he stayed until his death in 1930. In Brennan's last two elections (1925 and 1929), he received more votes than any other candidate. Content running the fire, police and other departments as public-safety director, he demurred from ever becoming mayor.[18]

Commissioner Brennan understood the value—political and societal—inherent in compromising to try to please the city's various factions. He refused to close the few movie houses that chose to show films on Sundays. Yet, to appease fanatics pressuring him to shut them, Brennan forced the movie houses to donate one Sunday's profits to a local charity every few weeks. William Ashby, founder of the Urban League of Essex County, said that Brennan always ensured that when it was the African American charity's turn to be the beneficiary, the money came from one of the larger movie houses. Brennan's door was always open to Ashby, and the commissioner sometimes asked him to stop by simply to chat—small acts of kindness that left an impression on Ashby, accustomed to second-class treatment in a racist world. Brennan, resting a leg on his oak table and sucking on one of the dozens of pipes he loved so much, "wanted nothing in particular," Ashby recorded in his memoirs. "He just wanted to talk to me. I would sit and listen to stories of his boyhood in Ireland—the brogue still so thick I could scarcely make out some of the words—and of his early life in this country."[19]

Brennan thrived under the nonpartisan structure of commission elections. Though a nominal Democrat, he never had organized backing from any political party. The commissioner had plenty of support, nonetheless, from people who viewed him as an honorable, genuine, self-made man who had their interests at heart. "What is the secret of Commissioner Brennan's success? Has he wealth? No!" one speaker said at a 1921 Brennan rally. "Has he courage? Barrels of it. Has he honesty, fidelity, and independence? Yes! All of these and more." Later, at the same rally, a woman addressed the crowd. "We like home-made things," she said. "We don't like machine-made goods. It's got to be ready made. That's Bill Brennan. He's a rough diamond. He has had no training but the training he received in the College of Hard Knocks."[20]

The commissioner was sometimes criticized as being too connected to labor, especially in light of his background with the fire department, unions, and trade groups. Time and again, though, Brennan instituted policies to rein in the power of the departments he oversaw. Brennan was outraged when Newark police and firemen unions attempted to secure a generous new pension in 1921. "You can put me down as no friend of theirs," he said, if "lending my efforts to help them put something over on the rest of the citizens." When Brennan became commissioner, first-year firemen received $800 a year. Four years and two raises later, they netted $1,800 annually.

The pension they sought was almost unheard of for the era: half salary after twenty years of service. "Imagine," Brennan said, "able-bodied men getting a thousand a year or more from the city and working in a bank at a couple of thousand more, taking work from men who need it."[21]

"A square deal for all; special privileges for none" was how Brennan summed up his political platform.[22] Police officers and firemen newly under Brennan's charge found it unusual that employees were actually promoted based on merit rather than patronage. "For the good of the service" was the pat response Brennan issued to anyone questioning a reassignment, promotion, or other change.[23] "He has tried to keep his department free from pernicious influences of all sorts," the *Newark Evening News* wrote in a 1921 endorsement of Brennan. "He has been fearless and capable. He has not forgotten that he owes responsibility to the people and to none other."[24]

After Brennan's 1921 reelection, he hosted an end-of-summer picnic to thank his supporters. The event soon became an immensely popular annual occurrence that symbolized the feel-good era of Newark in the early days of commission government. Tens of thousands gathered for a free day of merry-go-rounds, Skee-Ball, carousel rides, soda, peanuts, hot dogs, and ice cream at a Newark-area amusement park. Nearly a hundred thousand people attended the 1922 picnic at Irvington's Olympic Park. Brennan's picnics grew with each passing year. In 1928, invitations for the September 8 event at Newark's Dreamland Park went out to seventy-five thousand children and thirty-five thousand adults. Guests hopped on the miniature railway and the Ferris wheel, watched some twenty-five clowns and a Punch and Judy puppet show, listened to the drum-and-bugle-corps competition, and helped themselves to the staggering number of treats: 100,000 hot dogs, 75,000 packages of candy, 150,000 ears of corn, 7,500 gallons of ice cream, 5,000 gallons apiece of root beer, orangeade, and lemonade, as well as 75,000 toys.[25]

The picnics solidified Brennan's image as a man of the people, especially in the eyes of immigrants and the working classes. The "drys," who wanted Prohibition zealously enforced, consistently gave William Brennan grief, however. The commissioner thought Prohibition a foolish, prudish restriction on liberty. He took rudimentary steps to follow the law, but frequently argued matters were largely out of his hands. "What can I do?" Brennan asked in the fall of 1921, responding to Third Ward residents who wanted to shut a notorious neighborhood tavern called the Tub of Blood. "You see, under the old system of saloon licenses, I could do something. I could just revoke the license of the place. Now I can't do anything." An Anti-Saloon League official accused the commissioner of sitting on his hands. "The trouble is that Brennan lacks any disposition to interfere with such places," he said. "Saloons are operating quite openly, apparently without fear of the police."[26]

The following February, a coalition of Newark churches stormed City Hall, asking for Brennan's resignation. "The committee takes the position that vice is not being suppressed as it should," one speaker said. "There are two points: Inability and unwillingness." While people in the crowd heckled Brennan with shouts of "Give 'em a drink!" and "Throw 'em out!" the commissioner maintained the law was being enforced as well as it could be.[27]

A few days after the hearing, four African Americans died from drinking gin with wood alcohol in a saloon called the Side Pocket, located opposite the Tub of Blood. "It's hard to close such places unless we have conclusive evidence that a misdemeanor was committed on the premises," Brennan reflected. "There are no license laws on the basis of which we can close a saloon any more than we can close an ice cream parlor." Pro- and anti-Prohibitionists alike could have used the incident to support their cause—arguing either that the Volstead Act drove people to such dangerous lengths, or that such tragedies would be avoided if the law was vigorously enforced. Regardless, the *Evening News* reported that the morning after the people died, Broome Street's saloons were "filled with patrons, blacks and whites, laughing and talking and buying drinks, while nickel-in-the-slot machines ground out jazz."[28]

Arrests for Prohibition violations in Newark slowly accumulated: 83 in 1920, 198 in 1921, 233 in 1922. Few convictions ever occurred, however; there were less than a dozen in 1922, for example.[29]

Prohibition largely seemed successful only in turning normally conscientious citizens into law breakers because they wanted to relax with a whisky after work. The sober, virtuous utopia Prohibition advocates envisioned was never realized. Instead, the Volstead Act's most obvious creation was a vast underworld that amassed more money and power with each passing day—as well as a cooperative generation of policemen and government officials who were increasingly willing to look the other way.

———

In the early 1900s, when Newark's Third Ward was heavily Jewish, a tall, young tough named Abner Zwillman earned a reputation for defending Jewish peddlers and kids being harassed by hoodlums from other neighborhoods. Born in 1904 and raised on Charlton Street—a block west of the cobbled shopping thoroughfare of Prince Street, and four blocks from the notorious saloons of Broome Street—Abner came from a family of poor Russian immigrants, like most folks in the Third Ward. His father, Avraham, made a meager living selling live chickens in a public market stall, and Abner and six siblings were always hungry. As a composed and discreet adolescent, Abner ran errands for local politicians, bookies, and pimps in exchange for pocket change. By the time he was in his early teens, Abner Zwillman stood at a lanky six feet, two inches, olive-skinned, broad-shouldered, and handsome, with curly, black hair neatly parted down the middle. Third Ward residents had little reason to fear Zwillman's gang, the Happy Ramblers. Whenever Irish hooligans appeared on their turf, however, darting down Prince Street to raid the pushcarts or knock the skullcaps off of young Jews, a cry came out of "*Reef der Langer!*," Yiddish for "Get the Tall One!" *Langer* became anglicized as "Longy," Zwillman's lifelong nickname.[30]

Avraham Zwillman died during the summer of 1918. Longy had just completed eighth grade, and instead of going on to high school, the four-teen-year-old rented a horse and wagon. Rather than trying to peddle goods to the Third Ward poor, he chose a more lucrative option of touring wealthy neighborhoods and flirting with housewives while selling them fruits and vegetables. Within a year, in the course of his rounds Zwillman was supple-menting his income by taking penny and nickel bets for the illegal lottery, known variously as policy or the numbers game. Realizing that the hoods running lotteries were no tougher or smarter than he was, Zwillman soon established his own numbers game, which became the biggest in Newark. An organized network of barbershop, soda fountain, candy store, and saloon owners collected bets for Zwillman in exchange for a steady $30 a week.[31]

Zwillman effectively took control of Newark's numbers racket while still a teenager. By the beginning of the Roaring Twenties, he'd accrued connec-tions in politics and the police force to assure his business ran smoothly. An intimidating bunch of henchmen eagerly jumped to Zwillman's side and made bettors pay up, if necessary. Most importantly, Zwillman never wanted to be hungry again, and vowed to use his brains, energy, and muscle to make himself rich. In short, Longy Zwillman had the personality, skills, and desire needed to take advantage of the shady business opportunities that accompanied Prohibition.

At its peak, Zwillman's gang was importing 40 percent of the bootlegged liquor in the country, and Longy reaped in $2 million a year. Despite Zwillman's attempts to keep a low profile—quietly dishing out bribes, never wearing garish jewelry or driving expensive cars—the press began calling him "the Al Capone of New Jersey." A member of the Big Six (or the Syndicate), which included Charles "Lucky" Luciano, Frank Costello, Meyer Lansky, Bugsy Siegel, and other leading gangsters, Longy Zwillman consistently pushed for a professional approach to making money. He convinced criminal operations to divide up territories in a businesslike fashion, make peace with each other, and diversify investments to include legitimate interests, ushering in the age of organized crime.[32]

Newark's large breweries had no choice but to officially shut down with the advent of Prohibition. People wouldn't be denied, however. One brewery sold ingredients and instructions for making homemade beer. The Newark Public Library noted that pages on wine-making had been torn out of books. Many small breweries managed to keep churning out lager and ale, either by disguising their operations or paying off the right policemen.[33]

While U.S. brewers supplied speakeasies with beer, most Prohibition-era whisky came from Canada, and much of it came through Newark. Freighters from Canadian distilleries anchored a few miles off the coast, so as to be outside U.S. jurisdiction. Workers loaded liquor into waiting speedboats, which raced past on-the-take Coast Guardsmen into Newark, as well as ports in Ocean and Monmouth counties. In the beginning, the booze was loaded onto wagons and carted off to saloons and social clubs. Zwillman, always the innovator, bought a truck to distribute the bootlegged "hooch" more efficiently. "We started in the Third Ward, where we knew everybody," one of Longy's men later recalled. "We'd go around to the different joints to take orders. Longy would take his truck—we soon had three—down to the docks where he knew the people bringing stuff in. He'd buy a few hundred cases and bring 'em to a warehouse we had near Prince Street."[34]

Bootlegging was a dangerous business, especially in the early days. Zwillman developed a system to avoid hijackings, which were far more common than arrests. A Zwillman worker arrived at the port with half a $5 bill. If the contact on the docks didn't have the other half, guns would be drawn. One night, hijackers set up a barricade to block their trucks, but Longy had supplied his men with guns and instructions on what to do in such a situation. The first truck barreled through, and the men in all the trucks fired their weapons. "They thought Longy was some punk kid—he was only 17 years old—who'd run as soon as they had him hemmed in," another Zwillman associate said. "They never expected us to be ready with our own guns."[35]

Word spread that Longy Zwillman meant business in every sense. One obviously impressed player was Joseph Reinfeld, the owner of a tavern on High Street and Eighth Avenue. Though Jewish, Reinfeld was dark-skinned and tall and could have passed for Sicilian, which came in handy in his tavern, located in the Italian First Ward. A mostly Italian assemblage of loan sharks, brick-layers, politicians, gamblers, and members of the "Black Hand"—the crooked neighborhood bosses who were precursors to the mafia—were all regulars in Reinfeld's place. Joe Reinfeld asked Longy to become his junior partner. Reinfeld needed someone to distribute whisky from his connection in Montreal: the Bronfman brothers, whose surname appropriately means "liquor man" in Yiddish. In the 1920s, the Bronfmans merged their small distillery with another liquor manufacturer with a better-known name, Seagram's.[36]

The Reinfeld-Zwillman operation sold only top-notch whisky and, it was said, never watered it down like so many other bootleggers. Accordingly, they charged $30 per bottle, a whopping profit of $28 a pop. The partners became the biggest whisky importers on the East Coast. Reinfeld lectured his young partner in all aspects of business, notably bribery, which in Newark became an art form. "Any cluck can wave money in front of somebody he wants to buy. The trick is to learn who to bribe, and how much the guy is worth," Reinfeld was known to say. "A judge is more important than a prosecutor. A city attorney is more important than a cop. Some cops are important, though, because of the information they have, like when and where raids are planned. They're worth almost as much as a prosecutor."[37]

Reinfeld begrudgingly made Zwillman an equal partner in a tense Thanksgiving Day meeting in 1923. Longy had yet to turn twenty. As their business evolved, they chartered as many as thirty ships to cater to bootleggers all along the East Coast. According to the IRS, between 1928 and 1933, Zwillman and Reinfeld made about $40 million from liquor alone. Longy still controlled the numbers racket, which had spread from Newark into the surrounding suburbs. With business and political connections all over the state, Zwillman was approached by Meyer Lansky, Frank Costello, Lucky Luciano, and other New York crime bosses who wanted to expand their gambling operations to the west side of the Hudson River. Together, they opened a string of high-class casinos in Bergen and Hudson counties.[38]

An upstart First Ward gang leader named Ruggiero Boiardo temporarily disturbed Longy Zwillman's peaceful reign as Newark's underworld king. Boiardo grew up in Chicago, and in 1910, at the age of twenty, moved to Newark. For spells, he did masonry work and drove a milk truck. Eventually, Richie, as he was known, branched into lotteries, bootlegging, and shaking down merchants for protection money. Few homes had telephones in the era, and Boiardo always seemed to be talking to some girl or business associate from a candy store pay phone. When someone asked for Richie, the response was often, "He's in the phone booth." The last word, however, sounded more like "boot," which is where his nickname, Richie "the Boot" originated. Another theory had it that the "boot" was simply short for bootlegger.[39]

By the late 1920s, Boiardo's intimidating tactics, flashy persona, and obvious wealth made him a celebrity in the First Ward. Heads turned as Boiardo strutted into Eighth Avenue restaurants, his oversize belly stretching a pin-stripe three-piece suit to the limits. Around his waist rested a belt buckle studded with 150 diamonds and reportedly worth $20,000—easily ten times the annual salary of hard-working Newarkers. A five-carat diamond often sparkled from Boiardo's fat fingers, and a fifteen-diamond pin held his tie in place, just below a double chin. In some pictures, Boiardo appeared to have no neck whatsoever. His thick head of black hair was slicked neatly straight back above a fine Roman nose and dark, glazed-over eyes.[40]

At some point around a decade into Prohibition, the Boot's ambitions expanded beyond the First Ward. His henchmen began straying into the Third Ward—Zwillman territory—and demanding saloon owners buy their beer and liquor from Boiardo. A few bars were sprayed with machine-gun bullets. Some of Boiardo's boys also reportedly mugged men inside one of Longy's regular hangouts, the Third Ward Political Club. A gang war lasting several weeks followed, with failed assassination attempts of both leaders. One legendary story has it that two small-framed Italian would-be hitmen dressed in drag and presented themselves as hookers to (unsuccessfully) try to get into Zwillman's hotel room and knock him off. Before long, the two gang leaders decided bloodshed was bad for business. They declared a truce in the fall of 1930.[41]

To celebrate, Boiardo hosted a wild two-day party at Nuova Napoli, a Seventh Avenue banquet hall. About a thousand guests came to drink, eat, and pay their respects to the First Ward boss. The parade of fancy cars on Seventh Avenue looked like "an annex to an automobile show," the *Newark Evening News* reported. The crowd inside included Boiardo's wife and four children, local cops and city officials, and gangsters from as far away as Massachusetts, Nebraska, and Illinois. When Zwillman and ten of his men arrived at ten o'clock on the second night of festivities, a bleary-eyed Boiardo escorted them to a table, where they popped champagne and talked. Longy appeared in good spirits, but unlike several politicians, he refused press requests to pose for a photo with Richie. "G'wan, whaddaya want a picture for," Zwillman said. "Ain't it enough we're here together?"[42]

Less than two months afterward, during Thanksgiving week, Boiardo's driver, Joseph Julian, pulled up to 242 Broad Street, where Richie had recently begun renting an apartment after a fight with his wife. It was a little after 4 AM, at the tail end of a long Tuesday evening in nightclubs. Soon after Julian said good night, shotgun blasts erupted and slugs ripped into the car, as well as Boiardo's neck, mouth, arm, and chest. The unsuspecting Boiardo wasn't wearing his bullet-proof vest. Day broke a few hours later, and as word of the incident spread, First Ward undertakers approached the Boiardo family offering their services. By afternoon, however, while Boiardo drifted in and out of consciousness and avoided police questions, doctors said he would survive.[43]

Few people thought the attempted hit was the work of Abner Zwillman's goons—not because of the recent treaty, but because of the amateur approach taken by the would-be killers. They had rented an apartment across the street from Boiardo and apparently fired from about a hundred feet away. At such a distance, the shotgun's buckshot spread widely, inflicting only superficial wounds. Richie "the Boot" Boiardo would have to live with eight slugs in his body, but he would live.[44]

When City Hospital released Boiardo in early December, he was taken to police headquarters to be fingerprinted and photographed; in the mug shot, Boiardo's left arm is in a sling, and his head is wrapped in a cartoonlike mass of white gauze. Boiardo, who had been carrying a gun and a ten-inch knife on the night of the shooting, was arrested for carrying a concealed weapon, with bail imposed at $25,000. Police officers wondered if Richie might opt to remain in jail, where it would be more difficult for assassins to finish the job. "I'm safe in or out," Boiardo shrugged.[45]

Within two weeks of Boiardo's sentencing, three teenage boys spotted the body of a forty-two-year-old racketeer, ex-con, and former police officer named Adam Dresch floating in the Passaic River. Dresch's body was riddled with bullets, and there were obvious signs he'd been bound and severely beaten. The same day, Philip Rossi, a thirty-one-year-old former boxer, had been gunned down behind the Eighth Avenue club he co-owned. Neither incident could have been called a robbery, as both men still had valuables on their persons. Police believed that one or both of the killings were retaliations for the attempt on Boiardo's life.[46]

Fined $1,000 and sentenced to two and a half years due to the weapons charge, Boiardo never exactly served hard time. He was quickly transferred from Trenton State Prison to a minimum-security penal farm outside Bordentown. Throughout his stint in jail, reports circulated that someone who looked remarkably similar to Richie Boiardo appeared regularly in various First Ward haunts, especially on evenings and weekends.[47]

Longy Zwillman likewise couldn't completely avoid run-ins with the law. While Boiardo's trial was taking place, his Third Ward counterpart was serving six months for assault. These were minor setbacks, however. In the early 1930s, even as the gangsters sat behind bars and the end of Prohibition seemed imminent, Zwillman, Boiardo, and their cohorts tightened their grip on Newark politics and business.

One of the most blatant examples of the corruption that had infiltrated the city came during the November 1932 elections. The results in the Third Ward's Eleventh District suspiciously yielded fewer than ten votes for every Republican candidate and exactly 587 votes for Franklin Roosevelt and every other Democrat. Alleged fraud had similarly been discovered in five other wards. An inquiry began within days of the election, and by the end of the year, Essex County grand juries returned indictments against 113 people. Most of those indicted (eighty-three) were election officials, nearly every one with a Jewish or Italian surname. Trials began in early January, but the prosecutor's cases seemed hopeless. Early on in the investigation, twenty-seven suspect poll books—including all the Third Ward's results—had mysteriously disappeared from City Hall. No one was ever convicted.[48]

———

Newark's population growth had slowed—up marginally from 414,524 in 1920 to 442,337 in 1930. Still, most Newarkers were pleased with how far their city had come, and nearly everyone envisioned even brighter days ahead. In 1925, a rendering predicting what Newark would look like in 1975 showed a downtown teeming with skyscrapers. The vision seemed to be transforming into a reality on Broad Street by the end of the decade, what with the twenty-story New Jersey Telephone Building opening in 1929 and work nearing completion on the National Newark Building—a neoclassical gem and, at thirty-five stories, the state's tallest building.[49]

A world-class skyline seemed like the natural next step for Newark, considering the other monumental projects underway. In 1927, the city bought the abandoned Morris Canal and began draining and expanding it to accommodate a subway. A year later, with the world enthralled by Charles Lindbergh's first-ever transatlantic flight, the city hastily filled in acres of the Meadowlands to build an airport runway. Newark Airport soon boasted 125 departures and arrivals daily, making it one of the world's busiest airports through the early 1930s. The Holland Tunnel opened up automobile traffic between Jersey City and Manhattan in 1927, by which time plans had been formulated for the Pulaski Skyway, a remarkable highway resting atop a system of viaducts. When completed, drivers could travel from New York City to Newark's central business district, airport, or ship terminal in minutes.[50]

A one-liner making the rounds in the 1920s hinted that all was not well, however. "No one lives in Newark," it went. In certain circles, the silly joke was becoming a truism. Rich Newark families had begun fleeing for the suburbs in droves. As early as 1923, the *Newark Evening News* was pointing out a concern that should have been in the minds of wealthy businessmen leaving the city: "Is it going to be a desirable situation for the owners of the factory or its active managers to have nothing to say politically about the tax rates, police and fire protection or even the character of the government of the city in which they have invested their fortune?"[51]

Nonetheless, the escape route had opened thanks to road improvements and the increasing affordability of automobiles. In 1916, every Board of Trade officer was a Newark resident; a decade later, slightly over half the members of the Chamber of Commerce (the successor to the board) lived in the city. By 1930, more than two-thirds of the chamber's officers and directors lived outside Newark's borders. Newark's overall population had grown by about 7 percent in the 1920s, but the exodus of the well-off meant a slow chipping away of the tax base. There was no mystery about where those with the means had retreated. Many suburban towns within commuting distance nearly doubled in population during the decade. South Orange, for example, grew from 7,200 residents in 1920 to 13,630 in 1930.[52]

Newark's five incumbent commissioners ran for reelection in May 1929 under the joint slogan "Continued Prosperity." All five kept their posts, but the surprising runners-up revealed a definite shift among voters, who were more and more likely to be poor or middle class, and of Italian, Jewish, or African American heritage. Finishing a close sixth and seventh in the election were a pair of upstart politicians who appealed in particular to the two ethnic groups growing in power and prominence: Peter A. Cavicchia, an Italian Republican, and Meyer Ellenstein, a Jewish Democrat.[53]

Six months after the election, the stock market crashed, precipitating the Great Depression. The "continued prosperity" promised by commissioners seemed a cruel joke. Employment dropped in Newark by 25 percent between January and November of 1930. With investors out of cash or simply panicked, building in the city ground to a halt, leaving construction workers hit especially hard: nearly one-third were unemployed in 1930. Around the country that year, 26,355 businesses closed and 1,352 banks failed, making some $853 million in deposits worthless. Throughout that spring and summer, socialists and communists rallied in Military Park and other parts of the city to blame the depression on capitalism and demand jobs, taxes on the rich, and an immediate end to evictions. The numbers only got worse in 1931, with an additional 2,294 U.S. banks, worth $1.7 billion, going under. An estimated sixty thousand Newarkers—30 percent of its workforce—were without jobs that year.[54]

With each passing week, dozens more Newarkers couldn't make their rental payments and were evicted. Desperate thousands walked the streets begging for handouts or trying to sell apples from carts. Soup-kitchen lines stretched around blocks. One Newark mother described her family's day-to-day existence in a Social Services Bureau survey. "I used to sit and wonder if the people next door would send in something after they'd finished eating," she said. "Sometimes they would and other times they would have nothing left and we wouldn't eat. I'd tell the kids to drink lots of water and we'd wait for the next meal."[55]

As the group traditionally "last hired, first fired," African American workers suffered most in the 1930s. During World War I, with Newark's manufacturers running operations twenty-four hours a day and desperate for workers, African Americans had finally been able to land industrial jobs. While black men worked as longshoremen or unskilled laborers in steel-manufacturing plants, many black women moved on from domestic service to employment in factories making cigarettes or clothing. As word spread of opportunity in Newark, the city's African American population shot up from around 9,400 in 1915 to nearly 17,000 in 1920. A decade later, Newark's African Americans numbered 38,880, or around 9 percent of the total population.[56] (Chapter 6 offers a more detailed description of the Great Migration from the South and the growth of African American culture in Newark.)

Unfortunately, unlike the immigrant groups from Europe that managed to muscle into one or another line of work and move up the ranks, African Americans struggled to gain a stable foothold in many industries. Employers often set the ceiling for black workers firmly at the level of unskilled labor. As of 1930, more than two dozen unions officially banned African Americans from their membership. Other unions found creative, *Catch-22*–style methods to exclude blacks. Joining the union was possible, they'd say, so long as one had completed the proper apprenticeship courses—only African Americans weren't accepted in such courses. With their lowest-rung status, blacks accounted for 16.9 percent of Newark's unemployed in 1930, or twice their proportion of the city's total population. In other words, if you were black, you were two times more likely to be out of a job. The statistics worsened as time passed. Between 1930 and 1940, Newark added nearly seven thousand African American residents, yet the number of employed black males dropped from 13,308 to 7,990.[57]

Newark, like most cities, was completely unprepared to cope with the scope of poverty prompted by the Depression. Public relief rested in the hands of the Outdoor Poor Department, overseen since 1925 by a crony of Commissioner John Murray's named Frank La Fera. A former shoe salesman, La Fera had no experience in social work. A series of *Newark Evening News* exposés in December of 1930 revealed La Fera's organization as incompetent and corrupt. People in severe distress had obviously been ignored. Curiously, the one item relief recipients were steadily and amply supplied with was coal—nearly all of which was purchased by the city from a company controlled by La Fera's brother.[58]

La Fera was forced to step down from his post in early 1931, by which time Newark's commissioners had begun coordinating a fund-raising campaign. Most of the money raised came from municipal workers themselves; police officers, for example, agreed to give 2 percent of five days' pay. Five months into the program, with less than $60,000 raised, it was clear the efforts were inadequate. Giving work to the needy was always favored to a handout anyway, so the city began large-scale projects using plenty of manpower. Machines excavating the subway were abandoned and replaced with workers digging manually, increasing costs by $112,500 but employing twenty-five hundred at $4 a day. By the summer of 1932, when the city began supplying would-be farmers with seed and tools for planting vegetables in the Meadowlands, more than thirty-eight thousand unemployed Newarkers had registered for state-aided work relief programs. The number of openings far exceeded those registering, however: only about 10 percent of those signing up would ever work in the programs.[59]

———

Since the introduction of commission government, the knee-jerk reaction of Newark voters had been to favor incumbents. With the city in upheaval amid the Depression, however, a changing of the guard seemed in order. Building on his status as a top runner-up in the 1929 election, Meyer Ellenstein led the way.

Handsome, athletic, eloquent, and ambitious, Ellenstein was a natural politician. His life thus far—one every hard-working Newarker could aspire to—had been a story of pluck and determination, the very embodiment of the American dream. Born in New York City and raised in Paterson, Ellenstein dropped out school at age thirteen and began juggling various money-making ventures, working in a silk mill, boxing professionally, and selling shoes. He eventually started going to dentistry school at night and graduated in 1912, reportedly at the top of his class. While establishing a practice in New York City, he still sold shoes on the side. After marrying a Newark girl and moving to the Third Ward, Ellenstein decided dentistry wasn't his calling and began attending law school at night. He graduated from New Jersey Law School in Newark in 1925, again at the top of his class. Around this time, the energetic, charismatic, obviously driven Ellenstein involved himself in Third Ward politics. Some say that Longy Zwillman himself advised Ellenstein to run for office, telling him there was a lot more money to be made in politics than dentistry or law.[60]

After Ellenstein's fine showing in the 1929 election, many supporters argued that he should have been named a commissioner the following year, when William Brennan died. Instead, City Clerk William Egan—a longtime Brennan confidante rumored to be under the control of Longy Zwillman—was tapped to fill the spot. When Commissioner John Murray passed away in the fall of 1932 and another seat opened, Ellenstein finally landed a spot on the commission. Newspapers showed plenty of pictures of the dashing new commissioner with the easy smile and thick head of immaculately quaffed hair. The *Evening News* praised "Doc" as an excellent choice, while pointing out the fit Ellenstein was often "stripped for action," playing handball at local gyms. He was also an avid golfer and a passionate fan of Newark's baseball squad, the Bears. As if Ellenstein's life wasn't full enough, "he still obliges a few friends by extracting molars occasionally," the *News* reported.[61]

Relief work dominated Ellenstein's early days as a commissioner. Soon enough, however, he and his colleagues began gearing up for the 1933 election—which wound up being referred to as "the biggest political upheaval in the city's history." The rookie commissioner received twice as many votes as any other candidate and was the only incumbent to keep his post. Ellenstein was suddenly the commission's most experienced and most popular member, and his fellow new commissioners installed him as mayor. He immediately jumped into action as the city's most prominent cheerleader, making statements like "I haven't the slightest doubt that Newark will be one of the first cities in the country, and perhaps the first, to emerge from the depression."[62]

People rallied to the side of this man to whom success would apparently not be denied. In September of 1933, word came out that Ellenstein was trying to coax the stock exchange into relocating from Manhattan to Newark. The strategy ultimately failed, of course, but Newarkers had to love their mayor's bold vision and chutzpah. They cheered him on through his ongoing rivalry with New York Mayor Fiorello La Guardia, who wanted to see Brooklyn's Bennett Field replace Newark's airport as the region's main flight gateway.

Until the 1933 elections, Newark's commissioners had typically been a chummy bunch—perhaps too chummy, critics suggested. Each commissioner had controlled his fiefdom within the city with minimal oversight from his colleagues. In the short run, taxes stayed fairly low, the public seemed pleased, and the commissioners rarely argued. They became accustomed to a policy of "reciprocal noninterference," in the words of one watchdog group, with each commissioner free to run his department as he saw fit and occasionally indulge in pet projects.[63]

With Newark struggling through the Depression and a brash Mayor Ellenstein in charge, however, the transformed new commission was quarrelsome, often grandstanding and bickering about various initiatives and the general direction in which the city should be heading. The combative atmosphere was blamed as a reason why in the mid-1930s a group of New York financiers dropped plans for a $10 million development along Raymond Boulevard between Penn Station and Broad Street, which had included a ten thousand-seat sports arena, two theaters, a hotel, and dozens of shops. "I had a telephone call one day from one of the principals," an architect involved in the project said. "He told me, 'There's too much turmoil in the Newark City Hall to suit us; we'd better wait a while.'"[64]

Still, Ellenstein and his fellow commissioners did see through many large-scale projects, including the 1935 opening of Pennsylvania Station, heralded as "the largest railroad passenger-traffic improvement constructed in this vicinity since the completion of the Manhattan transfer in 1901."[65] The commissioners knew the city's seaport and airport still represented enormous potential. Even under the cloud of the Depression, Newark's airport flourished, setting a world's record with well over a hundred thousand passengers in 1933. That same year, the port hosted 450 steamers, 100 more than the previous year.[66]

Soon after the new commissioners assumed their posts, they quietly began buying up parcels of the Meadowlands around the port and airfield. News broke that in one of the deals, the city agreed to pay $190,000 for a 4.8-acre plot; two years prior, the owner had offered the same property for just $16,000. The commissioners rescinded their offer, but a taxpayer group's study revealed the overpayment as one tiny part of a series of questionable land transactions and city expenditures.[67]

The mayor and his fellow commissioners, as well as several other officials, were accused of no fewer than 134 illegal acts, most involving fraud that cost Newark taxpayers hundreds of thousands of dollars. As the report charged, a two-acre lot near the airport reportedly worth $7,000 had been purchased by the city for $78,000. The city paid $350,000 for another strip of land, along Raymond Boulevard, which would have likely sold for $60,000 on the open market. There was no accounting for what happened to some $50,000 worth of copper, rails, and other materials, which disappeared at the port. The city gave $92,000 to a contractor in a no-bid bridge-repair job that should have cost $15,000. There were smaller instances of graft as well: a $500 door in police headquarters, a $5,000 bathroom in the Newark Boys Home's superintendent's office.[68]

The New Jersey Supreme Court assigned a young professor at New Jersey Law School named Warren Dixon Jr. to investigate. In the fall of 1937, Dixon presented his case to a grand jury, accusing Ellenstein and other officials with "extravagant and wasteful dissipation of municipal funds in various and devious ways." Ellenstein pointed to his reelection that year as an indication people believed there was nothing to the charges. "The voters are the best jury," he said. "They gave their verdict in the last election."[69]

In December, the jury indicted twenty-seven people, including Ellenstein and all four of his colleagues on the 1933–1937 city commission, on charges of conspiracy to defraud and cheat the city. More than a year passed before the trial began. In the meantime, Ellenstein prepared for a tour of Europe on the city's dime, ostensibly to study airports overseas. A taxpayer group protested, stating the appropriation of funds for such a trip "will only serve to further the state of chaos that now exists in our city." Nonetheless, the commissioners approved $1,500 for the venture, and Ellenstein boarded the *Queen Mary* in late July of 1938. After listening to Ellenstein's justifications for the trip, Director of Public Safety Michael Duffy acquiesced, saying, "I wish I was going too."[70]

The trial finally got under way in January of 1939. Mayor Ellenstein took the witness stand in late March, armed with a briefcase full of documents that he occasionally consulted during slow, deliberate replies to questions. Though it seemed to have little bearing on the case, Ellenstein, in a low, calm voice, rehashed his life story, "a Horatio Alger saga of a poor boy rising by his own efforts to a position of prominence," the *New York Times* wrote. After discussing his teenage days working in a Paterson silk mill, years of night classes, and sixteen-hour days as mayor, Ellenstein testified he had no knowledge of one of the two land deals on which prosecutors focused the case. As for the other, the mayor explained, initial city appraisals of the property varied widely, one at $3,000 an acre, another at $25,000 an acre. At the time, Newark was trying to tempt the federal government into building an army base within city borders, and the land in question was deemed essential, Ellenstein said. Rather than hiring another appraiser, it was decided to pay a mean of the two other estimates.[71]

After thirteen hours of jury deliberations, jurors went to bed without rendering a decision at 1 AM one day in April. That night, one of the jurors, an Orange resident named Michael De Rosa, was diagnosed with appendicitis and operated on at Saint Michael's Hospital. The way New Jersey courts then operated, the sudden illness meant a mistrial had to be declared. A suspicious group of taxpayers looked into the ill juror's background and immediately turned up a heretofore unknown fact: De Rosa had a criminal record.[72]

Within weeks, another trial began concerning a Belleville man named Frank Matt, who had been charged with trying to bribe Xavier F. Du Mont, another juror in Mayor Ellenstein's trial. Matt allegedly offered $100, then $1,000, and finally $2,000 "to go easy on a verdict, especially where Mayor Ellenstein and Jules Tepper were concerned," Du Mont testified. (Tepper was a former corporation counsel for Newark.) During negotiations with Du Mont, Matt reportedly pointed out Michael De Rosa, the juror with the illness responsible for the mistrial, saying, "He's taking it. Why don't you?"[73]

In light of jury-fixing suspicions, judges brought in an outside jury, from Somerset County, for Ellenstein's retrial. After another twelve weeks of testimony, Mayor Ellenstein and his codefendants were found not guilty of all charges. An overjoyed Ellenstein shook hands in the packed courtroom and mounted the platform where the judge sat to address the crowd. "I am gratified for a just verdict," he said. "I will demonstrate by my conduct in office that the faith and confidence expressed by the jury in the verdict was justified."[74]

Voters pronounced a different verdict in the spring of 1941, when Meyer Ellenstein failed to be reelected to a third term. By then, a new round of scandals—kickbacks on everything from car-towing operations to laundry services at city baths—had blackened the city's reputation. Through it all, Newark officials had consistently taken a "prove it" stance, in the words of the Evening News.[75]

Four years after Ellenstein's ousting from City Hall, however, among a field of thirty candidates, he netted enough support to regain a commissioner's seat. Four years after that, in the election of 1949, Ellenstein was again the most popular politician in the city. He received more votes than any other man up for commissioner.[76]

———

Late on the evening of Wednesday, October 23, 1935, after the dinner crowd had come and left Newark's Palace Chop House and Tavern mostly empty, four grim-looking men walked through the seventy-five-foot barroom and settled in at a backroom corner table. Arthur Flegenheimer, aka notorious bootlegger and racketeer Dutch Schultz, selected the seat backing up against the room's green walls and facing its narrow entryway. After months on the run from authorities, Schultz had turned himself in at Perth Amboy in late September to face charges for income-tax evasion. He'd since taken up residence in Newark's Robert Treat Hotel, around the corner from the Palace and a few blocks from the many court appearances he'd have to make. As had become custom, Schultz and his three bodyguards gathered for steaks. Schultz's wife, Frances, who met her husband while working as a hatcheck girl in a Manhattan speakeasy, stopped in to see the boys at a bit after 9 PM. Soon thereafter, the eight booths surrounding Schultz's party emptied out. Dull electric lights filled the smoky room with a yellow haze. The muffled sounds of a jazz trio could be heard from the cabaret operating one floor above.[77]

Broad-nosed and broad-shouldered, with thin eyes and a formidable chin, Schultz had been born into a German Jewish immigrant family in the Bronx. As a troublemaking kid, he occasionally joined in smalltime thefts and schemes, serving time for the burglary of a Bronx apartment in 1919, when he was seventeen. Coming of age in the Prohibition era, he took advantage of the criminal opportunities available, running numbers rackets, demanding kickbacks from restaurants and saloons, and smuggling kegs of beer into New York via ferry. Adopting the name Dutch Schultz—which sounded tougher than Arthur Flegenheimer—he emerged as one of the biggest gangsters of the late 1920s, spreading his control from the Bronx to Harlem and Manhattan's Upper West Side. No matter how much money Schultz made, though, he proudly refused to pay more than $50 for a suit, and always looked, in the words of celebrated reporter Meyer Berger, "like an ill-dressed vagrant."[78]

Schultz retreated to the Palace's washroom a little after 10 PM, about the same time three men wearing dark overcoats and fedoras pulled low strode through the restaurant's main entrance on East Park Street. Moving briskly toward the backroom, one of the men eyed the bartender and said, "Lie down on the floor and stay there." Seconds later, a flurry of gunshots erupted, followed by the retreat of the three men, who quickly jumped into a black sedan that sped off. Two of Schultz's bodyguards pursued as far as the bar, but in their condition—one had been shot twelve times—only managed to fire off a few errant rounds, one into the cigarette machine, another into plaster above a window. Another bullet was lodged in the Public Service building across the street.[79]

Schultz had been shot only once, in the belly, either while still in the bathroom or just after reentering the dining room. When the police arrived, he was propped in a chair saying, "I don't know nothin.'" All three bodyguards died. Schultz held on until the following evening, when he too became delirious and passed away. The lone bullet that passed through Schultz had pierced his liver and caused internal hemorrhaging.[80]

Before dying, Schultz and his men provided no clues regarding their killers. It was widely believed that Lucky Luciano, Meyer Lansky, Longy Zwillman, and the rest of the Big Six ordered the hit. The group had allowed Schultz to run his rackets for years, but the Dutchman had recently been seen as a liability. By 1935, Schultz had been arrested a dozen times on charges that included gun possession, felonious assault, and homicide, but he'd only been sent to prison the one time, for burglary. The current charges, however, seemed likely to stick. The Big Six denied Schultz his request to kill Thomas Dewey, the ambitious young prosecutor from New York (and later, state governor) who relentlessly harassed Schultz and other gangsters. A high-profile assassination like that would attract too much attention, mob leaders thought. They decided to silence the unpredictable Schultz, who'd previously killed business associates without warning. Schultz might try to knock off Dewey without their blessings, they thought, or perhaps become a witness for the prosecution and implicate them in any number of crimes.[81]

Newark, of course, was Zwillman's territory. Longy, who was conspicuously miles away from the city on the night of October 23, reputedly engineered the killings. The city may have garnered a reputation for widespread corruption during the trials of Mayor Ellenstein, but the Palace shootings brought Newark to the heights of notoriety for gang activity.

All the attention brought on by the Schultz assassination apparently didn't change much for Zwillman, who continued on as Newark's undisputed underworld boss through the 1940s. After Prohibition was repealed in 1933, Zwillman discovered he didn't need bootlegging so long as he continued to control city officials, judges, and cops. For a long stretch, Zwillman lived in a luxurious East Orange apartment building where Wall Street and corporate executive types were his neighbors. He later moved into a twenty-room mansion in West Orange.[82]

Zwillman's former rival Richie Boiardo likewise fared well through the Depression and World War II eras. He literally built himself a castle in the First Ward's center of activity, the corner of Summer and Eighth avenues. Officially, Richie's son Anthony "Tony Boy" Boiardo served as proprietor of the family's lavish restaurant and banquet hall, Vittorio Castle. Behind the building's intricate red-brick façade—complete with four prominent turrets—murals lined the walls and only the finest white linens lay across tables. Politicians and celebrities were regulars. Yankee great Joe DiMaggio, who always seemed more comfortable in Newark than in the bustle and glitz of New York, periodically dined at the Castle with teammates Phil Rizzuto, Yogi Berra, and Joe Page, or perhaps with Richie Boiardo himself. Like Longy Zwillman, Richie "the Boot" left his Newark residence for an estate in the suburbs. (David Chase, creator of the HBO series *The Sopranos*, loosely based the show's fictional suburban gangster family on the Boiardos.) Decorating the grounds of the family's Livingston mansion, which was built with stone imported from Italy, were wrought-iron gates and elaborate sculptures—including busts of the family and one rendering of the patriarch himself atop a white stallion.[83]

The average Newark family, by contrast, experienced more than its share of hardships through the 1930s. Jobs funded by the federal Works Progress Administration for improving the airport, streets, parks, and sewers were snatched up quickly, often with the assistance of political connections.

Cheering for the Newark Bears proved a fine distraction. Yankees owner Jacob Ruppert bought the International League club and its Ironbound-area stadium in 1931 and immediately assembled first-rate rosters with soon-to-be Major Leaguers like Yogi Berra, Red Rolfe, and Joe Gordon. The Bears' 1932 and 1937 teams are regarded among the all-time best minor league squads. The latter squad featured hard-hitting slugger Charlie "King Kong" Keller, who would go on to be a five-time All-Star with the Yankees.[84]

Local charity groups, often organized along ethnic lines, helped Newarkers through the lean years. Over a twelve-month period in 1939 and 1940, for example, the newly formed Community Employment Service (CES), a Jewish welfare association, arranged jobs for 649 clients, including 90 refugees fleeing Nazi persecution in Europe. "I am only in this country 17 months," one refugee wrote in a letter of gratitude to CES. "If I look back I have accomplished a lot in this short time. Despair, misery, on the brink of suicide—and now I have found a wife, and built a home, and together we look forward to a better future."[85]

Even Abner Zwillman and Richie Boiardo dabbled in philanthropy, funding soup kitchens, delivering turkeys to churches, buying clothes for orphans, covering funeral expenses, and supporting entire families through rough streaks. Zwillman also employed a hard-nosed gang of enforcers, led by a stout, stogie-smoking former boxer named Nat Arno, to confront Hitler supporters in the 1930s. Armed with rubber hoses, clubs, and iron pipes, Arno's band overwhelmed Nazi sympathizers in street brawls in Newark, Irvington, and Union City. Whether the measures taken by Zwillman and Boiardo were motivated by genuine concern or calculated strategies for snagging political and popular capital didn't matter to most people. Criminals or not, Longy and Richie were viewed as neighborhood benefactors and protectors, even heroes.[86]

As with the rest of the country, no amount of effort in Newark could bring an end to the all-encompassing economic slump of the 1930s. Newarkers from all walks of life decided to take their chances elsewhere, making the 1930s the first decade in the city's history when population declined, from 442,337 in 1930 to 429,760 in 1940. The trend of the city's wealthy leaders deserting the city never ceased. Only 22 percent of Newark's Chamber of Commerce officers and board members lived in the city during the mid-1930s. With the onset of the 1940s, the figure dipped below 15 percent.[87] As of 1925, 40 percent of lawyers with offices in Newark lived in the suburbs; by 1947, the figure spiked to 63 percent.[88]

Years of economic malaise, city scandals, fiscal mismanagement, and a steady loss of rich taxpayers left their mark. In the spring of 1941, Newark residents viewed the prospect of what was then the city's highest-ever tax rate, $5.88 per $100 of assessment. Just six years before, the rate stood at $3.36. To the *Newark Evening News*, there was no mystery surrounding the exorbitant tax rise: "It is the fruit of years of bad government." Not only had hundreds of Newark factories closed during the Depression, the city was losing the competition for new industrial developments to neighboring towns with lower taxes and more available land. A General Motors plant, for example, which had been expected to be built in Newark, instead went to Linden. In 1940, when Kearny's tax rate was just $3.82, it issued more industrial construction permits than Newark, as did Linden, Belleville, and Elizabeth.[89]

While 20 percent of all New Jersey workers were employed in Newark in 1909, by the end of the 1930s, the figure stood at just 11 percent. Blue-collar jobs in particular had evaporated. As manufacturing of leather, shoes, and other traditional goods had slowed, factories making electronics, plastics, and other modern products took their place—but they often relied heavily on machines and equipment rather than manpower. In 1927, for example, the chemical industry's output matched the dollar value of textiles, yet chemical companies employed only one-third as many workers. As a result of the changing business landscape, only 34 percent of Newark's workforce made their living in manufacturing in 1940, compared with 50 percent two decades earlier.[90]

An economic reprieve came in the form of World War II, in which Newark's factories and shipyards kicked into action on a never-before-seen scale. Within weeks of Japan's attack on Pearl Harbor, the federal government purchased the Submarine Boat Corporation and began spending millions to modernize the World War I-era facilities. In the course of the war, the operation built $250 million worth of destroyers, escorts, and tank-landing ships. During peak times, it employed nearly twenty thousand mechanics and laborers and ran shifts twenty-four hours per day. The feds likewise took over Newark Airport, which served as the gateway for Europe-bound aircraft, gasoline, and millions of tons of cargo. Newark manufacturers hired thousands to keep up with colossal orders for radios, telephones, tents, and other goods. Newarkers themselves, of course, joined the cause, with some eighty thousand men and women serving in uniform. Tens of thousands more volunteered in Newark by babysitting children whose mothers worked in factories or dancing with servicemen biding their time before being sent into action.[91]

The war-related boost couldn't last forever. After the crowds packing downtown Newark's Four Corners to celebrate V-J had gone home, and the delirious excitement of victory had faded, the city had to face grim realities.

Taxes remained prohibitively high, and the city needed still more money to improve badly neglected schools and streets. An influx of workers had pushed the city to around 450,000 people, yet jobs in the future would not be nearly as abundant as in the war years. Not only was there a housing shortage, but a disturbing percentage of residences were in deplorable condition. Many poor families still lived in crumbling tenements that had been built in slipshod manner during the city's turn-of-the-century growth spurt.

The taint of pervasive corruption in politics and business had also never disappeared. In the fall of 1939, for example, news broke that the Newark Housing Authority (NHA) had hired a contractor for a demolition job, and that company in turn had subcontracted the work to Richie Boiardo. The Boot's crew, essentially, was on the city payroll. Longy Zwillman also got involved with several NHA projects. Using various dummy organizations, Zwillman supposedly financed NHA construction jobs with the proviso that building materials would be purchased by the city from his brickyards.[92]

Some Newark politicians didn't even bother to hide their association with gangsters. In 1950, Mayor Ralph Villani, who had campaigned with Meyer Ellenstein in the previous year's commissioner election, was a guest at the wedding of Tony Boy Boiardo. The First Ward's Saint Lucy's Church hosted the ceremony, and a 1,500-person reception was held at the Essex House, where a ten-piece band played and the decorations included a four-foot block of ice sculpted into a heart. Peter Rodino and Hugh Addonizio—both congressmen at the time, the former to preside over the Watergate hearings, the latter destined to be Newark mayor—also attended, alongside at least one Essex County freeholder and several City Hall underlings.[93]

A series of inquiries in the early 1950s shed some light on the web that ensnared politics and organized crime in Newark and other cities. A report summing up the famous Kefauver Committee hearings, which were televised for weeks, stated there was "evidence of corruption and connivance at all levels of government—federal, state, and local." The committee unearthed countless incidents around the country of criminal rings paying bribes directly to law enforcement officials so they would ease pressure on gambling or other illegal activities. Known gangsters contributed thousands for campaign efforts of politicians, sheriffs, and judges. Politicians and cops blatantly protected organized crime operations, which were sometimes run by their relatives. Police officers, city commissioners, and other public servants could inexplicably afford $100,000 summer homes and other extravagances.[94]

Longy Zwillman was among the hundreds of witnesses called to testify in Washington at the Kefauver hearings on organized crime. Zwillman admitted to bootlegging, but said he had long since operated exclusively in trucking, cigarettes, and other legitimate businesses. He came off as an earnest, polished businessman, especially compared to the other dim-witted thugs testifying. Yet in the hearing's aftermath, the government ordered Zwillman to pay nearly $1 million in unpaid taxes.[95]

Another Senate hearing, begun in July of 1951, subpoenaed Meyer Ellenstein as its first witness. He admitted to knowing Zwillman, but said the two never discussed business. In a follow-up appearance, Ellenstein discussed his finances. Ellenstein's commissioner salary was only $10,000, but he said he normally earned in the neighborhood of $70,000 annually. Seeing no conflict of interest, Ellenstein made the bulk of his money from public relations and consulting with corporations on labor problems. (Once Ellenstein was on a company's payroll, it had been discovered, strikes that had seemed likely were invariably called off.) Most of his clients conducted business in Newark. Prudential, for example, paid Ellenstein a $10,000 annual retainer, plus extra compensation for whatever hours he worked for the company. Ellenstein also received an automatic commission each time Anheuser-Busch—which Ellenstein had recently convinced to build a $20 million dollar brewery near Newark Airport—did business with a restaurant, furniture supplier, security agency, construction outfit, or any other firm introduced by him.[96]

Ellenstein denied any of his business relationships were improper. Investigators asked how he was able to do his job as city commissioner in light of all his other activities. Ellenstein said that his city responsibilities rarely required him to be present in City Hall, or anywhere in Newark. "I operate by remote control," he explained.[97]

—————

In the World War I era, Newark's reformers had believed a new form of government could be the solution to graft, patronage, political-boss control, and other urban ills. Three decades later, the commission system hadn't solved any of those problems for Newark—and in the meantime, new concerns and deeper levels of corruption had arisen. Perhaps, the latest round of reformers argued, yet another change to the government could be the remedy.

Meyer Ellenstein squeezed out yet another political victory in the May 1953 commissioner election, garnering the fifth most votes in a field of twenty-six candidates. Mayor Ralph Villani ran a poor sixth, due in part to the city's most recent scandal: the previous month, Villani was in court responding to charges he'd harvested campaign contributions through a "systemic shakedown" of city workers.[98]

Most importantly in that 1953 election, by a seven to one ratio voters approved the authorization of a committee to assess the commission-government system and recommend changes. The resulting study, released in September, unambiguously condemned the commission as a failure. "Municipal government in Newark has proved to be wasteful, extravagant, uncoordinated and not responsive to the basic needs of our city," the report stated. "There has been an overemphasis upon patronage, political bickering, and unwarranted appeals to racial and religious interests. The long range interests of the city have been sacrificed to political expediency."[99]

According to the report, the commission government had crushed "civic pride and the morale of municipal employees." The system "frustrated the efforts of good men in public office and has been a ready vehicle for those less mindful of their public trust. Many good citizens have been discouraged from even seeking public office." Nearly all the people testifying before the committee strongly advised a complete abandonment of the system. "No patchwork efforts can remove the inherent weaknesses of commission government," the report advised.[100]

Among the criticisms: the commission basically established five separate governments, which meant a duplication of staff and higher costs. The city's overall budget was essentially the sum of five different budgets, which were each created with minimal oversight. In 1952 Newark hit what were then all-time highs in terms of tax rates, personnel, and payroll (even though the city's population was about the same as in 1920). Newark's per capita spending in the early 1950s was $67.50, far higher than the average of $53.88 in U.S. cities run by a commission. Cities operating under council-manager or mayor-council forms of government, on the other hand, averaged expenditures of slightly over $34 per capita.[101]

Two months after the report's release, voters approved a change to a mayor-council system by a margin of about two to one. As a result, Newark was divided into five wards, in which each elected a councilman. An additional four councilmen were elected at large. All elections remained nonpartisan. Leo Carlin, a labor leader and reform-minded commissioner who called for an end to commission government at least as early as 1945, was elected as the new system's first mayor. In the most visible sign that change had taken place, Irvine Turner became Newark's first African American elected to a top position in city government as Central Ward councilman.[102]

The committee that had recommended the switch to a mayor-council system predicted a more transparent, ethical, and altogether superior system of government. "As never before, the citizens of Newark will have an opportunity to work together under the new charter to provide better local services and to seek solutions to the important problems of their city," the report had stated. "The attraction of new industry to the city and the realization of its full economic potential" was anticipated to follow. The progress already being made in post–World War II Newark would also certainly continue, the committee promised, especially the exciting work rebuilding entire neighborhoods. With the transformed new government, the report guaranteed in particular the "further development of the programs for rehabilitation of blighted areas and for slum clearance."[103]

CHAPTER 5

THE SLUMS OF TEN YEARS FROM NOW

A CITY TRANSFORMED THROUGH POSTWAR URBAN RENEWAL

On the crisp, intermittently sunny afternoon of October 12, 1956, a group of local dignitaries, community leaders, and families clustered in an empty lot in Newark's overwhelmingly Italian First Ward. Surrounding the gathering was an assemblage of imposing, brand-new thirteen-story brick apartment buildings. The eight identical structures—boxy and utilitarian, free of ornamentation other than neat rows of grated windows—jutted into the sky amid a neighborhood of four-story tenements, ramshackle factories, bakeries that welcomed customers bringing in their uncooked dough, and seafood markets that doubled as restaurants during lunch and dinner hours. Immediately west of the newly risen monoliths stood Saint Lucy's Church, universally regarded as the heart of the community. Once a landmark whose bell tower rose above its neighbors, the pale yellow church was now dwarfed by the brick buildings, each of which was easily twice as tall and three times as wide. Immaculate parking lots, freshly poured concrete curbs, and a sprinkling of tidy benches and streetlights filled the gaps between the high-rises.[1]

The first three hundred tenants had moved in the previous autumn, but city officials decided to wait until all 1,556 units were complete to hold an official dedication. And there seemed no more fitting occasion than this Friday in October. After all, it was Columbus Day, and these were the Christopher Columbus Homes public-housing projects.

Dedication day fell during an exceptionally festive period for the neighborhood. October had traditionally been the month in which the New York Yankees were crowned with their latest championship, and the people of the First Ward had followed the team especially closely since the early days of the great Joe DiMaggio. The pride of Italians everywhere—and a frequent First

Ward visitor—DiMaggio retired after the 1951 season, but the neighborhood remained crazed for baseball.

Streets buzzed with World Series talk in early October 1956. It was a legendary match-up of two area teams: the Yankees led by Mickey Mantle versus Pee Wee Reese, Jackie Robinson, and the rest of a Dodgers squad that had won its first championship the previous season. When school let out, children could roam any street in the First Ward and hear the broadcast from the radios of every tenement and shop; many stores also posted scores in their windows. Two days before Columbus Day, the Yankees wrapped up the seven-game series with a 9–0 victory at Ebbets Field. The biggest hero was Yankees catcher Yogi Berra (also occasionally spotted in the First Ward), who hit two home runs in the final game, and who memorably leaped into Don Larsen's arms after the pitcher completed a perfect Game 5.

As always, however, the First Ward's marquee autumn event was the Feast of Saint Gerard, hosted by Saint Lucy's. For three days in mid-October, a procession of thousands flowed through streets lined with archways of electric lights and vendors offering hot zeppoles, calzones, clams, mussels, nuts, and sausages. Young girls wore virginal white, while many boys dressed all in black in imitation of Gerard, the unofficial patron saint of mothers.

It was said that praying to Saint Gerard yielded miracles: women unable to conceive found themselves pregnant, and infants on the verge of dying recovered in days. Mothers named children Gerard or Gerardine, out of gratitude. During the procession, women carried enormous candles—the weight was supposed to be equal to the size of the person being prayed for, usually a child—and piously walked barefoot or crawled on their knees through the streets. Everyone followed the nearly life-size statue of Gerard, which was sculpted in Italy and sent to Newark in 1898. With the statue's pale face, and eyes turned upward as if thinking only of God in heaven, Gerard always appeared devout (and somewhat sickly). Before too long, a cloak of greenbacks covered the saint. Down Sheffield and Garside streets, up to Clifton Avenue, the crowd roamed, stopping for donations at businesses, tenements, and homes. Occasionally, someone lowered a flower-covered basket filled with money from a fire escape. A special golden box collected donated rings, jewels, earrings, necklaces, and pendants.[2]

Whereas Saint Gerard's Feast was a largely Italian event, the entire city celebrated Columbus Day. Newark children of all ethnic backgrounds marched in the parade and entered essay contests with topics such as "What Can the Youth of Today Gather from Columbus to Advance the Cause of Democracy?"

The 1956 Columbus Day parade had begun with a police unit trotting on horses from Lincoln Park down Broad Street, passing grandstands at City

Hall just before noon. The fifteen thousand marchers included the Knights of Columbus Color Guard; bands, majorettes, and cheerleaders from five high schools; thousands of grammar school children, notably the kids in maroon uniforms from Saint Lucy's School who had spent weeks practicing walking five abreast at Branch Brook Park; and a convertible that drew plenty of hoots and whistles because in it was Hillie Merrit, the chestnut-haired "Miss Rheingold of 1956," sponsored by the beer company.

Surely, plenty of people had a laugh about the article in that morning's *Evening News*, featuring a First Ward resident named Christopher Columbo—who wasn't celebrating his birthday that day, the paper noted. "Sure, I've taken some kidding about it since school days, but it's always been good-natured," said Columbo. As a new twist to the usual double-takes Columbo received, strangers had recently begun showing up at his Summer Avenue home requesting apartments in his namesake housing project. "It always turns out somebody told them I owned it," said Columbo.[3]

At the Columbus Homes project's dedication that afternoon, Mayor Leo Carlin hailed the buildings as a key step in the "face-lifting of Newark" and praised the "men of vision of today who were responsible for the project." Another speaker, state senator Clifford Case, remarked that he always welcomed Columbus Day as a reprieve from partisan politics in the middle of campaign-season battles. (Presidential contender Adlai Stevenson, for example, had just been in Newark challenging President Eisenhower to "take the leadership" on a move to ban hydrogen bomb tests.) The bipartisan support of the Columbus Homes, Case pointed out, was a fine example of what good political leaders can accomplish when they aren't jousting with each other for votes.

Indeed, the redevelopment of the First Ward had the universal support of Newark's leaders. The public first heard in January of 1952 about how forty-six acres of the densely populated neighborhood would be torn down for new housing. Estimated to cost $40 million, the development made headlines as New Jersey's largest, most expensive housing project. It had been welcomed as a godsend by local newspapers and politicians largely because the federal government was anteing up most of the money. Boosters saw an easy, cost-effective opportunity to upgrade old tenements and businesses. "The program is the product of bold, imaginative planning," a *Newark Evening News* editorial read. "It will bring a desperately needed improvement in the living quarters of a large number of slum dwellers."[4]

The *Italian Tribune*, which would have to move its Eighth Avenue office because the street would disappear due to the Columbus Homes, said the project "will aid over 3,000 families, in the most worthwhile gesture ever

put into operation for the benefit of so large a group."[5] Every notable politi-
cian, including the city's most influential Italians—former mayor Ralph
Villani and two congressmen, Hugh Addonizio and First Ward native Peter
Rodino—never wavered in backing the development.

The only two buildings allowed to remain in the redevelopment area,
which measured a half mile by a thousand feet, were the McKinley School
and Saint Lucy's Church. The church's pastor, Father Gaetano Ruggiero,
also addressed the crowd on dedication day. To many First Warders, the
neighborhood was simply unimaginable without Ruggiero. Born into a
family of ten children on the island of Salina, he served as a chaplain to the
Italian army in World War I. He came to Newark in 1921 as assistant pastor
under Father Joseph Perotti, who had watched the Saint Lucy's community
bloom since taking the helm of the parish in 1897 with a few dozen poor
Italian families and a small, wood-frame church. Perotti collapsed at the
altar in 1933 and died shortly thereafter, and Saint Lucy's had been overseen
by Father Ruggiero ever since.[6]

A kind, gregarious leader, Ruggiero always seemed to be visiting a sick
widow, chatting with schoolchildren, giving the blessing at a social-club
dinner, hosting a Halloween party, or administering countless weddings,
baptisms, and funerals. When kids in the neighborhood broke a window
of the rectory or school while playing ball, Ruggiero's response was usually,
"Well, that's OK. The poor boys have nowhere else to play." On his rare days
off, Ruggiero and Father Joseph Granato or another young Saint Lucy's priest
drove first thing in the morning to Manasquan and fished in a rowboat until
after dark. They cooked the fresh flounder, eel, and clams with men at one of
the First Ward's many social clubs for the night's dinner. There was usually
plenty left over to give to the nuns who taught at Saint Lucy's.[7]

When agitated, however, Ruggiero—short, lean, and wiry, with a strong
wide chin and an imposing bald skull—could transform into a combatant
intense enough to earn him the nickname "Little Napoleon."

As Ruggiero stepped to the microphone on the Columbus Homes' dedication day, politicians and housing officials immediately seemed uncomfort-
able. They winced, grimaced, and stared at the ground. "Believe it or not,"
Ruggiero said in a thick Italian accent, "my first remark is a protest, and a
very strong one."[8]

Referring to a recent newspaper article, Ruggiero started off by objecting
to his neighborhood being slandered as "the worst slum" in the country.
"Our decent people can see the malicious stupidity at such a statement," he
said. "But malice and opportunities make you see things which are not." He
then spoke of the many "good, honest people" who "on a false pretense were
unjustly ousted from their homes."

Like most Newarkers, the priest had initially welcomed the redevelopment as it was first presented. But after years of listening to "countless telephone calls and the indignant remarks of the people of the First Ward, my people," Ruggiero said, he'd promised "that at the proper time, a solemn protest would be raised. And here I stand this afternoon before you to voice the indignation of my people, indignation that is my own, one thousand percent."

———

Father Ruggiero's comments brought to light an underlying, and undeniable, truth—one that politicians and Newark Housing Authority (NHA) staffers seemed to hope people would overlook, or even forget. No one familiar with the city could argue with another of the priest's statements: "You don't need to travel throughout the country to find real slums. All you need is to walk ten minutes from this very spot to find them."

Compared to many spots in Newark, the First Ward, which after the switch from commission to city-council government became part of the North Ward, was hardly the city's worst neighborhood. No one knew this better than the men most responsible for the "face-lifting": Villani, Addonizio, and Rodino, as well as the NHA's executive director, Louis Danzig. All four men were noticeably absent from the Columbus Homes dedication ceremonies.

While Italian politicians gave the redevelopment key support, Danzig engineered the building of the Columbus Homes, as well as every other housing project during his two decades as head of the NHA. Danzig bore a fair resemblance to actor Telly Savalas, only with hair. More often, Danzig has been called Newark's version of Robert Moses, the domineering, never-elected figure who oversaw decades' worth of road, park, housing, and other projects in New York, immortalized in *The Powerbroker*, a biography by Robert Caro. A graduate of Newark's Central High School, Danzig went on to New Jersey Law School and was admitted to the New Jersey bar in 1930. He practiced law until 1942, when he joined the NHA to become a manager at two of the city's older, smaller housing projects, first at John W. Hyatt Court, in the Ironbound, and later at Pennington Court, near the airport.[9]

In 1946, Commissioner Ralph Villani appointed Danzig as his executive clerk. The city agencies overseen by Villani included the NHA, and Danzig handled renting and maintaining all city-owned buildings. Danzig was soon on a first-name basis with the city's most powerful players in real estate and construction. Two years after Danzig joined forces with Villani, the Essex County prosecutor threatened to bring a case against the NHA for playing favorites and improperly selecting tenants. Villani, hoping to avoid a scandal, asked for the resignation of the NHA executive director, Dr. Carl Baccaro.

Villani immediately named Danzig, who by then was already regarded as a brilliant, tireless administrator, as the NHA's new director.[10] "The change was a surprise," wrote the *Newark News*. "Baccaro told the authority in a letter of resignation that he feels it is time he went back to his first love, dentistry."[11]

Well aware of Villani's precarious situation, Danzig made a few demands before accepting his new post. Based on what he'd learned at the NHA and in housing courses at Columbia University, NYU, and the New School, Danzig knew that to truly be effective he needed more authority than the job usually afforded. He requested a five-year contract, rather than the standard one-year agreement, so he couldn't be dismissed on some politician's whim. He also sought control to appoint all of the top levels of his staff, as well as the full, unquestioning support of City Hall when choosing housing-project sites. What Danzig asked for was carte blanche to run the NHA as he saw fit, with minimal chances for interference. Villani, desperate to avoid more controversy and bad press, acquiesced.[12]

Danzig's reign at the NHA was dynamic from the beginning. Before officially taking command, he sent orders for the authority's main office to be reconfigured, with departments shifted, new walls erected, and fresh paint in every room. Danzig made sure to tell the press that the work was being done at minimal cost because NHA labor and materials it already owned were used. To complete the job, a number of NHA workers "volunteered" to slave over the Fourth of July weekend, a newspaper article noted, so the office would be ready for the new boss's first day.[13]

All that Danzig knew about housing, health, and urban planning indicated that slums were a danger not only to residents, but also to society as a whole. "The slums do not wait," he said in one of many pitches to drum up support among realty, business, and civic associations. "They creep like a paralysis until they engulf the entire city and then they spread to the suburbs. If the situation continues, the time will come when the slum dwellers will rebel against their conditions and then it may be too late to control them."[14]

Danzig's theories were shared by most housing experts and urban planners. After World War II, leaders all over the country turned their attention to fixing tired old cities where housing was both dilapidated and short of supply. With soldiers returning from service and starting families, the housing problems were all the more pronounced. Newark's population, for example, swelled in 1948 to an all-time high, just under 450,000.

The NHA released a study in 1946 (before Danzig took over) to prove that the slums were dangerous and expensive. The report argued that there was a "tremendous differential which exists between the revenue from the slum and the costs of servicing it." A table detailed how much Newark could save annually by replacing its slums with housing projects: tuberculosis cases would reportedly be cut from 405 to 201, reaping in a savings over $1 million; infant deaths would decrease from 179 to 149, saving the city $217,200 (figuring that the capital value of each boy and a girl was then projected at $9,000 and $4,000 respectively); fatal home accidents would plummet from thirty-eight to zero, saving $171,000; and in the future, the city would average 115 home fires rather than 430 a year, saving $179,000. In conclusion, the NHA stated that slums cost the city $14 million annually. "The only way of stopping blight and preventing huge sums of money from being poured out needlessly is to completely eliminate the slums and blighted areas," the report stated. "This may be a painful operation, but it is the only way in which our cities can survive."[15]

The manner in which Newark had grown—in piecemeal, haphazard fashion, with a factory here, tenements thrown up there, various trolley lines strewn about almost randomly—was traditionally blamed for many of the city's mid-twentieth-century problems. The Central Planning Board (CPB), created in 1943 during the mayoralty of reformer Vincent Murphy, spent four years studying every corner of the city in order to present a comprehensive strategy for more coherent future development. The CPB discovered that one-third of all Newark dwelling units needed major repairs and/or lacked private bathrooms or a private water supply. Newark still came up short in terms of parks, with only one acre per 513 people, when the minimum accepted ratio was one to a hundred. For the time being, however, it was determined that housing and streetscapes should be the focus. To ease congestion, the CPB declared, some streets needed to be widened while others should disappear. Vast areas of slums in the Ironbound and the North and Central wards needed to be completely razed. "Sporadic efforts to reclaim small areas will not solve the problem," the 1947 CPB report stated. "It must be done on a comprehensive basis as a part of a long-range program of municipal improvements."[16]

As soon as a Meyer Ellenstein–led coalition wrangled control of City Hall in 1949, though, the CPB's recommendations fell out of favor. The board was viewed as a band of Mayor Murphy's "good government" people, and Ellenstein and his allies largely ignored their calls for all-encompassing planning strategies.[17]

Huge (if isolated) urban-renewal projects, however, would soon be off the ground thanks to the federal Housing Act of 1949, which stated every American deserved "a decent home and a suitable living environment." The government's efforts weren't solely concerned with creating new housing. The landmark act's preamble stated that its goals were to "remedy the serious housing shortage" and eliminate "inadequate housing through the clearance of slums and blighted areas."

Private investors knew that there was rarely any money to be made in clearing slums and building new housing. Most cities couldn't afford large-scale clearance projects on their own dime either. So, to prod slum clearance along, the federal government would foot most of the bill to buy areas deemed "blighted" and construct new low-rent public housing on part of the freshly cleared land. The remaining land would be sold off to private investors, with the idea that they'd build stores, businesses, and apartments and houses for middle- or high-income buyers. All told, the federal government would cover two-thirds of expenses, and the city in question would finance the balance.

The legislation fostered grand rebuilding in line with influential urban visionaries such as the Swiss architect Le Corbusier. For decades, he and others had been proposing to remake cities in dramatic form, usually mixing towering high-rises with vast open spaces. "Our streets no longer work," wrote Le Corbusier. "Streets are an obsolete notion."[18] Most cities—Newark obviously included—had grown organically, even arbitrarily, and the results were "not worthy of the age," according to Le Corbusier. "They are no longer worthy of us." He wanted to see the chaotic city flattened so it could be rebuilt according to his orderly, geometric ideals. Among his recommendations was the elimination of two-thirds of the average city's existing streets. Winding roads and alleyways would have to disappear; only intersections at perfectly right angles were acceptable.[19] Le Corbusier so despised congestion and disorder that in 1925 he proposed destroying virtually the entire Right Bank of the Seine in Paris, suggesting a few dozen glass towers in its place.

Urban planners contended that with a decrease in the number of streets, cities could save money by cutting back on services. In particular, police forces could be reduced because there would be fewer streets to patrol. Together with designers such as Ludwig Mies van der Rohe, who was famous for his declaration "less is more"—and not quite as well known for designing three glass twenty-two-story buildings that bookended the Columbus Homes (the Colonnade, built in the late 1950s)—Le Corbusier maintained that orderly architecture would result in an orderly, law-abiding, and sophisticated citizenry.

Newark leaders had a long history of characterizing slum tenements not only as dangerous or unhealthy, but as magnets for crime and immorality. "These dwellings naturally attract the poor, the ignorant, careless and criminal part of the community, where generally a total disregard of accepted methods of decent living are tolerated and sometimes preferred," a city health officer wrote in 1944.[20]

Louis Danzig also believed that poor living conditions bred criminals, and sound, attractive homes therefore must create a wholesome populace. One NHA report published under Danzig's supervision could have been a motto for the theory: "Good houses make good citizens."[21] At speaking engagements in the early 1950s, Danzig emphasized the fact that over the NHA's decade-plus in existence, there had been no truancy or delinquency in any of the city's housing projects. Incredibly, there had never been a fire or a single accident on public-housing grounds, nor even one call to the police, Danzig claimed.[22]

From Danzig's perspective, his job was to attract as much federal money as possible, as quickly as possible, to clear as many acres of slums and build as many housing projects as possible. He rarely ever paused to wonder whether these projects would ultimately improve neighborhoods. Harold Kaplan, a graduate student who worked at the NHA in the 1950s and authored a 1963 book praising the organization, wrote that the authority quickly "came to place greater emphasis on winning some kind of clearance than on obtaining clearance strictly in accordance with their initial purpose."[23]

Louis Danzig was an experienced attorney and an expert on housing law; he had even sat in on the Federal Housing Authority's (FHA) hearings and helped write the 1949 legislation. Once the act passed, many cities hosted extended debates on the merits of clearing neighborhoods, or at least waited for federal money to pay for fact-finding surveys. Danzig, on the other hand, dipped into the NHA's coffers to immediately get to work.

With a clear mission in mind, Danzig implemented a number of other NHA policies to speed up the normally tortoiselike processes involved in slum clearance. Discussions regarding potential redevelopment sites were always behind closed doors. Opening up the conversation to the public was too risky. It increased the chance some group would interfere. In Harold Kaplan's assessment, "Limited participation and low visibility seem to be necessary" for NHA efforts to yield results. Danzig wanted guaranteed approval from politicos and planning boards before any information was passed along to the affected neighborhoods—and by then, the ball would be rolling and it would typically be too late to alter plans. The critics who voiced complaints about the NHA's tactics or slum clearance in general were consistently panned as selfish obstructionists who didn't have the needs of the city at heart.[24]

The emergence of a powerful, driven figure like Danzig was hardly the only reason post–World War II Newark aggressively and wholeheartedly embraced public housing. The city's failure to annex more territory meant that there was limited open land upon which to build. Slum clearance would finally provide opportunities for new construction. Whereas families who lived in a neighborhood for generations would be likely to resist urban renewal, Newark's population was largely in flux in the late 1940s and early 1950s. Large numbers of African Americans moved in during the era (chapter 6 describes the migration more fully), and whites shifted neighborhoods or moved out of the city entirely. The knee-jerk reaction of Newark politicians, who by then were accustomed to the patronage-related windfall that came along with such city initiatives, was to welcome any large-scale development with open arms and few questions.

Newark residents themselves also seemed eager to upgrade the city's old, neglected residences. A series of 1949 articles in the *Newark Evening News* decrying slum conditions culminated in a meeting of five hundred clergy members, civic group leaders, politicians, and citizens seeking to eliminate blighted areas. Simple rehabilitation would be useless in many of the slum areas, Commissioner Stephen Moran declared. "We must rip down, clear off, and build new housing," he said to the crowd.[25]

Louis Danzig, while testifying in Washington at the 1951 National Housing Conference, estimated that Newarkers embracing public housing outnumbered those against by a margin of at least ten to one. The NHA executive director pointed to a vote the previous year as an indication of just how supportive Newark was of public housing; a referendum had been approved to appropriate fifteen acres of Branch Brook Park for a low-rent housing project. (Ultimately, the Essex County Park Commission didn't allow the land to be used.) "Doubtless to the envy of many in his audience," an *Evening News* editorial wrote of Danzig's appearance in Washington, "he could point to a minimum of opposition in Newark. There has been none of the fierce resistance which has blocked slum clearance in some cities."[26]

To varying degrees, New York, Chicago, Detroit, Washington, D.C., Pittsburgh, St. Louis, New Haven, and other cities also leapt at the opportunity to rebuild with federal cash. As a result, freshly constructed housing projects dotted the landscapes of poor urban areas such as Harlem in Manhattan and Chicago's South Side. Other cities—particularly wealthy, largely suburban ones—refused federal money because they were wary of stipulations that went along with it. These protective communities wanted to retain full control over what was built, how it was built, and who the residents would be.[27]

By 1956, when the Columbus Homes officially opened, the NHA operated 7,385 apartments in the city. Since Louis Danzig had taken charge of the authority, the number of public-housing units had more than doubled, up from 3,008 at the end of World War II.[28] Before too long, with a leader hell-bent on pushing redevelopment, and a city willing to allow him to do so, Newark built more public-housing units per capita than any other U.S. city.[29]

The Columbus Homes were so substantially different from previous Newark projects that it was difficult to predict their impact. The Newark Housing Authority had come into existence in 1938 thanks to funding from the federal Housing Act of 1937, a Depression-era initiative with the lofty goal of putting people back to work and creating affordable places to live. Mayor Meyer Ellenstein and the four other commissioners each appointed someone to the newly formed NHA board. The positions were unpaid, but that didn't seem to be a problem. Officials were in charge of hiring managers, janitors, clerks, stenographers, and other jobs involved in NHA projects, and the power and opportunities that came along with dispensing patronage were in many ways better than a salary.[30]

Stephen Crane Village and Pennington Court opened in 1940, followed soon by Seth Boyden Court, James M. Baxter Terrace, John W. Hyatt Court, and Felix Fuld Court. These initial projects were low-rise buildings, with 236 to 612 units apiece. Public housing represented progress for the working classes, and residents initially took great pride in the places they called home. One father of eight even wrote a theme song for his housing project, with the chorus: "Baxter Terrace to you I shall be true/ I'll always dwell within thy gates, no other place will do."[31]

With the exception of Baxter Terrace, located just northwest of down-town, all the early housing projects were built on the outskirts of the city. Like most Newark neighborhoods, each project was unofficially segregated by race: Jews predominantly lived in Seth Boyden Court in the Weequahic section, while Italians filled the majority of Crane apartments near Branch Brook Park, and so on. As of 1949, African Americans represented 40 percent of Newarkers eligible for public housing, yet they accounted for only 7 or 8 percent of the city's units. Well into the 1950s, Baxter Terrace was the only project where African Americans were the majority.[32]

Within months of the 1949 act's passing, NHA staff had targeted sixteen dilapidated areas and ranked them according to blight. Yet Danzig did not take the next rational step and suggest clearing the worst area first. "The key question about any redevelopment site was whether a private firm could make a profit on middle-income housing in that area," wrote Harold Kaplan. "If the answer was negative, no redeveloper would buy the site, and no FHA official would agree to insure mortgages for construction."[33]

Under such criteria, projects suggested for the most blighted ghettos, such as in the largely African American Central Ward, were more likely to be turned down by the FHA. Danzig didn't want to risk defeat with his first large-scale proposal, so the NHA disregarded its initial study and started from scratch. What the authority now sought was "site feasibility," in Kaplan's words: an area with housing that was poor enough to qualify as a slum, but in a sufficiently decent neighborhood—and plainly, one where whites were the majority—to attract developers. The NHA found just such a location in the densely populated First Ward. "In short," Kaplan wrote, the neighborhood "was not sufficiently blighted or interracial to repel redevelopers or the FHA."[34]

The First Ward development drew the unanimous support of all five Newark commissioners. Ralph Villani called it a "tremendous boon" for the neighborhood and for Newark in general. Meyer Ellenstein, then revenue and finance director, pointed out that the transformed area was expected to bring triple the tax revenue into the city's coffers. Public Safety Director John Keenan said the development would mean "enormous benefit" for the First Ward, noting that "good housing goes hand in hand with good police work to bring about a reduction in crime and juvenile delinquency."[35]

Housing officials and newspapers likewise rejoiced upon the project's approval. The *Evening News* published a cartoon with a colonial-looking gentleman wearing a Puritan hat as a stand-in for old Newark; the fellow looked in a mirror aghast at the large black blotch on his face captioned "First Ward Slums."[36] Fred Stickel Jr., a commissioner of the NHA who for years had tried and failed to persuade private developers to build in Newark's slums, said the proposal was "like a dream come true." Reverend Thomas Finnegan, chairman of the NHA, said that a "cancer" was being removed from the city. William Hayes, also a reverend and NHA member (who would be the namesake of another huge housing project), said the announcement was his happiest moment in ten years on the housing board. "We're really going places," he said, "and I'm 110 percent for it!"[37]

The condemned section of the First Ward included 1,371 apartment units and 1,362 families. An NHA survey revealed that 91 of the apartments had no private toilet, 751 units had no private bath, 1,040 didn't have central heating, and 702 were without hot water. The area's 469 buildings, which covered 56 percent of the land at ground level, were supposed to be replaced with 26 buildings occupying only 20 percent of the space.[38]

"A rundown, antiquated area of 46 acres north of the Lackawanna tracks ... was chosen for the city's first venture in redevelopment," a 1952 NHA report stated. "The tract will be replanned to eliminate unnecessary streets and to create open space for grass and parking."[39]

The problem was that many First Warders vehemently disagreed that their streets were unnecessary, or that their beloved neighborhood was a slum.

They weren't alone. Herbert Goldberg, a former State Association of Real Estate Boards president, said that while he generally favored redevelopment, he didn't believe it was accurate to call the First Ward a slum. "A lot of good buildings," he said, "would be coming down."[40]

Certainly, some of the area slated for destruction ranked among Newark's poorest and most filthy streets; few people would be sad if the winding stretches of dark, crumbling tenements on Aqueduct Alley and Drift Street disappeared. The "cancer" to be razed, however, also included Sheffield Street's tiny markets, mom-and-pop candy shops, and pastry, butcher, and pork stores. The tenement backyards on tiny D'Auria Street, where residents planted flowers and grew oranges, apples, figs, peaches, and grapes, would fade into history.

The First Ward—at the time, the fourth-largest Italian enclave in the country—was of the sort that as soon as children turned eight (sometimes even younger), parents let them walk the streets unsupervised to run errands or play. Mothers called children in for dinner from second- or third-floor windows. Few people locked their doors. In part because the tenements were so cramped, sidewalks and alleys doubled as family rooms for the entire community.

The most unfortunate loss, as noted by the *Newark News*, was that "Eighth Avenue, main artery of the Italian-American community there, will disappear along with its restaurants, bakeries, groceries and seafood places which attract a large clientele not only from the neighborhood but also from other parts of the city and the suburbs."[41] Over the years, a few top-notch eateries had sprouted on the avenue, including Richie "the Boot" Boiardo's ornate Vittorio Castle, as well as Vesuvius, a fine-dining establishment with a view of Saint Lucy's Church from an immaculate side garden. Eighth Avenue had proved elegant enough to attract visits from the likes of Jackie Gleason, Jayne Mansfield, Jack Dempsey, George Raft, Marilyn Monroe, and Joe DiMaggio, as well as countless politicians, businessmen, and members of the underworld.[42] The street was also chock-a-block with bocce courts, political meeting halls, and social clubs like the Giuseppe Verde Society, which in 1927 donated the statue of Christopher Columbus that was proudly placed in Washington Park.[43]

Outraged that their neighborhood would be transformed, and that thousands of people would be tossed from their homes without a vote, First Ward residents mounted a protest. They demanded to speak to Mayor Villani, a tan, balding dandy known for dressing in only the finest suits. Villani was always up for a good photo op, perhaps waving a flag to start soapbox derby races on Sheffield Street, or carving an eight-foot-long provolone at an Eighth Avenue grocery store.[44] Though he wasn't from the First Ward, Mayor Villani was Italian and had received overwhelming support in the neighborhood. Surely, First Warders believed, the mayor would be looking out for them.

Two weeks after the redevelopment project announcement, some five hundred First Warders met with officials at City Hall. "I'm trying to make life easier for you people," Mayor Villani assured the crowd. "May God strike me dead if I want to harm anyone." Speaking alternately in Italian and English, the mayor recalled his own hardships as a child in the slums. "Our family lived in two overcrowded rooms without central heating, without baths, and a toilet in our backyard," he said. "I don't like to see human beings living in houses where you are afraid of breaking a limb in dimly lit hallways." The politicians presented a united front, with Congressman Hugh Addonizio chiming in that "Newark has the nation's second worst slums," and that immediate action was necessary. Peter Rodino implored the crowd to not be selfish and to consider the future of the city's children. He urged the crowd to avoid spreading "discontent and bitterness."[45]

The meeting at City Hall lasted nearly three hours. Villani and his colleagues dutifully listened to the concerns of First Ward business owners and residents. There was no chance the politicians were going to let the people make or break the development, however. Prior to the gathering, Villani was in fact lobbying to quash a bill in the state legislature that would have allowed voters to approve or reject slum clearance and urban-renewal projects.[46]

Before the meeting wrapped up, Villani staked his career on the fact that rents in the new, modern public-housing apartments would be less expensive than their old cold-water flats. "Nobody will be thrown out on the street," the mayor promised. "Ralph Villani wouldn't let that happen, not to his people. There is nothing to get excited about. We won't hurt anyone. Some day you people will build a monument to me for what I'm trying to do for this city."[47]

Rent prices, however, weren't the main concern. According to federal regulations at the time, about two-thirds of residents about to be displaced—the people who were living in supposed slums and would ostensibly most benefit from new housing—actually earned too much money to be accepted as tenants in low-rent projects. Ironically, they were too well-off to qualify for the new units intended to solve their "housing problems."

First Ward residents weren't ready to accept their fate. Within weeks of the project's announcement, several hundred citizens gathered at the McKinley School, next to Saint Lucy's, to discuss how to proceed. A volunteer named Rocco Rotunda summarized each speech in Italian. "The people are peeved at having been denied their constitutional rights by not having been consulted before the redevelopment plan was approved," said Joseph Melillo, an attorney who emerged as the group's leader and would later win a city council seat. Joseph Glenn, a private investigator who lived on Seventh Avenue and worked closely with the police precinct in the area, disputed the claim that the ward had troubles with crime. "The streets in this neighborhood are the safest in the city at night," he said. The group, which called itself the Save Our Homes Council (SOHC), proposed an alternative plan to wholesale clearance of the neighborhood. Tear down only buildings that are "really slums," they suggested, and then provide "liberal loans to property owners" to install or improve heating systems, bathrooms, and plumbing.[48]

Residents faced an uphill battle. The city's political structure was such that even a minor figure wouldn't risk joining the protestors for fear of retribution. Many Italian social organizations also decided it wise to get behind redevelopment. In early March, delegates from the Federation of Italian-American Societies of Newark, representing thirty social organizations, passed a resolution supporting the First Ward project. The men in these organizations understood that large-scale developments like the Columbus Homes brought with them employment and opportunity. If the destruction of Eighth Avenue brought with it jobs, then it was that much easier to swallow the idea that low-income projects could fix Newark's housing problems, and maybe even help bring about an end to crime and disease as well. People were also aware of who doled out rewards in Newark. Among the social organizations' document of support was the statement: "Further resolved that copies of this resolution be sent to Congressmen Rodino and Addonizio expressing thanks to them for the active role they took in the U.S. Congress in support of the legislation which will make the redevelopment possible."[49]

Opponents of the projects still created enough of a stir to merit a powwow with the Central Planning Board on May 1, 1952. "The importance of the meeting is great," wrote the *Italian Tribune*, in mid-April. "And the importance of residents attending and casting FAVORABLE comments on the proposed program is even greater. The chance for better living for themselves and future generations hangs in the balance. We urge readers to support the project."[50]

By all accounts, the meeting was testy. Board Chairman Peter Cavicchia repeatedly hammered his gavel to quiet boos from the crowd. Louis Danzig and top-level NHA staffers stressed that turning back now would be a grave mistake. "Progress cannot be stopped," argued Danzig. "This is the direction we must go."[51]

Joseph Melillo, representing the SOHC, presented a petition with eight hundred signatures of residents and business owners opposed to clearing the site. The group submitted photos of dozens of beautiful homes slated for destruction, as well as statistics demonstrating that crime and disease in the First Ward were far lower than the city average.[52] "The people of the First Ward don't want the homogeneous life of their community destroyed," Melillo said. His comments revealed another concern: most Italians didn't want other ethnic groups to move in and change their neighborhood. "This section has been the center of the Italian-American community for 50 years."[53]

When a Congress of Industrial Organizations (CIO) union tried to address the crowd, a heckler shouted, "You CIO boys are sure fine ones to talk about this project. You say you're for it and then probably will go out and strike on another housing project. What have you got to say about that?" Others in the crowd stood up and shouted at NHA leaders, union men, and the planning board. Cavicchia said the board would soon make "a thorough inspection" of the area and quickly adjourned the meeting.[54]

Three weeks later, the board voted unanimously to push forward. There were no official accounts of their inspection. Rumor had it that Rodino led the group to his old neighborhood, paying particular attention to the most rundown streets. Upon hearing of the vote, Melillo repeated yet again, "It seems a crime and a waste that so many good homes must be torn down. Some method should be found to tear down some deplorable sections of the First Ward, like Aqueduct Alley."[55]

Planning Board Chairman Cavicchia replied that it was indeed a pity that some good buildings had to be razed. Unfortunately, the way federal funding worked, it was an all-or-nothing proposition. No money was available for piecemeal clearance and redevelopment initiatives. Besides, Cavicchia rationalized, "Progress tears down something good sometimes to bring something better."[56]

———

All along, the NHA maintained that its rebuilding efforts would slow or reverse the population shift to the suburbs. But, as it turned out, approximately 15 percent of First Ward residents left the city for good the moment they were displaced. More than half the businesses in the clearance zone ceased to exist after the wrecking ball came.[57] Some who protested evictions became legendary, like the old woman who swung a lead pipe at policemen as they coaxed her into vacating her bakery on Christmas Eve. Most people sadly and uneventfully gathered their belongings and left.

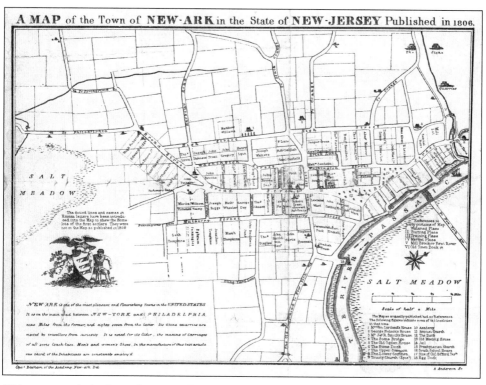

This map, made in the early 1800s, shows the original plots occupied by Puritan founders, and the seal on the bottom left features a shoemaker. Newark earned a great reputation for shoe manufacturing, shipping most of its good to the South. (From the Collections of the New Jersey Historical Society, Newark, New Jersey.)

NEWARK,
(EAST OF MULBERRY ST. 1820-5)

A lithograph of downtown circa the 1820s. After the Revolution, Newark transformed into a teeming industrial hub, largely due to its prime location. (From the Collections of the New Jersey Historical Society, Newark, New Jersey.)

Seth Boyden, Newark's great nineteenth-century inventor. (From the Collections of the New Jersey Historical Society, Newark, New Jersey.)

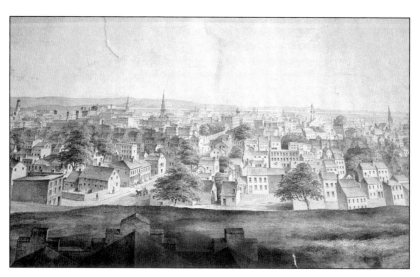

A lithograph from the pre–Civil War era, showing Newark in its early days as a city. (From the Collections of the New Jersey Historical Society, Newark, New Jersey.)

William Wright, a leading saddle manufacturer, Newark mayor, and U.S. senator who sympathized with the Confederates during the Civil War. (From the Collections of the New Jersey Historical Society, Newark, New Jersey.)

William Wright's grand mansion sat on Park Place facing Military Park. (From the Collections of the New Jersey Historical Society, Newark, New Jersey.)

Newark's bustling "Four Corners" at the cobbled, trolley-laden intersection of Market and Broad streets, circa 1910. (From the Collections of the New Jersey Historical Society, Newark, New Jersey.)

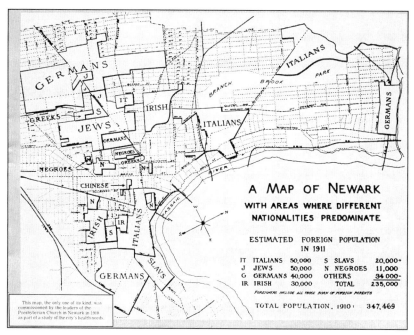

Various ethnic groups formed enclaves throughout the city, as demonstrated in this early-twentieth-century map. (From the Collections of the New Jersey Historical Society, Newark, New Jersey.)

One of the ways Newark became much more than a manufacturing city was by attracting shoppers, particularly to its huge downtown department stores—notably Bamberger's, Plaut's, and (shown here) Hahne & Co. (Courtesy of the Newark Public Library.)

Irishman William J. Brennan was Newark's most popular commissioner during the freewheeling 1920s. (Courtesy of the Newark Public Library.)

The 1933 swearing-in ceremony for newly elected city commissioners, including Mayor Meyer Ellenstein (with hand raised, closest to the microphone). All five faced federal charges for defrauding the city in shady real estate transactions. (Courtesy of the Newark Public Library.)

Mayor Meyer Ellenstein, shown in 1936, was said to be handpicked to run for office by Abner "Longy" Zwillman, Newark's most powerful organized-crime boss. (Courtesy of the Newark Public Library.)

Looters helping themselves to goods in a Central Ward store during the 1967 riots. (From the Collections of the New Jersey Historical Society, Newark, New Jersey.)

Two African American boys walk past National Guardsmen during Newark's July 1967 civic disturbance. The image was captured by Life *photographer Bud Lee, who also shot the magazine's iconic cover depicting a child lying on a street bleeding from a gunshot wound. (Courtesy Bud Lee/The Serge Group.)*

In the wake of the riots, Newark voters elected the divisive "law and order" candidate Anthony Imperiale as a councilman. Imperiale is shown at left preparing for a 1969 motorcade in support of Police Director Dominick Spina. (Courtesy of the Newark Public Library.)

Kenneth A. Gibson, shown in June of 1970, made history as the first African American elected Newark mayor. (Courtesy of the Newark Public Library.)

Opened in downtown Newark in 1997, the New Jersey Performing Arts Center was the clearest sign that the city's renaissance was no myth. (Photo by Richard Termine, courtesy of NJPAC.)

In 2002, Governor James McGreevey (right) promised Newark a new sports arena and endorsed Sharpe James (left) in his quest for a fifth term as mayor. (Photo by Robert Sciarrino, courtesy of the Star-Ledger.*)*

After a politically motivated scuffle broke out at a 2005 basketball tournament, Cory Booker (left) and Sharpe James (right) had to be separated by a police officer providing security for James. (Photo by Ed Murray, courtesy of the Star-Ledger.*)*

Newarkers praying during a memorial service at Mount Vernon School, where three young residents were murdered in 2007. (Photo by Saed Hindash, courtesy of the Star-Ledger.*)*

Newark aglow on October 25, 2007, opening night for the Prudential Center. The arena is expected to be the cornerstone of a vastly improved downtown. (Photo by Frank H. Conlon, courtesy of the Star-Ledger.)

The transition wasn't easy, even for people expecting to get new apartments in the Columbus Homes. "We are particularly concerned over the predicament confronting the many families who are compelled to seek living quarters elsewhere while the development plan is going on," wrote *Italian Tribune* columnist Vince Tuggolo in January of 1953. Just a few months after the paper had overwhelmingly prodded First Warders into getting behind the project, Tuggolo decried the "trying experience" of those forced to move, particularly the "greater portion of these people, who will become ineligible under the present Housing laws to qualify for rooms or an apartment in the newly erected projects." Tuggolo also questioned the "statute of limitations" facing anyone who did qualify for housing. Residents paid proportionately more rent as their salaries increased, and faced eviction if income increased over a certain level. "If conditions are that difficult," he asked, "why then seek living quarters in housing at all?"[58]

In July of 1955, as the Columbus Homes were nearly ready to welcome its first residents, the NHA announced a new round of slum clearance for the old Third Ward. Tuggolo noted the sense of déjà vu. The city was again turning "deaf ears to the cries and legitimate protests of the people," Tuggolo wrote. Residents and business owners had been protesting the destruction of homes and stores on Prince Street, which was once the main shopping drag of Jewish Newark and, in Tuggolo's view, still "has been doing a fabulous business these many years."[59]

Unlike protests over the First Ward project, the more recent demonstrations were subdued and short-lived, partly because the people of the Third Ward were among the poorest in the city. Most would be eligible for public housing. Besides, the residents were mostly African Americans, who had reason to believe their complaints would be ignored. "Fifteen years from now we'll be right back where we started from," one black leader stated, to no avail. "Most of the Negroes will be living in overcrowded, no longer new, public housing projects within the Central Ward."[60]

As more urban-renewal projects got under way, criticism of Louis Danzig and the NHA mounted. Just a few months before the Columbus Homes' dedication, Central Planning Board member Joseph Zeller voiced a growing concern about the heavy density of residents and the strict income limits in high-rise projects. He wondered aloud if the NHA was "creating the slums of ten years from now," and criticized the authority for not giving the board sufficient time to review project plans before being forced to vote.[61]

Danzig responded with a letter saying he was "amazed" to hear such statements. He blamed federal regulations as the reason board members didn't have more time to review projects. "The cost of slum sites is so great in Newark that we are obliged to build high-rise buildings if we are to obtain federal funds at all," Danzig explained.[62]

While everyone agreed that Newark desperately needed new housing, finding tenants who were both qualified and interested in living in the projects became a chore. Time and again, Louis Danzig turned into a salesman to pump up his authority's latest building. To fill spots in the 730-unit Otto K. Kretchmer Homes, which opened in the summer of 1953, the NHA expanded the inspection time for potential tenants from four to seven days a week. The 1,450-unit Hayes Homes, the Central Ward high-rises that would become infamous during the 1967 riots, were billed as the "newest and greatest achievement in low-rent housing" when they opened.[63]

Trying to fill the Columbus Homes during the summer of 1955, Danzig gave would-be residents the hard sell. "This is a real bargain we are offering," he said. "Imagine—brand new apartments averaging 4.6 rooms renting for an average of $40 a month, with the rent charge including gas, electricity, heat, hot water, gas range, and refrigerator." If these units were on the open market, Danzig claimed, the monthly rent would be well over $100. "If that doesn't make our apartments a genuine bargain, I don't know what does."[64]

Eventually, the NHA filled the Columbus Homes, though not in the way many Italians anticipated. Early rumors had it that one reason Italian politicians agreed to let Danzig build the project was because the NHA promised most of the units for Italians—at the same time it supposedly agreed to a 10 percent cap on African American residents. (It was also widely assumed that Newark politicians and their underworld cronies would make a fortune via demolition and construction contracts involved in urban renewal.) As the Columbus Homes' opening drew closer, however, Louis Danzig repeatedly stated that all races would be welcomed in every Newark public-housing project. Often, African Americans were the only people who were interested in living in the project and who didn't surpass the income restrictions.[65]

In time, Louis Danzig and his housing authority would come under fire from both blacks and whites in Newark. To whites, upset with the way blacks dominated residency in the city's public-housing projects, the NHA stood for the "Negro Housing Authority." To blacks, angered by being pushed out of neighborhoods for redevelopment, urban renewal came to mean "Negro removal."

For all the controversy, public housing in Newark circa the mid-1950s helped many families immensely. A NHA report described one such family, the Walskys. Alfred Walsky returned to his wife, Mae, in 1945 after serving in World War II, the young couple moved into a cold-water flat with her father. They stayed for eight years and had three children. "It was a nightmare," said

Mae. "Every day we carried kerosene up from the basement. We got sick of the smell from the oil stove. There was no wash basin in the bathroom, only a tub and toilet." A friend suggested that Mae apply for an apartment in the projects, and the Walskys moved into the Thomas J. Walsh Homes in 1953. "Things began to change right away," said Mae. "Here we have a living room, three bedrooms, a kitchen and a bath—all clean and modern. The children have made new friends and play wherever they like. They sleep better."[66]

Many First Warders still stuck in cramped, cold-water flats were jealous of the people who lived in Columbus Homes. The high-rises were not only equipped with huge new apartments, but laundry rooms and common areas that hosted everything from ballet lessons to kids' arts and crafts. Residents formed softball leagues and dance groups, organized roller-skating parties, and even created their own monthly newsletter.[67]

Ultimately, however, stacking low-income families on top of each other in unwelcoming, resentful neighborhoods that didn't have parks, police, or local services to handle them was a recipe for failure. Just two months after the Hayes Homes' dedication, a project spokesman told the city council that "tenants are not safe on the grounds at night because of fights, robberies, and attempted rapes. Gangs of teenagers have engaged in battles and drunks from nearby saloons sleep in hallways and basements." The NHA hired guards to patrol only after receiving a petition signed by fifteen hundred residents.[68]

Omens at the Columbus Homes also appeared early. One month after the dedication, a twenty-two-year-old man and two teenagers were arrested for assaulting a seventeen-year-old boy at the projects. The boy was cut with a knife on both cheeks and had bruises all over his body.[69] By the summer of 1957, problems became apparent on several fronts at Columbus Homes. In June, two adults and two children were trapped in an elevator between the third and fourth floor for an hour before police let them out of a trap door. Bands of unsupervised teenagers roamed the hallways, leading to a tenant petition requesting that a police force be established at the project. "A great many of us," the petition read, "are in constant fear for ourselves and our families."[70]

As early as the spring of 1957, Danzig himself implicitly owned up to difficulties with the projects. Approaching federal authorities, he pled that the NHA "must be given the money and staff to provide more than just brick and mortar for tenants." The NHA needed help because of "broken families, poor housekeepers and vandalism," Danzig said, as well as "maintenance and management problems."[71]

In 1962, Gerald Spatola, an NHA member whom Mayor Carlin had recently decided not to reappoint, went public, criticizing Danzig's "arbitrary policy to present vast numbers of items for approval by authority members without affording the members a reasonable opportunity to study them." Danzig's methods had "reduced me to the status of a rubber stamp, with no independence of thought or decision," said Spatola, whose requests for project details in advance were never met. "I did not receive an agenda until the day of the meeting, and yet I was asked to approve a project involving millions of dollars without the opportunity for adequate study or orientation."[72]

In light of the backlash mounting against the NHA, Louis Danzig, and City Hall, Congressman Hugh Addonizio crushed Leo Carlin in the 1962 mayoral election. Italians and African Americans, the two groups most affected by urban renewal of the 1950s and 1960s, constituted Addonizio's base of support.[73]

———

By the time Hugh Addonizio became Newark's mayor, a book written by a mild-mannered New Yorker named Jane Jacobs boldly decreed that post–World War II public housing and urban planning represented "the sacking of the cities" rather than their salvation. "Let's look what we have built with the first several billions," Jacobs wrote in her urban studies classic, *The Death and Life of Great American Cities*, published in 1961: "Low-income projects that become worse centers of delinquency, vandalism and general social hopelessness than the slums they were supposed to replace."[74]

Unlike the typical order-obsessed urban planner, Jacobs celebrated the chaos of street life, with its colorful mix of people, industries, offices, shops, apartment buildings, and homes. She argued that streets full of activity were not only more interesting, but safer for residents and better for businesses.

Throughout her book, Jacobs delved into Boston's North End, "an old, low-rent area merging into the heavy industry of the waterfront, and it is officially considered Boston's worst slum and civic shame." The neighborhood's problems included high density of residents, little parkland, and tiny blocks. "Twenty years ago," Jacobs wrote, "when I first happened to see the North End, its buildings—town houses of different kinds and sizes converted to flats, and four- or five-story tenements built to house the flood of immigrants first from Ireland, then from Eastern Europe and finally from Sicily—were badly overcrowded, and the general effect was of a district taking a terrible physical beating and certainly desperately poor."[75]

Jacobs's words could have also accurately described another Italian neighborhood: Newark's First Ward. Yet, whereas that section of Newark was transformed by urban renewal, no official action was taken in the North End. Curiously, the Boston neighborhood changed on its own, as Jacobs noted on a visit in 1959. "Dozens and dozens of buildings had been rehabilitated," she wrote. "Instead of mattresses against the window there were Venetian blinds and glimpses of fresh paint. Many of the small, converted houses now had only one or two families in them instead of the old crowded three or four." Everywhere she looked, even down narrow alleyways, she saw "more neatly repainted brickwork, new blinds, and a burst of music as a door opened. . . . The streets were alive with children playing, people shopping, people talking."[76]

The turnabout of Boston's North End occurred, simply enough, because people living and working there cared enough about the area to improve it. Newark's First Ward residents never had the chance to do the same. Amazingly, Louis Danzig and the NHA installed policies that actively discouraged Newark property owners from making improvements. If landlords cleaned up their properties, it would be more difficult to argue a section was blighted. Even if the NHA was able to condemn the area, improved buildings pushed up the NHA's acquisition costs. Neither scenario was in line with Danzig's mission, so he argued that inspectors shouldn't even bother enforcing code violations in the worst slums.[77]

A self-fulfilling prophecy followed the NHA's arrival in a neighborhood. "They come around and start doing their survey, and before you know it, tenants are scared and move out," one landlord said in a survey in the early 1960s. "Then the property goes to hell and you're left without income for three years before they make a settlement."[78]

Landlords saw little incentive to rehab their rental units. The ensuing tax hikes following any improvement would probably outweigh the additional money they would be able to charge in rent. Slum conditions snowballed around the city as landlords in poor and borderline areas also pointed to the NHA as a reason they refused to fix up apartments. Why spend the money when the building would probably be flattened within a few years? "If there wasn't urban renewal coming, I think I would probably re-side the house," an owner of a group of cold-water flats said. "It sure needs it, and I'd put in central heating. It seems to improve the quality of the tenantry."[79]

In the book that included the landlord interviews above, a housing expert is quoted as making what would seem to be an obvious statement: "Clearly housing conditions are not improved by demolishing occupied substandard housing if, in the process, the total supply of accommodations which the displaced family can afford is reduced. To as great an extent as possible, demolition should be the consequence of abandonment, not the cause of it."[80]

Newark was, in fact, guilty of evicting more people than it accommodated in public housing. Between 1959 and 1967, 3,760 units were built. At the same time, approximately twelve thousand families were pushed out of their homes to make way for public housing, highway, and other urban-renewal developments. Some poor families were forced to move several times in just a few years—because when they were displaced, the only spots they could afford were in other slums that would also soon to be razed. What's more, those eligible for "low-income" public housing often faced higher rents than they had in the past; Third Ward African American families, for example, paid $50 or $55 a month in public housing, compared to $25 or $30 for their old homes.[81]

The already shifting racial makeup of neighborhoods was pushed into overdrive with the onslaught of urban renewal. Blacks represented just 8 percent of Clinton Hill residents in 1950, and nearly half the neighborhood a decade later. In one western section of Newark, twenty thousand whites moved out in the 1950s just as sixteen thousand non-whites arrived as residents. Young families were well represented among the newcomers, and the newcomers quickly dominated the school system. Weequahic High School, which in the 1950s consisted overwhelmingly of college-bound Jews, increased from 19 percent African American in 1961 to 70 percent in 1966. The number of African Americans at West Side High, which accounted for 33 percent of the student body in 1961, was over 80 percent in 1966.[82]

Other parts of Newark remained nearly as segregated as the surrounding suburbs. Even with an influx of African Americans in the Columbus Homes, northern Newark was 85 percent white as of 1960. Although the number of non-whites living in Vailsburg more than doubled in the 1950s, there were still only 250 African Americans in the neighborhood in 1960, compared to over 34,000 whites.[83]

Newark had hoped to plug the leak of wealthy and middle-class white residents, but if anything Louis Danzig, with the assistance of local politicians and federal housing policies, widened the hole in the dam. About a hundred thousand white Newarkers—more than one-quarter of the population—left the city in the 1950s.

Danzig, along with officials in many cities, blamed federal policies for white flight. "These families properly belong to the cities," Danzig said in a TV interview, but low-rate mortgages in the suburbs were simply too attractive to pass up. Financing for urban projects had dried up, leaving cities like Newark in the lurch. "It's high time that one arm of the government stops spending money unless the second arm of the government was going to go carry through the project and issue commitments for reconstruction, particularly in the housing field."[84]

Danzig's arguments had some validity to them, but that didn't stop criticism of him and the NHA throughout the 1960s. Former chief magistrate
Nicholas Castellano, during a 1966 mayoral election run versus then-mayor
Hugh Addonizio, charged that Danzig was a "willing captive tool of the
present administration," and accused him of "playing politics at the expense
of the safety and welfare of housing project tenants." Robberies, rapes, and
assaults took place nightly in the projects, Castellano said. "The housing
director has converted his domain into a political machine which goes into
operation whenever the present master in City Hall pushes the button. In
doing so, he has permitted the project buildings to deteriorate disgracefully
and become breeding grounds of every conceivable crime."[85]

Complaints about racism in Newark's public housing multiplied to the
point that the New Jersey Advisory Committee called a two-day meeting in
June 1966. Among other things, Danzig and the NHA had been accused of
segregationist practices, based on the fact that blacks represented more than
90 percent of tenants in four poorly maintained high-rise projects in the
Central Ward (Felix Fuld Court, Hayes Homes, Stella Windsor, and Scudder
Homes). At the same time, the non-white populations at Stephen Crane
Village and Bradley Court—low-rise projects in the suburban outskirts
of the city—were less than 10 percent. The white-majority buildings were
"country clubs," in the words of those living in projects dominated by African
American residents. James Kennedy, of Hayes Homes, said that while people
in the Crane and Bradley projects were "fighting for air-conditioning—we're
fighting for living conditions."[86]

"Any Negro family that wants an apartment in the two so-called country
club projects can have one," Danzig told his inquisitors. When asked for an
explanation in the disparity of races from one project to another, Danzig's
reply drew a chorus of hoots and boos. "People," he said, "are more comfortable with their own."[87]

CHAPTER 6

BOUND TO EXPLODE

GENERATIONS OF FRUSTRATION
BOIL OVER IN THE SUMMER OF 1967

A rather commonplace incident occurred on the night of Wednesday, July 12, 1967. At approximately 9 PM, police pulled over a forty-year-old taxi driver heading west on Fifteenth Avenue near South Ninth Street. The patrolmen, John DeSimone and Vito Pontrelli, were of Italian descent, which was to be expected in a police department that was 90 percent white and dominated in particular by Italians. The man pulled over was African American, also unsurprising. By the mid-1960s, more than half of Newark's population was black, including nearly everyone living in the Central Ward neighborhood where the incident took place. Even the cab driver's name was generic: John Smith.[1]

Also typical of the era, the two sides told very different stories regarding what happened. In the police version, Smith's cab tailgated Pontrelli and DeSimone's patrol car and flicked the high beams on and off for a block. The taxi then "shot around us at the intersection of Fifteenth Avenue and South Seventh Street and went approximately one block on the wrong side of the street," DeSimone stated. The police pulled the taxi over, and Smith answered license and registration requests with insults and curses. Moments later, police said, Smith opened the cab door and began punching DeSimone in the chest and face. The patrolmen forced Smith inside the police car but never handcuffed him, supposedly because the taxi driver was putting up too much of a struggle. While Pontrelli drove the half-dozen blocks to the Fourth Precinct, his partner and Smith fought. At one point, Pontrelli testified, Smith struck him at the wheel. Smith refused to get out of the patrol car at the precinct and therefore had to be dragged inside. At around 9:30 PM, John Smith was booked, charged with the use of loud and offensive language, assault and battery, and resisting arrest. The following morning police presented him with various traffic citations, including driving with a revoked license and failure to stay on the right side of the road.

Like many of Newark's African Americans, Smith came from the South. Born in Warthen, Georgia, his parents moved to North Carolina when he was a child. Smith joined the army, where he played the trumpet. Upon being discharged, Smith moved to Newark to follow his dream of becoming a professional trumpet player. He took music classes in New York City by day and hacked for Safety Cab Company at night, taking an occasional shift off to play a gig. Driving a taxi certainly didn't seem like a good career for Smith; he'd been involved in six car accidents in 1965 and another one in 1966. At the time of his arrest in the summer of 1967, he listed his address as 214 Seymour Avenue, which was about a ten-minute walk from the Fourth Precinct. Standing a thin five feet, seven inches, Smith sometimes wore a goatee and midsize, bushy Afro. Few Newarkers knew much about Smith before or after the summer of 1967. He was a soft-spoken, unassuming man who blended anonymously into Newark's Central Ward.[2]

In Smith's telling of the events of that Wednesday evening, he picked up a female African American passenger in his cab near City Hospital, drove south on Sixth Street, and turned right onto Fifteenth Avenue. A block ahead, he encountered a double-parked police car. After slowing down, signaling, and passing the patrol car, Smith was pulled over. He pled his case to the officer, saying, "You were double-parked and I thought you were working and I just made a normal pass." An obviously angry police officer opened the taxi door, told Smith he was being arrested, and then insulted the passenger and ordered her to get out of the cab. On the way to the precinct, the patrolman in the front passenger seat turned around and punched Smith several times. The driver told his partner to stop, saying, "No, no, this baby is mine."

"There was no resistance on my part," Smith said at his bail hearing. "That was a cover story by the police. They caved in my ribs, busted a hernia, and put a hole in my head." Smith said he had been struck in the groin in the police car, and when they arrived at the station house he was buckled over in agony, unable to get out. He was dragged inside. The two arresting officers and seven or eight other cops kicked and beat him, first behind a closed door at the precinct, and later in a holding cell. They muscled Smith's head over the cell's toilet and splashed its rank water into his face. "While my head was over the toilet bowl I was struck on the back of the head with a revolver," Smith said. "I was being cursed while they were beating me."[3]

Plenty of witnesses saw the police wrestle Smith into the Fourth Precinct. Each arresting officer clutched one of Smith's arms, and another cop grabbed Smith's legs to help haul the taxi driver inside. Directly across Seventeenth

Avenue from the Fourth Precinct sat the Hayes Homes, a 1,450-unit, eight-building high-rise public-housing project very similar in appearance and design to the North Ward's Columbus Homes—except that virtually all Hayes Homes residents were black. People watching the ugly spectacle from project windows alerted neighbors and called local civil-rights organizations. By 10 PM, three dozen African Americans gathered outside the precinct in protest. Rumors quickly spread throughout the projects—and through much of the city, thanks to Smith's cab driver colleagues—that Smith had been paralyzed, or even beaten to death. "He's gone, brother," people said. "They killed him."[4]

Someone had to get into the precinct to check on the taxi driver, pleaded Hayes Homes resident and tenant leader Esta Williams. Her husband, she said, had been brutalized inside there two years before. The growing crowd, now about seventy-five strong, approached the station house. Police allowed entry to about a dozen people, including Robert Curvin, a young activist who worked for the Congress of Racial Equality, or CORE. Curvin observed Smith lying in his cell—alive but in severe pain. The group asked the precinct leader, Inspector Kenneth Melchior, an obvious question: Why hadn't the prisoner been allowed to see a doctor? As midnight approached, Smith was taken out through the precinct's rear door and loaded into a patrol car bound for Beth Israel Hospital, where it was discovered he'd suffered a broken rib and other less serious injuries. People followed the police car driving Smith to the hospital because, in the words of Curvin, "Frankly no one trusted the police enough to take someone to the hospital even in a situation like that."[5]

A dozen policemen attempted to disperse the crowd still outside the precinct, but some thirty taxi cabs blocked the street and the protestors numbered at least 250 people. Curvin, along with Don Wendell of the local branch of United Community Corporation (UCC), the federally funded antipoverty organization, and other activist leaders, urged the people to go home peacefully and attend a formal protest the following morning at City Hall. As they addressed the crowd, a Molotov cocktail slammed into the Fourth Precinct. Police rushed out of the station house, wearing riot helmets and wielding night sticks, and surrounded the building.

African American leaders asked for another chance to calm the crowd. Standing atop a car with a police bullhorn to his mouth, Curvin called for a demonstration. Some people began to leave for an all-night vigil at City Hall, but attention turned to a fire that had broken out in an abandoned car across from the Hayes Homes. Policemen and firemen tending the burning car were pelted with stones and fled. Soon young black men dashed through the streets in small groups, hurling rocks, bottles, and other projectiles at the station house, patrol cars, and police officers.

Eventually, police were able to secure the immediate area around the Fourth Precinct. Several women who lived in Hayes Homes said they were chased inside their buildings by police officers and beaten in darkened hallways. A few dozen carloads of African Americans arrived at City Hall by 2 AM to protest Smith's arrest and demand his release, but Police Deputy Chief John Redden convinced them to go home; after all, no city officials were there to hear their protests. Other groups who'd been dispersed from the station house began looting, first striking Harry's Liquor Store, a block away from the Fourth Precinct on Belmont Avenue (later, Irvine Turner Boulevard). Looters also smashed the windows and helped themselves to liquor and beer at Jack's Tavern, on Seventeenth Avenue. "Originally, only the most aggressive, the boldest of the guys would go in," said UCC Board President Timothy Still. Others joined in the looting as they saw police cars zooming past without even slowing down to investigate. "All the people saw that the cops didn't care, so they went in, too."[6]

By 4 AM, quiet returned to Newark's streets. While the rioting had been ugly, the destruction wasn't too severe. Damage to buildings and businesses was estimated at about $2,500. A total of twenty-five people had been arrested on charges such as looting, possession of stolen property, breaking and entering, and the vague misdeed "idling." No guns had been fired, and other than the taxi driver John Smith, no one was seriously injured.

Early that morning, the UCC's Don Wendell heard Police Director Dominick Spina addressing officers on the Fourth Precinct's steps. "The situation is normal," Spina said. "Put the windows in early in the morning; get the place cleaned up. Just return it to normal and don't treat it as a situation, because once you begin to look at problems as problems, they become problems."[7]

————

Spina's longtime ally Mayor Hugh Addonizio took the same approach, characterizing the fracas as an "isolated incident." In fact, the mayor and the police director had a long history of downplaying all signs of racial tension. The previous April, Dr. Martin Luther King Jr. had referred to Newark and a few other U.S. cities as "powder kegs" which could "explode in racial violence this summer." Spina reacted to King's remarks in typical fashion. "I don't believe there will be any violence whatsoever," Spina said. "Complaints of police brutality are at their lowest ebb and the police in the city have already been alerted to any potential problem areas." Addressing Dr. King's comments, an Addonizio spokesman issued the statement: "This is not the first time that this kind of nonsense prediction has been made for Newark. Three previous times such predictions proved false and they undoubtedly will prove false again."[8]

As always, Mayor Addonizio was following his political instinct, which had led him to fantastic success thus far. A born and bred Newarker, Addonizio grew up and still lived on Hazelwood Avenue, in the westernmost part of Vailsburg, near the South Orange border. He attended Saint Benedict's Preparatory School and West Side High School, was named quarterback on the 1934 all-state football team, and received an athletic scholarship to Fordham University. Addonizio served in the army for almost the entire duration of the U.S.'s involvement in World War II, seeing action in Sicily and North Africa and landing on Omaha Beach in the invasion of Normandy. After being discharged in 1946 with eight battle stars and the Bronze Star, he ran for Congress in New Jersey's Eleventh District, which included parts of the Oranges and Newark's South, West, and Central wards. The war hero squeaked out a victory and won six more consecutive terms, largely due to the loyal backing of his district's Italians and African Americans. His mayoral elections in 1962 and 1966 were blowouts, each won by margins of more than twenty thousand votes.[9]

Hugh Addonizio earned a reputation as a political heavyweight—one as confident, crafty, and ambitious as any in the state. Few other politicians could match him in terms of sheer moxie. In 1965, the fifty-one-year-old mayor witnessed bank robbers on Clinton Avenue trying to escape after an $8,700 heist. Addonizio and his driver chased them in the mayor's car until the thieves crashed into a utility pole. Before running off, one robber scurried up to the mayor's car and shot a bullet through the windshield. "I wasn't particularly frightened," said Addonizio, a five foot, seven inch, two hundred-pound bear of a man with a bulbous nose and a large bald head. "If I had a gun, I would have shot back."[10]

By the summer of 1967, Addonizio was gearing up to run for governor two years later. Campaign buttons had already been made. Well aware of the negative impact news of a riot could do to his chances for higher office, the mayor was reluctant to admit his city had gotten out of hand following John Smith's arrest. "There was no riot alert," the mayor told the press on the morning of July 13, 1967. "We're concerned but not unduly concerned." The officers who arrested Smith would be reassigned to administrative duties pending an investigation, Addonizio said, but there were no plans to increase patrols or call in help from the state police. The ever-confident mayor gave every indication the "isolated incident" would blow over. "This is a difficult situation," he said, "but apparently it has no significance as far as relating it to any other problem."[11]

In reality, the chaos following the arrest and pummeling of John Smith occurred mainly because the incident was so typical of what African Americans had come to expect in Newark. People were fed up with the fact that, a century after the Civil War had ended, police brutality and discrimination were still commonplace. After World War II, the combination of white flight and an influx of black people had dramatically transformed Newark, yet the city's power structure still remained almost entirely in the hands of whites. Frustration was at a peak, and any minor incident had a chance of setting off an angry spree of violence and looting.

Racism, of course, was not unique to Newark. Actually, one of the reasons so many African Americans had moved to Newark was because, compared to other cities, it was considered a welcoming haven with a fair amount of opportunity for people of color.

By and large, Newark's black population came to the city from the South in one of the waves of migration begun in earnest around World War I. Somewhere between three hundred thousand and one million black southerners fled to the North between 1910 and 1920. There's little mystery why they left. A farm worker in the South earned perhaps seventy-five cents for a long, grueling day laboring in the fields. "I had to chop cotton, pick cotton, pick peanuts up and stack 'em around," one female migrant to Newark recalled of her early days in the South. "We had to go to the fields, sun-up every day, and come out, sun-down. We didn't go like you go eight hours here and you finish your day's work."[12] During the war years in Newark, by contrast, a dye-plant employee made $2.75 per day, and the company paid for his passage from the South and provided a rent-free room on arrival.[13]

An African American man could not only make a better living in a northern city, he could expect to enjoy a better life, with fewer of the societal restraints that governed every move in the South. "They're treated more like men up here in the North," said one black minister from Philadelphia, addressing the reasons for the mass migration. "There's prejudice here, too, but the color line isn't drawn on their faces at every turn as it is in the South." In other words, as one black migrant wrote in a letter to a friend still down South: In the North you "don't have to mister every little white boy comes along."[14]

At the very least, by leaving the South an African American would decrease the chances of getting lynched. Between 1889 and 1919, vigilantes in Georgia, for example, hanged one black person per month, on average. William Ashby, a leader of the Urban League in Newark, grew up in rural Virginia and one day saw a black man strung up in the woods. "There on the end of a rope, over a limb of a sycamore tree, on a gray morning, hung a man," Ashby wrote in his memoirs. "He was quite dark. His mouth was open. His red tongue stuck out as if he wanted to say something. Perhaps he wanted to ask, 'Why have you murdered me?'"[15] Prejudice was to be expected in the North, just not to such a brutal degree. "I didn't come North lookin' for flower beds," was how one Newark migrant and mother of ten summed up the situation. "But I did come here not wanting my children to be killed like they was bein' killed down there."[16]

As those remaining in the South received letters and money from friends and family who had already migrated, more and more African Americans headed north to join them. World War I-era migrants from southwestern Georgia and neighboring parts of Alabama wound up in Newark in large numbers. "It seems impossible that a Negro is left in Dothan, Alabama," a Newark social worker wrote in 1917.[17]

Black migrants would later joke that they wound up in Newark by mistake; they'd been trying to get to New York and confused the two. The truth was that Newark was attractive to black southerners not only because jobs were abundant, but the city had a well-established African American community with its own churches and social services. The public schools were desegregated, and at least early on, many neighborhoods were likewise racially mixed. African Americans had traditionally grown in proportion to Newark's overall population and accounted for only 3 or 4 percent of the total through the early 1920s. At that point, the continued arrival of tens of thousands more African Americans coincided with the departure of many of Newark's wealthy white citizens for the suburbs. By 1930, black residents constituted just under 9 percent of the city, numbering 38,880 and growing.[18]

To a newcomer from the rural South, Newark offered excitement at every turn. Even getting around town by public transportation was a thrill. "Oh Lord, to come up South Orange Avenue on that trolley car, that was something," recalled Mildred Arnold, who at age ten moved from South Carolina to Newark with her family in 1924. "I never rode on a trolley before; I had never even seen a trolley. I was saying to myself, 'What is this? We can ride this?'"[19]

The transition to city life for the "country folk" could often be difficult, however. With their particular way of dress and slow, drawn-out speech, they were easily marked as targets by con artists and coaxed out of what little money they had saved. Many African American women, whose only work experience had been picking cotton, had no idea what was to be expected of a domestic in a rich suburban home. In the South, when a farm worker built up a sweat he simply took off his coat and shirt. Many new arrivals did likewise when overheated at work in Newark's factories and freight yards—and promptly came down with grippe or, worse, pneumonia.[20]

Landlords routinely charged African Americans high rents for awful apartments, and since Newark regularly experienced extremely low vacancy rates, there wasn't much choice but to pay up. Initially, there was no distinct black section of Newark. By World War II, however, nearly two-thirds of the city's African Americans were concentrated in a small sliver south of Orange Street and west of High Street. The crumbling old Third Ward, long a Jewish enclave, completely transformed within a few decades as black families replaced the Jews heading to Weequahic or suburban towns. From 1910 to 1940, the number of black residents in the Third Ward shot up from under fifteen hundred, or about 4 percent of the neighborhood, to over sixteen thousand, or 63 percent.[21] Most businesses in the Third Ward and other rapidly changing neighborhoods remained in the hands of white owners, however. And regardless of where African Americans settled down, there was one other constant: the housing they inherited was in poor shape. The Central Planning Board estimated that in 1945, more than half of the city's black residents lived in "unhealthful and unwholesome quarters," which needed major repairs or lacked private baths, toilets, or water supply.[22]

Overall, in the first few decades of the twentieth century, African Americans experienced what might be considered third-class citizenship, a rung below immigrants from eastern and southern Europe, who were themselves viewed as a separate caste from the older immigrant groups who basically ran the city. Fairly typical of northern cities in the era, Newark's public services were segregated in one form or another. Swimming pools, for example, were open to African Americans only during limited hours when whites weren't present. Jim Crow sections were the only seats opened to blacks in most of Newark's movie theaters. Many department stores refused to allow African Americans the standard courtesy of trying on garments before purchasing them.[23]

Even with the racist state of affairs, African Americans carved out better lives for themselves in Newark than they could have expected in the South. The Third Ward became the exciting center of black life. A string of clubs west of Broad Street constituted a mini-Harlem, where African Americans socialized over cocktails amid a stylish, upscale crowd. The "colored entertainment" included singers in zoot suits, comics dressed in blackface telling bawdy jokes, and first-rate big bands. The old Rink, which hosted the city's Industrial Exhibitions in the 1870s, became a black vaudeville house named the Orpheum Theater, where the show might include a performance by tap dancer Bill "Bojangles" Robinson or a tug-of-war featuring heavyweight boxing champ Jack Johnson. The vibrant scene helped launch the careers of countless African American entertainers, most notably a pair of singers: Miss Rhapsody, born in the East Ward as Viola Wells and known as "Newark's Number One Brown Gal" for her signature song "Brown Gal"; and Sarah Vaughan, a product of the Mount Zion Baptist Church choir and Arts High School, who was bound for status as a jazz legend. Many of Newark's clubs were owned and operated by black entrepreneurs, including a few women like Eurlee Reeves. Universally known as Mrs. Reeves, she was a Georgia native who in the 1930s transformed a hotdog and beer joint on Warren Street into the Nest Club, a cozy, welcoming hot spot that catered to African American clientele and served as a home-away-from-home to dozens of singers, dancers, musicians, and vaudeville performers. For the late-night crowd, after-hours clubs dotted Broome Street, a stretch that also served as one of Newark's most notorious red-light districts.[24]

On summer Sunday afternoons, African American couples, families, and friends packed chicken and potato salad, dressed in their finest clothes—suits for men, flowery dresses and big hats for women, everyone with their hair done just right—and ventured into the Ironbound to see the Newark Eagles play at Ruppert Stadium. To many, the Negro League team's games were tremendous sources of pride, "full of noise and identification" and "greetings over and around folks," in the words of Newark poet and activist Amiri Baraka, who attended games as a boy with his father. Eagles players were "legitimate black heroes" to Baraka (born Everett LeRoi Jones) and to so many others. Players were larger-than-life inspirations and yet accessible figures who celebrated victories with fans at the team's hangout, the Grand Hotel, a two-story lodging establishment for blacks on West Market Street. "They were extensions of all of us," Baraka wrote of the Eagles, "in a way that the Yankees and Dodgers and what not could never be."[25]

Effa Manley, who owned the team with her husband, Abe, a 1920s boot-legger who became a major player in Harlem society, was an even larger presence than the players in the Eagles organization, serving as business manager as well as the face of the team—and a gorgeous face at that. Effa Manley was thin and light-skinned; some speculation had it that she was not African American but entirely white. Always photographed with eyebrows perfectly sculpted, she could have easily passed for a model or movie star. Legend has it, she personally gave the signal for an Eagles' batter to bunt by crossing her sexy legs from her stadium box seat; one player was reportedly so distracted by his boss, he never noticed the pitch zipping toward his head, which knocked him unconscious.[26]

Well aware that the business of baseball relied to a large degree on image, Effa Manley insisted Eagles players appear neat and professional on and off the field. She issued the new, glowing-white uniforms to players in the infield—because they were closer to the crowd—and chastised players if they had so much as a smudge of mud on their shoes. At a time when women of color rarely aspired to anything more than working in a factory or becoming a housewife, Effa Manley was a smart, hard-nosed businesswoman. After Jackie Robinson broke the color barrier by playing for the Dodgers, and other Major League teams began snatching up more players from the Negro Leagues, Effa Manley was the first owner to demand compensation for the players being taken. She also did her share to help the civil rights cause, promoting boycotts of businesses that wouldn't serve blacks and volunteering as treasurer of Newark's local chapter of the NAACP. Under Effa Manley's leadership, the Eagles put together some remarkably talented rosters. Three players on the 1946 squad, champs of the Negro League World Series, were eventually named to the National Baseball Hall of Fame: Larry Doby, a second baseman who grew up in Paterson and became a seven-time All-Star; Monte Irvin, a hard-hitting shortstop and graduate of East Orange High School; and Leon Day, a pitcher with a blazing 95-mile-per-hour fastball. In 2006, Effa Manley herself became the first woman ever elected to baseball's Hall of Fame.[27]

Life might have been better in the North for a person of color, but still there came a moment in every African American Newarker's life when an ugly, unmistakable truth came to light. Glass ceilings in workplaces and society in the North may have been higher and less obvious than those in Georgia or Mississippi, but they existed nonetheless.

Often, the moment when prejudice became a reality shocked Newark's young African Americans, who until then had likely played unassumingly with white kids in their neighborhoods. The childhood experiences of Edward Williams, who would go on to be Newark's first African American to be a captain, and later an inspector, in the police department, were fairly typical. Williams grew up in the 1930s in the Third Ward on West Kinney Street, around where the Hayes Homes would eventually be built. His childhood neighbors were Jews, Poles, Germans, and African Americans. One Saturday night, Edward's mother, who worked as a domestic in the suburbs, gave him and his older brother each a dime. It was double the usual amount, so rather than going to the movies three blocks from their house, the boys walked past the stores on Springfield Avenue to the fancy Savoy Theater. They paid and started walking to their seats when a tall African American usher stopped them. "You boys know better than that," he said. "Now turn your asses right 'round and get up to that balcony." Soon thereafter, Edward and his brother tried to go swimming in a public pool, where a white man at the entrance turned them away, with the gruff phrase: "No Niggers in here except on Fridays."[28]

The boys left the pool hurt and confused. Edward's brother kicked a dog on the way home. Young Edward Williams found himself wondering whether every time white students were giggling at school they were secretly ridiculing him. "My white teacher was warm and sensitive," he thought. "She would sit beside me and help me with difficult problems; she would encourage me when I needed it, and she would compliment me when I deserved it. Was this the enemy?"[29]

In his memoirs, the Urban League's William Ashby offered a story demonstrating the sometimes unintended consequences of discrimination. For years, Newark sent poor children free of charge to a summer camp at Avon-by-the-Sea on the Jersey Shore. The camp's first five weeks were reserved for whites, and one final week was offered to African Americans. Even the camp's admission tickets were printed on different colored paper for whites and blacks. The Urban League helped distribute tickets for the black week, and one day a group of ten-year-old boys who lived in central Newark on Colden Street arrived, asking Ashby if they could attend. Ashby handed out tickets to all except the lone white boy in the group. "You didn't give Tony none," the group's leader said to Ashby, who tried to explain why the young white man couldn't attend camp the same week as his friends. The boys began to leave, and then stopped and returned to toss their tickets at Ashby. "Here mister," said one, his arm around the shoulder of his white pal Tony. "Take your ticket. If my friend can't go, I don't want to go."[30]

Eventually, kids exposed to racism and segregation embraced them as the status quo. "Adults fed us various poisons that pushed us apart as we grew, naturally," wrote Amiri Baraka, whose best friends early in life were white. "By high school, almost miraculously, the relationships we'd had on the street level and in grammar school had disappeared." Baraka's closest friend, for example, was an Irish kid known as Augie D. They played basketball and baseball together. Augie's house was the first in their neighborhood around Dey Street to have a television, and kids of all ethnicities piled inside Augie's house to watch. Augie loved to comb his hair, and one day his black friend asked to borrow his comb. "Don't mix the breeds," Augie responded, casually shooting his buddy down.[31]

The further an African American ventured into society, the more walls he encountered. Many bars and restaurants were completely off-limits. In 1931, William Ashby was put in charge of throwing a party honoring Joseph H. E. Scotland, who had recently completed his twenty-fifth year working for

Essex County, most of it as custodian of mortgages. Called "Judge" by most people, because he was a justice of the peace, Scotland was widely respected and admired throughout the state. Most restaurants and banquet halls in Newark refused to host the event, however, because Scotland was black. "Oh, I know Judge Scotland," one Jewish restaurant owner said. "He's a fine man and I think he should be given a party. But I'm sorry, I can't help you. You see, I have a steady dinner trade. If I did what you wish, I should have to close my place to my regular diners. I know they would not like it." In broken English, a manager at an Italian restaurant in the First Ward responded to Ashby's request by saying, "I can no rent to color people. He no know how to act in fine place like these."[32]

After returning from service in the navy in World War II, Edward Williams walked into a Newark bar with a white friend. At the time, Williams was a father of three and had just joined the police force. The bartender ordered Williams out, prompting his confused friend to say that he was over twenty-one. "I don't care if he's 121," said the bartender. "We don't serve colored in here."[33]

Both world wars had been promoted to black men as an opportunity for advancement; they could prove themselves as good as any men, the armed-service recruiters proclaimed, and fight for freedom and justice. What became more apparent than ever to returning African American servicemen, however, were the hypocritical differences between the freedom and equality preached by the government and the racist society confronting its black citizens. Sometime around the end of World War II, a sentiment boiled up and spread throughout Newark and all of black America. Ashby summed up the feeling as: "I'm tired of all this goddam crap. Tired of hearing the white man say, 'I can't serve no niggers in my restaurant.' Tired of being told, 'I ain't got no place for colored in my hotel.' Why, hell, I've been to Europe. Hitler leveled his bullets at me. Missed. I went to the Pacific. Mr. Hirohito sent his madmen at me to blow me to hell in their planes. I'm still here. Why don't I tell the white man, 'Take your goddam boot off my neck! Get the hell out of my road so that I can pass!'"[34]

———

The civil rights movement followed as a natural outgrowth of the mindset described by Ashby. By the mid-1960s, however—after years of work by Dr. Martin Luther King Jr. and other African American leaders, after Rosa Parks refused to give her bus seat to a white man, and after the Freedom Riders, the March on Washington, and Civil Rights Act of 1964—the black poor in cities such as Newark viewed the movement with a degree of skepticism. It had not changed their lives, by and large. For many, peaceful civil rights efforts had succeeded only in raising false hopes.

Nationwide in 1966, blacks were twice as likely as whites to be unemployed. The median income for a black family was only 58 percent of the average white family. Segregation remained the unofficial policy of many areas even in the North. In the mid-1960s, for example, of the 150,000 people living in four Newark suburbs—Bloomfield, Harrison, Irvington, and Maplewood—only about 1,000 were African Americans. Some of Newark's middle-class black families had been able to move to suburban towns including East Orange and Montclair, but the city they left behind became poorer and more desperate.[35]

As early as 1963, Police Director Dominick Spina insisted that the Newark police force was "completely integrated," and the New Housing Authority's Louis Danzig claimed that integration in public housing was "a fact and it is working."[36] Yet easily observable facts—a 90 percent white police department, housing projects obviously divided along racial lines—told another story. As Newark's black population grew, the city as a whole, and the public schools in particular, became more, rather than less, segregated according to race.[37]

The frustrations of limited work options and awful housing were felt most acutely by the African Americans remaining in Newark and other older, rusting urban areas. Beginning with World War I, Newark's overall population hovered for four decades at around four hundred thousand. During that time, the number of white residents fell in almost exact proportion to the number of blacks moving into the city, with African Americans taking over as the majority sometime in the mid-1960s. Of all major U.S. cities, Newark experienced the biggest influx of African Americans relative to its overall population.[38] The city that they moved into was one steadily on the decline. Manufacturers were leaving Newark for areas with lower taxes, less corruption, and better, newer infrastructure. Solid union jobs and apprenticeship programs were seldom available to black workers. In 1967, African Americans constituted well over 50 percent of Newark's population and yet of the 1,787 apprentices registered in Essex County, only 150 were black. White-collar employment was even more unlikely. In the 1960s, only 20 percent of Newark's black males worked in offices, compared to 43 percent of the city's white men. Considering the city's high school dropout rate was 32 percent—and the figure was probably higher because more than a quarter of students transferred, and they weren't tracked to see if they actually continued their educations—prospects for the future weren't remotely promising.[39]

Unfair, sometimes brutal treatment at the hands of the police and the courts had always been an issue among African Americans. As Newark's slums became increasingly black and the authorities remained overwhelmingly white, they came to view each other as enemies. Curtis Lucas's 1946 pulp novel, *Third Ward Newark,* told a story black Newarkers could certainly appreciate. Two young black women are abducted, raped, and left for dead by a pair of white men, and no one is ever brought to justice for the crime. Lucas wrote of police who were "callously indifferent to the looks of hatred that the colored people gave them."[40]

One incident that drew the attention and anger of the black community occurred in the Central Ward in the late summer of 1954. While walking down Springfield Avenue, a heavyset twenty-nine-year-old black man named Edward Taylor saw two policemen across the street confronting a group of African Americans on the sidewalk. When Taylor stopped to watch what was happening, police told him to keep moving. As Taylor told it, he was unable to hear the officer and crossed the street. He was arrested for telling the officers "in loud and abusive language," according to police, that the people on the sidewalk were doing nothing wrong. Taylor, who turned out to be the director of the New Jersey Negro Labor Council, testified that the two arresting officers beat him on the sidewalk and at the station house—the Fourth Precinct, where John Smith would be taken in 1967. With a broken nose, a cut lip, and a badly bruised right eye, Taylor said that the officers planted a five-inch knife on him to justify the arrest. He also argued that a man of his size, weighing three hundred pounds, with fallen arches and shortness of breath, was simply incapable of putting up much of a fight, yet Taylor was convicted of assault and battery, interfering with policemen, and other charges. At the end of the trial, the judge explained that the many witnesses testifying on Taylor's behalf seemed nervous on the stand, and there had been some contradictions in what was said. The two policemen, on the other hand, appeared sure of themselves and told the same story, the judge said.[41]

Another incident in early 1959, in which a black man stopped for traffic violations wound up needing thirty-seven stitches and several days in the hospital to recuperate from a police beating, sparked a forum of 250 African American ministers and businessmen. A *Newark News* reporter gathered quotes from leaders denouncing police brutality and discrimination against black people, but the story never ran in the newspaper. A *News* editor decided the story was too inflammatory.[42]

Still, Newark newspapers of the 1950s and 1960s were filled with stories of routine traffic stops or arrests for minor violations that mysteriously escalated and ended with a black man injured or dead. There were also plenty of reports of alleged African American criminals gunned down from behind by law enforcement. One night in the summer of 1965, an officer named Henry Martinez—who later became a long-serving city councilman—shot and killed twenty-two-year-old Lester Long, who had fled from police after being pulled over for traffic violations. Officer Martinez changed his story several times, first saying his gun had gone off accidentally, later that he'd carefully aimed and fired. After incidents such as the Long killing, Newark's African Americans felt they couldn't trust anything the police told them. The hatred festered. "The police were simply Devils to us, Beasts," Amiri Baraka wrote.[43]

Led by CORE and other civil rights groups, Newark African Americans in 1965 lobbied for a civilian review board in the hopes of stopping police brutality. Mayor Addonizio and the police department opposed the measure. They pointed out that over the past five years, police arrested more than a hundred thousand people, but only twenty-eight complaints of brutality had been made—and of those, the police had deemed every one unsubstantiated. CORE chairman Fred Means called the figures "very definitely misleading," arguing that African Americans didn't file complaints precisely because they were so frightened and distrustful of the police. In one way or another, the cops would always succeed in dismissing cries of brutality. An ACLU spokesperson likewise called the complaint statistics "fairly meaningless," stating that "for every complaint that's made, there are 50 or 100 that aren't made."[44]

That same summer, several African American leaders voiced concerns over the likelihood of a violent uprising in Newark. Executive director of the Urban League of Essex County James Pawley was one of many to call Newark a "powder keg," and identified the police as "the one big danger, as I see it." William D. Payne, a civil rights activist and youth organizer who would later be a New Jersey assemblyman, feared "a very serious possibility of racial violence" because none of the underlying issues of the black community had been addressed. "The cautious, responsible leaders are losing faith in negotiations," Payne said, while others were forming self-defense groups in preparation for what seemed like an inevitable clash with authorities.[45]

At the time, outbursts of racial violence and looting—"riots" in mainstream eyes, "rebellions" to others—were all but expected in U.S. cities once the weather warmed. There had been fifteen such incidents in 1964, nine in 1965, and 1966 would see thirty-eight more. Police brutality complaints were often the starting point of disturbances, including the two most serious riots up until that point, in Harlem in 1964, and in 1965 in the Watts section of Los Angeles, when thirty-four people were killed over a six-day span.[46]

Traditional protests and demonstrations had failed to yield many lasting, concrete results for African American citizens. Countless episodes of police brutality continued to go unpunished. Disillusioned with what they saw as the civil rights movement's failure to live up to the hype, and yet still desperate for solutions, many African Americans in Newark and elsewhere increasingly sympathized or openly supported radical militant leaders who didn't necessarily restrict themselves to peaceful means. "There are 22 million African Americans who are ready to fight for independence," Malcolm X said in a 1964 speech in New York. "I don't mean any non-violent fight, or turn-the-other-cheek fight. Those days are over. Those days are gone."[47]

Even among the many whites in and around Newark who supported civil rights, horror and indignation arose upon hearing the more provocative, threat-laced comments from Malcolm X, Stokely Carmichael, Amiri Baraka, and other black leaders—and those were the sorts of comments that most often made headlines. Baraka was always one to test—and cross over—boundaries, suggesting in one rambling essay from 1965 that white women should be raped, and that all whites "know in their deepest hearts they should be robbed."[48]

"Black Power," the new phrase repeated often in the African American community, inspired fear and anxiety among whites, as did a few widely publicized incidents in northern New Jersey. In one, several Black Muslims, who began appearing in Newark in significant numbers in the early 1960s, were implicated in the wild 1965 bank robbery in which Mayor Addonizio gave chase. Two Black Muslims in their twenties were arrested after the getaway car crashed, and soon thereafter police raided the mosque they belonged to on South Orange Avenue, breaking through the building's glass door when no one answered.[49] The episode seemed to prove what much of white America strongly suspected—that black militants were a dangerous, lawless bunch. Many citizens not only encouraged authorities to deal severely with such groups, they wished the police would use even more aggressive tactics.

The fact that by mid-1967 Newark had not already experienced a severe race riot surprised many observers. Tensions heightened early that summer, when hundreds of African Americans disrupted Board of Education meetings to protest Mayor Addonizio's decision to appoint James Callaghan—a councilman and former labor official with no college degree—to the lucrative post of board secretary. Wilbur Parker, the city's African American budget director, protestors argued, was far more qualified for the job. Parker had a CPA and extensive education training.[50]

In early June, a brawl nearly broke out at a city planning board meeting over the proposed New Jersey College of Medicine and Dentistry campus. The school's trustees had been reluctant to build in Newark, but Mayor Addonizio and city planners would not be denied. They promised the school 150 acres—

far, far more space than was necessary—for the campus, and the area selected was in the Central Ward. Many families found out about the planned campus via eviction notices from the Newark Housing Authority, the organization that for years had been ousting them from their homes and placing them in crowded public-housing projects. While the city said that perhaps three thousand people would be displaced, opponents of the school's construction estimated the figure at twenty-two thousand. Crowds of angry demonstrators held rallies and jeered decision-makers at public meetings, but it seemed they were powerless to stop or change plans already set in motion.[51]

The buildup of broken promises and ugly rhetoric stirred widespread distrust between the races. At any moment, it seemed, the coil that precariously maintained the peace in place could snap. "Allegations of prejudice, discrimination and racism, real or imagined, polarized the black and white citizens of Newark, with the whites thinking that outside agitators, communists, criminals, and hoodlums were inciting Negroes to violence," wrote Edward Williams, the city's highest-ranking black police officer in the 1960s. "Attitudes were fixed on both sides. There were whites on the police force that had never mingled with blacks in social situations. They had learned racism and prejudices at home from their parents and relatives who they believed and trusted." At the same time, the black community wasn't going to buy "the story that the police were going to treat everybody the same," Williams wrote.[52]

Mayor Hugh Addonizio appeared confident that he understood his city best, and that he could keep any matters under control. The South and Central wards, where trouble seemed most likely, were among Addonizio's most loyal bases of constituents dating back to his days in the New Jersey Senate. Upon arrival in office, Addonizio rewarded his friends, becoming the first mayor to appoint African Americans to prominent administrative posts. Newark's best-known black politician, Councilman Irvine Turner, was an Addonizio protégé, and one of the mayor's strongest allies. To the NAACP and other civil rights groups, Turner was a flashy, unprincipled demagogue, motivated mainly by his desires to stay in office and keep his powerful friends in City Hall happy. Turner welcomed the coming of each Central Ward housing project as a feather in his cap. He often praised Mayor Addonizio's efforts to ease tensions between blacks and the police. In July of 1965, while civil rights leaders saw race riots looming for Newark, Turner claimed credit for the previous summer's calm, and assessed the current state of race relations by saying, "Looks pretty good to me."[53]

The growing, undeniable consensus among African Americans, and much of the city for that matter, was that Addonizio, Turner, and the rest of the municipal government were shamelessly crooked. In the eyes of many,

Addonizio ran the city hand in hand with organized crime leaders and "a crew of niggers and Negroes crawling around him that would make any honest person's hair stand on end," as Amiri Baraka wrote.[54]

"There's a price on everything at City Hall" became a familiar chorus. Newark officials seemed shockingly friendly with organized crime figures. Abner "Longy" Zwillman, the city's crime boss since the 1920s, was long gone, found hanged in the basement of his West Orange home in 1959. (The death was officially ruled a suicide, despite wrist marks that indicated Zwillman had been tied before being strung up.) But the Boiardo crew was still very much alive. Insiders said that the real man in charge of Addonizio-era Newark was not the mayor, but his old friend, Tony Boy Boiardo, son of Zwillman's old partner, the infamous Richie "the Boot" Boiardo. For years, city agencies in Newark had been referred to only half-jokingly as "the steal works." Graft was assumed, political connections and payoffs were guaranteed routes to success, and from the perspective of Newarkers of all races, the city's leaders had collectively sold them out.

———

Mayor Addonizio met with a group of African American politicians, civil rights organizers, and assorted other representatives on Thursday afternoon, July 13, 1967, the day after disturbances centered on the Fourth Precinct. The group, who later characterized the meeting as "long" and "inconclusive," issued three demands: the suspension of the two officers who arrested John Smith; the establishment of a panel to investigate the previous night's disorder; and the promotion of a black police officer to the position of captain. Addonizio asked for a couple of days to consider the requests, steadfastly clinging to the theory that tensions would subside. "The people are fantastically aggrieved," warned CORE's Robert Curvin, who attended the powwow with Addonizio. "You can look at it as an isolated incident if you want to, but it's not just Smith the taxi driver whose arrest Wednesday night touched off the disturbance."[55]

Throughout Thursday afternoon, the neighborhood around the Fourth Precinct was flooded with leaflets with the heading "STOP! POLICE BRUTALITY," announcing a rally at the station house at 7:30 that night. By the early evening, a handful of TV cameras were ready to roll, and a small group of picketers paraded in front of the precinct. A much larger group, numbering around three hundred, assembled to watch from across the street near the Hayes Homes. Within minutes of the first speaker addressing the crowd, bottles and rocks lofted from the housing project crashed into the precinct. Rally organizers scurried to safety. One woman then approached the station house with a long metal pole and methodically bashed the building's street-level windows.[56]

The onslaught of rocks and other projectiles continued as a few dozen policemen brandishing nightsticks stormed out of the station house. Backup from other precincts quickly arrived. A rock smashed through the window of one police van, sending splintered glass into the eyes of a sergeant riding inside. Garbage cans and stones crashed into patrol cars. A block away from the main action, near the General Electric plant, a car burst into flames. Responding firemen were met with rocks tossed from across the street and from twelve stories up, atop the Hayes Homes. As Tom Hayden, a white civil rights activist based at the time in Newark, later observed, the projects proved to be "a useful terrain for people making war."[57]

Looting and vandalism ensued, mainly along a fifteen-block section of the Central Ward's main shopping thoroughfare, Springfield Avenue. Young men picked up ash cans, hurled them through plate-glass windows, and ran off with radios, TVs, and bottles of liquor. "There were shifts of people at work," wrote Amiri Baraka, who drove slowly down Springfield in a Volkswagen van that night, before being pulled over, beaten, and arrested by a group of police officers that included an Italian high school classmate of Baraka's. "The window breakers would come first. Whash! Glass all over everywhere. Then the getters would get through and get to the getting. Some serious people would park near the corner and load up their trunks, make as many trips as the traffic would bear. Some people would run through the streets with the shit, what they could carry or roll or drag or pull. Families worked together, carrying sofas and TVs collectively down the street. All the shit they saw on television that they had been hypnotized into wanting they finally had a chance to cop."[58]

Smoke poured out of a toy store set on fire. The shelves and racks of dress stores and laundromats were emptied. "I saw people whom I had known for years to be law-abiding citizens caught up in the fever of lawlessness," wrote police officer Edward Williams, who as one of the few blacks in the department worked with community relations. "Openly, I saw a mother carrying a lamp she had taken from a store window and her young son following behind her with the matching shade. Fathers and sons were operating in teams, ripping away protective screens from liquor store windows and carting away merchandise by the cases."[59]

Police focused on containing the damage to Springfield Avenue. At one point, twenty cops around Springfield and South Tenth Street pointed their guns at a second-story window where a white man held a shotgun of his own, perhaps with the idea of stopping the looting. "Drop it!" police shouted. "Just drop it!" The area quieted briefly around midnight, leading Mayor Addonizio and Police Director Spina to believe the situation was "pretty well in hand" in the mayor's words. He hadn't asked for help from the state police, whose log book summed up the situation in Newark soon after midnight: "Bands of eight to 15 people traveling on foot and in cars, looting and starting fires. Four policemen injured, four new areas have broken out in the past 15 minutes. There is still no organization within the Newark Police Department."[60]

As early as 10:10 PM, Newark policemen had begun dialing the state police for assistance. Newark cops were told such requests had to come via the mayor. At 2:20 AM, with the entire fourteen hundred-person Newark Police Department called to duty and the city still out of control, Addonizio finally relented and called Governor Richard Hughes. Until then, there had been a scant few unsubstantiated reports of gunfire, but no one had been shot or killed. Sometime after midnight, however, as crime sprees spread to different sections of Newark, looters broke into a Sears, Roebuck on Elizabeth Avenue and made off with twenty-four rifles. Addonizio felt he had no choice but to call for help, and, in the words of Governor Hughes, the "quite upset" mayor "insisted on the deployment of the state police and National Guardsmen to the maximum extent possible."[61]

Governor Hughes, Mayor Addonizio, Director Spina, and leaders of the state police and National Guard met before daybreak on Friday, July 14. After some arguing, it was decided that Spina would remain in charge of Newark's police, while the state troopers would lead the National Guardsmen in a joint operation. The arrangement was a disaster. The general leading the National Guard maintained that his units were *not* under the command of the state police. Each of the three groups operated on different radio frequencies. Routine information regarding fires, looter activity, or the movement of law enforcement squads wasn't shared. Confusingly, the city was divided into six, then eight, and finally twelve sectors to be patrolled, and there weren't enough maps to go around. Only Newark policemen and firemen received calls from citizens, and state police and National Guardsmen were generally unsure what to do other than follow local authorities and provide support. National Guardsmen had received a total of eight hours of riot training, which concentrated mainly on crowd control, so the more than five thousand New Jersey troops sent into Newark were unprepared to cope with the chaos on their hands. The city's police force was even more clueless, without any riot training whatsoever. Director Spina later testified that he purposefully decided against such training because it would only "incense the Negroes" and result in "more problems than it was worth." Thus, the entirety of the police department's preparations for quelling a riot consisted of ordering twenty-five new shotguns, which arrived in Newark in early July, 1967.[62]

Governor Hughes, who for the duration of the disturbance appeared exasperated behind his Buddy Holly eyeglasses and a loosened necktie, ordered several emergency regulations on Friday, July 14. Cars were banned from Newark roads between 10 PM and 6 AM. A civilian curfew extended from 11 PM to 6 AM. All sporting-goods stores, bars, and liquor stores were closed, and the sale or possession of alcoholic beverages was prohibited. By early afternoon on Friday, blockades had been set up and manned with a mix of guardsmen and state and local police at 137 intersections around the main riot areas. Normal city activity ground to a halt. Fires dotted downtown and areas west, and for a time, traffic had to be detoured around Broad Street because of an out-of-control blaze between Branford Place and Market Street. Jurors at the Essex County Courthouse were given the day off. Employees at City Hall, PSE&G, banks, insurance companies, and most other businesses were sent home by lunchtime. Prudential decided not to open at all, and early in the morning had alerted all nine thousand of its workers at the downtown headquarters that they should stay home.[63]

The looting had continued in the Springfield Avenue area through the night and into the light of day on Friday. Hoarding everything from lamps to liquor, as well as groceries, cribs, dressers, clothing, and baby carriages, Central Ward residents trotted down filthy, brick-paved streets and sidewalks littered with shattered glass and broken metal gates. As late as 1 PM, people were openly snatching items from a jewelry store.[64] By then, a pattern emerged revealing that the looting wasn't completely random. White-owned stores with reputations for taking advantage of black customers were targeted first and robbed and vandalized. By contrast, African American shops and restaurants—some of which were spray-painted with "SOUL BROTHER" or other words signifying a black-owned business—were left unharmed.[65]

Law enforcement pushed farther into the riot areas, and arrests and injuries piled up. More than nine hundred people were arrested on Friday alone. At first, Newark police seemed reluctant to fire their weapons. After the Thursday night rally at the Fourth Precinct escalated to throwing rocks and looting stores, Deputy Chief John Redden made an announcement over the police radio: "Firearms may be used when your own or another's life is in danger and no other means are available to defend yourself or apprehend an offender." Director Spina—Redden's superior—followed that message with one of his own. "If you have a gun, whether it's a shoulder weapon or whether it is a handgun, use it."[66]

By daybreak on Friday, three Newarkers, all black, were dead: sixteen-year-old James Sanders, slain by a policeman's shotgun blast after robbing a Sampson's Liquor Store at the corner of Springfield and Jones; twenty-eight-year-old Tedock Bell, another looter, shot while fleeing from cops; and Mary Helen Campbell, forty, died when her car collided with a fire engine. That morning, forty-year-old Jessie May Jones was killed with a bullet to the back of the head on the front stoop of her Fairmount Avenue home.[67]

Surreal, apocalyptic scenes filled the weekend. Tank sightings became routine. Jeeps covered with barbed wire parked in the middle of streets to serve as checkpoints. In tense standoffs, white police forces pointed bayoneted rifles at groups of angry, unarmed African Americans who refused to shuffle on home. A black man on a street full of looters hollered at a teenage boy, "I told you not to come down here," and then slapped the young man after he whined, "Everybody else is!"[68] Police cars eased slowly down roads with rifles pointed in every direction from the windows. Newspapers were filled with photos of giddy, smiling looters, projecting an atmosphere that Governor Hughes compared to laughing at a funeral. A white businessman whose store hadn't yet been looted was spotted painting the word "SOUL" on the window. "What else can I do?" he said. "If they don't get me tonight, they'll come around tomorrow. I can't think of anything else to do."[69] A confectionary store set up a grill on one riot-torn street corner and did brisk business selling barbecued ribs. At police headquarters, officers taunted a woman picked up for looting and invited the media over to snap photos as they piled up electric irons, a hair dryer, and other items at her feet. "Smile, Miss Looter, you're on Candid Camera," one police officer said, as the woman cried and tried to hide her face.[70] Fire department officials in Engine Company 6 looked out the window and saw dark figures directly across the street brashly throwing Molotov cocktails into a Springfield Avenue baby-goods store. National Guardsmen poured out of trucks to greetings of glass bottles and rocks crashing at their feet, tossed from nearby housing projects.[71]

Many of the National Guard troops lived in middle-class, 99 percent white towns and had never been to Newark; some were from as far away as South Jersey. Few socialized with blacks, and all feared for their safety, especially in light of the reports circulating among law enforcement agencies. One story had it that a car with North Carolina plates filled with dynamite was en route to the riot area. An FBI report from Buffalo stated that twenty or thirty carloads of black youths were spotted heading from Detroit to Newark. Rumors similarly streamed through the African American community—that the police had formed concentration camps, that authorities were plotting to poison the water supply.[72]

All of the stories fed into the idea that Newark wasn't merely in the middle of a racial disturbance: this was war. There were even, apparently, snipers, just like the ongoing war in Southeast Asia, which Americans viewed nightly on TV. From the moment the Newark police received backup in the form of hundreds and hundreds of state police and National Guardsmen, word spread that snipers were targeting law enforcement officers and firemen. From July 14 to 17, there were no fewer than seventy-nine reports of sniper activity.[73] "Every time you think things are under control, sniping breaks out," said Mayor Addonizio after meeting with Newark clergymen to brainstorm ways to end the violence. "It's like Vietnam."[74]

At 7:30 on Friday night, Police Detective Fred Toto was shot and killed, reportedly by a sniper holed up in the Stella Wright housing project. Around the same time, firefighters—who over a five-day stretch received 364 calls, when ordinarily a dozen calls constituted a busy day—were on Prince Street battling blazes in a string of three-story brick structures that had been looted the night before. The firemen said snipers were shooting at them from fourteen stories up at the nearby Scudder Homes project, prompting police to evacuate the building before blasting away hundreds of rounds with revolvers and machine guns. Dozens of families who had fled their apartments watched from the street as bullets chipped away at the bricks and shattered nearly every window on the top six floors. No snipers were found. Police said they must have escaped through the building's cellar.[75]

As news spread that night of Detective Toto's death and the shootings of two other policemen, who would survive, the authorities increasingly turned on the offensive. "The line between the jungle and the law might as well be drawn here as well as any place in America," Governor Hughes said on Friday evening. In the few hours between the time Toto was slain and midnight, four African Americans were shot and killed, including ten-year-old Eddie Moss, who was riding in a car when a bullet hit him behind the right ear. At midnight on Friday, the body count stood at fourteen, all but one from bullet wounds.[76] About a hundred civilians suffered gunshot wounds before daybreak on Saturday.

Reports of snipers continued through Saturday night, and police and troopers continued returning fire at the elusive phantom gunmen. Shots sporadically sprayed fire houses. Gunfire around Engine Company 6, one block from the Hayes Homes, grew intense enough on early Saturday evening that officials abandoned the building. Calls came in regarding a sniper on top of the Columbus Homes in the North Ward, and police rushed to the scene and began exchanging fire with men who turned out to be National Guardsmen. Seven more people were killed on Saturday, including Michael

Moran, a forty-one-year-old captain in the fire department. Late on Saturday night, Eloise Spellman, a mother of eleven living in the Hayes Homes, was in her tenth-floor apartment when she died from a shotgun blast in the neck. Authorities said she was caught in crossfire between National Guardsmen and a sniper.[77]

Doctors and nurses in area hospitals worked triple shifts to keep up with the casualties. More than three hundred riot-related injuries were treated on Friday, and an additional four hundred on Saturday. Most of the injuries were caused by glass—thrown bottles, shards from broken store windows—and countless cuts had to be stitched. The city's prison system was likewise overwhelmed trying to cope with the mass arrests—more than sixteen hundred before order was restored. African Americans chained together in fours were transported to holding cells in everything from Essex County sheriff's vans, to ambulances, and even rented trucks. When regular jails filled, detainees were cordoned off into iron cages that normally served as storerooms in an old city armory.[78] "This is really mass production," said one sheriff's officer processing those arrested.[79]

The streets quieted considerably on Sunday, July 16, when downtown was nearly deserted and a comparatively small number of people (120) were arrested. James Ruttledge, a nineteen-year-old black man, was the only person killed by gunfire. Police said that on late Sunday afternoon they interrupted Ruttledge in the act of looting a Bergen Street tavern. He was shot at least six times.[80]

Late on Sunday, Governor Hughes and other government decision makers met with community activists and African American leaders, who repeatedly told the authorities that the presence of the state police and National Guard was doing more harm than good. Earlier that day, in the wee hours before daybreak, citizens witnessed at least a dozen separate incidents in which law enforcement officers broke the glass, robbed, or shot their guns at previously unharmed businesses emblazoned with "SOUL BROTHER" or other messages of African American solidarity. The owner of a clothing shop on Clinton Avenue said that troopers smashed the window of his store, where a sign read, "This Is Not a Race Riot." Leon Ewing, a home-repair contractor who lived above his shop on Bergen Street, looked out his window at two state police cars and a National Guard truck. "At first I thought they were shooting up into the air," Ewing said. "But then they stopped outside the restaurant across the street and just shot into it."[81] Nancy Ferguson, owner of a furniture and appliance business, confronted three policemen outside her shop, also on Bergen Street, after she heard guns being fired at around 3 AM. "Step aside," police ordered. "We will kill you." Ferguson testified that she said, "Well, I am here to die." Police left, walked around the corner, and shot their guns into the furniture store.[82]

Black-owned businesses weren't the only targets. Eighteen bullets were found lodged in the Black Muslim mosque on South Orange Avenue—the same mosque that police had busted open in 1965 because its members were involved in the widely publicized bank robbery broken up by Mayor Addonizio. "There were no snipers in our building, and it was late at night," the mosque's minister, James 3X, said. Gustav Heningburg, then a Trinity Cathedral public-affairs official, said at the time that the black community was less frightened by the rioters than by the police, who were "going through retaliation rather than protection."[83]

Per Governor Hughes's order, nearly all of the state troopers and National Guardsmen began leaving Newark at mid-afternoon on Monday, July 17. A group of citizens, concerned that it was too early for the pull-out, signed a petition asking the mayor to keep the troops patrolling the streets, but it wasn't Mayor Addonizio's decision to make. Police arrested an additional seventy people on Monday, and one of the disturbance's most tragic deaths occurred just before 1 PM, when twelve-year-old Michael Pugh was shot while emptying a garbage pail on the sidewalk in front of his house on Fifteenth Avenue. Pugh's family said the bullet, which hit Michael in the gut, came from the direction of a group of National Guardsmen gathered one block away.[84] Even so, the worst of the violence, and nearly all of the $10 million in property damage, was in the past.

———

Why? The media attempted to get to the heart of that big question from the first hint of disorder. Why did demonstrations so swiftly evolve into the chaos of rock-throwing, looting, and vandalism? From the mainstream perspective, there was no viable justification whatsoever for such rampant lawlessness. "What happened in Newark last night and early today was nothing less than criminality, initially disguised as protest," the *Newark News* wrote in an editorial on Friday, July 14. "How this outbreak can serve the cause of civil rights, including more jobs and better housing for Negroes, is impossible to understand." A *News* editorial two days later blamed "marauding bands of criminals acting under the guise of protest" for the widespread destruction and loss of life. "Protest was the level under which shootings, arson and robbery were wantonly carried out . . . in large part by a desire for jobs. Could anything be more senseless or illogical?"[85]

In the same line of thinking, Governor Hughes said, "Many of the looters would have [stolen goods] every day if they could. They just wanted the fur coats and television sets. They weren't upset about injustices."[86] A *Chicago Sun-Times* cartoon showed two dark figures carrying looted booty down a street lined with broken windows and burning buildings, as well as a body lying on the sidewalk. The caption read "Freedom March—1967 Style."[87]

Some conservative Newarkers of color—older folks in particular—basically agreed with the mainstream assessment. "It doesn't make sense, all this drinking and looting and carrying on," said Joseph Davis, a black forty-one-year-old landscaper. "Discrimination isn't at the bottom of this. It's just violence."[88]

From the perspective of most of Newark's black community, however, rioters weren't simply taking advantage of the chaotic environment. "These people couldn't speak, and now they're speaking in the only way they know how," said Fred Means, a former head of CORE. When asked by a reporter why the riot happened, a young, neatly dressed African American man on Market Street said, "You'll find your answer in the hearts of the men who run this country. That's all I have to say." Another black man, twenty-nine-year-old William Smith, believed that the riot "doesn't solve anything, but we were due for it," he told a reporter. "When you suppress something, it's bound to explode."[89]

The theories that outside agitators or a relatively small number of hardened criminals were responsible for the riots didn't hold up upon inspection. No proof ever came to light that the looting and violence were organized or coordinated in any way. "Yes, it was agitation, agitation of neglect and harassment and prejudice," one young black mother said. "People want to blame outsiders so they can pretend that the niggers on their own plantation are too happy to riot."[90] Of the approximately sixteen hundred people arrested, all but a few lived in Newark or surrounding towns. The majority (73 percent) was employed, and only 20 percent had previous convictions.[91]

One generalization that could be made of the looters is that they were overwhelmingly young. Half were twenty-four or younger, and three-quarters were under thirty-three. Compared to older African Americans, who grew up with racism and discrimination as assumed, unalterable facts of life, younger generations who came of age with the civil rights movement viewed the unjust state of affairs with a heightened sense of outrage and disgust.

"We ain't riotin' agains' all you whites," a twenty-four-year-old African American named William Furr said to a *Life* magazine reporter on Saturday, July 15. "We're riotin' agains' police brutality, like that cab driver they beat up the other night. That stuff goes on all the time. When the police treat us like people 'stead of treatin' us like animals, then the riots will stop." In between loading goods stolen from a liquor store into a car on Avon Street, Furr offered the reporter a beer. "If the cops show up, get rid of it and run like hell," Furr said. Moments after Furr spoke with the reporter, police arrived. Furr ran down the sidewalk, and an officer in a yellow riot helmet fired his shotgun, killing the twenty-four-year-old man who actually lived in well-to-do Montclair, not Newark. People who tried to come to his aid were beaten with the butts of police shotguns and rifles.[92]

The Furr incident was one of many from July of 1967 that made little sense—at the time, or in retrospect. Stealing cases of beer wasn't going to help end discrimination or corruption, or to win African Americans jobs. The overreaction by police wasn't going to stop the riot, and it certainly wouldn't ease racial tensions. If anything, the harsh police tactics only inflamed hatred and resentment between blacks and whites.

Newark, just a few short miles from the media capital of the world, was summarily deemed the epitome of a city gone wrong, a clear display of the complete breakdown of race relations. *Newsweek* called Newark "a textbook example of a city in crisis." Russia's state newspaper took the opportunity to criticize the capitalist system, commenting that the Newark riots were caused by poverty and unemployment that wouldn't exist under a Communist regime.[93] The cover of that week's *Life* was even more infamous than the story inside of William Furr. In the photo, a twelve-year-old black boy named Joe Bass laid flat on his belly on a Newark street, with his cheek planted into the blacktop and his left arm twisted at a painfully awkward angle. He wore a long-sleeve striped shirt, jeans frayed at the knees, and filthy, tattered canvas sneakers. The boy had just been shot—by police gunning for William Furr—and ripples of blood stained the street around him.

A week later, the cover of *Life* showed the silhouette of police troopers patrolling amid a backdrop of buildings aflame in Detroit. That city's riot—one of 128 racial disturbances in the United States in 1967, including those in Plainfield, New Brunswick, Englewood, and elsewhere in New Jersey—was the summer's most destructive, surpassing Newark's in terms of deaths (43) and arrests (7,000).

Newark may not have been left with the stigma of hosting the worst race riot in U.S. history, but the bad blood between whites and people of color in the city would be a bitter, lasting legacy. Governor Hughes ordered that a commission create a report studying the causes and circumstances of the 1967 riots in New Jersey, and some of the most telling details were how differently the races perceived the events that had just taken place. "Attitudinally, whites and Negroes are in two almost separate worlds," the groundbreaking report said. As to the underlying reasons for the riots, African Americans most often named bad housing, unemployment, breaking of official promises, and police brutality. Whites surveyed, on the other hand, put completely different causes on the top of their lists, including outside troublemakers, criminals and hoodlums, and the search for excitement. Likewise, whereas African Americans were far more likely to characterize the behavior of law enforcement during the riots as "too tough," a large proportion of whites believed police were too soft with the rioters.[94]

Even the statistics—supposed facts—from the commission report can and have been viewed from varied perspectives. The most commonly quoted number of deaths in the riot is twenty-six, but only twenty-three of those deaths came from gunfire. A woman killed in a car crash with a fire engine, as well as a narcotics overdose and a sixty-eight-year-old woman's heart attack have also regularly been attributed to the riot. It has widely been assumed that police forces were responsible for all of the shooting deaths, but their bullets did not kill twenty-three people. Within a week of the riot's end, for example, a thirty-two-year-old black man confessed that while drunk and firing a gun at cars on the morning Friday, July 14, he inadvertently shot and killed Jessie May Jones on her front stoop.[95] Among the hundreds arrested, many were charged with possessing weapons such as shotguns, pistols, knives, brass knuckles, firebombs, and at least one machine gun.[96]

Because Newark policemen often used their own guns rather than those issued by the department, there was no way of knowing exactly who killed who, or even how many bullets local police shot. State police and National Guardsmen, on the other hand, tracked their every shot, and the number of rounds fired was astonishing: 2,905 and 10,414 respectively. "The amount of ammunition expended by police forces was out of all proportion to the mission assigned to them," the commission's report stated.[97]

At the same time, the report found no definitive proof of snipers. At best, "there may have been some organized sniping activity once the riot had reached its Friday peak," the report stated. No snipers were ever arrested, even with the governor offering clemency to any looter with information leading to the capture of a sniper. A *Life* reporter supposedly met with some snipers during the riot, but the gunmen only admitted to shooting up in the air to distract the police. Certainly, many of the "snipers" were in fact bumbling law enforcement officers firing on fellow men in uniform due to poor communications and altogether chaotic, terrifying circumstances. If any snipers did exist, they were awful shots. Only one policeman and one fireman were killed during the riots; all others who died were black civilians.

Regardless of the facts, and regardless that both sides of the conflict had exhibited less than honorable behavior, most people involved in the riots defended their actions at the time, and for years to come. They were entrenched in their beliefs—on the one side that the black community was increasingly being taken over by ignorance and lawlessness and therefore needed to be controlled, and on the other that the authorities were corrupt racists who eagerly dealt out vigilante justice and suppressed people of color. A city thus divided could not hold itself together for long. Some sort of resolution had to occur, and the next natural step seemed to be for the largest ethnic group in Newark to seize control.

African Americans not only constituted the majority in Newark, they were also clearly desperately pushed to the brink. "Almost suicidal" was how a leading African American psychologist interviewed on WCBS radio during the riots characterized the community actively participating in the disturbance. "In some unconscious, or maybe not so unconscious, incoherent way, the rioting people are saying, 'We want this destroyed.' They're saying, 'It's the only way we'll get change.'"[98] Dr. Martin Luther King Jr., while supporting the use of federal troops to suppress riots, agreed with the psychologist's point of view. "Revolts come out of revolting conditions," King commented after violence erupted in Detroit. "A riot is the language of the unheard. It is a suicidal act—that last desperate act—when the Negro says, 'I'm tired of living like a dog.'"[99]

One of the many startling photographs taken during the Newark riots showed poet-playwright LeRoi Jones (Amiri Baraka) after his arrest. The image was displayed around the world during the summer of 1967, and would be made into posters that decorated radical students' dorm-room walls for decades. In the photo, Jones sits in a wheelchair and stares into the camera with a fierce, determined scowl. His head is covered in bandages—the result of a thorough clubbing by police, Jones said—and he is handcuffed to his wheelchair. A week after his arrest, Jones, who was rapidly emerging as an icon and a spokesperson in the black community, told reporters that a transfer of power in his hometown would be the inevitable result of his people's struggle. "We will govern ourselves," he said, "or no one will govern Newark, New Jersey."[100]

CHAPTER 7

THE WORST AMERICAN CITY

A TRANSFER OF POWER AND THE DIRE 1970S

In New Jersey Governor Richard Hughes's view, "any other site" would have been preferable to Newark to host the first-ever Black Power Conference.[1] Regardless, in midsummer 1967, some 1,300 representatives of 190 African American organizations gathered to discuss the state of black America, foster unity among the disparate groups coming from thirty-nine states, and plot a course for empowerment.[2]

The conference opened as scheduled on Thursday, July 20, 1967. The National Guard and state police had pulled out of Newark only a few days earlier. Block after block in the Central Ward still looked like a war zone, with dark, empty stores smoldering in ashes, buildings pocked by gunfire, and broken glass and refuse everywhere. Around the nation, racial disturbances had either erupted or would soon in spots such as Cincinnati, Ohio; New York City's Spanish Harlem; Cambridge, Maryland; Plainfield, New Jersey; and most violently of all, Detroit. Destruction, looting, and killing may have ceased in Newark, but anger and tensions remained dangerously high. On the Black Power Conference's opening day, delegates physically removed a white reporter from a press event, pushing him through a ground-floor window. Two days later, delegates who didn't want the media at one session smashed TV cameras and threw chairs at three dozen newsmen, including a few African Americans. Bruised and bleeding reporters escaped through a window. Some were chased by delegates down an alley to shouts of "We don't want Whitey here!"[3]

Most delegates disapproved of the assaults on the media, according to a conference spokesperson, who called the incidents symbolic of the "self-destructive syndrome of oppressed people."[4] A fair share of conference attendees, however, either supported or refused to condemn such attacks. For that matter, the conference's diverse assortment of African Americans—with delegates from the moderate NAACP and Urban League, as well as representatives from far more militant, revolutionary groups—agreed upon little else other than the fact that the system of racial oppression in the United States needed to be addressed.[5]

The real differences among delegates came to light as they debated in workshops devoted to topics such as "Black Power through Economic Development" and "Black Professionals and Black Power." As *Newsweek* pointed out, "the array of costumes" worn by attendees dramatized the range of philosophies represented. For example, Ron Karenga, head of the black nationalist organization US, which was born in the wake of the Watts riots, wore "orange on pale green kimono-like shirts," while delegates from more conservative groups "looked drearily conservative in business suits."[6] Afros and dark sunglasses were popular among young hipsters, but there were also a number of delegates with short, straightened hair and thin, old-fashioned mustaches.

One contingent sought the quickest, most practical means for improving the lives of black people—methods for "pumping the system for all it's worth," as one put it. Others wanted nothing short of revolution through quasi-socialist arrangements. "You've got to change the whole system," an elderly delegate said. "I don't want to be exploited by a black man any more than I want to be exploited by a white man." Another called capitalism "the most successful system of enforced exploitation in the world" and "the latest model of slavery."[7]

Whenever debates devolved into chaos, calls for harmony were sounded. "I want to know if Black Power is about love and unity and R-E-S-P-E-C-T," one woman wearing a colorful, flowing robe cried out to calm an argument.[8]

One particularly sensitive issue—the ongoing racial disturbances in U.S. cities—was the elephant in the room that couldn't be ignored. "We have to distinguish between riots and revolts," said US chief Ron Karenga. "Riots are illegal. A revolt is legitimate because it is what a people must do in order to express self-defense, self-determination, and self-direction."[9]

One proposed resolution, to "strongly endorse the black revolution in all its glorious manifestations," which presumably included violence, arson, and looting, was tabled after a series of arguments. Instead, a statement was issued supporting the creation of paramilitary defense units for black communities.[10]

Religion was another divisive topic. After spirited debate, Christianity was labeled "a white religion that had taken the diamonds and minerals of the world in exchange for the Bible—a bad deal."[11] Curiously enough, Dr. Nathan

Wright, the head of the conference's planning committee and unofficial host of the gathering, was, in fact, a Newark-based Episcopalian minister.

Consensus or not, by the time the four-day conference ended, delegates adopted a mixed bag of eighty resolutions. They included calls for a national holiday to celebrate black heroes such as Malcolm X, a nationwide "buy black" movement, the creation of a black university with subsidiary schools in every U.S. city, and a "Hell no, won't go!" approach to the draft. One workshop urged a boycott of the 1968 Olympics by all black athletes and spectators unless Muhammad Ali was reinstated as boxing champ. (Ali had recently been stripped of his crown for refusing military induction based on his religious convictions as a Muslim.) Delegates officially rejected the word "Negro" and sought national discussions to partition the United States into two countries, one black and one white. Resolutions supported Arab claims against Israel and North Vietnamese efforts to counter bombing by U.S. forces. After a discussion on pregnancy, a resolution passed refusing all birth-control programs. "We are quietly eliminating ourselves for these white people," one speaker said, drawing a standing ovation.[12]

The venting in conference forums put a muddled array of opinions on display. Despite what an adopted resolution stated regarding planned pregnancies, for example, many black women viewed a boycott on birth control as another source of oppression—by black men who would give their women little say on whether they should have children, or how many they should have. Still, most conference attendees believed a strong semblance of union was necessary. Black Power would be most powerful if it had unanimous support. There was no room for dissension, many delegates believed. They adopted an unbending resolution reading: "Every black church and all religious institutions that do not join the black revolution shall be boycotted, ostracized, criticized, publicized and rejected by the black community."[13]

———

During the conference, crowds never tired of cheering the frequent mentions of Black Power movement heroes such as boxing champ Ali and Robert Williams. The latter, author of the 1962 book *Negroes with Guns*, had been among the first activists advocating violent (not passive) self-defense. The NAACP suspended Williams for his aggressive stance, and he had fled the United States to live in exile in Cuba and, at the time of the conference, in China. Another of the movement's most popular figures was a Newark native and one of the many people arrested during the city's recent civic disturbance. He was also a conference attendee: poet-playwright LeRoi Jones, who later renamed himself Amiri Baraka.

A thin five-foot, eight-inch figure, Baraka was a charismatic whirlwind of activity, always juggling a handful of projects—writing essays and poems, organizing protests, brainstorming Afrocentric educational programs, raising money for theater projects. His energy seemed boundless. While on trial for a weapons charge, he busied himself in court by writing a play satirizing black celebrities. Few people were more comfortable in front of a crowd. At the podium, his voice rolled smoothly and his hands swiftly fluttered while enunciating one of his poems, quoting Malcolm X, or speaking off the cuff about jazz, colonial history, or Marxism. He frequently wore a bushy beard, and, based on photos from the 1960s, his brow seemed permanently furrowed. Baraka, or Jones as he was known in his early years, earned his first literary successes alongside white Beat Generation friends such as Allen Ginsberg. By the mid-1960s, Baraka became an avowed black nationalist, turning his back on his white bohemian artist peers as well as his first wife, who was also white. Baraka's various incarnations were marked by dramatic changes to his artwork, political stances, and lifestyle. He would leap full-fledged into one or another belief system only to drop it suddenly and completely—and expect his followers to do the same. Yet despite the inconsistencies, the tiny man with an enormous presence always managed to project an air of the utmost confidence, pressing forward with his hunched-over stride and asserting his views with unwavering conviction.

From Baraka's perspective, being arrested and bludgeoned by police during the summer of 1967 propelled him more determinedly than ever in his shift from artist-intellectual to militant activist. "I felt transformed, literally shot into the eye of the black hurricane of coming revolution," Baraka wrote in his autobiography. "It was a war, for us, a war of liberation. One had to organize, one had to arm, one had to mobilize and educate the people."[14]

In the years following the Newark riots, race seemed to drive Baraka's every action. Yet not long beforehand, the man had attempted to live an existence that essentially transcended traditional racial boundaries. Born in Newark in 1934 and raised in a middle-class family, the young Baraka befriended kids of all ethnicities. After high school, he attended Rutgers-Newark and later, Howard University, but was nearly as unhappy among Howard's elite black bourgeoisie as he was with the largely white student body at Rutgers. To the disillusioned, mischievous, hip young Baraka, both schools were square. In one well-known story from his Howard days, Baraka and a friend found a prominent spot to split a watermelon as a way to mock the racial stereotype. The college's president wasn't amused with the prank, and Baraka was eventually suspended and sent back to face his disappointed parents in Newark.[15]

After a stint in the air force, the young man who always felt like an outsider gravitated to New York City's Greenwich Village in its mid-1950s Beat Generation heyday. He studied literature at Columbia University, wrote poetry, socialized in intellectual circles, and worked at a jazz magazine called *Record Changer*, where conversations about Kafka with a co-worker named Hettie Cohen evolved into a romantic affair. Cohen was an artsy Jewish woman in her twenties who felt alienated from her traditional Queens family. She fell in love with her fellow lost soul, the man she called Roi, despite the scandal then inherent in a mixed-race relationship—or perhaps partly because of it. Cohen became pregnant in 1958, and as per their bohemian lifestyle, they decided to marry in a Buddhist temple. Hettie's family disowned her.[16]

A few months before the couple wed, they began jointly publishing a literary journal called *Yugen*, "profound mystery" in Japanese. Early issues of *Yugen* included works by its editor, LeRoi Jones, as well as Allen Ginsberg, Gary Snyder, Jack Kerouac, Gregory Corso, Robert Creeley, and other cutting-edge writers who would one day become mainstays in college English courses. Hettie and LeRoi Jones's West Twentieth Street apartment became a hangout for *Yugen* contributors as well as musicians, writers, and artists of all colors.[17]

As Hettie raised their daughter, and became pregnant with another, her husband's career began to take off, with poems and essays in literary magazines such as *Evergreen Review*. In 1961 his first book, a collection of poetry called *Preface to a Twenty Volume Suicide Note* was published with the dedication "This book is Hettie's." By 1963, LeRoi Jones's acclaimed book on jazz, *Blues People: Negro Music in White America*, had been published. He'd earned status as a minor celebrity; the magazine *Ebony* featured a picture of the rising literary star. The Jones's marriage was disintegrating, however, due partly to LeRoi's philandering, and probably more so to his increasingly antiwhite sentiments. "Some people were beginning to say that hypocritical Roi talked black but married white," Hettie wrote in her autobiography. "Others, more directly, said he was laying with the Devil."[18]

LeRoi Jones's play *Dutchman*, a one-act verbal sparring session on a subway between a black man and a white woman who eventually kills him, opened in the spring of 1964 to widespread accolades. The *Village Voice* gave it an Obie Award as the season's best Off Broadway play. When Howard University asked the playwright to attend a special performance of *Dutchman*, Hettie Jones asked her husband if she could tag along on the trip. "I can't take you," he replied. When Hettie asked why, LeRoi's response effectively ended their rocky marriage. "Because you're white," he said.[19]

Spurred on by the assassination of Malcolm X in early 1965, LeRoi Jones moved to Harlem and founded the Black Arts Repertory Theater (BART). A working theater and school, it was dedicated to celebrating African American liberation through music and drama. With money raised from Jones's plays, as well as $40,000 from a federal antipoverty program, BART took over a four-story brownstone and hosted art and history classes for four hundred Harlem youngsters. The theater showed productions scripted by Jones and others, typically laced with racist jabs. White men were often portrayed as homosexual. Jones's play *Jello* parodied Jack Benny's radio program, only in the BART performance, Benny's black chauffeur killed all of the whites.[20]

"It's simple," Jones said, explaining his societal visions to a magazine writer during his BART era. "Harlem as an independent state with its own laws—black laws—and its own culture—black culture. And it will be the only future in this country—the black future. If any whites should still be around, they might be allowed to wander through the black world as tired, placid tourists."[21] In another interview, the media quoted Jones as saying, "I don't see anything wrong with hating white people."[22] News broke that federal money was being used for Jones's race-baiting productions, and BART's days were all but numbered in mid-March 1966. Following a lead from a shooting incident, police raided BART's building and discovered rifles, ammunition, and a practice shooting range.[23]

Police arrested six black nationalists associated with BART. But by the time of the raid, Leroi Jones had already abandoned the theater and school to which he devoted so much time and passion. Just after Christmas of 1965, he had moved back into his parents' home in Newark.[24]

Jones picked up in New Jersey the work he had started across the Hudson, founding the poetry-publishing operation Jihad Productions and opening a community theater group called Spirit House. The theater, in a three-story tenement on Stirling Street in the Central Ward, sat about fifty people. In contrast to the grim, gray street scene outside, the Spirit House's interior smelled of incense and was painted in vibrant yellows, greens, and oranges. A group of nonprofessional actors called the Spirit House Movers performed plays by Jones and other black playwrights. Jones lived upstairs with a new African American wife, Sylvia, and their growing family. Like her husband, Sylvia was a writer and activist who, in the late 1960s, would discard her "slave name." She became Amina—meaning faithful, the name of one of Muhammad's wives—Baraka.[25]

Police often appeared at the Spirit House, breaking up rehearsals, snatching scripts, and generally harassing folks associated with the group, which Newark authorities viewed as radical, racist, and dangerous. Jones funneled his frustrations into promoting black culture. He stenciled a fist and the words "Black Power" all over Newark streets, but at least initially didn't get involved in politics. That changed after the playwright met Ron Karenga while Jones was teaching at San Francisco State College in the spring of 1967.

The son of a Baptist minister, Karenga was a brilliant, popular student. By the mid-1960s, he had served as the first black student-body president of Los Angeles City College and received a master's degree in political science from UCLA. The killing of Malcolm X and the 1965 outburst in Watts led him to change his name from Ron Everett to Maulana (Swahili for "master teacher") Ron Karenga. He began wearing African-style clothing and founded the black militant organization US (as opposed to "them"). Years afterward, Karenga would be best remembered for creating the African American holiday Kwanzaa. Karenga and Jones immediately saw eye to eye on the importance of creating and promoting an authentic black culture, or cultural nationalism, as the movement came to be known. Though Karenga was only in his mid-twenties when the two met—Jones was seven years his senior—he had far more experience in community activism. Karenga assumed the role of older brother and mentor, even guru. Jones's speeches, writings, and interviews in the late 1960s were sprinkled with some variation of the phrase, "as Karenga says."[26]

The Newark poet became a minister in the faith Karenga created, Kawaida, which included principles such as unity, self-determination, cooperative economics, and creativity. Karenga's philosophies were also overtly chauvinist. A woman was never to use birth control or question her man, let alone attempt to be a leader in her household or community. "What makes a woman appealing is femininity but she can't be feminine without being submissive," Karenga preached. "The role of the woman is to inspire her man, educate their children and participate in social development. Equality is false; it's the devil's concept. Our concept is complementary."[27]

Jones's perception of his life's mission changed after coming under the influence of Karenga. "I had never before tried to organize black people on concrete bread and butter issues," Jones said.[28] One night during the Newark riots, while Jones sat in jail, bullets shattered the windows of his home, sending his terrified wife, with their newborn son, into a closet for safety. The following evening, someone broke into Spirit House and vandalized the theater. The Joneses presumed the police were responsible for both acts. Shortly afterward, upon the suggestion of a group of black Sunni Muslims, the couple changed their names. LeRoi's was originally Ameer Barakat, meaning "the Blessed Prince." Karenga proposed that Jones alter the name slightly to make it sound more Swahili. The new name symbolized Baraka's new sense of purpose. While he would always be an artist, he would now turn his attention far beyond the theoretical world of culture and intellectualism. He pursued practical, tangible changes for his family and the greater black community. His main goal was nothing short of orchestrating the African American takeover of Newark's power structure.[29]

Spirit House began hosting casual gatherings of local political players on Sunday afternoons. Some radicals and militants attended, but most of the regulars were from the middle class and fairly mainstream. They included Harry Wheeler, a schoolteacher who floated among politicos for years, and Ken Gibson, a low-key civil engineer who came in third place in the 1966 mayoral election. The Sunday afternoon group called itself the United Brothers. Another organization, Black Community Development and Defense (BCD), which was based on Karenga's US, also began attending meetings. Following Karenga's suggestion, the two groups, as well as several others, formed the Committee for Unified Newark, or CFUN.[30]

Toward the end of March 1968, Dr. Martin Luther King Jr. toured Newark as part of his Poor People's Campaign. He gave talks at African American churches, discussed the pros and cons of supporting Lyndon Johnson or Robert F. Kennedy for president, and addressed fourteen hundred teachers and students at South Side High School. "Stand up with dignity and respect," King said. "Too long black people have been ashamed of themselves. Now I'm black, but I'm black and beautiful." In the middle of King's hectic day, which also included visits to Paterson and Jersey City, he took the time to stop by Spirit House and meet with its director. Commenting on their closed-door afternoon meeting, Baraka said that he and King "talked about unifying the black people." At 10 o'clock that night, a crowd of nearly a thousand greeted Dr. King at the Newark's Abyssinian Baptist Church and cheered wildly as he said, "The hour has come for Newark, New Jersey, to have a black mayor."[31]

On April 1, 1968, John Smith, the taxi driver whose arrest in Newark the previous summer helped ignite a riot, was convicted by an all-white jury of assaulting a police officer. Three days later, Dr. King was murdered in Memphis, reportedly by a white racist high school dropout named James Earl Ray. More than a hundred cities exploded in angry demonstrations, some violently so, over the assassination of America's most famous, most highly respected civil rights leader. In Newark, fires tore through twenty-six buildings the day after King's assassination. Two weeks later, arsonists set a blaze that ranked as one of the worst in Newark's history, destroying thirty-four buildings and leaving 650 people homeless.[32]

Even considering the fires, Newark remained somewhat subdued, with no major violence. At least part of the credit for the peace can be attributed to the efforts of Amiri Baraka and other black leaders. They had decided that, of the two paths to justice famously suggested by Malcolm X—the ballot or the bullet—the former seemed the wiser approach in Newark, where some 60 percent of the population was black. "Don't be a chump—Be cool—Cool. Support the United Brothers and their black convention," a flyer posted in the spring of 1968 read. "Don't riot. Don't do what the man wants you to do. Come together as blacks and support blacks. Take this city by the ballot. This is not punking out. This is being smart."[33]

To keep the peace, and in doing so hopefully increase the chances of CFUN candidates winning in the fall city council elections, Baraka agreed shortly after Dr. King's death to appear on a local television broadcast. On the show, he discussed the state of the city and race relations with Anthony Imperiale, an Italian strongman known in his native North Ward as "Big T," despite standing only five feet, six inches. Imperiale, a squat 230-pound black belt in karate and former marine, known for wearing ill-fitting suits and an absurd toupee, had created the North Ward Citizens Committee after the 1967 riots rocked Newark. Often called a racist vigilante organization, the all-white group regularly sent members wearing green helmets out to patrol the streets in vans, ostensibly to protect citizens from muggings or worse. African Americans and Puerto Ricans periodically reported the group dishing out insults and beatings without provocation, and complained that the police never stepped in to stop them. Members of the North Ward group received gun training and karate lessons, and its leader did his best to match black nationalists in terms of blunt militant rhetoric. "If they come to burn our homes this summer," Imperiale said, speaking of potential rioters in 1968, "we'll shoot to kill."[34] In a speech in Nutley a month after Dr. King died, Imperiale called the civil rights leader "Martin Luther Coon."[35] When addressing an audience he often dropped the line, "When the Black Panther comes, the White Hunter will be waiting."[36]

On the TV program, Imperiale and Baraka—representatives of opposite extremes who both rode the Newark riots to newfound power and influence—jointly denounced white leftist groups Students for a Democratic Society (SDS), led by Tom Hayden, and the Newark Community Union Project. The two organizations and other outside groups were the troublemakers causing much of the racial unrest in Newark, Baraka and Imperiale agreed. To Baraka, SDS and others were just "white boys pimping off the black struggle."[37] As a black nationalist, he saw nothing wrong with denouncing any white person, even someone like Tom Hayden, who had been devoted to ending discrimination and improving the inner city. Imperiale, an avowed hater of communists, who celebrated the work of Joseph McCarthy more than a decade after the senator had been censured for his "commie" witch hunts, was more than happy to seize any opportunity to blame the Left for trouble. With the assistance of Baraka, Imperiale was also able to pit one group of liberals against another. Like Baraka, Imperiale regarded Hayden and other activists as unwanted interlopers. Shortly thereafter, the extremists on opposing sides of the racial divide succeeded in driving Hayden and other outsiders from Newark.[38]

Whites and blacks alike were surprised by Baraka's comments and his apparent mutual understanding with Imperiale. "It was a very happy occasion for me to find myself in total agreement with LeRoi Jones," one Newark police official said.[39] Baraka offered further explanation for his positions, saying that he had more respect for Imperiale's honesty than the fake earnestness of white liberals who lied and broke promises. Most important of all, Baraka said, nothing should be allowed to jeopardize the pursuit of African American power in Newark. "We are out to bring black self-government to this city by 1970, and the ballot seems to be the most advantageous way," he said. "We are educating the Negro masses that this city can be taken without a shot being fired."[40]

In late June of 1968, the United Brothers and CFUN sponsored a political convention to elect candidates for city council. Karenga's fingerprints were all over the campaign, which he personally anointed with the slogan "Peace & Power." Many older, more conservative African Americans involved in politics felt alienated by the cultural nationalist preachings of Karenga. They weren't interested in wearing dashikis or learning Swahili phrases. They simply wanted to see progressive, qualified black people representing them in political office. It soon became apparent that Baraka's influence was limited, and that the black community didn't entirely trust him. The people may have also been apathetic or simply disorganized. Elections were held in August for a committee overseeing slum rehabilitation in thirteen Newark districts. Each district elected its own representative, and in Baraka's district he received just twenty-eight votes. (The top vote-getter in Baraka's district netted only 118 nods.) Tony Imperiale, on the other hand, was not only elected as his district's representative, he received the most votes of any committee candidate in the city.[41]

A few months later, Imperiale also won a seat on the city council, along with another first-timer, Anthony Giuliano, a Newark police detective and Patrolmen's Benevolent Association president who led the resistance against a civilian review board. Both had run as "law and order" candidates, appealing to white voters who were outraged that the governor's post-riot report put the blame for the previous summer's disturbances at the feet of city government and the law enforcement officers who had put their lives on the line. Many old-time Newarkers frequently wondered: What about the rioters themselves? And the people they called "outside agitators"? How could the governor's commission say those groups bore little or no responsibility for what happened? From the perspective of rightwing voters, the best chance for salvaging their city was through leaders who would crack down on crime and violence on Newark streets.[42]

The men supported by Baraka, the United Brothers, and CFUN for city council all lost. Their candidates received 73 percent of votes cast for the council in the South Ward, and 86 percent in the Central Ward, but the election was citywide. Unlike Giuliano and Imperiale, Baraka's candidates didn't have enough pull around Newark as a whole. Upon closer inspection they apparently didn't even earn the confidence of all that many folks in the South and Central wards, a large number of whom entered the booths to cast votes in the presidential election only. Over 60 percent of voters in the South Ward, for example, didn't bother checking the name of any candidate in the 1968 city council elections.[43]

———

Change was inevitable in the fallout of the 1960s riots, and Newark's initial step was a shift to the right. Calvin West and Irvine Turner remained the only two African Americans serving on the city council, and both were beholden to Mayor Addonizio. Either many black voters hadn't abandoned hope in Newark's old leadership, or they simply didn't believe any of Baraka's suggested new leaders could fix their dysfunctional city.

The mayor and his allies argued that turning the city over to radicals wouldn't be wise. Black conservatives and moderates should still support the current administration, Addonizio maintained. He pointed to progressive, post-riot measures he had taken that were already improving race relations. Less than a month after the riots, Edward Williams became the first African American police captain. After Governor Hughes's commission report was released in February of 1968, Mayor Addonizio followed one of the report's suggestions by appointing Williams in charge of a police precinct in a predominantly black neighborhood. The precinct Addonizio handpicked was the Fourth, where the previous summer's riots began.

Much of Newark's police force was outraged that the Fourth Precinct's current captain would be transferred to make way for Williams. Dozens of policemen picketed City Hall. Williams saw the move as no different from previous appointments in which ethnicity was a factor, like that of a Jewish captain who'd been given command of the Fifth Precinct when Weequahic was largely Jewish. He was disheartened at the sight of his "brother officers" protesting his appointment. "I had broken bread and drank booze with some of the same cops that were on the picket line," Williams wrote in his memoir. "I felt nausea stirring in my vitals."[44]

Nonetheless, on March 1, 1968, Williams made history by taking command of Newark's Fourth Precinct. Newspapers in Las Vegas, Baltimore, St. Louis, and elsewhere around the country noted the appointment. Congratulatory messages flooded in to Williams from as far away as Canada, Australia, and Ghana. At the start of Williams's uneventful first shift as commander, in which he oversaw eighteen white and four black policemen, the captain reflected on the Fourth Precinct, which he used to walk past as a boy. "We used to lower our voices when we passed it," he said. "It looked so formidable. And we all believed they had a whipping machine for kids in the basement, a machine that gave kids a spanking."[45]

The governor's report had also brought to light the rampant illegal gambling operations in Newark. Under pressure to combat the city's reputation for corruption, Mayor Addonizio created a special gambling unit. The new nine-man unit was headed, appropriately, by Deputy Police Chief John Redden, the man who had testified to the post-riot commission about Newark's well-known bookmaking and numbers games. Redden had also been an outspoken critic of Police Director Dominick Spina, particularly with regard to the department's lack of preparation for riots, and for Spina's overall poor handling of the disturbance.

Busting up Newark's gambling operations was easy. All the undercover officers had to do was walk into storefronts that accepted bets—it was an open secret where they were—and, after a brief discussion, start making arrests. A couple of weeks after the special unit was created, Redden's men raided a luncheonette and confiscated a paper bag with nearly $7,000 in cash and $500 in lottery bets, as well as a dozen tickets to Mayor Addonizio's birthday party.[46]

In mid-April, Director Spina dissolved Redden's short-lived gambling unit, citing a "desperate manpower shortage" in the department as the reason.[47] Mayor Addonizio was conveniently out of town when the decision was announced. Reached for comment on vacation in Miami Beach, Addonizio said, "Spina discussed it with me before I left. He said they hadn't produced anything." Just the opposite was true. In its six short weeks of existence, Redden's squad had arrested twenty-two people and seized two shotguns, six handguns, $10,000 in stolen merchandise, and over $16,000 in cash. This was more confiscated gambling money than the entire police department had collected over the past three years. To Redden's men, there was no mystery as to why the special unit was disbanded. "We were stepping on too many toes," one said. "We were getting too close to big people," said another.[48]

Spina's dissolution of the gambling squad raised a red flag to Essex County prosecutors, who immediately prepared an investigation. In July, a grand jury handed down an indictment on four counts of nonfeasance—in other words, failure of Director Spina to perform his duties. Mayor Addonizio refused to accept Spina's resignation, which the police director offered. The mayor defended his old friend, stating that Dominick Spina "has one of the most difficult jobs in the nation and he has, in my judgment, dedicated himself to it with a devotion most men will never know or understand."[49]

With the Spina trial under way in early November of 1968, several members of the disbanded gambling unit testified about the ease of breaking up lottery operations. Patrolman Harold Gibson, brother of Ken Gibson, the city engineer aspiring to the mayor's office, discussed how members of the squad sat in unmarked cars and watched bets openly being taken by businesses. Harold Gibson and other squad members said that several people nabbed for involvement in illegal lotteries handed over green cards when they were being arrested. "I'm just an old numbers player and I'm okay," one man told the officers, producing the card in the hopes they would let him off. A few days after the squad members' testimony, the judge told the jury that they must disregard any mention of the curious green cards. They were inadmissible, he ruled. The trial never reached the jury anyway. On November 7, the judge stated that the prosecution had failed to provide sufficient proof of Spina's guilt. The judge said the police director could not be held responsible for "violations of law by his subordinates." All charges were dismissed.[50]

Regardless of the Spina trial outcome, prosecutors smelled blood. At the time, Assistant State Attorney General William J. Brennan III—son of the U.S. Supreme Court justice and grandson of the long-serving, Prohibition-era Newark City Commissioner Bill Brennan—was leading a special investigation of organized crime in the state. About a month after dismissal of the Spina case, a casual remark from Brennan to a group of journalists made national headlines. Based on what he'd unearthed in his investigations, Brennan said organized crime had "infested virtually every facet of public life in New Jersey."[51]

When the Essex County prosecutor's investigation began the previous spring, Addonizio initially told all city personnel to cooperate fully. By mid-December of 1968, however, the mayor was actively fighting subpoenas to turn over his financial records.[52]

A full year passed before the indictments were handed down. At a federal grand jury hearing in early December of 1969, Mayor Addonizio invoked the Fifth Amendment and refused to answer questions about accepting kickbacks. Within a week, seventy people—primarily city officials and underworld operatives—were indicted for involvement in gambling operations, a $50-million-per-year business in Newark, according to prosecutors, and in city-contract payoffs and other schemes. Hugh Addonizio and Anthony "Tony Boy" Boiardo topped the list of men indicted for income-tax evasion and five dozen counts of extortion. "We found a city of impacted rackets," one Justice Department official said. "At some point, the rackets grew from public nuisance to an alligator devouring the city."[53]

Three current city councilmen were indicted: Frank Addonizio, a distant cousin of the mayor's, and the council's only two African American representatives, Calvin West and Irvine Turner. Four former councilmen were also charged, including James Callaghan, the man at the center of controversy in the months before the riots. It was Callaghan whom Mayor Addonizio had wanted to name as Board of Education secretary over a more qualified black man, Wilbur Parker.[54]

On the other side of the kickback system, Mario Gallo, an owner of pipe, crushed stone, and gravel companies that did work for the city, was indicted. There were also a few men charged due to connections with Valentine Electric Company, another outfit that frequently contracted with the city. Tony Boy Boiardo was listed as a mere salesman with the company, but most people understood that he and his father controlled the entire operation. After the younger Boiardo joined the company, its business quickly skyrocketed from averaging $1 million per year up to $11 million annually. Valentine focused operations in Newark, but it also nabbed contracts from Jersey City and was involved in the building of a scandal-plagued post office in Kearny. For several years, about half the electrical contracts for the Newark Housing Authority went to Valentine. The situation got to the point that other electrical companies didn't bother submitting bids to the NHA.[55]

Judges, city lawyers, and officials of public works and other city services were likewise indicted. Though the NHA was involved in many of the payoff scenarios, Louis Danzig, the long-serving housing-authority executive director, was not on the list of those charged. Always regarded in political circles as a brilliant operator, Danzig had left his post at an opportune time, several months before the mayor, councilmen, and so many other players with whom he associated were indicted.

Newark's abominable housing situation had often been named as a cause for the 1967 riots, and in their wake, the community increased pressure on Danzig to make improvements. Testifying before the governor's post-riot commission, Danzig admitted that high-rise projects were "the worst housing that you can build for large families." Overall, though, he offered remarkable praise for the NHA. "Housing conditions in Newark are now better than they have been in our time," he maintained. "The greatest improvement has been made in recent years by means of urban renewal and the public housing program."[56]

In April of 1969, residents at the high-rise Scudder Homes projects declared a rent strike after months of pleading with the NHA over a long list of grievances, including plumbing problems, broken windows and door locks, and insufficient police protection. "We're going to win this battle," said tenant Charlotte Jackson. "If Louis Danzig doesn't like it, he can get the hell out, and we're here to see that he does."[57]

Three months later, Danzig resigned. "For the present, I have done all I can do in this office," he said. "The dream of a new city for the people in Newark's future is beginning to take clear shape." Newspapers rehashed the sweeping urban renewal projects from the Danzig era: $350 million of new construction, 5,674 public-housing units, expansion of Rutgers University and of the Newark College of Engineering, as well as several privately owned residential buildings including Brick Towers—which, in the future, would come to embody urban neglect, according to a resident and ambitious political upstart named Cory Booker. Despite anecdotal and statistical evidence strongly to the contrary, Louis Danzig took his exit while declaring the city's housing program in "a most favorable situation."[58]

Danzig's impromptu departure caught Mayor Addonizio off guard. "After 20 years in politics, the mayor is never shocked anymore," one City Hall source said. "But this time it is safe to say that he was greatly surprised."[59]

After the indictments, the *Star-Ledger*, Newark's Chamber of Commerce, and countless Newark community leaders asked Mayor Addonizio and the other implicated officials to step down, but they refused. All fourteen of the main players pled not guilty, posted bail, and awaited trial. Addonizio confidently stated he would be acquitted of all charges. "I am returning to City Hall to continue to run the administration of the city's affairs effectively and efficiently," said Addonizio, after making his plea. "This is a very difficult city to administer. I am trying to do the job and solve the problems."[60]

The 1970 mayoral election loomed less than six months in the future, and the beleaguered Addonizio had yet to comment on whether he would seek a third term. Many Newarkers believed the mayor would enter the race, despite the scandal rocking City Hall. And as crazy as it seemed, people knew that even while Mayor Addonizio faced dozens of criminal charges, thousands in fines, and more than a thousand years in prison, he stood a good chance of pulling off a victory.[61]

———

The 1968 city council elections had ended in obvious failure for the African American political faction led by Amiri Baraka. The group's campaign had garnered limited support, even among the black community. Baraka himself was viewed as a large part of the problem. The poet-activist not only alienated rightwing and liberal whites alike, he was regarded with suspicion by conservative and moderate blacks. Baraka's approach was too radical, too intolerant, too impractical, and often too bizarre for many people to embrace and follow.

The dictatorial style of the United Brothers and other organizations also put people off. Before the 1968 election, for example, one man entered the United Brothers headquarters to drop off a $600 donation. After the man signed in, guards threw him up against a wall because he dared to break off a conversation with a United Brothers officer. "Do anything necessary to keep him in line," a United Brothers staffer told the guards.[62]

To Baraka, the only acceptable alliances were among black-liberation groups. Rather than working with white, liberal, hippie idealists in Newark, Baraka helped push them out of the city. "We 'support' the white revolution of dope and nakedness because it weakens the hand that holds the chain that binds Black people," Baraka wrote. "Just because the slavemaster has long hair and smokes bush does nothing to change the fact that he is and will be the slave master until, we, yes, we free ourselves."[63] African Americans who did not endorse black nationalism were not only fools, Baraka argued, they were traitors. "The Negro artist who is not a nationalist at this late date is a white artist, even without knowing it," Baraka wrote in 1969. "He is creating death snacks, for and out of dead stuff. What he does will not matter because it is in the shadow, connected with the shadow and will die when the shadow dies."[64]

Some people couldn't get behind Baraka because so many of the man's antics and rants were "out there," even by 1960s standards. In a *Negro Digest* interview, Baraka voiced odd theories such as the evolution of African Americans into a different species of man. He called capitalism "just a word—a euphemism for evil. It doesn't exist as any kind of viable economic philosophy."[65]

"We came from an invisible world and we are going back to one," he said, mystically, in that same interview. "Art is supposed to put you in contact with that invisible world, for a moment, and then it retreats. Like when you go to sleep, you lose sight on this world; and when you awake, you lose sight on the other world. But they exist all the time on different levels—like a target; there are rays and rays of different kinds of existence."[66]

The cult of personality around Maulana Ron Karenga, the founder of the black militant US organization and Baraka's mentor, grated on many black Newarkers. Baraka ordered members of CFUN, the organization that selected candidates for the 1968 city council campaign, to follow Karenga's Kawaida philosophy and regularly recite the doctrine's seven principles. After speaking at meetings, CFUN members were expected to end by stating the phrase: "If I have anything of value or beauty, all praise is due to Maulana Karenga, and all mistakes have been mine."[67]

Many African Americans never bought into the cultural nationalism of Karenga and Baraka. The Black Panther Party, for example, derided cultural nationalism as "pork chop nationalism"—window dressing that wouldn't bring about true political freedom. The two organizations argued over which group was authentically black and about which political candidates to endorse.[68]

As the rivalry between the Black Panthers and US heated up, Karenga's behavior grew increasingly strange. Believing the FBI, the Panthers, and others were out to get him, Karenga countered his paranoia by popping pills that left him in a stupor. For a spell, a machine gun sat propped in Karenga's living room pointed at the front door. A shootout in early 1969 on the UCLA campus between Karenga's followers and a group of Black Panthers left two Panthers dead. Karenga himself was arrested in the fall of 1970 for torturing two of his young female followers—who supposedly had information about attempts to poison the US leader. The women testified that Karenga ordered them to disrobe, and that he and other US members beat them with electrical cords and karate batons, and poured laundry detergent into their mouths. A hot soldering iron was allegedly placed to the face of one woman, and the big toe of the other was squeezed in a vise. A psychiatrist testified that he considered Karenga "both paranoid and schizophrenic with hallucinations and delusions." Karenga denied his guilt and spent several years in jail after being convicted of felonious assault and imprisonment.[69]

Unlike Newark's 1968 black political convention, in which Baraka had taken the lead under the strong influence of Ron Karenga, the US founder was nowhere to be seen in the buildup to Newark's 1970 mayoral election. Baraka, regarded as too polarizing a figure to run a campaign with the wide appeal necessary for victory, likewise took a backseat to more moderate leaders. Robert Curvin, the CORE leader who had tried to quell demonstrators at the Fourth Precinct after cabdriver John Smith's arrest, headed a committee of minority leaders organizing a convention to name candidates for city office.

It had been decided early on that the convention would not be limited solely to African Americans. Blacks may have constituted the majority of Newark's population, but a large portion was too young to vote. More than half were under twenty-one, compared to about one-third of whites. A disproportionate number of African Americans who were old enough to vote weren't registered to do so, partly due to the frequency with which poor people changed residences. One estimate stated that if thirty thousand black voters registered in a voting drive in Newark, about ten thousand would be unregistered three years later because they'd moved. If the mayoralty was decided strictly along a black-white vote in 1970, the white side would win. Puerto Ricans, who represented about a tenth of Newark's population, joined the convention with the idea that together, the oppressed people of color could finally take City Hall. The Black and Puerto Rican Political Convention, as it came to be known, drew from a broader population than Baraka's 1968 convention, but as Anthony Imperiale, Hugh Addonizio, and many other critics pointed out, it wasn't inclusive. All whites were excluded.[70]

A junior high school in Newark's South Ward hosted the convention over three days in mid-November of 1969. It was an exceptionally tumultuous period in Newark and all over the country, with race relations tense, antiwar protests reaching a peak, and the counterculture dividing older generations from young.

Earlier that month in a Chicago courtroom, Black Panther national chairman Bobby Seale, on trial for conspiracy to incite a riot at the Democratic National Convention with the rest of the Chicago Eight, was held in contempt for speaking out of turn. The judge sentenced Seale to four years on contempt charges, and separated his conspiracy trial from the others. For several days afterward, on the judge's order, Seale sat through court hearings while gagged and strapped to a chair. Young female protestors dressed as witches pranced outside the court building, screaming out curses and drawing encircled X's on the windows.[71]

The remaining Chicago Seven, as well as their lawyer, William Kunstler, asked the judge to end hearings early on Friday, November 14, so that they could attend the following day's massive antiwar demonstrations in Washington, D.C., San Francisco, and elsewhere. Charter companies in New Jersey reported hundreds of requests for buses to bring protestors to the marches and rallies in the national capital, and many buses left directly from Newark college campuses after Friday protests in the city. In the buildup before the main demonstrations, Peter, Paul and Mary, Pete Seeger, and the cast of *Hair* sang in Times Square, and luminaries ranging from actor Tony Randall to Dr. Benjamin Spock to conductor Leonard Bernstein offered support for the peace movement as dozens of white doves were released. More than 250,000 people marched down Washington, D.C.'s Pennsylvania Avenue to protest the Vietnam War policy of President Richard Nixon, who reportedly spent the afternoon watching the Ohio State–Purdue football game. More than 100,000 demonstrated in San Francisco, and smaller groups of protesters voiced opposition to the war in cities around the world, including Paris, Rome, London, and West Berlin.[72]

Newark's black and Puerto Rican convention took place the same weekend as the major anti-Vietnam demonstrations. The issues discussed in Newark were mostly local—unemployment among the city's people of color at double the rate of whites, student dropout rates of 32 percent, housing and overcrowding problems, the highest maternal mortality, infant mortality, and venereal disease rates in the country. Volunteers sitting behind rows of narrow tables helped hundreds of citizens register to vote. African American politicians and celebrity activists made appearances, among them comedian Dick Gregory, actor Ossie Davis, and Richard Hatcher, the mayor of Gary, Indiana. "Black power is not radical, frightening or unique," Hatcher said in a speech. "Other ethnic groups have been doing it since this country's beginning." Brooklyn's Shirley Chisholm, the first black woman elected in Congress, also spoke. "We're through with tokenism and gradualism," she told crowds. "We want our share of the American dream now."[73]

The convention was billed as "The Community's Choice," but delegates were presented only with a single option for mayor and few choices for city council. Kenneth Allen Gibson, the civil engineer regular at Urban Brothers meetings at Baraka's Spirit House and respectable third-place finisher in the 1966 mayoral election, received all 283 of the delegate votes cast for mayor candidate, with no one running against him. Sharpe James, the athletic director for Essex County College, and Alvin Oliver, a director at the antipoverty group UCC, likewise received no-opposition endorsements for council races in the South and East wards respectively. There wasn't much of a competition for the Central Ward city council position, in which Rev. Dennis Westbrooks won 238 of the 247 delegate votes.[74]

That's not to say other men of color didn't want to run for office. Harry Wheeler, another attendee of Urban Brothers meetings at Spirit House, announced his mayoral candidacy the week before the convention, which he boycotted. Newark assemblyman George Richardson, also a no-show at the convention, would also run for mayor. Willie Wright, president of the United Afro-American Association, entered the campaign for councilman in the Central Ward without the endorsement of the convention he called "rigged." The gathering was "purposely designed to lead black people and white people to believe that there is unity where there is only chaos," Wright said. "If this is the black community's idea of self-determination, then I fear for the future of black politics."[75]

There was nothing all that unusual about the back-room politics that evidently played out at the convention, down to the lone Puerto Rican representative, Ramon Aneses, tapped to run for an at-large council spot. The ringing endorsement of thirty-seven-year-old Ken Gibson seemed curious, however. Before the delegate vote for a mayoral candidate, twenty-two attractive women wearing shiny gold dresses—Golden Gibson Girls, they called themselves—paraded in front of delegates waving banners. The display was the only thing remotely flashy about Gibson, a quiet, plodding man who had slowly ground his way to an engineering degree over twelve years of night school. Gibson had a doughy physique, sleepy eyes, a whispy mustache, and the close-cropped hair and outdated fashion sense that hipper, Afro-wearing men mocked. "We gon' have to slick bro Gibson up a bit," Rev. Jesse Jackson said at an appearance with the Newark mayoral candidate. "He gon' have to grow some hair and get rid of these old-fashioned shoes."[76] Gibson wasn't a particularly good speaker, and had never won any political office or been the administrator of a large organization. He was certainly no visionary. His agenda consisted mainly of unexciting issues like efficiently delivering services and restoring the people's trust in government. His statements were rarely bolder than lines like: "What I think I could do is create a climate of respect and honesty."[77]

Somehow Gibson had built up overwhelming support among people of color. His previous run for mayor gave him name recognition, which helped. He may not have been anyone's first choice, but he was someone that all African Americans and Puerto Ricans could live with as mayor. Gibson's dullness, in its own way, was seen as a virtue. People knew he would run a subdued, inoffensive campaign that might even attract some white voters. "We're going to conduct a campaign to appeal to everyone in the city," Gibson said after accepting the convention's nomination. "We are not going to say anything bad about anybody."[78]

————

"A radical black, a militant white and a man under a 66-count federal indictment are the forerunners in Newark's mayoral race," was the lead sentence in a nationally published newspaper article in the spring of 1970.[79] Of the three, Gibson, tagged as the "radical black," despite his fairly mainstream platform, was the only attendee of a televised debate in early May. Councilman Tony Imperiale and Mayor Addonizio opted out. Gibson and four other mayoral candidates (two white and two black) sat behind a curved table making statements into the TV camera. "Why is it that Mayor Addonizio isn't here today?" asked Alexander Matturri, the state senator positioning himself as the lone Italian candidate who was both moderate and trustworthy. "Is he afraid to speak up? Is he afraid of the questions to be asked?"[80]

As promised, Gibson maintained a calm, respectful demeanor, though he did offer the backhanded insult that only he, Imperiale, and Addonizio stood any real chance of victory. Assemblyman George Richardson didn't refrain from attacks, lumping Gibson in with militants, as Imperiale, Police Director Spina, and others regularly did throughout the campaign. "We cannot afford the all-black politics of a LeRoi Jones-oriented government headed by Mr. Gibson," Richardson cried out.[81] The other two candidates with seemingly no prayer of being elected were former schoolteacher Harry Wheeler and John Caulfield, Addonizio's former fire department chief, an Irishman in a city that was bound to elect an Italian or an African American. "The campaign was a circus," wrote one reporter covering the duration of the campaign. "I considered that I was gazing down at an array of clowns who were frantically calling attention to themselves amid the chaos."[82]

Ken Gibson clung to the low-key approach in the campaign, dishing out statements rarely more boastful than, "I couldn't be any worse than Addonizio."[83] It was up to Gibson's supporters to inject much-needed passion into the race. The posters they dreamed up couldn't be ignored by the black community. "Take the Man's Money, But Vote for a Brother!" one read. Another pictured Tony Imperiale holding a gun with the warning: "Register and Vote or This Will Be Your Mayor!" Still another invoked the riots, showing a policeman over a dead black child and the words "Register & Vote! Never Let This Happen Again!"[84]

For the good of the Gibson campaign, the polarizing figure of Amiri Baraka stayed mostly behind the scenes. He used his renown to attract dozens of celebrities into Newark to endorse Gibson and raise money. James Brown played a benefit at Newark's Symphony Hall one week, followed by Bill Cosby the next. Stevie Wonder, the Temptations, Max Roach, Harry Belafonte, Dustin Hoffman, Sammy Davis Jr., Flip Wilson, Jesse Jackson, and other well-known figures praised Gibson at political rallies. The Gibson candidacy became a national cause, with black politicians around the country giving endorsements and offering assistance.[85]

Hugh Addonizio did his best to portray himself as the sensible, experienced, moderate choice in between two extremists—Gibson, "the hand-picked choice of LeRoi Jones," in the mayor's words, and Imperiale, "a so-called candidate who huffs and puffs and disgraces our city by his boasts of guns, tanks, dogs, and vigilantes."[86] Addonizio and his city council cronies, which still included African Americans Irvine Turner and Calvin West, ran on a "Peace and Progress" slate and appealed to their base, the city workers they employed. Even though the city was nearing bankruptcy, the mayor's team approved substantial raises for Newark employees, including a hefty $4.3 million pay hike for teachers as part of the 1970 strike settlement. The mayor wasn't conceding the African American vote to Ken Gibson. Dozens of black clergymen supported Addonizio in 1970; the mayor's hold on welfare money and patronage jobs likely had something to do with it.[87] Addonizio also paid for full-page ads in black newspapers. One ad claimed that unemployment had been cut in half the previous year. Another showed Addonizio with his "old Congressional friend," the deceased President John Kennedy, alongside a photo of the mayor giving a tour of City Hall to some black children.[88]

In the buildup to the May election, signs around the city for all seven candidates were torn down or painted over. One night, someone smashed the windows of John Caulfield's Central Ward headquarters. Hecklers occasionally called Ken Gibson a nigger or a baboon. Young black men, reportedly followers of Amiri Baraka, regularly disturbed George Richardson at public meetings and shouted at him to drop out of the race. Harlem's former congressman Adam Clayton Powell, a Gibson supporter, chimed in to criticize Richardson as an "Uncle Tom" and "Addonizio's Prat-boy."[89]

The real ugliness, however, didn't surface until after the May election, which Gibson dominated with nearly 40 percent of the vote. Gibson won every ward except the North, and received more votes than Addonizio and Imperiale combined. Still, a majority was necessary to win the mayoralty outright. A runoff election in mid-June between the two top vote-getters, Gibson and Addonizio, was necessary. Race immediately jumped to the forefront, with anyone crossing the color divide deemed a traitor. "If *we* vote, *we* win," an Addonizio poster declared. Despite the ban on police department officials making political endorsements, the mayor's henchman, Director Spina, called the election a "black-versus-white situation," and implored crowds to back Addonizio. "For the white man in Newark," Spina said, "this is a matter of survival."[90]

By the time candidates were rallying voters for the runoff, Mayor Addonizio's criminal trial had begun. The mayor spent his days in a Trenton courtroom and sped back to Newark each evening to campaign. "The charges will blow away," he promised, claiming the indictments were typical of the stereotype associating all successful Italians with organized crime.[91]

The juxtaposition of front-page stories about the upcoming election and the ongoing federal trial may have been the best campaign publicity Ken Gibson could have asked for, but he also received key endorsements. The *Star-Ledger* supported Gibson, noting he "reasons carefully, calmly and seemingly soundly," and also that he "repeatedly has said the volatile LeRoi

Jones would not be included in his administration."[92] Clifford Case, U.S. senator from New Jersey, backed Gibson, as did two of Gibson's opponents in the mayoral general election, George Richardson and former fire chief John Caulfield. The latter paid dearly for endorsing a black man. Anthony Imperiale called Caulfield "the scum of the earth."[93] Crowds spat at Caulfield and greeted him with shouts of "nigger lover." At one appearance, a mob manhandled Caulfield and his wife. Rocks showered their car as the couple drove away. When Caulfield picked up the phone, voices often promised to burn down his house and kill his children.[94]

At an Addonizio rally in a North Ward restaurant a few days before the election, Tony Imperiale fired up the crowd against the onslaught of Gibson and his supporters. "They're not going to destroy our city! Over my dead body!" he bellowed. "I say all this as a councilman, as a citizen, and as a vigilante! You've got to fight! How in hell can you look in your children's eyes if you don't fight? Fight for your lives! If Gibson was a good man, I'd work for him. But this is Communism versus democracy!"[95] Mayor Addonizio voiced a similar call to action. "You all know what is involved here," the incumbent said. "Everything you hold sacred—your homes, your families and your jobs. We cannot let leaders of race hatred take control of our city. You all know what I'm talking about."[96]

A few days later, on election night, angry Italian men in Addonizio's campaign headquarters overturned tables, shoved reporters, and destroyed TV cameras, yelling, "We're going to burn this town down unless we get every foot of film."[97] They apparently didn't want their images captured on the historic night that a black man was elected mayor of Newark. Gibson netted 55,097 votes, including about 7,000 from whites, compared to Addonizio's total of 43,086. In a rare, clever quip, Gibson said, "When Robert Treat, the man who founded Newark over 300 years ago came here, I'm sure that he never realized that someday Newark would have soul."[98]

Jubilant crowds of black people flooded around Gibson's Broad Street headquarters and danced in the streets. "Our joy literally knew no bounds," Baraka later wrote. "We had won! We had kicked those Crackers' ass!"[99] A bus driver parked his vehicle and joined crowds of hugging, high-fiving strangers. A few revelers climbed on top of the bus and strutted in celebration. White policemen watched as cars honked and people raised their fists. In the ecstasy of the moment, black Newarkers compared the election victory to the Emancipation Proclamation, Joe Louis's defeat of German Max Schmeling in the boxing ring, and Times Square festivities at the end of World War II.[100]

Addonizio's city council allies lost their elections, yet only three black and Puerto Rican convention candidates won council posts: Earl Harris,

Sharpe James, and Dennis Westbrooks. Italians held the six other seats, and therefore they controlled the majority. The Gibson camp was obviously pleased with the overall election results, but early on adopted a measured, realistic stance. "There's a sense of euphoria that things are going to change," said Gibson's campaign manager. "But frankly it's going to take years to get things accomplished."[101]

———

Three weeks into Ken Gibson's administration, his predecessor was found guilty on sixty-three counts of extortion and one charge of conspiracy. A jury needed only six hours of deliberation to convict Hugh Addonizio, former public-works director Anthony LaMorte, and two mafia players involved in the notorious Valentine Electric Company. Of the original fourteen men jointly indicted, these four were the only ones whose trials ended in July of 1970. Two of the indicted passed away before they could be brought to trial; one died in a car crash shortly after agreeing to cooperate with the prosecution. Several other defendants, including former councilmen Irvine Turner and Calvin West, had their trials severed due to health ailments or other reasons. The most recent case put on hold was that of the tan, dapper, round-faced Tony Boy Boiardo. In early July, soon after a witness explained the elaborate system of payoffs orchestrated by Boiardo, a judge declared a mistrial for the mob boss. Doctors said Boiardo suffered a heart attack. Though he would live for another eight years, Boiardo somehow never quite regained his health to the extent he could stand for trial.[102]

The star witness for the prosecution in Addonizio's trial was an engineering contractor named Paul Rigo, who testified that over the years he'd personally paid more than $250,000 in kickbacks to Newark officials and mob players. Rigo produced a payoff diary and explained the codes—"P plus 2," for example, meant "the Pope" (the code name for Addonizio) received $2,000. Rigo stated that during one conversation, Hugh Addonizio explained why he'd decided to leave Congress and run for mayor of his hometown. "There's no money in Washington," Addonizio reportedly said, "but you can make a million dollars in Newark." Testifying in his own defense, Addonizio swore that none of what Rigo and others said was true. Under cross-examination, however, Addonizio couldn't deny his longstanding friendship with Tony Boy Boiardo; the two had frequently been seen dining together and hanging out by hotel pools on vacations in Florida and Puerto Rico. Addonizio also admitted that many of his travel expenses and gambling debts were paid by "old personal friends," including construction executives with dealings with Newark.[103]

On September 22, less than three months removed from the Newark mayoralty, fifty-six-year-old Hugh Addonizio clasped his hands together and stared at the courtroom floor while the judge read his sentence: ten years in prison and $25,000 in fines. "An intricate conspiracy of this magnitude could never have succeeded without then Mayor Addonizio's approval and participation," the judge said, calling the crimes "as calculated as they were brazen, as callous and contemptuous of the law as they were extensive."[104]

———

From the moment Ken Gibson took office, it was clear he wasn't the radical that alarmists made him out to be. Two of the highest-level appointments went to moderate white men with long histories in Newark. John Caulfield assumed his old role as fire chief, surely due in no small part to his well-publicized endorsement of Gibson. For police director, Gibson named John Redden, a twenty-three-year department veteran, deputy chief under Dominick Spina, and leader of the short-lived special gambling unit.

Mayor Gibson's initial steps in office aimed mainly at bringing efficiency to city government. He targeted employees who collected two or three city salaries, usually one of which was a "no show" job. Many old-timers in City Hall were openly hostile to the new mayor. "I want you to know that I worked for Addonizio's reelection," one city worker told Gibson. "He lost but as far as I'm concerned he is still my boss."[105] The measly thirty-hour week some city employees worked was entirely insufficient, Gibson opined. Seeing as the mayor couldn't change their contracts, he mandated that Newark workers sign in and out at their offices to ensure the city at least got a full thirty hours of work out of them. Later, the frustrated mayor installed time clocks to better track city workers.[106]

By the fall of 1970, Ken Gibson and his staff had gathered a clear, and disturbing, picture of the extent of corruption and financial mismanagement left behind by Addonizio's cabal. Virtually every city contract had been inflated by 10 percent to factor in kickbacks. Men accustomed to the old regime approached the new mayor and openly offered thousands of dollars in exchange for favors. After the teacher-strike settlement, Addonizio's people had buried $21 million in school expenses so that taxes wouldn't have to be raised before the election. Overall, Newark faced a $60 million deficit, including the very real prospect of not being able to keep schools open through 1971.[107]

"History has played another of its cruel jokes on the Negroes," said a *Newsweek* cover story about newly elected African American mayors in cities such as Washington, D.C.; Dayton, Ohio; Cleveland; and Newark.

"The mantle of power, now finally within their reach, may no longer be adequate to the problems that come with it." In other words, by the time a city was filled with enough black residents to elect one of its own as mayor, the municipality was probably broke, or close to it.[108]

Making matters worse for Ken Gibson, the Italian-majority city council fought nearly every one of his decisions, blocking the hiring of an accountant, killing a special audit of city finances, and rejecting Gibson's nominees for municipal judges. The mayor couldn't even count on the support of African Americans, many of whom were disappointed they hadn't received jobs and hadn't seen immediate improvements in their neighborhoods. Amiri Baraka led the loud and frequent criticisms of Ken Gibson for not appointing a black man as police director and for not hiring more blacks, in general.[109]

"No one has danced in Broad Street recently," a *Star Ledger* article read in late 1970, noting the marked change in atmosphere since election night just half a year earlier.[110] The city was bankrupt or would be soon. Time and energy that should have been used to remedy the city's ghastly financial situation was often sidetracked by petty squabbles. Mayor Gibson, for example, was drawn in as mediator when Amiri Baraka organized a boycott of Portuguese businesses in Newark because, far away on the other side of the Atlantic Ocean, Portuguese merchants had recently invaded Guinea.[111]

Early on in the Gibson administration, a pattern had been established in which each time the mayor appeased one interest group, he invariably angered another. He faced knee-jerk hostility from entrenched white power brokers on one side, and frustrated black masses calling him a sell-out and a hypocrite on the other. Observers from all walks of life viewed Ken Gibson as a political lightweight, not nearly experienced or savvy enough to handle the monstrous tasks that needed tackling.

If Ken Gibson wasn't aware of just how ungovernable the city he inherited was, his eyes were opened in his first spring as mayor, when Newark reached an extreme in terms of dysfunction and divisiveness. A series of incidents occurring during a little over a week in 1971 reveal what Ken Gibson, and the city as a whole, was up against.

At a little after 9 PM on Thursday, April 1, a sixty-year-old black man said goodbye to his son, a policeman, and began walking to a friend's wake in the Central Ward. The old man had been born in Alabama, where at age twelve he quit school and began working long days in the fields to help feed his four brothers and five sisters. Like so many other Southern African Americans, the man later headed north. With his wife and two sons in tow, he arrived in Newark in 1940 and found employment as a butcher in a meat-processing plant, where he still worked three decades later.[112]

Somewhere near the corner of Farley and Clinton avenues, six young black men surrounded him. "What you got, old man?" one asked, as the pack pushed him and grabbed for his wallet. The man had suffered three heart attacks and knew running wasn't an option. Believing that the young men might very well kill him, the old man pulled out a penknife and flailed it at the muggers, slashing one across the belly, another on the hand. When he tripped over a low fence, the hoodlums kicked and beat him with fists and a tree branch.[113]

With blood dripping from his mouth and one swollen eye starting to close—injuries that would eventually need eleven stitches—the man entered a shop and asked to use the phone. The storekeeper refused, not wanting to get involved. Another store also turned down his request for help. Someone finally called the police after recognizing the bloodied old man. He was Willie Gibson. One of his sons was police officer Harold Gibson. His other son was Mayor Kenneth Gibson.[114]

From his hospital bedside, Willie Gibson raged against the justice system after learning a few of his assailants were juveniles who had recently committed crimes only to be freed into the custody of their parents. A fifteen-year-old boy arrested in the Gibson incident had mugged a woman on South Broad Street less than two weeks before. "There have got to be some changes in this particular part of the law," Willie Gibson said, in a sentiment that would be repeated for decades. "If kids are old enough to snatch purses and beat people, they should go to jail." The elder Gibson said the parents of children who commit crimes should be held legally and financially accountable, and, although there was no precedent to do so, he announced plans to sue the parents of the juveniles who mugged him. "If a dog bites you, you're responsible for the dog," he said. "A vicious child has no more rights than a vicious dog, and the parents should be responsible."[115]

To Willie Gibson, however, the most disappointing aspect was the unwillingness of people to assist an old man who'd obviously just been assaulted. "The worst part about it all was that nobody wanted to get involved," he said. "If someone didn't recognize me as the mayor's father, would anyone have called the police?"[116]

A short distance away from where the mayor's father was jumped, another ugly episode revealed precisely why people may have been reluctant to get involved. On the same night of the Willie Gibson mugging, John Graybush, a sixty-eight-year-old man with horn-rimmed glasses, a thick head of gray-black hair, and a ruddy, deeply wrinkled brow, was nearing the end of his 4 PM–midnight shift driving bus No. 25 westward on Springfield Avenue. A native Newarker, Graybush left the city in the mid-1950s along with so many other middle-class whites. With his wife, six sons, and three daughters, Gray-bush moved to Union, but held onto his city-bus-driver post. By 1971, he'd been at the job for twenty-seven years. When three young men on his bus attacked a sixty-year-old woman, ripping the pocketbook out of her hands, Graybush instinctively jerked the wheel to the side of the road and ran back to help her. One of the muggers, a sixteen-year-old boy, yelled at the driver to back off and then fired a single bullet into Graybush's chest. He died an hour later, leaving a wife, nine children, and sixteen grandchildren behind.[117]

In their way, Willie Gibson and John Graybush were Newark archetypes: the black southern migrant and the white resident who'd fled but maintained ties with the city. Both men could lay claim to being part of a harder-working, more respectful generation than the one reaching its prime in the 1970s. Newark had changed significantly since these two old-timers had come of age. As Mayor Gibson pointed out after the attack on his father, Newark was now a place where "anyone's mother, father or sister can be mugged."[118] The outgrowth of a new, more desperate and more vicious breed of criminals was a gloomy sense of hopelessness and fear among the people, who were increasingly—and understandably—cautious about fighting back.

On the night Willie Gibson was attacked, the mayor couldn't get to the hospital to see his father because he was engaged in discussions to end the city's nine-week-old teachers' strike. Until recently, Gibson had generally maintained a hands-off approach to the strike, during which about two thousand of Newark's forty-four hundred teachers and half of the city's seventy-eight thousand students hadn't gone to school. Not wanting to overstep his bounds, Gibson had allowed the board of education, the Newark Teachers Union (NTU), and appointed mediators to hash out the issues. The result was more than two months of bickering and posturing, and one of the ugliest strikes in the nation's history. Finally, after being criticized for "failure to assume leadership" by city council president Louis Turco and others, Gibson began strong-arming the union and the board of education into accepting the contract then on the table. "Nine weeks is too long," Gibson announced, calling for teachers to return to schools soon. "If the teachers who are supposed to do it won't, then we will get teachers who will."[119]

On Friday, April 2, the same day word spread about the Willie Gibson mugging and bus-driver killing, some apparent good news reached the city. The board of education and NTU leaders had reached a tentative agreement that would end the strike. By that time, the main sticking points were seem-ingly minor issues. Teachers wanted to be responsible for fewer nonprofes-sional chores, such as monitoring hallways and guiding children to and from buses, and have the option of seeking binding arbitration in disputes with principals or the board of education. They also sought a guarantee that the 347 teachers suspended during the strike would get their jobs back.[120]

Both issues—chores and arbitration—had already been decided in the prior (1970) strike settlement, in the teachers' favor. Since then, Mayor Gibson had appointed three members to the board of education, which in the 1970–1971 school year was led by a nonwhite majority for the first time. Several board members, including newly appointed president Jesse Jacob, regarded the previous year's settlement contract as a grave mistake. Many people believed the one-year contract, signed when Mayor Addonizio was running for reelection and desperate for positive media coverage, had taken far too much power out of the hands of the board. Jacob called the old agreement "asinine" and "outlandish."[121] With Ken Gibson as mayor, the board decided to fight to restore the old policies, essentially negating those aspects of the 1970 settlement. The union wasn't about to give back hard-won concessions, hence the strike.

That's how the teachers' strike played out on the surface. As with almost any confrontation in 1970s Newark, however, the underlying reasons for the strike largely came down to race. Most teachers were white, and even though the head of the NTU was a black woman—Carole Graves—a disproportion-ately high percentage of those striking were white. Striking teachers worried that without binding arbitration, they'd be subject to the whims of the board and school principals—both of whom, it was believed, were heavily influenced by racial politics. Teachers might be transferred or fired with little recourse. On the flip side, black militants argued that control of the schools needed to be wrested away from white teachers who lived in the suburbs, didn't have a vested interest in Newark, and cared for little other than their salaries and benefits. Many people viewed Ken Gibson's appointment of the openly anti-labor Jesse Jacob as the mayor's way to bully the teachers' union, or perhaps even break it. Everyone knew that the NTU wouldn't budge on policies it had fought over just a year earlier; no union would. Jacob and much of the black community argued that teachers unwilling to pitch in through certain nonprofessional chores were clearly insensitive to the needs of their students. Those close to the standoff maintained that black militants didn't particularly care about nonprofessional chores or arbitration, however. These issues certainly didn't seem significant enough to justify forty thousand kids being out of school for nearly three months. The policy battle was simply a ploy to force a strike, which might break the union and allow the board to gut the 1970 contract and take firmer control of the schools.[122]

The first strike, in 1970, had been fraught with the tension, emotion, and angry rhetoric inherent in any labor clash. Yet there was a certain amount of dignity among the participants. Black and white teachers alike went on strike for standard reasons like wage increases and job security, but also with the goal of creating better environments—for themselves and for their students. One of the major issues was limiting classes to a maximum of thirty children. (Until then, fifty, sixty, even seventy kids might be crammed into a single room.) Rather than being a black-white battle, the 1970 strike was basically a classic labor-management confrontation. Most working-class Newarkers, regardless of race, gave teachers their respect if not outright sympathy. The strike may have been illegal, but teachers at least had the conviction to stand their ground. At a hearing in which dozens of teachers were sentenced to ten or more days in jail, several teachers addressed the court by citing the experiences of others who had broken the law over principle, including Plato, Sir Thomas More, and the revolutionary founding fathers of the United States. "I prefer to be in contempt of this court," one teacher said, "rather than face the contempt of my students."[123]

The 1971 strike, by contrast, began with bloodshed. On February 2, the first day of organized picketing, carloads of young black men pulled up in front of the NTU office and attacked fifteen striking teachers with fists, broom handles, lead pipes, and other weapons. Six teachers had to be taken to hospital; two teachers were injured badly enough to be kept overnight. One woman suffered a fractured skull. A male teacher needed 126 stitches; he'd been beaten with a Wiffle ball bat lined with nails. Blood had streamed down his face and speckled his button-down shirt, where a small circular NTU pin rested.[124]

It was assumed that Newark's black-militant segment was responsible for the attacks. Teachers responded by bringing knives, screwdrivers, ice picks, and other weapons to pickets. They also viciously harassed teachers still working. Cars in school parking lots were fair game. Strikers flattened tires, poured soap powder down carburetors, and smashed windows. One teacher admitted shooting out the same car's windows with a BB gun seven times. The striking teachers smeared gum over school door locks. They hollered insults and threw pennies at scabs. Someone came up with a concept called the "wild bus ride," in which fifty or sixty teachers rented a bus, drove to a school, and vandalized cars and pelted nonstriking teachers with eggs. They would then surround the school so no one could leave. Fights broke out when husbands arrived to pick up their wives trapped inside the building. Teachers breaking the strike lines weren't even safe at home, where they received threatening phone calls. Scabs sometimes got up in the morning to find windows broken in their home and insults spray-painted on their car.[125]

On Monday, April 5, the strike entered its tenth week. That night, the

North Ward Parent-Teacher's Association hosted a gathering primarily of Italians, including former councilman Anthony Imperiale, council president Louis Turco, and board of education member John Cervase. An Addonizio appointee, Cervase was a lawyer from the wealthy Forest Hills section of the North Ward. He had traditionally taken a conservative stand on most issues, opposing sex education and the ban on prayer in schools. He'd also generally been antiunion. Frightened by what might happen if Jesse Jacob and the militant blacks wielded more power, Cervase became the board's strongest supporter of the strike. Cervase and Jacob clearly hated each other. At the North Ward PTA meeting, Cervase told how Jacob had recently taken a swing at him. Cervase, Imperiale, Turco, and others impressed onto the crowd the importance of going to City Hall the following night, when the board of education would vote on the teachers' contract.[126]

The meeting on Tuesday, April 6, was an unabashed fiasco. Nearly a thousand people crowded into the 450-seat city council chambers. The first argument began when Jesse Jacob, the muscular board president, tried to open up the floor to the public, which he said was required by law. Cervase interrupted Jacob, stating there was no such law, and called for an immediate vote. Their spat escalated. Cervase griped that he was sick of being called a liar. Jacob responded with taunting reminiscent of junior high: "You lied. You lied. You lied." The crowd, which was mostly black, chanted, "Cervase got to go! Cervase got to go!"[127]

Eventually, at about 8:45 PM, the first of nearly two hundred people scheduled to address the board stood ready at the microphone. He was Dr. E. Wyman Garrett, a thirty-seven-year-old dentist and former board member with a neat, puffy Afro, dressed in a black suit and a ruffled, powder-blue shirt. Garrett began by promising revenge on two board members who he accused of selling out their votes. "We are going to make sure you don't get back on the board," he said, before moving on to the subject of teachers who'd been picketing. "When the teachers come back to school they better have a cop escorting each one each day, because when they don't there is going to be trouble." Each speaker was supposed to be allowed only ten minutes, but because of constant interruptions—board calls for people to clear the aisles, as well as shouts from the crowds of "Right on, doctor, right on!" and "We want the kids back in school!"—Garrett had the floor for about forty minutes. He demanded a rejection of the contract by the board, who he said were partly racists, partly Uncle Toms. "Come on niggers, get off your knees and stand up," Garrett said. "You honkeys run your schools the way you want to on your side of town and we'll run our schools on our side of town."[128]

About fifteen other speakers gave their ten minutes of input, mostly calling for the board to vote no. The supply of whistles, catcalls, and racial slurs from the audience seemed inexhaustible. "I am sick of banging this gavel!" Jacob cried out. As if to dispel any illusions regarding the real subtext of the board's decision, a white woman at the microphone addressed Jacob specifically. "I hope you realize what's going on here tonight," she said. "Blacks against whites. Whites against blacks."[129]

Around 11 PM, a white teacher approached the podium, yelling, "Jesse, here I am, come and get me!"[130] Fights erupted all over the room. Scrums of people were knocked to the floor and mashed up against walls. Window blinds crumpled in a heap near where one group tussled. Microphones, chairs, and electrical wiring were destroyed. A *New York Times* reporter who refused to turn over his notebook to four black men was punched in the stomach. The men then took the notebook, as well as the reporter's wallet. Police rushed in to break up the fights, and the board adjourned for the night.[131]

The following evening, Wednesday, April 7, the meeting continued at Symphony Hall. Outside the building, dozens of cops and paddy wagons stood ready. Inside, policemen searched gym bags and briefcases before allowing people to enter; one man was arrested for trying to bring in a concealed vacuum-cleaner hose. The procession of speakers picked up where it had left off. "If you pass this contract, you're asking for trouble," one black mother said, threatening the board. "These teachers will be going back to the suburbs every day but you'll be here 365 days a year." LeRoi Jones was called to speak, but apparently wasn't in attendance. One woman at the microphone repeated the same five words more than a hundred times: "Do not sign the contract. Do not sign the contract. Do not sign the contract . . ." Jacob eventually said her time was up, though by then the crowd had taken up her chant.[132]

Many speakers addressed one particular board member. Charles Bell, a Gibson appointee, was the lone black board member to tentatively approve the contract. Still, Bell admitted his loyalties were divided. He believed strongly in unions, and yet felt that blacks should be able to run their communities and their school systems as they saw fit. "We were both black before we were born, do you understand, brother Bell?" one speaker said. "I hope you don't sell us out because they're using you. Bell, come home, brother. Come back black."[133]

After a brief recess, the board returned, and all eyes gazed on Charles Bell, the first man to cast his vote. He rambled about there being "no such thing as a victory for either party," and about "a time we do not totally personally agree but my vote must reflect the people I represent." Ultimately, Bell said, "I must vote for the survival of a city and therefore I vote no." Crowds cheered, hooted, and hugged. They stood on top of chairs and pumped fists high in the air. The rest of the board voted along racial lines: all told, four whites in favor, and four blacks and one Puerto Rican opposed. "If this be the year of attrition, then let it be," said Jacob, after casting the final, deciding vote to reject the contract, and ending the meeting with one more bang of the gavel. "In the words of the Negro spiritual, 'Free at last, free at last, praise God almighty, free at last.'"[134]

As the crowd funneled out of the building, police arrested Dr. Wyman Garrett, the dentist. The *Times* reporter had fingered Garrett as one of the men who had assaulted and robbed him the night before. "It's so obvious," Garrett said of the charges. "They would never arrest a white physician." Police also arrested Councilman Dennis Westbrooks, an Amiri Baraka ally and one of the candidates endorsed by the black and Puerto Rican convention. Westbrooks and four juveniles were charged with obstructing the aisle and refusing to let people by at the meeting.[135]

The arrests kicked off a new controversy. On Thursday, April 8, Westbrooks, dressed in a colorful, African-style shirt, and a full-bearded, sunglass-wearing Amiri Baraka sat behind microphones at a City Hall press conference, demanding the removal of Police Director John Redden. "Redden must be fired," Baraka declared. "The majority of the community is fed up with this racist turkey." According to Baraka, the past few days proved Redden could not "control the zombies Spina trained to eat black flesh." The city needed "a police director . . . who can not only control the psychopaths and licensed killers who wear police uniforms, but who can also relate to the majority community of blacks and Puerto Ricans." Speaking of Mayor Gibson, Baraka said, "He's trying to please the devils and the angels at the same time, and it can't be done."[136]

The mayor had steadfastly defended John Redden since first proposing him as police director. The media, state prosecutors, and people involved in the post-riot governor's commission often praised the Redden appointment as Gibson's smartest move. If anyone could clean up the Newark Police Department, they said, it was the tough, blunt Irishman with the pointy chin, deeply receding hairline, and husky, six-foot frame. A native Newarker, Redden joined the department after returning from a stint in the navy during World War II. He worked his way through the ranks, consistently getting top scores on department exams. He earned a reputation as a bright, honest, hard-nosed cop. While leading Newark's short-lived special gambling unit, Redden demonstrated he was unafraid of confronting far-reaching criminal operations. Even so, Newark's city council initially voted unanimously to reject Redden as police director. The black councilmen apparently opposed Redden because he wasn't black, while the Italians opposed Redden because he couldn't be controlled. The council eventually came around and accepted Redden after reaching some compromises with Gibson. Once in charge of the department, Redden reassigned hundreds of beat cops and high-ranking officers in the hopes of stirring precincts out of their complacent, corrupt ways. The new director also created initiatives to recruit new officers solely from Newark, aiming specifically to bring more African Americans and Puerto Ricans into the department.[137]

No matter the criticism from Baraka and the black community, Gibson offered his "unqualified, 100 percent support" to John Redden, calling him "the best police director in the history of Newark." Gibson also took a bold potshot at "self-appointed leaders making a lot of noise," presumably meaning his old ally Amiri Baraka.[138]

Sunday, April 11, was Easter. In light of the tense week, fifteen clergymen had quickly organized an afternoon prayer service "to remind all Newarkers that we are one community with a common interest in the future of this city."[139] A crowd of five hundred blacks and whites bowed their heads on a warm, sunny day on the steps of City Hall. Among the speakers calling for an end to hate-filled rants and racial polarization was an eighth grader named Reginald Clark. He was allowed to address the crowd as a representative of a group who too often had been overlooked during the ugly struggle: the students. "Lord, we pray to You to help end the strike for the city's sake, and especially for the students' sake, because it is holding us back most of all," Clark said. "It is holding us back from being the future leaders of this community."[140]

Mayor Gibson attended the service but did not speak. In the day's newspapers, however, amid articles about the possibility of a state takeover of Newark schools, Gibson's letter to the board of education and the NTU was made public. The mayor called for an end to the strike, as well as to the racist rhetoric. "Demagoguery has replaced conciliation," Gibson wrote. "Energies which could otherwise be channeled into productive service are being spent on activities destined to bring about confrontation of a most destructive and undesirable nature."[141]

The following day's newspapers included a rare, extended public statement from Police Director John Redden. In businesslike fashion, Redden presented some irrefutable facts. Since 1960, Newark experienced more crime per capita than any big city in the nation. Whereas in 1950 there were 24 criminal homicides in Newark, in 1970 the city experienced 143, and 1971 was already shaping up to surpass that figure. "These crimes do not have their origin in the police department," Redden said. "The majority of these crimes originate in our community. It is our own who make the streets unsafe to walk. It is our own who are going to have to respond to the problem." Redden went on to echo a growing sentiment: "The present tensions parallel the conditions that existed before the riots in 1967." The previous week, Councilman Sharpe James and Urban Coalition president Gustav Heninberg had said essentially the same thing. "The guns are being loaded again by those who would plunge this city into the same type of apocalyptic convulsions it exercised in 1967," Redden warned. "The problem is not whether or not I remain as police director. Among the many distasteful assignments I have had as a police officer, this is the most distasteful. The problem concerns a decision on public policy." The police director ended his message by calling for normally "aloof" citizens to get involved, for the sake of the city's future: "It is decision making time."[142]

———

For Newark schools, decisions were made on April 18. During Easter week, parent groups, community activists, clergymen, and politicians lobbied for peace. Mayor Gibson appeared on television and issued statements demanding a compromise. The contract was adjusted slightly, calling for teachers to "voluntarily accept" a few nonprofessional chores as part of their jobs. Binding arbitration would remain in the teachers' favor, and the 347 suspended teachers would be reinstated. Charles Bell and one other African American board of education member reversed their votes at an April 18 meeting, giving the yeas a 6–3 edge. When teachers approved the contract later that evening, the standoff was over. At eleven weeks, it had been the longest-ever teachers' strike of any large U.S. city, and certainly one of the most vicious labor strikes in American history. Bitterness and hostility would remain for decades. "I don't think anybody scored a victory," said board president Jesse Jacob, who voted no on the final contract. "I say children got kicked in the teeth."[143]

John Redden stayed on as police director after the strike. Frustrated by being placed in the middle of another ugly racial confrontation, in the fall of 1972, he resigned. This time, factions were battling over a housing development. A group led by Amiri Baraka had been able to secure Housing and Urban Development approval, funding, and a local tax abatement for a sixteen-story, 210-unit apartment that included a 300-seat theater and community rooms. Named for the black-nationalist philosophy Baraka had adopted, Kawaida Towers was slated for a site near Lincoln Avenue, deep in the Italian North Ward. Several leading Italian politicians initially supported

the project, due to be built by an Italian contractor. North Ward councilman Frank Megaro, who would later dubiously claim to have not known
Baraka was involved, actually introduced the tax abatement to the council,
which approved the motion. At the October 1972 groundbreaking, however,
an emerging North Ward community leader named Steve Adubato led a
demonstration against the apartment building. Adubato accused Megaro
and others of betraying the North Ward. Who had approved such a project?
he asked. Why was an African American–oriented tower being built in the
Italian North Ward? Why wasn't it being called Garibaldi Towers?[144]

Pickets accompanied the laying of the foundation in early November.
The leader of the Newark PBA openly supported anti-Kawaida demonstrators and called for policemen to join them. Most of the picketers were old
Italian women, along with teenagers wearing white armbands. Chants of
"Nigger go home!" and "Go back to the jungle!" greeted black construction
workers. Anthony Imperiale, then a state assemblyman, chained himself to
a fence at the site one morning. A judge concerned about violence ordered
a halt to construction. By the end of the month, Frank Megaro and his
Italian city-council colleagues backtracked and rescinded the project's tax
abatement. Around Thanksgiving, when construction began again, 350 white
demonstrators blocked eight construction workers from the building site.
A newspaper photo showed Imperiale, with lamb-chop sideburns reaching
almost to his double chin, wagging a fat finger at Police Director Redden,
who looked downcast in a fedora and beige overcoat.[145]

Yet again, Redden was disgusted. Both sides of the confrontation gave the
police department endless grief. Imperiale claimed policemen were too rough
with demonstrators; Baraka questioned why protestors weren't arrested, as
they surely would have been if they had darker skin. The police director
issued another rare public statement, his prickliest to date. "The arrest of
the kids, housewives and old men who are so liberally represented in the
group of demonstrators" was not an answer, Redden said. "A situation has
been created which has two major factions in this city at each others' throats.
It was created by an administration which has permitted divisiveness and
confrontation. It was confirmed by a City Council which is either too inept
or too lazy to do its job. As usual, the Police Department is in the middle. The
department can neither treat nor solve this mess. It is a political problem and
must be solved by that process." As he had during the teachers' strike, Redden
called for level-headed business and community leaders to get involved and
override extremists like Imperiale and Baraka. "They had better be heard
before the self-serving leaders on both sides turn Newark into the biggest
dung heap on the East Coast."[146]

Shortly afterward, Redden announced his resignation, effective at the end of the year. The police director said he'd reconsider and stay longer if certain leaders took positive steps to ease tensions, but he had little hope that might actually happen. "It's like the Missouri farmer who beat his mule over the head to get him to listen," an exasperated Redden said, explaining his decision to leave.[147]

Building at the Kawaida Towers site stalled due to protests, legal battles, and the tax-abatement issue. Mayor Gibson in particular wasn't willing to fight for the project, especially not with an election looming. It slowly became apparent that the Kawaida Towers would never be built. In 1976, the site's foundations were buried for good.[148]

Mayor Gibson won the 1974 mayoral election, running as the candidate representing all of Newark. He refused to attend the follow-up to the original black and Puerto Rican convention because of its no-whites policy and was victorious without the group's endorsement. Gibson received more than 50 percent of the votes in the general election—about ten thousand more votes than the runner-up, Anthony Imperiale—so that there was no need for a runoff.[149]

The newly elected 1974 city council promised that the old era, in which meetings were interrupted by name-calling, filibustering, and posturing, was over. Dennis Westbrooks, the Baraka ally who once led a group of protestors depositing dozens of bags of trash on City Hall's steps, lost his election to Jesse Allen, a moderate backed by Mayor Gibson. (In fact, not one of the nine council candidates endorsed by Baraka's black and Puerto Rican convention won in 1974.) Louis Turco, the young former council president often viewed as a future mayor, was also gone. He'd pled guilty to federal income-tax charges related to his $100,000-a-year gambling debts and, after initially fighting to stay on the council, resigned in March of 1974. A month later he was sentenced to a year in prison.[150]

"The circus is gone," Councilman Anthony Giuliano said at the first meeting of the transformed city council. As if to prove things would be different, the council, still a 5–4 white majority, elected Earl Harris as the first black council president. "The first order of business will be business, not nonsense," said Harris.[151]

Even with a reelection victory and a newly hopeful political atmosphere, Ken Gibson was hardly optimistic in his assessment of the city. Decades of corruption, incompetence, and racial strife, as well as industrial and residential abandonment, had left Newark at, arguably, an all-time low. More and more "for sale" signs popped up in front of large homes in upscale white neighborhoods like Vailsburg and Forest Hills. Middle-class blacks with the means also avoided Newark when choosing where to live. "I have to think about schools for my children," said one African American mother who worked in the city and lived in West Orange. "Newark is so crazy, like a city that caught some sort of incurable disease, how could I really live here?"[152] Looking back on his first four years in office, Gibson couldn't say much more than, "We haven't had a riot, but very little has actually been done."[153]

Soon after the mayor uttered those words, the city in fact did have a riot, on Labor Day weekend of 1974. The initial confrontation began when Essex County police forces tried to break up a dice game at a Puerto Rican festival. Police were pelted with rocks in the ensuing melee, which escalated into two days of violence resulting in two deaths, at least five dozen people injured, and three dozen arrested. In one instance, police arrested six people riding in a car with twenty-five Molotov cocktails. Looters hit Seventh Avenue stores, near the Columbus Homes projects. More than two dozen buildings burned down. Puerto Rican leaders passed along much of the blame for the outbreak to oppressive conditions in Newark, where unemployment rates among Puerto Ricans topped 25 percent.[154]

All U.S. cities struggled through the 1970s. Boston was plagued with racial violence related to federally mandated busing aimed at desegregating schools. Baltimore's inner harbor, after years of neglect, consisted mostly of abandoned, rotting warehouses. New York teetered on bankruptcy, and President Gerald Ford seemed unwilling to bail it out, prompting the famous *Daily News* headline: "Ford to City: Drop Dead." By the mid-1970s, the perception was firmly established that in America, suburbs were king, and urban areas were corrupt and dangerous.

During this nadir for all American cities, some fell lower than others. None fared worse than Newark. The city seemed to have fallen apart even more quickly than it had skyrocketed to riches and industrial prominence a century before.

When *Harper's* magazine published an article in 1975 on "The Worst American City," it revealed what many people already knew. Newark was the worst of the worst, ranking among the worst five cities in nineteen of the study's twenty-four categories such as per capita violent crime and infant death. The city had the nation's lowest percentage of high school and college graduates. It had the lowest percentage of home ownership, and was among the worst cities in terms of housing quality and overcrowding. Newark also had the least acreage of public parks per resident—just four feet by four feet for each Newarker—as well as the lowest percentage of amusement and recreation spots per person. "The city of Newark stands without serious challenge as the worst of all," the study said in summary. "Newark is a city that desperately needs help."[155]

PART III

REBIRTH

Talk of a renaissance in Newark began soon after the 1967 riots ended. Still, by almost every indication, the city struggled through formidable hardships in the 1970s and 1980s. The population dropped by about fifty thousand in each of those decades, and Newark failed to shake its reputation as the epitome of a ghetto. Voters eventually lost faith in Kenneth Gibson. The even-tempered mayor may have been the right man to steady the city during the divisive post-riot era, but after four terms in office, Gibson seemed incapable of leading Newark to the next stage of recovery. The person voters chose to do just that was Sharpe James, a brash, boisterous councilman first elected alongside Mayor Gibson in 1970. The successes, challenges, and controversies of the early James years are the subject of chapter 8.

While Sharpe James was undoubtedly an outspoken and influential cheer-leader for Newark, he also faced nearly constant criticism from inside and outside the city. Most of the gripes centered on the heavy-handed methods used by James to retain power, as well as highly publicized government corruption scandals that occurred under the mayor's watch. Several council members and a pair of top James aides would be convicted of federal crimes in the 1990s. Observers increasingly questioned why crime rates weren't lower, why the public schools were so remarkably dysfunctional, and why residents couldn't see the impact of Newark's widely heralded "renaissance" in their neighborhoods. People also wondered how Mayor James, a three-decades-plus veteran public servant, could afford a yacht and millions of dollars worth of real estate. Chapter 9 covers the bitter battles of an upstart reform-minded newcomer named Cory Booker to wrest the mayoralty away from James, who by the mid-1990s was New Jersey's most powerful African American politician.

   The Booker years, described in chapter 10, have not been without troubles. A group of frustrated city workers and diehard Sharpe James supporters led a short-lived campaign to recall Mayor Booker. The gruesome, execution-style murders of three young Newarkers caught national headlines. Despite drastic changes in the police department, the city's overall murder rate remained exceptionally high during Booker's first full year in office. Even so, the concept of a Newark renaissance has become undeniable. The city was simply too valuable a hub for transportation and commerce to remain tangled in despair and economic malaise forever. With a new downtown arena, a hot real estate market, a fresh sense of hipness about the city, a charismatic, widely beloved mayor in City Hall, and a population that at long last is growing, all signs indicate Newark will continue to blossom.

CHAPTER 8

SHARPE CHANGE

A NEW MAYOR CHARTS
THE MEANDERING ROAD TO RECOVERY

In Newark, as in most cities, one sure way of telling that an ethnic group had arrived as a significant political force was the election of one of its own as mayor. Newark's Irish, Jews, and Italians successively took great pride when someone within their ranks finally seized the reins of power at City Hall.

No group had ever been as sharply and widely discriminated against as African Americans, and arguably no group ever felt as strong a sense of glory as Newark's black community did when Ken Gibson was elected. The 1970 run for mayor was not simply another political campaign. It was a cause—locally and nationally—taken up with almost religious fervor. And when the first African American was at long last given charge of the city, there was no understating the hope in the hearts of Newark's people of color. As Gustav Heningburg, TV host and political advisor to Gibson and other mayors, put it, the overly simplistic feeling during the 1970 election amounted to: "All we need is a black mayor and Monday morning he will solve all our problems."[1]

The black and Puerto Rican coalition had battled vigorously to take over Newark government. Ken Gibson and Newark's new leaders understood the city they had won was troubled, but over the years it became apparent they'd underestimated just how dreadful the conditions truly were. The people who had pushed Gibson into office had also overestimated the inexperienced new administration's ability to deal with Newark's long list of deeply entrenched problems.

During the Gibson years, African American leaders succeeded in switching the names of some schools and streets to reflect their culture and heritage. High Street, for example, became Martin Luther King Boulevard; schools were rechristened in honor of black heroes such as Marcus Garvey, Rosa Parks, and Harriet Tubman. Yet figuring out how to affect deeper institutional changes to the city's business structure, school system, and neighborhoods was far more complicated.

Newark's African Americans may have united to elect Ken Gibson, but the idea that there was consensus in the black community as to which direction the city should pursue was a myth. Mayor Gibson, for example, opposed groups seeking to fly the black liberation flag at public schools, as well as the insertion of the names of black heroes at the expense of historic Newarkers such as Robert Treat. "Why change names?" asked Gibson. "Why change Robert Treat, the founder of Newark? You can't change history by changing names."[2] Gibson, who made his career largely as a compromiser, was also criticized incessantly by hard-line African Americans disgusted by what they perceived as the mayor's constant appeasement of Newark's Italians, corporations, and other interests.

In many ways, the city's predicaments were too large and too numerous for the community to solve by itself—especially in a city as divided as Newark. As a result, by almost any measure, Newark in the Ken Gibson era fell into worse shape than it had been in the tumultuous, corrupt 1960s.

The population dropped by fifty thousand between the 1970 and 1980 censuses. Statistics from the early 1980s showed that about one-third of Newark residents lived in poverty, compared to 22.5 percent in 1970. During the ten years after the riots, while employment rose dramatically in nearly all of New Jersey, including Essex County as a whole, one out of four jobs in Newark disappeared. About two-thirds of the jobs remaining in Newark were held by people living outside the city. Dozens of companies found it impossible to stay in business in Newark, including several once-stalwart institutions closely associated with the city. The *Newark Evening News* ceased operations in 1972, as did brewer P. Ballantine & Sons, closing its thirty-eight-acre Ironbound plant. Orhbach's and Hahne's department stores deserted the city, and while Bamberger's remained, it downgraded the quality of its goods to match the limited buying power of its changing customer base. Grand Union grocery store executives, in a trend-setting move copied by other supermarket chains, decided that there was not much money to be made in the inner city and closed all of its Newark locations.[3]

When a 1973 study revealed that Newark had the poorest housing conditions of all large U.S. cities, Robert Notte, the new Newark Housing Authority director, could do little other than call the findings "very valid."[4] At the time, the NHA was struggling to summon up money owed to PSE&G, which had contacted federal authorities and threatened to cut off service at city housing projects. Public-housing residents refused to pay rent in a long, drawn-out strike unless the awful, dangerous living conditions were remedied. More than ten thousand Newarkers signed a petition requesting that the Columbus Homes be phased out and demolished; some 20 percent of the project's units had already been abandoned, even though the complex was less than twenty years old.[5]

Private homeowners hadn't fared much better. Thousands of houses were destroyed to make way for I-78 and various urban-renewal projects. From 1972 to 1976, Newark foreclosed on more than a thousand homes annually, on average, compared to about a hundred per year in the late 1960s. A depressed real estate market, combined with thousands of fires, resulted in an overall 12 percent drop in assessed value of property in Newark; during that same period, values skyrocketed in the suburbs.[6]

Hundreds of experienced teachers grew disgusted by tense battles with colleagues and the board of education, as well as the increase in drugs, violence, and disrespect in schools. Teachers by the dozen either used connections to assume responsibilities with limited student interaction or left Newark altogether. To fill the openings left behind, the race-conscious board heavily recruited people of color who oftentimes were not qualified. By the end of the 1970s, about half of Newark's public-school teachers were not certified.[7]

The city's finances deteriorated steadily. Public universities and other tax-exempt entities accounted for about two-thirds of the land within Newark's borders. Corporations were increasingly offered tax abatements as enticements to keep operations in the city. Property owners who did pay taxes were incapable of covering the bills for police protection, schools, and other municipal services. Many owners had already "torched" or abandoned their buildings rather than try to keep up with the exorbitant tax rates. Bloated city-agency budgets certainly didn't help the situation. Federal executives criticized the NHA as "wasteful" and "top-heavy" and threatened to pull funds unless Newark's housing agency streamlined operations.[8] The school budget ballooned from $30 million in 1960 to over $150 million by the end of the 1970s.[9]

Facing imminent financial collapse, the Gibson administration increasingly looked to handouts from state and federal sources. In fiscal year 1978–1979, for example, the state covered 64 percent of the cost of Newark's school system, and federal funds kicked in another 10 percent. By contrast, state aid covered only 14 percent of Newark's school budget in 1960–1961.[10]

No matter how much money poured into the city, however, Mayor Gibson seemed powerless to alter Newark's image as an urban jungle. Racial views and distorted media coverage certainly contributed to the perception, but many people came to the same conclusions based on what they'd seen with their own eyes. "There is almost no way to enter Newark without facing the fact that the city needs some work—badly," wrote a *New Jersey Monthly* contributor—in a 1979 issue dedicated to praising the city's "real, live, honest-to-God renaissance," no less. (Cover headline: "Surprise! Some Nice Words about Newark.") "McCarter Highway goes past some smelly industrial plants that turn the stomach. Ditto Raymond Boulevard. But even this is better than a westward approach. South Orange Avenue, Springfield Avenue—these two arteries take cars past sights that turn the mind and the spirit."[11]

Stanley Winters, an urban-history professor at New Jersey Institute of Technology, in a *New York Times* article from the era entitled "Newark: Don't Let It Die," recounted one of his journeys into the city via the No. 25 bus, the same Springfield Avenue route upon which bus driver John Graybush was killed in 1971. "It's a strange world of ghostly shops, battle-scarred buildings and bygone people," Winters wrote of the Central Ward scenery. "There is something for everybody: charred storefronts, plywood windows, broken glass, iron shutters, illegible signs worn by weather and age."[12]

"Newark has the will to fight, but it can't go it alone," Winters wrote. "The basic problem is whether her immediate neighbors, and indeed the whole society, are prepared to share the task of helping it face the 21st century."

The public soon tired of dumping money into cities such as Newark, however. Conservative politicians often pointed out that the hundreds of millions funneled into America's cities in the 1970s had yielded few tangible, lasting improvements. Newark had used federal and state money to hire hundreds of new police officers, bringing the department to an all-time peak in 1974 of 1,640 cops, or 4.7 officers for every thousand residents—one of the nation's highest ratios for large cities, which averaged 3.4 cops per thousand people. Despite the increased police force, Newark crime rates decreased only marginally. In a 1977 survey, a quarter of Newarkers said they had personally witnessed a crime in the preceding year. In the Central Ward, over one-third of residents said they'd seen a crime committed, though only 10 percent of those actually called the police.[13]

As popular sentiment turned against cities, funds that Gibson had been accustomed to receiving evaporated, and the mayor didn't have a viable Plan B. After federal cutbacks in 1978, Gibson announced layoffs of 450 city employees, including 225 cops. Police officers protested by calling in sick and spreading rumors of a strike. After one Patrolmen's Benevolent Association union meeting, the windows of forty-six police vehicles were mysteriously shattered. "If that is the only way they can alert the public to our problem," said the PBA president, while admitting no wrongdoing, "then it is a necessary evil." Nonetheless, the layoffs took effect on New Year's Day of 1979.[14]

Whenever Mayor Gibson was called out for doing too little for Newark—
and he heard the criticism constantly—he responded by pointing out that all
cities struggled. Newark's troubles were no different from those of New York,
Boston, Philadelphia, Baltimore, and other cities. No mayor could snap his
fingers and solve his city's problems. Sustained effort was the only solution,
Gibson maintained, and who better than him to guide the way? Lately, he
had taken up running marathons, a sport that perfectly suited his grinding
approach. "I don't assault problems," said Gibson. "I wear them down. In
times of crisis, my pulse rate slows down."[15]

After four years of Ken Gibson as mayor, 80 percent of residents in a 1974
survey said they'd seen no improvement in Newark. Perhaps even more
disturbing, 28 percent of whites and 36 percent of blacks wished to move
out of the city. Even so, most people did not seem to blame Mayor Gibson.
Nearly two-thirds of African Americans and about 40 percent of whites gave
him favorable job ratings. Voters, in turn, tended to give their low-key, steady,
if uninspiring, mayor the benefit of the doubt, electing him easily to second
and third terms. Gibson outdistanced opponents with majority votes in the
1974 and 1978 primaries, meaning there was no need for a runoff in either
year. In 1978, soon after serving as president of the U.S. Council of Mayors,
the heavily favored Gibson netted a whopping 70 percent of the vote.[16]

Gibson, like any politician, often pointed out the achievements during his
years in office. Gateway I and II, a pair of multimillion-dollar high-rise office
complexes built on urban-renewal land around Pennsylvania Station, had
been completed in the early 1970s. Prudential and PSE&G never abandoned
the city, as many had expected them to do; PSE&G even built a slick new
glass tower across from Military Park to serve as its downtown headquarters.
In 1977, Newark established its first historic district, west of Washington
Park along James Street, where dozens of brick Victorian homes were being
renovated, just as similar old neighborhoods were being fixed up in Hoboken
and Jersey City. Thousands of Portuguese immigrants reinvigorated the
Ironbound, restoring homes and opening restaurants, travel agencies, and
other businesses.

Many Gibson-era improvements came with caveats, however. Glass-
enclosed tubes connected the train station and the two Gateway buildings,
so that commuting office workers wouldn't ever have to set foot on the
street. The design gave added heft to Newark's reputation as a dangerous
place in which unusual measures were necessary to keep people safe.
Prudential and PSE&G hadn't deserted Newark, but both companies
employed far fewer workers in the city in the early 1980s compared to a
decade earlier. Progress in the James Street historic district occurred at a

snail's pace, with buildings haphazardly refurbished over the course of a decade. The revamping of James Street and the Ironbound were also largely self-contained. Improvements failed to spread to surrounding areas, and in many ways residents even at these desirable addresses had the same problems as people in other parts of town. Burglaries and car thefts plagued James Street homeowners for years; some residents emptied their vehicles of car seats and other items nightly and even left their car doors open rather than have thieves break in and damage their cars. "We could use a grocery store," said one James Street resident, offering a complaint to be heard for decades. More problematic, after years of extensive urban-renewal projects had decimated Newark's old neighborhoods, the city didn't have many other areas worthy of restoring.[17]

By the fall of 1981, the widespread perception was that Ken Gibson had lost his energy and sense of mission. "I'm not a manager of hope," Gibson said, always the realist, always ready to point out the limits of his power. "I'm a manager of resources."[18] The mayor seemed eager to move on. He entered the Democratic primary for governor and came in a respectable third. Crime rates spiked in 1980 and 1981, and Gibson vehemently denied there was any correlation between the increase and recent cuts in the police department.[19]

The unthinkable had also occurred. A genuine scandal tarnished the reputation of Ken Gibson—the industrious fellow who earned his engineering degree over a dozen years of night school, the teetotaler who never stayed out late, the man who many viewed as the lone honest figure in Newark politics. In July of 1981, vandals stole a valve from Newark's far-flung water system, and a pipe burst as a result. In the aftermath, a tidbit of information leaked: years beforehand, in a patronage appointment aimed at gaining favor with Italian city council members, Mayor Gibson had hired a former councilman, Michael Bontempo, as chief of security for the city's water supply system. The main problem with Bontempo, who collected $115,000 over seven years in his post, was that he was rarely ever in Newark, or even in New Jersey. He lived in Florida.[20]

To much of Newark's black community, the scandal was symptomatic of a large problem they had with Ken Gibson. The mayor had turned his back on his base, critics said. He spent far too much time trying to please the Italians, the city council, insurance executives, developers, and federal officials rather than dealing with housing or poverty or other issues important to his African American constituents. The aloof, sullen mayor always seemed to be out of town or unavailable, they grumbled. As early as the mid-1970s, community leaders complained the mayor allowed cronyism and political maneuvering to take precedence over reform. "Gibson is up in the Gateway Center eating," one said. "He's fat now. In 1969 he was out in the street with us—talking about the people needed housing."[21]

Mayor Gibson offered few apologies for his distant demeanor, flatly saying, "If I tried to talk with everyone my work would never get done."[22] In his campaign for an unprecedented fourth term, Gibson bragged about the city's latest coup, in which Prudential would soon break ground on Gateway III, an eighteen-story glass office tower. (Again, there were caveats: the building would have elevated walkways like the other Gateway structures, and the contract stipulated that Prudential receive a fifteen-year property tax break.[23]) Many of Newark's African Americans were frustrated with the mayor's policies and personality, but were unsure where else to turn. "Things have happened in Newark that, if they happened under a white administration, the people would be rioting in the streets and saying, 'Hey, whitey don't care,'" said Councilman Sharpe James. "Now people don't know what to do. They don't know how to fight a black administration."[24] The charismatic James, in his typically colorful turn of phrase, explained black voters' evolution during the Gibson era: "They danced in the streets in 1970. They walked to the polls in 1974, and they crawled to the polls in 1978. There's been an erosion of voter support. Their quiet protest is they simply do not come out and vote."[25]

Leading up the May 1982 election, Gibson ran his standard, realistic—pessimistic, some might say—campaign which essentially said: "I'm as good as Newark voters can expect." "We have not solved all the problems of Newark," the incumbent said, "but I dare say nobody could in 12 years, and nobody will be able to do it in the next 12 years."[26] Gibson failed to win a majority of votes in the general election, as he had in his previous two runs for mayor. He faced the second-place finisher, City Council President Earl Harris, in a June runoff. "Newark voters face a depressing choice," a *Times* editorial stated. At the time, both the incumbent and his challenger were under indictment for conspiracy and misconduct due to the hiring of Michael Bontempo in the no-show water-system job. (Council President Harris had signed off on the patronage post as well.) They were "also parties to stagnant and ineffective leadership," the *Times* stated. "Newark's schools are worse than ever, crime is rampant and city government, if generally less corrupt, hardly well managed."[27]

Gibson edged Harris with 52 percent of the vote to win a fourth term. Later that year, a deadlocked jury caused a mistrial for charges related to the Bontempo episode, and Gibson's indictment was thrown out. Despite a somewhat sullied reputation, Gibson remained mayor and a formidable political power with broad, well-organized support. But the mayor's struggles—the patronage scandal, the crime increase, the stalled economy, the public's

growing impatience with the mayor's blank, unenthusiastic persona—
exposed weaknesses that the right candidate could target and attack.

––––––

On paper, not much differentiated Ken Gibson from Sharpe James. Both
were moderate Democrats in their fifties who had been educated in Newark
public schools and New Jersey colleges and who were endorsed by the
original Black and Puerto Rican Political Convention. They'd assumed their
first political offices as allies in 1970—Gibson as mayor, James as South
Ward councilman—and occupied rooms one floor away from each other
in City Hall.

By the early 1980s, however, their career trajectories were heading in
opposite directions. While support for Ken Gibson fizzled, Sharpe James's
popularity soared. In 1978, no candidate even bothered to oppose the heavy
favorite South Ward incumbent. Four years later, James received more votes
than any other council candidate and became the first ward representative
to move up to an at-large council position.

The personalities of the two men could also not have been more different:
Gibson, the quiet, white-haired engineer, versus James, the trim, strong-jawed
athlete and coach with the quick wit and winning, gap-toothed smile. During
the 1970 campaign, Gibson focused on delivering services and restoring a
sense of trust and honesty in City Hall. James, who had been a finalist in the
1960 Olympic track tryouts, handed out leaflets listing his record as track
coach during his last year at West Side High School ("crushed Irvington
17–44 . . . trounced Barringer 21–36"). Gibson ran marathons and was happy
to complete the race. James played tennis, often arriving at city meetings in
sneakers and sweat suits, and always asked for a rematch in the rare case he'd
lost. Whereas Gibson earned a reputation for being distant and humorless,
the gregarious, back-slapping James worked crowds relentlessly and seldom
turned down an opportunity to engage a would-be supporter. "Sharpe James
is ready 24 hours a day to meet and explore a possible solution to the problem
at hand," a campaign flyer stated. "His home at 38 Wilbur Avenue is under
the open door policy." Gibson spent much of his time shaking hands in
Washington and Trenton, attempting to attract federal and state aid. James
instead always seemed ready to leap into action in Newark, physically if need
be. Frustrated that a large portion of African Americans and Puerto Ricans
were failing the police department's physical exam, James himself took the
test (and passed).[28] Even their names spoke volumes about their respective
styles—one mundane, the other "Sharpe!"

In his 1982 run for a fourth term, Ken Gibson promised no major innovations to his approach of steady leadership—and on that account the mayor delivered. Newark basically received more of the same. In the past, Newarkers had applauded Gibson's "calmness." After more than a dozen years with Gibson at the helm of a middling, crime-ridden city, however, the word tossed around more frequently was "lethargy."[29]

The mayor had also grown increasingly powerless, as he often pointed out himself. Since coming into office, Gibson had lost control of school-board appointments. Board of education members were now chosen by the public—in elections in which, as it turned out, less than 10 percent of registered voters actually cast ballots. Those who voted were more often than not union members themselves, and as a result, "The board is completely controlled by the union," Gibson said.[30] In 1985, despite the appalling failure of Newark's educators, the board approved record-breaking salary increases for teachers, totaling 23 percent over three years, among other perks. Gibson accused the board of "surrendering its management prerogatives," but could do nothing to stop them.[31]

Through the mid-1980s, Newark's tax rates hovered at around $12 per $100 of assessed valuation, one of the highest rates in New Jersey, up 50 percent compared to the Addonizio era.[32] Mayor Gibson, when asked about solutions to tax issues and economic woes, said, "Our job is to pick up the garbage, sweep the streets and provide some measure of police and fire protection, and we can barely do that." His administration seemed to have no answers for Newark's troubles. "What can police do about poverty?" said Police Director Hubert Williams, when asked about ways to crack down on street crime. "What can police do about unemployment?" Alfred Faiella, a young Gibson aide who would become a player in Newark politics through the millennium, offered a non-solution solution, inadvertently pointing out the hopelessness of the Gibson era. "Me, I pray for another gas crisis," he said. That way, he figured, people would be forced to commute via public transportation to jobs in hubs like Newark, rather than drive to work in the suburbs.[33]

Frustrated that the city was either too overwhelmed or too inept to help the people, more and more community and faith-based groups took matters into their own hands. Saint Benedict's, the central Newark prep school that was founded in 1868 and educated successive white ethnic groups, closed briefly in the troubled early 1970s, then reopened with a new sense of mission to recruit local African American and Latino students—who flourished in sports and academics, with extraordinarily large percentages going on to higher education. Organizations such as La Casa de Don Pedro and Steve Adubato's North Ward Educational and Cultural Center established day care centers, job-training programs, and children's baseball leagues.

The New Community Corporation (NCC), Newark's most wide-reaching nonprofit agency, was born in the aftermath of the 1967 riots. William Linder, a young priest at Queen of Angels Catholic Church in the Central Ward, founded the organization in the church basement with a small group of parishioners and board members. After raising $100,000 from donors and the state Jaycees, NCC purchased two acres of mostly vacant Central Ward land and began inviting poor families to help design their own houses. By 1975, residents moved into 120 handsome low-income, low-rise apartment buildings surrounding a playground. Despite the NCC's positive impact on the neighborhood, politicians and black militants often criticized Linder and his organization. The NCC didn't play according to the rules set by local powerbrokers, and it embarrassed politicians by doing work that should have fallen under the government's domain. Supporters of the NCC were occasionally threatened for their involvement with the organization. Yet the group managed to dramatically expand its operations over the years, eventually growing into the largest nonprofit agency in New Jersey. By 1990, NCC and its subsidiaries had opened more than two thousand housing units and a Pathmark supermarket on Bergen Street, as well as the Priory, a Southern-style restaurant that hosted jazz musicians in the back of an old church on West Market Street.[34]

As city government continued to prove ineffectual, people who were once among Mayor Gibson's most ardent supporters also increasingly tired of his tortoiselike approach. What was a prudent course during the unruly 1970s seemed outdated and unproductive in the fast-paced, enterprising 1980s. Perhaps an aggressive, energetic character such as Sharpe James—the hare to Gibson's tortoise—could boost the city's image and jump-start new life into its blighted streets.

James had grown increasingly critical of his old ally, Mayor Gibson. "Many of us have no confidence in this administration," James said in a 1984 housing discussion. At the time, 15 percent of Newarkers—22,500 people—lived in public housing, and 6,500 more languished on waiting lists. Yet, because of funding problems and mismanagement, one-third of Newark's existing public-housing units were uninhabitable and therefore they lay vacant.[35]

James entered the 1986 run for mayor, telling voters "Newark Needs a Sharpe Change." He dared Gibson to visit the Columbus Homes or other projects and ask residents what they thought of the mayor's performance. James, whose seventeen-year-old son, John, had recently been robbed and shot in the leg while waiting for a bus, also hammered away at Gibson for doing little to solve Newark's high crime rates, among other issues. "We have 70,000 fewer people than in 1970," James said. "Newark is now Fear City and

Dope City, with the prostitutes and drug pushers operating all over the city at all hours."[36]

Even so, the mayor remained the favorite, with the Gibson machine reaping in over $400,000 in campaign funds, more than double the amount raised by James. Gibson posters far outnumbered those calling for the election of James—especially in the North Ward, where the mayor, once viewed as a savior of Newark's people of color, now had the loyal support of North Ward Italians, including the controversial Anthony Imperiale.[37]

Sharpe James, as a sixteen-year veteran city councilman, shared responsibility with the mayor for Newark's laggard economy and other troubles, and offered no groundbreaking solutions in his campaign. He wanted to increase the number of police officers, improve housing, and lower unemployment—all steps Gibson also wished to take should there be public money to do so. "Mr. James may be more energetic than Mr. Gibson, but he seems no more imaginative," a *Times* editorial stated.[38] To voters, however, James's energy, style, and charisma—and, more importantly, the fact that he clearly wasn't Ken Gibson—were apparently enough. The challenger soundly beat the incumbent in the May election, netting 55 percent of the overall vote, meaning no runoff would be necessary.[39]

"This is not a victory for Sharpe James—this is a victory for Newark residents," said James on election night. "They have issued a mandate for a better life in Newark."[40] That life included ordinary neighborhood amenities like grocery stores and movie theaters, which James promised to deliver once he was mayor. (At election time, Newark had just one of the former and only X-rated versions of the latter.) From the beginning, James also stated his intention to get a downtown arena built, as sure a sign as any to the former coach and track star that a city was prospering.[41]

On inauguration night in Symphony Hall, James, wearing oversized, black-framed glasses that were in style at the time, took his oath resting a hand on the Bible held by his wife, Mary. In his speech, which was interrupted by applause thirty-five times, Mayor James stressed the importance of family values, morality, and responsibility in government. He spoke playfully, with lyrical phrases similar to those of the nation's leading African American figure, Jesse Jackson. "We must crack down on crack," said James, calling attention to the latest, most dangerous inner-city drug of choice. "Will power must replace pill power.... We must turn to each other and not on each other."[42]

In ways big and small, the mayor promised to revamp the city's image and bring a new sense of dignity, honor, and pride to City Hall. He vowed to establish a strict code of ethics for all officials, and mandated courteous phone manners and proper dress codes among city workers. That included James himself, who traded in his shorts and tennis shoes for sleek pin-striped suits.[43]

The election of James hadn't been heralded with quite the level of "We Shall Overcome" optimism present in 1970. Still, Mayor James offered Newark something that his predecessor hadn't been able to summon in years. "Our victory," said James, "provides hope for all who share a belief in a better tomorrow."[44]

————

"Are you ready?" shouted Mayor Sharpe James, wearing a tuxedo and top hat, his voice booming into a microphone. "Yeah!" came the response from the Meadowlands' Brendan Byrne Arena, which was filled with excited, squirming youngsters from Newark, all staring at their dashing new mayor. "Are you *ready*?" the man in the spotlight cried out again, pumping up the crowd. "Yeah-h-h-h!" the people cheered.[45]

"Now, on with the Greatest Show on Earth!" James bellowed. He tooted a whistle and out whirled jugglers, elephants, acrobats, unicyclists, and clowns. This night, in the fall of 1986, the mayor served in a role he seemed born to play: honorary ringmaster for Ringling Brothers and Barnum & Bailey's "Newark's Night at the Circus."

Sharpe James relished being the carnival barker in the center of the circus—at Brendan Byrne Arena and, in a larger sense, as Newark's most boisterous and prominent cheerleader. From the beginning, there was no mistaking the new mayor for the staid, old killjoy Ken Gibson. Mayor James established himself as the anti-Gibson, socializing, cracking jokes, making appearances, and tossing around hugs and high-fives. Everywhere James went, comments followed to the effect of: "You'd never see Ken Gibson do that."[46]

Nothing seemed capable of holding the upbeat, hard-charging Mayor James back. At the reopening celebration of a South Ward grocery store—no minor occasion in Newark—James trolled the aisles for a ribbon and scissors, which no one thought to bring for the ceremonial cutting. "All right, we need shoelaces or a ribbon," James said, hustling through the frozen foods section. "Or maybe we'll put a body across the door and cut it. Hey," James said, joshing one shopper, "can we put you across the door?" The mayor himself wound up darting across the street to borrow scissors from a day care center.[47]

On the strength of his personality, political savvy, and sheer will, the relent-less Mayor James cultivated "a sense that good things are about to happen" in Newark, according to a *Times* editorial assessing his first months in office.[48]

"If nothing else," James said, "we've created a new sense of excitement about being in Newark. We've given a new direction. We've been very visible. We've been very active."[49]

Most businessmen, residents, and observers seemed to agree that with Sharpe James as mayor, a brighter future lay ahead. Even outlandish plans seemed possible. Six weeks after James was sworn into office, a diminutive forty-five-year-old developer named Harry Grant pulled into Newark with a proposal to construct the tallest building in the world, a 121-story structure with a green and golden façade. The Grant USA Tower, he wanted to call it. Born in Iraq as Uri Chvavis, he lived in Israel and Canada before settling in the mid-1970s in New Jersey's Bergen County. He fancied the name Harry Grant after spotting it in a phone book, and duly took it for his own. Grant navigated his way into the construction business and built shopping centers and upscale homes, primarily in northern New Jersey.[50]

Yet Harry Grant always had much bigger dreams. Occasionally, he pondered the likelihood of building malls and office complexes in outer space. In 1984, the man who always griped about traffic on the George Washington Bridge put together a proposal to build a five-mile tunnel ("The Grant Tunnel," naturally) beneath the Hudson River just north of the bridge. The Port Authority rejected the vague plan as infeasible. At a public auction, Grant scooped up Newark's abandoned crumbling old Central Railroad depot, just north of City Hall, for $1.2 million. It was here that Grant wanted to build his tower, along with a complex that included three million square feet of office space, a five-hundred-room hotel, piano bar, observation deck, convention center, parking garage, and a sixty-thousand-square-foot mall adorned in Italianate marble. The Renaissance Mall, it was dubbed, signifying the city's rebirth.[51]

"I have half a billion dollars ready and waiting," Grant said at the time.[52] People were skeptical about the figures Grant quoted—he seemed to underestimate costs for construction and what the tower would have to charge for office space—but such creative accounting seemed typical of many cocksure entrepreneurs. As signs of good faith, Grant personally paid to cover City Hall's dome in twenty-four-karat gold and spruce up parts of downtown with flags and new brick sidewalks, all the while he was negotiating for tax abatements, permits, and other arrangements with the city. One year, he donated a five-story Christmas tree to be erected outside City Hall.[53]

The developer won people over with his swagger and free-spending ways. Like Newark's mayor, Grant was prone to talking about himself in third person. "No one in the United States can bid against Harry Grant," the man rumored to come from a rich Baghdad family would say.[54] Also like Sharpe James, Grant was one to indulge in silly word play to woo support. "Everything I do is 'granted,'" he'd say with a wink through his oversized glasses.[55]

According to Grant, the mall would be completed by 1987, and the tower would open in 1991. Held back by transit studies and financing issues, however, the project remained hypothetical well into late 1980s. Still, Mayor James, the city council, and the chamber of commerce heralded the coming of "Hurricane" Harry. *Greater Newark: A Microcosm of America*, a book published by the chamber in 1989, promoted Grant's mall as "the newest jewel of the downtown shopping district."[56]

Within a few years in office, Sharpe James could point to some tangible signs of his city's successes. Between 1980 and 1988, housing prices rose 50 percent, not as sharp an increase as the 300 percent gains in Jersey City or Hoboken, but a respectable gain nonetheless. Unemployment in Newark circa 1988 stood at 7.9 percent, still double the state average, but a significant drop from the 12.2 percent it had been when James took office. Property-tax collection rates improved from a dismal 80 percent to 95 percent by 1990. The market for office space had gotten new life due to decisions by companies like Blue Cross–Blue Shield, which moved twenty-five hundred workers from the suburbs to downtown Newark. The state had also approved plans for a $180 million arts center to be built in downtown Newark.[57]

Riding the wave of economic progress, Sharpe James cruised to a second term in the 1990 election. In an unprecedented turn of affairs, no one dared oppose him.

Even with a dominant hold on City Hall, Mayor James seemed powerless to solve many problems that were deeply entrenched in Newark's fiber. The Gibson administration, like Hugh Addonizio's people before them, had played with the city's financial statements leading up to the 1986 election, and the $30 million surplus that Gibson had bragged about suddenly turned into a $20 million deficit once Sharpe James became mayor. James sent layoff notices to thousands of city workers and successively raised tax rates to uncharted new highs: $14.46 per $100 of value in 1988, up to $16.98 by 1991. That year, the mayor threatened to raise rates to $19.90, meaning a property owner would pay taxes equivalent to the total value of his home in a little over five years. Newark's public schools seemed on the verge of collapse, despite the fortune being dumped into the system. In 1990, for example, the board of education passed a school budget topping $420 million; it had been $247 million as recently as 1984. The 1990 budget accounting for all other city services and personnel, by contrast, totaled $346 million. About 50 percent of Newark public-school students didn't complete high school, and a state takeover, threatened for years, seemed more and more likely.[58]

Newark's crime problems never faded. The city's reputation for street crime actually worsened during the James years. From the late 1980s through the early 1990s, Newark held the dubious distinction as "the nation's car-theft capital." Later, Newark became the "carjacking capital of the world" when that phenomena made news in the early 1990s. Irvington generally held the nation's second highest car-theft rate, and Elizabeth, another of Newark's bordering towns, ranked in the top ten. "Driving a car has become akin to taking a stagecoach across the Wild West," one assemblyman from Orange said while pushing for tougher penalties.[59]

By November of 1992, 111 people had been killed that year in the Newark area in car-theft related incidents. Perhaps most disturbing, more than half the thieves in Newark were juveniles: 57 percent of those caught were under seventeen, and some were as young as ten. The situation grew so out of control that at one point the city purchased 1,750 anti-car theft devices, and Mayor James conducted random drawings to give them away to residents.[60]

To combat the city's dire crime problems, James hired a street-savvy, twenty-five-year veteran of the Boston police department named William Celester as police director. Celester, who came to Newark in 1991, had once been a teenage gangster who went by the name "Blast" and ran in Boston's poor Roxbury area with a crew called the Marseille Dukes. He spent several months in jail in his teens before eventually turning his life around and working his way through the ranks of Boston's police force. With his background, Celester could identify with Newark's troubled youths and therefore better handle them, it was believed. Celester's life story was also held up as an example which Newark kids might try to emulate.[61]

Those children were increasingly likely to be poor, despite Newark's well-publicized revitalization. A study by the antipoverty group United Community Corporation (UCC) showed that the percentage of poor families in Newark rose in every ward between 1970 and 1990: from 15.5 to 22 percent in the North Ward, for example, and from 30.8 to 34.5 percent in the Central Ward. Of the thousands who had left the city, about three-quarters disappeared from the impoverished, predominantly black Central and South wards, which had respectively lost about ten thousand and twenty thousand residents. Newark's so-called renaissance hadn't touched these people, or the struggling poor who remained in the city. One photojournalist working in the mid and late 1980s chose to document the Central Ward as the epitome of a slum, where moms stayed up through the night so rats wouldn't bite their children, and where an eight-year-old girl worried about being raped and complained of pushers trying to sell her pills. "Mostly, what I have seen reminds me of Dante's inferno," the journalist wrote, amid photos of dejected faces and filthy, graffiti-strewn apartments.[62]

The James administration complained that the 1990 census drastically underestimated Newark's population, particularly with regard to Latinos. Still, the statistics revealed Newark as the incredible shrinking city, with a mere 275,000 people. The figure represented a drop of more than 16 percent since 1980, and the fewest number of residents since the turn of the century.[63]

———

Harry Grant decided to host a "grand opening" ceremony in 1989 at his Renaissance Mall. However, when Newark politicos and businessmen toured the mall in hard hats, they found half-built ceilings and walls. The escalator worked, but that was about the only fully functional aspect of the site. Duct work and electrical wires hadn't been covered, and none of the stores were occupied. Grant's spokespeople refused to name any retailers that had actually signed contracts to operate in the mall. Still, Grant promised the mall would open in March of 1990. Horse-drawn carriages departing from the mall on tours of the city would commence soon thereafter. The confident developer also continued to speak in his characteristic third person. "Big-boy Harry made up his mind to come to the city," Grant said of Newark, "and to show to the world that it can be the number one city in the world."[64]

A serious falling out between Harry Grant and Newark occurred in autumn of 1989. Grant had hired men—mostly homeless, as it turned out—to install Belgian block sidewalks along Broad Street. But after Grant's crews finished the agreed-upon job, Hurricane Harry ordered them to keep on going. His workers tore up sidewalks and laid new bricks on two extra blocks, even after members of the James administration told Grant to stop. After the men continued laying sidewalks—after dark, without permits—the city pressed criminal trespass charges.[65]

Excavation for Harry Grant's tower began in early 1990. By the spring, with the Renaissance Mall still not remotely ready to open, creditors began foreclosure proceedings on Grant's properties because he'd defaulted on loans. Grant declared bankruptcy, seeking Chapter 11 protection for four of his companies and himself personally. He owed creditors nearly $63 million, including $12 million for the mall project. The real estate market's downturn caused all the trouble, Grant said.[66]

The city later spent $50,000 to redo Grant's shoddy sidewalks and another $200,000 to fill in the city-block-size hole dug for the tower foundation. Taxpayers also footed the bill to buy back the site in bankruptcy court.

Meanwhile, the shell of the Renaissance Mall would stand for more than a decade as an embarrassing albatross hung around the city's neck.[67]

The Harry Grant fiasco may have been a fluke, but a more enduring problem continued to dog Newark. Details of city officials' shameless behavior and nonsensical use of taxpayer money often made news. City council members had been given hefty raises in the 1980s with the idea that the positions be considered full-time jobs, yet most council representatives still collected second and even third salaries, often from city or Essex County agencies. Five staffers were employed to work for the council as a group, and each council member was allowed to hire five additional full-time aides. (The staffs of state legislators, by contrast, typically consisted of one or two aides with salaries totaling about one-fourth of each Newark council member's staff.) Without apology, council members stocked their staffs with family members, employing nephews and wives, even children home from college on summer and winter breaks. Council members received cars, spent freely on food and travel, and, in a bizarre practice, allocated thousands to a fund that required almost no oversight. Council members said they often dipped into the fund and handed out money directly to Newark residents. "I don't know how many people walk in off the street and say, 'Can I borrow $10 or $20?'" Council President Henry Martinez said. "I give it to them. If people say, 'I need $150 to pay my rent,' I go into my pocket. I don't account for it, so I've lost it."[68]

Council-member spending was usually, but not always, legal. Marie Villani, the tiny grandmotherly woman who had served as an at-large council member since taking over her husband's post when he died in 1973, pled guilty in 1993 to federal charges of misusing city money and resigned from the council. Her son Allen was also implicated in the scandal, which involved submitting bogus bills to the city. The two were sentenced to three months in prison and each fined $5,000.[69]

The scandals continued in February of 1994, when federal officials unsealed indictments against City Council President Gary Harris and Ralph Grant Jr., also a council member and an ordained Seventh Adventist Church minister. The men were charged with accepting thousands of dollars in bribes to arrange municipal contracts for a towing company.[70]

People also began asking more questions about Mayor James's apparent financial windfalls. During his years on the city council, Sharpe James projected the appearance of a tightfisted reformer. He voted against a pay increase and refused to accept a city-owned car, saying it was a poor use of taxpayer dollars. So how was it that by the early 1990s, Sharpe James could afford to buy five homes? What about the $160,000 yacht?[71]

James's newfound wealth became a topic harped on by mayoral contenders in the 1994 election. Unlike in 1990, when James won reelection unopposed, several candidates entered a fiercely battled 1994 campaign. The challengers included William Payne, brother of Congressman Donald Payne; Dr. Colleen Walton, a podiatrist and vice chair of the Essex County Democratic Committee; and Ras Baraka, a twenty-five-year-old school-teacher whose campaign was managed by his father, poet and activist Amiri Baraka. Windows at Baraka's Halsey Street headquarters were smashed. Payne complained that voters feared endorsing him because they believed the James administration would seek revenge. After James questioned Walton's medical credentials at a forum hosted by the teacher's union, the doctor filed a defamation lawsuit. Leaflets disparaging various candidates flooded the streets. One, titled "King James—Millionaire Mayor," questioned why the mayor refused to disclose his tax returns.[72]

Mayor James said his wealth was simply the result of wise investments and a frugal lifestyle. People who questioned him were either jealous or racist—no one would wonder how a white man bought some real estate—or simply playing politics.

James campaigned in 1994 largely by rehashing Newark's achievements under his watch. The National Civic League had designated Newark an All-America City. Another group rewarded Newark with a first-place finish in a competition for America's most livable city. James had gleefully turned many of the city's misbegotten high-rise housing projects into dust. Four buildings at the North Ward's Columbus Homes were razed two months before the 1994 election. (More than forty high-rise projects would eventually be demolished by the mayor.) Sharpe James could also claim Newark was home to the nation's fastest-growing airport and a rapidly increasing corporate presence. Plans for hundreds of market-rate condos were in the works, as well as an amazing coup for the once-depressed city: ground had broken on the $180 million arts center, due to open in 1997.[73]

The opening of a modern, six-screen movie theater probably meant more than an arts center to the average Newark resident. Located in the heart of the 1967 riot zone, at Springfield Avenue and Bergen Street, the movie house was the first of its kind to operate in the area in twenty-five years. Before the theater opened in the spring of 1993, people had to drive to Millburn or Short Hills to catch a movie. The return of such an ordinary pleasure meant that life in the troubled city might truly be returning to normalcy.[74]

By the 1994 election, Mayor James had become known as a savvy maverick leading America's urban revitalization and answered requests to give speeches on the topic around the country. A government trade newspaper had named

Sharpe James New Jersey's "most valuable public official." He could brag of impressive political support. The mayor held enough sway at the state level that in 1991 New Jersey Governor Jim Florio appointed his wife, Mary James, a Newark public-school teacher, to a part-time, $83,000-per-year patronage position on the Crimes Compensation Board. Mayor James, named president of the National League of Cities in 1994, was friends with Jesse Jackson and President Bill Clinton, who had welcomed him to a night in the Lincoln Bedroom. The 1994 campaign, while viciously fought, easily went to Sharpe James, who won 64 percent of the vote.[75]

Insulted that none of his challengers called to congratulate him, James called the campaign "the dirtiest" he'd experienced in his twenty-four years in politics. At an election-night celebration at the Robert Treat Hotel, the mayor oddly compared his bitter victory to another, far nobler political contest on the other side of the world. Nelson Mandela, a prisoner in apart-heid-era South Africa for nearly three decades, had just become that nation's first democratically elected president, and its first-ever black leader. "Nelson Mandela did not win for himself," James said. "He won for the people of South Africa. Tonight, it's not a celebration, but a renewed commitment to work together and make Newark a better city."[76]

———

Players in Newark political circles have an uncanny talent for lingering around the fringes of power for decades. They throw their support behind candidates at opportune moments so that they're perfectly positioned to snag patronage jobs, trade favors among businessmen and officials, and oc-casionally put money in guaranteed investments. Calvin West is one example of just such a political operative. West came from a politically connected family. His sister, Larrie Stalks, was a secretary for Hugh Addonizio while he was in Congress. After Addonizio won the mayoralty, Stalks was named secretary to Newark's Central Planning Board. Later, as the director of a low-income housing complex and register of deeds and mortgages in Essex County, she organized a network of supporters and became something of a political kingmaker among Newark's African Americans. (After retiring, Stalks pled guilty in 1995 to accepting kickbacks of as much as $200,000 in exchange for steering housing security contracts to certain firms.[77]) In 1966, Stalks's brother, Calvin West, became the first black man in Newark to win an at-large city council seat. He and Irvine Turner, the long-serving Central Ward councilman, were Newark's top-ranking African American officials during the Addonizio years. Both were strong allies of Mayor Addonizio, and in 1969 both were indicted for extortion and conspiracy alongside the mayor and assorted city officials and mobsters.

Whereas Hugh Addonizio was quickly convicted, West, Turner, mob leader Anthony "Tony Boy" Boiardo, and others managed to get their trials delayed and eventually dropped. Still, the scandal contributed to West, Turner, and others losing in the 1970 elections. Sharpe James had been among the slate of reformist "Community Choice" candidates to push Addonizio, West, and others out of office. Technically, at least, James and West were on opposing sides. West was part of the corrupt, unproductive regime that Sharpe James and Ken Gibson replaced. Yet lo and behold, years later, Calvin West surfaced in City Hall as a deputy mayor and top aide in the Sharpe James administration.

From his influential post, West stood poised to take advantage of other opportunities, like when Jon Corzine spent nearly $35 million in his 2000 run for U.S. Senate. In addition to the five thousand to seven thousand people Corzine employed to campaign in the streets of Newark and other cities for $75 a day, the candidate hired Calvin West as one of forty-odd higher-paid "consultants." West and others gathered at the Robert Treat Hotel—where Sharpe James always hosted his parties and where Corzine had rented out an entire floor for over $200,000—to discuss strategy. In 2001, Governor Jim McGreevey, another high-profile official who owed favors to Sharpe James and Calvin West for their support, appointed West as the governor's "North Jersey field representative." The job, which paid more than $100,000 annually, hadn't existed before McGreevey created it for West, who was an old friend. Several years later, the new governor—Jon Corzine—was facing pressure to cut back on government spending and dissolved the unnecessary North Jersey representative post.[78]

E. Wyman Garrett was another interesting character who resurfaced periodically to make news. During the notorious 1971 teachers' strike, Garrett, a dentist and former board of education member, gave perhaps the angriest of all the speeches. He threatened board members, warned striking teachers they'd need police escorts if they attempted to return to schools, and told "honkeys" to stay out of the black community's business.[79] By 1987, the dentist had become an obstetrician-gynecologist, embroiled in a controversy related to the many abortions he performed. Some forty patients had filed complaints against Dr. Garrett. In one instance, a fetus survived the operation; in another, a fourteen-year-old girl died. Garrett pled guilty to gross malpractice and his medical license was revoked.[80]

E. Wyman Garrett, the former dentist/doctor/board of education member/all-around rabble rouser, dropped the title "Dr." in the late 1980s and became a lobbyist who specialized in working for clients seeking assistance from Newark politicians. Garrett represented waste-industry businesses, among other clients. In 1989, a savings and loan company called Metrobank paid $200,000 to the consulting firm run by Garrett and his wife. Garrett's job was to lobby Newark officials to give a tax abatement for a condominium conversion overseen by Metrobank's Newark subsidiary, Forest Hill Terrace. Garrett said he discussed the matter personally with Councilman Henry Martinez, Mayor James, the mayor's chief of staff, Jackie Mattison, and other officials. A few months after Sharpe James's fund-raising committee received $10,000 and various council members received smaller checks—either directly from Metrobank or from Garrett's company—the city council OK'd the tax abatement. The thirty-year agreement amounted to a tax break of $28 million.[81]

Of course, at the time of the agreement the public knew almost nothing about E. Wyman Garrett's negotiations with city officials. The nefarious dealings made news only in the fall of 1994, when Garrett was called to testify before federal investigators.[82] In the aftermath of the indictments of councilmen Grant and Harris related to municipal towing contracts, prosecutors had expanded their probe and slowly been connecting the dots to figure out how and when money traded hands in Newark. Hundreds of subpoenas flooded into City Hall in the months after Sharpe James was elected to his third term. James initially told council members, city agencies, and all of his aides to cooperate fully with the investigation.

By early 1995, Mayor James seemed less willing to assist investigators, who he now accused of focusing on his administration because he was black. As the federal probe continued, a fair-election commission issued a twenty-seven-count complaint against James. It stated that hundreds of thousands of dollars raised by the mayor's charity was essentially being used to fund campaigns for James and his allies—which was illegal, unless the money was properly reported to state election authorities. The findings of more than $900,000 in improperly donated money ranked as the worst-ever breach discovered in the election commission's two decades in existence. Much of the money had been generated during James's annual birthday parties, lavish affairs in which guests paid $200 to $500 a head to socialize with New Jersey's most powerful African American official. For anyone hoping to do business with the city of Newark, attendance and an opening of the wallet at these events was all but mandatory. James's organizations were fined $44,000 and later wound up being disbanded.[83]

Evidence presented in the trial of councilmen Harris and Grant, meanwhile, indicated that Newark's city government was as corrupt as it had ever been. "City Hall is like a supermarket," said the voice of Frank Megaro, unknowingly being recorded by a federal informant. "Everything is for sale."[84] Megaro, a Newark councilman during the early 1970s, and Bobbie

Cottle, a former Newark police officer, had pleaded guilty to bribery and agreed to testify for the prosecution against Grant and Harris. Cottle and Megaro represented an outfit called K&K Towing Company. They handed bags of cash to councilmen Harris and Grant at City Hall, Newark hotels, or other meeting places, with the idea that the council members would steer municipal contracts to K&K.[85]

The main informant in the case was Charles Geyer, a businessman who owned parking lots and an office building in Newark and owed the city millions in back taxes. Geyer said he first went to federal authorities after Alfred Faiella, executive director of the Newark Economic Development Corporation and a longtime Sharpe James crony, tried to extort $100,000 from him in order to make Geyer's tax troubles disappear. (Faiella refused to testify, citing Fifth Amendment protection against self-incrimination.) Cottle, the former cop, had earlier approached Geyer and asked him to help K&K win city contracts. Geyer began wearing a wire and recorded dozens of phone calls and meetings with the involved parties. Jurors listened to at least three incidents in which Geyer personally handed the councilmen several thousand dollars in cash.[86]

In March of 1995 a jury convicted Harris and Grant on all charges, including counts of conspiracy, extortion, and mail fraud. Both men protested their innocence. Four African Americans sat on the jury, which delivered a unanimous verdict, yet Grant argued that the courts were biased against black men. Harris and Grant, the two latest Newark public servants convicted of crimes committed while in office, were each sentenced to thirty-three months in prison.[87]

Everyone waited for the other shoe to drop. In the hours of taped conversations presented at trial, Cottle and Megaro regularly claimed that Sharpe James, mayoral appointees, and nearly every city council member could be bought. They were all "on the pad," voices said. Time and again, conversation bubbled to the effect of *How do you think the mayor could afford his yacht?* No evidence directly implicated the mayor of wrongdoing, but everyone expected more indictments.[88]

For the moment, at least, attention turned to the long-awaited state takeover of Newark's hapless public-school system. The post-riot governor's commission had recommended the takeover way back in 1968. Threats had been consistently lofted at Newark's board of education, warning that improvements had to occur. Yet signs of incompetence and corruption, of board members expensing tropical junkets and people being hired without qualifications, never ceased. On the same day Harris and Grant were convicted, for example, two school supervisors were arrested and charged with taking $80,000 in bribes from a contractor. When the contractor put in bathroom stalls without doors, no one asked him to finish the job, so students had no choice but to use the facilities with no privacy.[89]

Apparently most Newarkers were either uninterested or too skeptical to believe that anything could be done to fix the schools; even with the threatened takeover looming, a mere 4 percent of the electorate had voted in a recent school-board election. The system was spending the most money in New Jersey—more than $10,000 per child, most of it state money—yet three-fourths of Newark students failed the High School Proficiency Test. Statewide, three-fourths passed the test.[90] "That is a description of failure on a very large scale," said a judge in mid-April of 1995, ordering that the state finally take over Newark's schools.[91]

———

The other shoe dropped on November 9, 1995. Federal agents armed with search warrants raided the offices and homes of Jackie Mattison, Mayor James's chief of staff, and William Celester, Mayor James's handpicked police director. Cartons full of documents were seized. Mattison was married and had two children, but lived most of the time with his longtime girlfriend, a Newark hairdresser named Janice Williams, whose house was also raided. It was there, under the floorboards, that agents discovered $156,000 in cash.[92]

Within hours of the raid, Sharpe James boarded a plane to Los Angeles to attend a frivolous contest sponsored by HBO for the nation's funniest mayor. James was the only mayor to appear in person. He told his joke, which involved the Pope driving a limousine. HBO awarded James $1,500 for Newark's homeless. A Broad Street vendor summed up the outrage many Newarkers felt with James's disappearance. "It's like your house is on fire and you go to a picnic," the vendor said. "I mean—your chief of staff? How can you go out of town at a time like this? It is just not responsible."[93]

When James returned to Newark, he placed William Celester on leave— paid. The police director, who had allegedly pocketed confiscated money from drug dealers, used city money to pay for vacations to Mexico and Bermuda, and demanded subordinates fork over hundreds of dollars if they expected promotions, continued to receive his $95,000-a-year salary while the investigation progressed. Mayor James took no action against his trusted aide Jackie Mattison, whom the mayor defended as a man of "honesty and integrity" and "an exemplary member of my staff." James said he had "complete confidence" in Mattison. "There is nothing he's done wrong."[94]

As chief of staff, Jackie Mattison was the mayor's right-hand man. Mattison arguably knew more about Newark's inner workings than even Sharpe James.

Insiders understood that the quiet, unassuming aide was the gatekeeper through which all city contracts, appointments, money, and influence flowed. Mattison, the forty-five-year-old cousin of James's wife, Mary, joined the mayor's administration from the beginning, signing on as an aide in 1986. At the mayor's suggestion, Mattison ran and won a state assemblyman's seat. He'd since breezed through five election victories, the last one immediately before the federal raid. Mattison pulled in $87,000 a year as James's top aide, and another $35,000 as a state legislator. With duties bringing him to Trenton, Mattison served as the mayor's liaison with all branches of state government. He also oversaw Mayor James's birthday parties and coordinated fund-raising for charities and political campaigns.[95]

Only when the indictment against Mattison was handed down, in late January of 1996, did Mayor James remove his chief of staff from his post. James, who said he "was saddened" by the indictment, didn't ask for Mattison's resignation or even place him on leave. Instead, the mayor reassigned him to the department of health, where Mattison could continue to collect his salary. Mattison was charged with nineteen counts of conspiracy, extortion, and bribery. He'd collected more than $17,000, prosecutors said, in exchange for lining up contracts for William Bradley, a broker who was also indicted. In exchange for the kickbacks Bradley paid to Mattison's girlfriend and the mayor's chief of staff directly, Bradley snagged control of a $43 million retirement fund for city workers and insurance contracts with the Newark school board.[96]

Sharpe James, usually a garrulous man who welcomed the spotlight, had kept a low profile since the federal subpoenas began flying. Through the summer and fall of 1995, he consistently offered no comment on the investigations, other than to decry the racism of the media and prosecutors. At one dedication ceremony, James showed his face only after police ensured him that no journalists were present. In late November, a few weeks after the federal raid—and mere hours after the *Star-Ledger* warned it was going to court to obtain public documents James refused to turn over—an eviction notice was posted on the newspaper's office at City Hall. A week after his friend and aide Jackie Mattison was indicted, the mayor dedicated much of his forty-two-page state-of-the-city speech to blasting the "hostile and racially charged media."[97]

The indictment of William Celester followed that June. He pled guilty to three charges of fraud the following month, admitting he had illegally taken nearly $30,000 from an account that was supposed to be available for paying off confidential drug informants. Instead, from almost the moment he arrived in Newark, Celester tapped into the account and started writing checks to cover personal expenses—presents for his wife and girlfriend, gifts for office workers, tropical vacations, his wife's car insurance. The disgraced former police director later tried to explain that his wrongdoings were simple mistakes. "That's the way the account was used," he said. "There were never any guidelines on that account."[98]

Celester also admitted to filing false tax returns and illegally siphoning another $30,000 in "donations" from subordinates. At Celester's sentencing hearing, a 1992 memo surfaced in which Newark's police director promised to "wipe out all corruption" in the police department, "no matter how miniscule or isolated." Sentencing guidelines recommended twenty to twenty-seven months in prison for the crimes, but the judge ordered Celester to jail for thirty months. "He was selected to come in and clean up the situation," the judge said, "and he only made it worse."[99]

In early 1997, with his former police director in jail, his city's school system in state hands, and his chief of staff's criminal trial under way, Sharpe James boasted in his state-of-the-city address that he'd met or surpassed all of the goals set for the previous year. James all but guaranteed he'd run for a fourth term as mayor in the speech, which bristled with confidence and a bit of fury. "If I was white, I would be mayor of the decade," he said.[100]

Jackie Mattison never testified in his own defense, but his girlfriend, hairdresser Janice Williams, took the stand in exchange for immunity. One day, Williams told the court, she'd simply come home and discovered stacks of hundred-dollar bills under the floorboards and in the attic. Her father, a taxi driver, had previously owned the home, so she supposed that the hidden loot was somehow his. Jackie Mattison had absolutely nothing to do with the money, Williams said, even if there were several notes that read "10K" in Mattison's handwriting among the cash. And the money given to her and Mattison by the broker William Bradley? They were loans, not payoffs. The jury didn't believe the defense's story and convicted Mattison and Bradley on all charges. After the jury rendered its decision, Mattison finally resigned from his position in the James administration, which at that point was paying him just under $95,000 per year. He was later fined $25,000 and given the maximum sentence of forty-one months.[101]

———

Newark's 1967 population stood at just over 400,000. Over the next thirty years, about 140,000 people—one out of three residents—left the city. The 1997 population estimate of 259,000, down from 275,000 at the 1990 census, meant that people continued to move out of Newark, even during the city's much-heralded "renaissance."

Conditions for those who remained were grim. Per capita income among residents was $9,424, about half the state average. More than 37 percent of Newark kids lived in poverty. Student test scores hadn't budged since the state takeover of public schools. In the late 1960s, crime had often been cited as a prime reason why Newark's middle-class families moved to the suburbs. Three decades later, the city's violent crime rates had doubled—so had the average number of cars stolen each year, even with the overall population drop. According to FBI statistics, as recently as 1995 Newark was ranked, per capita, as the most violent city in the United States.[102]

Newark's department stores, once a magnet for suburban shoppers, had all disappeared. Macy's, which had taken over Bamberger's and its Market Street site, was the last to go, closing in 1992. Broad Street largely became the domain of steel-shuttered discount stores and sidewalk vendors selling cheap clothing, hot dogs, or bootlegged CDs and movies. One couldn't walk a few blocks without encountering an abandoned building—the crumbling old hulk of the Hahne's department store, Westinghouse's contaminated brick factory near the Broad Street train station. Perhaps worst of all was the empty façade of Harry Grant's Renaissance Mall, an eyesore whose name served as a constant reminder of unreached ambitions.

Signs of improvement were apparent in some areas, however, with a pair of modern movie multiplexes, one in the Central Ward and another farther out near the city border. Shiny new supermarkets, national drugstore chains, strip malls, and condo developments had also begun dotting worn-out old neighborhoods. After years of urban renewal initiatives, some forty thousand students attended Newark's five colleges, bringing with them much-needed youthful energy to the city. The airport expansion, once considered a catastrophic waste of money, had successfully laid the foundation for Newark International to supplant La Guardia and JFK as the metropolitan area's busiest airport. The market for office space around the Gateway buildings and Penn Station was booming, with mere 3 percent vacancy rates.[103]

Even with the positive signs, though, the much-quoted phrase that "Wherever American cities are going, Newark will get there first" hadn't quite borne out. Newark may have led the nation's urban decline, but it, in fact, lagged behind the ensuing revitalization. Seattle, which lost more than sixty thousand people in the 1960s and 1970s, had since lured families and young professionals back in the technology-booming 1980s and 1990s, when seventy thousand residents were added. Sports complexes, museums, arts centers, revamped historic districts, and other major initiatives had brought the masses into previously struggling downtowns of cities such as Baltimore, Cleveland, and Pittsburgh. In New York City, areas once considered dangerous slums—the Lower East Side, downtown Brooklyn, Park Slope,

Harlem—underwent rapid gentrification and became hot places to live and invest. Young, well-to-do residents likewise poured into Hoboken and Jersey City. The latter welcomed more than ten thousand newcomers in the 1990s as it came closer to leapfrogging Newark as the state's most populous city.

Even Mayor Sharpe James admitted that Newark's naïve post-riot leadership, of which he was a part as a councilman, deserved some of the blame for the city's hardships and snail-paced recovery. "The tragedy was that we didn't have the skills, knowledge and vision to move the city," James said. "We had failed at many projects."[104]

All those mistakes were in the past, Mayor James contended. The October 1997 opening of the New Jersey Performing Arts Center (NJPAC) in downtown Newark was the most obvious example that the often-discussed revival wasn't mere bluster. Since 1986, when then-governor Thomas Kean first commissioned an organization to look into building an arts complex somewhere in the state, Sharpe James lobbied strongly and often for Newark as the site. James held the power of endorsements over the heads of Democratic state legislature candidates; if they didn't support placing the arts center in Newark, then James didn't support them for office. "Lincoln Center was built in an area formerly known as Hell's Kitchen, and people came," James said, answering the many skeptics who argued that NJPAC would struggle to bring in crowds because of its downtown Newark location.[105]

Eventually the state jumped on board, ponying up more than half of the center's $180 million price tag. Corporations and philanthropic organizations also put their faith, and their money, into the project. Prudential, the insurance and financial company whose fate had been intertwined with Newark's for more than a century, and whose tax breaks and community commitment had often been questioned, led corporate investment in NJPAC with $6.5 million. Pepsi chipped in $500,000, ensuring it would be the center's only beverage supplier for five years. Continental Airlines, the offspring of Newark-based upstart People Express, donated $250,000. Newark's Andrew Carnegie came in the form of a quiet, silver-haired man named Raymond Chambers, a West Ward native and Rutgers University-Newark graduate who amassed $200 million in the financial world by the mid-1980s—and began giving away his fortune in the 1990s. Through his various philanthropic endeavors, Chambers steered some $12 million to the NJPAC cause.[106]

"No city can revive without a middle class," Chambers said. "And you can't have a middle class without an after-dark life." Prudential chairman and CEO Arthur Ryan agreed, saying, "A city doesn't function if it's open only eight hours a day."[107]

Bringing sophisticated, wealthy people back to downtown—more bluntly, bringing them into the heart of the poor, black city, after dark, no less—was the way to propel Newark to the next level of revitalization, NJPAC backers believed. "This is the big idea: to change the way people think about Newark," said NJPAC president Lawrence Goldman. "It's not the place where you get your car stolen; it's where you go to concerts."[108]

To Goldman, who took over the NJPAC project after serving as vice president at Carnegie Hall, building a first-rate facility in Newark was a necessity if the gamble was going to pay off. In order to guarantee a proper construction job, Goldman disqualified anyone attempting to secure contracts through political connections—no minor feat in graft-ridden Newark. The result was a stately facility acclaimed as one of the country's finest places to hear music. "After Carnegie Hall and Symphony Hall, in Boston," NJPAC's main room, the 2,750-seat Prudential Hall was "the best orchestral space in the Northeast," a *New Yorker* critic wrote. "With its classic horseshoe shape, glowing dark-wood interior, and warmly resonant acoustic, it exudes the personality of a nineteenth-century room."[109]

Buoyed by NJPAC's opening and other coups—a $22 million minor-league baseball stadium and Rutgers' new $55 million law school building were both in the works—Mayor Sharpe James regained his swagger, if he'd ever lost it. Months had passed since the convictions of the mayor's police director and chief of staff, and still James hadn't been indicted. It seemed as if Sharpe James was in the clear. No longer avoiding the media, the mayor returned to his rascally, wise-cracking routine, at one point kissing on the cheek a male *Times* reporter who asked about corruption.[110]

"Celester? Sharpe James is your hero. I am your Sherlock Holmes," Mayor James told the *Times* reporter, talking about himself as usual in third person. An audit ordered by James had led to the revelation that Newark's police director, William Celester, was crooked, after all, and the mayor explained he deserved credit for bringing Celester down. James also said he'd never been anything but helpful when FBI agents came looking for Jackie Mattison's files. "I opened the door for them and said, 'Would you like a tuna fish sandwich?'" James said. "So am I a part of the problem or the solution?"[111]

Sharpe James clearly wasn't making all of Newark's problems disappear. When he first became mayor, he promised that city employees would no longer be required or even expected to donate to political campaigns, as had been standard protocol. "City Hall will function as a business, not as a social or political club," James said at his inauguration.[112]

In practice, things worked quite differently. By the eve of the 1998 election, Newark's bloated municipal government ranked as the city's fifth largest employer. Either out of loyalty to the man to whom they owed their liveli-hoods or fear of what that man might do if crossed, Newark's four thousand municipal workers consistently flushed Sharpe James's campaign coffers with donations. One study showed that between the 1994 and 1998 elections, two-thirds of James's campaign funds came from current or former city workers. Donations tended to spike each year in late February, right around the mayor's birthday bash at the Robert Treat Hotel. Cops, firefighters, housing-authority staffers, city lawyers, and labor unions were the most likely to contribute, and top appointees generally handed over the most generous amounts.[113]

Would-be political competitors complained that, in light of James's donation vacuum, there were few other sources in cash-strapped Newark from which to tap. "What he wants to do is block out the ability of anyone to raise money," said one council member.[114] Mayor James steamrolled over three poorly financed challengers in 1994, and no matter the proven corruption rampant in his administration, 1998 seemed to be shaping up the same way. James raised hundreds of thousands more dollars for the 1998 campaign, and his challengers were no more formidable than they'd been in 1994. Two council members, Mildred Crump and Ronald Rice, entered as mayoral candidates and tried to call attention to the crime, school failure, and corruption under the James administration. They were hopelessly overmatched, however. Combined, their campaigns totaled $170,000, compared to James's $1.6 million.[115]

The *Star-Ledger*, in its 1998 mayoral endorsement, painstakingly came to "a conclusion that is not pleasing but is at the same time inescapable," and gave its nod to a fourth term for Sharpe James. "Warts and all, he is the best we are able to get at this moment in history."[116]

In a perfectly choreographed photo op a few days before the election, Mayor James ate hot dogs and popcorn, sang "Take Me Out to the Ballgame," and planted a shovel into the dirt at a groundbreaking ceremony for the city's new minor-league baseball stadium. James didn't seem concerned that the stadium's eleven-acre site hadn't actually been purchased yet. He chastised the "naysayers," who didn't have faith in him or the return of professional baseball to Newark after a fifty-year absence. "We say to them we believe this is a city poised for greatness, and we believe the renaissance is for real," James said.[117]

As expected, the mayor cruised to another election victory, winning 56 percent of the vote. Only one-third of registered voters bothered to cast ballots in the uneventful contest. Sharpe James celebrated gleefully at his Broad Street campaign headquarters, leading supporters in a chant taunting his just-crushed opponents. "Dumped Crump! Fried Rice!" they cheered.[118]

CHAPTER 9

A RENAISSANCE
FOR THE REST OF US

CORY BOOKER CONFRONTS THE POWER STRUCTURE

A couple of days after Newark's May 1998 general elections, Mayor Sharpe James rounded up a handful of close advisors and city council allies for a feast at Don Pepe's, a Spanish fine-dining establishment adorned with pastoral murals and glass chandeliers, renowned for its lobster and sangria. In a back room overlooking the slow-flowing, brown waters of the Passaic River, they gathered not so much to celebrate the mayor's latest blowout victory at the polls, but to plot strategy for the upcoming city council runoff elections.[1]

Mayor James had won his contest easily enough to avoid a runoff, but several long-serving council members hadn't fared as well. The power of incumbency was always particularly strong in Newark. Once someone landed on the city council, he or she tended to stay there for decades. There's an old joke that goes something along the lines of, "Newark politicians leave office in only one of two ways: death or conviction." Yet in the May election, Henry Martinez, who'd become Newark's first Latino council president in the course of serving as the East Ward's representative for twenty-four years, lost in his run for a seventh term. Martinez was then only the third council incumbent in three decades to lose a reelection bid. (The East Ward, which included the heavily Portuguese Ironbound neighborhood, fell to Augusto Amador, a PSE&G executive and native of Portugal.) Three other incumbents and two new candidates backed by Mayor James had each failed to net 50 percent of the vote and therefore faced runoffs in June.[2]

To a council unaccustomed to turnover, five new members would potentially be the greatest upheaval in city government since the historic 1970 elections. Even though Mayor James had breezed to a fourth term, the strong results for upstart council candidates represented a throwing down of the gauntlet to the city's status quo political structure, including the kingpin at the top. The mayor, held in awe as a power broker who swept allies into office with a few words' endorsement, viewed the insurgency as an affront. "My victory is not complete," the mayor said, until his slate of candidates also won their races.[3]

The push for reform in city government, brewing for years, had picked up in intensity in the mid-1990s, when members of the James administration and two councilmen were convicted of federal crimes. At one point, community activists rallied to recall several council members. The *Star-Ledger* helped inspire the movement, printing a story detailing city officials' high salaries and profligate spending. The council budget, an astronomical $9.1 million, was unparalleled among U.S. cities of comparable size. Jersey City, for example, had a population nearly the same as Newark's, yet the budget for Newark's clerk and city council was seven times as large. In 1995, the council had voted themselves 5 percent guaranteed annual raises. While the median household income in Newark stood at $19,000, council members collected salaries of $75,000 and up, higher compensation than what similar officials received in much bigger cities, such as Philadelphia and New York City. Most of Newark's council received other income from second or third employers and/or pensions, typically from previous careers also funded by taxpayer money. Council members also received city cars and spent lavishly on travel, meals, cell phones, and other expenses. Flowers and fruit baskets ordered by the council, for example, cost taxpayers an average of $1,500 per month.[4]

The council's hefty budget became an issue during the 1998 campaign. Several upstart candidates promised that they'd fight to scale back pay and perks, if elected. Ras Baraka, the teacher and son of poet-activist Amiri Baraka, who'd run for mayor in 1994, was one of the reform-minded candidates eager to challenge the power structure. "They brought this on themselves," said the younger Baraka of council members whose positions were in jeopardy. "They don't prepare any young people to take the baton. They want to be there forever. To me, I feel like I've committed a crime because I love my community and want to run for office, for God's sake."[5]

To Mayor James and his allies, another idealistic young council candidate seemed potentially more troublesome even than Ras Baraka. The candidate, twenty-nine-year-old Cory Booker—a Rhodes Scholar and Yale Law School graduate with GQ looks and a six-foot, three-inch, thickly muscled frame— was like nothing ever seen before in Newark politics. Outsiders were always viewed with suspicion in Newark's huddled political circles, and being raised in one of the city's poor neighborhoods had almost become prerequisite to running for office. Most serious contenders traditionally navigated their way to prominence by establishing careers as police officers, teachers, or in other public-sector jobs. They dutifully campaigned for city elders in election after election until being approved as candidates themselves.

Cory Booker had taken a much different path before running for a city council seat. Born in Washington, D.C., Booker grew up in Harrington Park, a wealthy North Jersey suburb twenty miles and a proverbial world away from the tough streets of Newark. His parents, both IBM executives active in the civil rights movement, were the first African Americans to integrate the affluent all-white neighborhood where they raised their two boys, Cory and Cary. Cory followed his days as a standout high school athlete and student by attending Stanford University, where he played tight end on the football team, served as student-body president, and graduated cum laude. Next came a couple of years in the early 1990s at Oxford University as a Rhodes Scholar, and then three years at Yale pursuing a law degree. While still at Yale, Booker began commuting from New Haven to Newark to make inroads as a tenant-rights' advocate. Until then, Cory Booker's main connection to the city had been through an uncle who operated a dental practice in town. Upon receiving his law degree in 1997, Booker moved to Newark full-time and continued advocacy work for tenants and the homeless.[6]

Booker established himself in the heart of the city's poorest neighborhood, the Central Ward. He became a leader of a group of young community-minded professionals who called themselves the Breakfast Club. Booker also spoke his mind at city meetings, lobbied officials to support his tenant initiatives or other reforms, and made connections with Newark's many grassroots organizations.[7]

Cory Booker claimed he originally had no political aspirations. He said his work in Newark was simply his way of realizing the lofty expectations instilled by his civic-minded forebears, who'd always preached, "To whom much is given, much is expected." From the time Booker arrived in Newark, however, friends and acquaintances told him that he should run for office. In a story often repeated by Booker, a fiery old woman named Virginia Jones prodded him into becoming a council candidate. Jones, president of the tenants' association at the dilapidated sixteen-story Brick Towers, where Booker would live for eight years, asked the earnest young man, "Boy, are you here to be a lawyer or are you here to help the community? If you're here to help the community, you are going to be our candidate."[8]

To jaded Newarkers, there was something fishy about this young crusader from the suburbs. His resumé and background, his overly sincere manner, the fact that he never drank alcohol or ate meat, the way he unleashed corn-ball phrases like "Jiminy Cricket" in lieu of vulgarities, the tale of his calling to politics—it all seemed too perfect, like he'd been following a playbook written by Bill Clinton and other ambitious, calculating political superstars. From the time Cory Booker was in elementary school, the word constantly passed around was that the handsome, charismatic young man would one day be president. In Newark, people believed Booker would somehow use the city as a stepping stone in his quest for higher office. Or perhaps, as some hinted, this mysterious outsider was a complete fraud with darker intentions.

On the other hand, George Branch, the sixty-nine-year-old, four-term Central Ward council incumbent Booker hoped to unseat, had been around long enough for voters to know him and his authentic, up-from-the-streets Newark credentials well. Branch had first made a name for himself as Buddy Gee, a crafty boxer who amassed a 28–8 record as a pro. Branch had lived in Newark since 1941 and been active in Central Ward politics dating back at least to the 1960s. In 1973, the retired prizefighter earned a bit of political clout donning his old gloves and going a few rounds in a charity match with Mayor Ken Gibson. In 1982, Branch seized the Central Ward council post, and he had held on to it ever since.[9]

Branch supporters had apparently overlooked the 1988 scandal in which the councilman was indicted for extorting $1,500 in exchange for selling city lots at a discount to a restaurateur.[10] After listening to tape recordings of the kickback transactions, a teary-eyed Branch reportedly confessed to an FBI agent, "You got me."[11] Ten days into Branch's trial, however, a judge dismissed the case due to a technicality. Prosecutors had failed to prove the payoff involved interstate commerce, a necessary element to the federal charges Branch faced.[12]

George Branch went on to win two more city council elections before meeting Cory Booker as an opponent in 1998. Branch's supporters—Mayor James included—gave him credit for leading the Central Ward's recovery efforts by deftly trading favors with businessmen and other city officials. During Branch's long era in office, townhouse developments, a movie theater, and other businesses came to occupy previously vacant lots in the struggling neighborhood best known as the center of the 1967 riots. Senior citizens in particular were loyal to Branch, an unashamedly unlettered man known for wearing a sleek tailored suit underneath a straw fedora hat.[13]

The media jumped onto the Branch-Booker matchup as a melodrama whose results would foretell the future of the city. It was a battle of the tough, old political-machine hack versus the earnest, young do-gooder; the streetwise, homegrown dinosaur versus the outsider who was book-smart but unschooled in gritty urban politics. Sharpe James characterized it as a contest between "the Rhodes Scholar and the road scholar."[14]

The closely followed race featured some of the year's ugliest political propaganda. One leaflet, showing the challenger morphing into a wolf, was headlined "Cory Booker is a WOLF in Sheep's Clothing!!!" The flier included tidbits about Booker's privileged upbringing in an all-white community and hinted that Booker, who "now lives with a white male in a secluded mansion," was gay. Another piece of literature claimed Booker received campaign money from hate groups.[15]

Branch refused to comment on the origin of such information, though he often questioned his challenger as an unproven Johnny-come-lately. "I would feel much better if I was running against someone who lived in the ward, worked in the ward, got schooled in the ward, and cared about the ward for his whole life," Branch said. "He's just a new person on the block. I was here in the middle of the riots in 1967, taking children out of the streets. I've made history in the ward. I'm the one who made it possible for people like him to move here and feel safe."[16]

"I want to give honor to Mr. Branch, who has been the councilman since I was 12 years old," Booker countered. "But it is time to pass the baton to someone with new vision and new talents."[17]

Campaigning for Newark's May elections traditionally began only in April, but Booker began knocking on Central Ward doors as early as January. Calling for reform, he harped on the overpaid, underperforming city council. Booker also raised $150,000 for his campaign, about $50,000 more than the incumbent. Newarkers were both awed and suspicious of Booker's well-financed campaign, which ran largely on money from Booker's friends at Stanford and Yale and other sources outside Newark. Barbra Streisand, of all people, was an early supporter. Booker met the criticism for his outside funding by questioning the ethics of his opponent, who accepted money from some of the city's shadiest landlords. "When you're struggling to get something in your apartment fixed," a Booker flier said, "the last thing you want to have to worry about is whether your councilman owes a favor to your landlord."[18]

Branch received 340 more votes than Booker in the May general election, but a runoff followed in June because the incumbent failed to win a majority. Booker predicted the results of that contest would forge "a new political consciousness that will forever change the way business is done in Newark."[19]

From the moment the May election results started circulating, the North Ward Cultural Center's Steve Adubato's phone was ringing. Known in the late 1970s as the "prince of the North Ward" and "Newark's other mayor," Adubato had never been elected to anything. For decades, though, he remained a formidable political power in Newark and around the state, with close ties to governors, congressmen, and county and municipal officials. With the allegiance of old Italians, Latino groups, and other factions, Adubato could be relied upon to deliver blocks of voters. His support could mean victory for any of the candidates forced into a runoff, so people lobbied Adubato early and often. In the Central Ward, Adubato's political machine represented about one-quarter of the votes, so he could easily shift the outcome to Booker or Branch.[20]

Initially, Adubato didn't endorse either man, though he hinted that the incumbents should be concerned by the pressure imposed by upstarts such as Booker. "The most feared thing in the world is the unknown," Adubato said after the May election. "The city council here is constant. It never, never changes."[21]

The campaign building up to the June runoff grew increasingly bitter. Fliers showing Booker and asking, "Who is this masked man?" were posted on telephone poles and mailed throughout the ward. Branch supporters called Booker an opportunistic carpetbagger and implied he was white or gay or running his campaign with money from the KKK. Eventually, Steve Adubato decided he liked Booker, despite his misgivings that the young Rhodes Scholar might soon drop Newark to run for national office. Adubato's endorsement went to Booker, and so did the Central Ward council seat. In a rare upset of a sitting councilman, Cory Booker beat George Branch by 656 votes.[22]

———

Ras Baraka and Cory Booker may have both been calling for widespread reforms, but the two men were not remotely friends or allies. The Barakas viewed Booker with as much suspicion as Newark's old political regime did. Ras Baraka chose not to align himself with another candidate. While he received endorsements from Nation of Islam ministers, famed poet (and longtime friend of his father's) Maya Angelou, and several labor unions, Baraka ultimately lost his bid for the council. Still, in the biggest electoral turnover in decades, four new faces landed on the 1998 city council.[23]

Three of the rookies—Cory Booker, Augusto Amador, and Mamie Bridgeforth—vowed to immediately fight for more rigorous oversight of city expenses, including the scaling back of council members' salaries and perks. "That's bullshit," Donald Tucker, a council holdover who'd clung to his position since 1974, said of the proposed reforms. "I'm not interested in cutting the salary. I have no problem freezing it, but the discussions at this point haven't even started."[24]

Before the rookie members could officially join the council, the incumbents and lame ducks made clear what they thought of attempts to rein in their perks by passing a last-minute "emergency" resolution that set aside nearly $200,000 for new cars for themselves. The new Ford Crown Victorias would replace identical models purchased four years earlier for the council. Booker, Amador, and Bridgeforth all publicly declined one of the new $22,000 cars.[25]

Cory Booker, in fact, turned down any city-expensed car, even a used one. It was the beginning of a career marked by austere, uncompromising stands that earned Booker a reputation as either a highly principled reformer or an overly dramatic publicity seeker, depending on one's perspective. In Booker's early days in office, he called for an end to the huge bills for meals at council meetings and the street festivals they sponsored. Battling to lift the ban on citizens' right to speak at council meetings, Booker lectured his colleagues on the importance of free speech. In another contentious issue, Booker stood firmly against the tens of thousands of dollars council members were planning to spend on a cultural visit to Ghana, especially because the trip was to be led by a black-studies professor known for spouting anti-white, anti-Semitic rhetoric.[26]

In his first full summer as a councilman, Booker staged his first major demonstration. Harkening back to the 1960s, when his parents walked in civil rights marches and attended sit-ins, Booker and a few aides set up a tent and slept on cots outside Garden Spires, a broken-down 550-unit housing complex known for its awful living conditions and rampant drug transactions. Hoping to take the area back from drug dealers, Booker even fasted during his "sleep-in." Over the course of a few days, hundreds of church leaders, college students, and regular citizens joined the councilman in the tent, many of them spending the night. Neither Booker's council colleagues nor Mayor James showed their faces, however. In a petty display, the police director, Joseph Santiago, refused to give Booker's group overnight protection because the councilman violated protocol by asking for help from a local police captain rather than top administrators.[27] "The resources of the police department are controlled by the police department, not the councilman," Santiago said.[28]

After more than a week of bad publicity, Mayor James finally appeared with Booker at Garden Spires to announce an on-site police command post for the housing complex, as well as the building of a new park adjacent to the site. An exhausted, sick-looking Booker—twenty-five pounds lighter due to his hunger strike—thanked the mayor graciously. Booker, surprisingly, called James "the father of Newark." Until then, the two men were known mostly as being each other's worst critics, and speculation had already begun that they'd be rivals in the 2002 mayoral race. The mayor seemed startled by Booker's unexpected praise. Amid two hundred people crowding into the tent, Councilman Booker and Mayor James hugged. In an even more stunning turn of events, the mayor, normally a vengeful man who held power with an iron grip, talked about the need to "pass the baton" to younger political leaders. "Just as there was a Ken Gibson and Sharpe James, there will be a Cory Booker and others," said the mayor. In a touching scene, Booker and James were boosted by a cherry picker into the air, where they cut down a pair of boots hanging from a wire—a symbol that drugs were sold in the area.[29]

By the following summer, Mayor James seemed tired and somewhat envious of the young councilman whose antics were drawing attention away from the mayor's "renaissance." With $30,000 in donations, Cory Booker had bought a battered 1987 RV and began parking it in different drug locations around the city. Then he'd simply wait for the media and police to take notice and help chase off the dealers.[30]

Booker's conspicuous actions attracted national attention, with features in *Time* and on *60 Minutes*. He also drew plenty of local enmity. The day Booker started driving his RV, a four-page anonymous letter landed in the hands of every city leader. "Booker himself hates Newark," the screed read. "He is a mere publicity-stunt hound dog who is against everything and for nothing."[31] Council members said Booker's RV tour "lacked substance," and that the delusional young councilman thought he was Superman.[32]

Taking the long view, Sharpe James said that back when he was a rookie councilman, he too had been an idealistic, perhaps naïve young man on par with Cory Booker. The mayor also stated Booker had much to learn. "Grandstanding, I, too, was a grandstander," said James. "I was the good guy. They were the bad guys. I refused to take a city car when I came onto the council. In the end, I had a city car. When the other council members were taking trips, I wouldn't. In the end, you have to take the trips to do the work of the city."[33]

———

In the fall of 1997, Arthur Stern, chairman of the Manhattan-based office developer Cogswell Realty Group, received a phone call from a realtor. There was an office tower on the market in Newark that Cogswell might want to see, the realtor said. Stern asked around the office to see if his partners were interested. "I don't do Newark," one replied bluntly, leaving it up to Stern and other colleagues to decide if they wanted to investigate. Stern, a tan, trim man with slicked-back hair, had never set foot in Newark. "The only thing I knew was 11 o'clock news footage of carjackings and muggings," Stern later recalled. "That's all you ever heard about Newark."[34]

Stern and a small party agreed to check out the property to see if Newark really was as bad as its reputation. Nervous they'd attract too much attention—the dangerous sort of attention—Stern and his associates changed out of their suits into jeans and T-shirts before making the afternoon trip from Manhattan to Newark. Driving into town, they kept their distance from other cars, especially at red lights, fearing a carjacking. They parked near the thirty-four-story Broad Street building up for sale, and periodically returned to make sure the car hadn't been stolen.

Opened in 1930, 744 Broad was once the state's tallest, most prestigious tower. The Cogswell people discovered an Art Deco gem that had fallen apart over decades of neglect, most recently while the building was owned by powerful landlord Harry Helmsley. (Some people said that Helmsley and other landlords helped cause downtown Newark's decline because they kept their highly visible buildings in such shoddy condition.) Murals of historic Newark inside 744 Broad had faded and suffered water damage. A slipshod drop ceiling covered ornate original plasterwork. The bathrooms were filthy, the lighting system barely functional. Elevators worked in curious fashion. One would hit floor six only to arrive at floor eight and have to walk down two flights. Only 19 percent of the offices were occupied, and many of them were used by telecommunications companies that filled the rooms with equipment and few people. But beyond the grime and the desolate ambiance, Stern saw enormous potential. The tower had "great bones," as architectural connoisseurs say, with fantastic gilding, gorgeous details, and grand Art Deco touches that one didn't find in modern buildings.[35]

"Here was a building crying for attention," Stern thought. More importantly, "the city wasn't what people said it was." Visiting on a beautiful October afternoon, Stern felt safe on Newark's streets, and saw as much potential in the city as he did in 744 Broad. He and his party walked past Military Park, donned hard hats, and toured NJPAC, which was nearing completion. The visitors were impressed. Before they returned through the Lincoln Tunnel, Stern and his partners had already lined up financing and theoretically agreed to purchase 744 Broad and pour $60 million into a renovation. They knew a much cheaper rehab could net quick and easy profits, but decided that a facelift wouldn't be the smartest investment. The top-shelf law firms, architects, and software companies Cogswell hoped to attract away from the Gateway buildings would only relocate to a first-rate building.

A couple of months after Stern's tour, his company purchased 744 Broad for an estimated $6 million—a mere $11 per square foot. Donald Trump, by contrast, had just bought a building on Manhattan's Fifth Avenue for about

$500 a square foot.[36] The National Newark Building, as Cogswell renamed 744 Broad, underwent a renovation that included the installation of period chandeliers, restored murals, and exterior lighting atop the building that glowed brilliantly after dark. The revamped tower was 82 percent full by early 2001. As the *Times* then wrote, the National Newark Building was "as good a symbol as any of the revival of the office market in the downtown core of this formerly heavily industrial city."[37]

The National Newark Building's turnaround was one of many improvements that might be attributed to the "NJPAC effect." The arts center that Sharpe James had fought for so vehemently was yielding results in the form of a hot downtown office market. Investors opened their eyes to the area's safer image and prices that were a fraction of similar buildings in Jersey City or Manhattan. A dozen or so of Newark's office buildings traded hands around the arts center's opening, with prices escalating as time passed. Gateway II, for example, sold for $35 million in 1996, and then promptly resold for $78 million just eighteen months later. All the while, Newark's downtown office rental rate crept higher, from under $17 a square foot in 1996, on average, up to over $27 a square foot in 2000.[38]

The downtown renaissance seemed to snowball with the much-acclaimed 1999 return of pro baseball, when the Newark Bears moved into their freshly completed minor-league stadium. In the modern world, though, perhaps there's no better sign of a city's achievement, or at least its normalcy, than the presence of a Starbucks. The coffee chain opened its first Newark location in 1999, on the ground floor of Cogswell's National Newark Building. Other national chains slowly followed, notably Home Depot, Kmart, and Old Navy, the last leasing space for one of its clothing shops in the old Bamberger's department store on Market Street.[39]

Newark also attained a certain level of hipness, with an emerging café scene along the Ironbound's Ferry Street, an influx of young residents drawn by cheap rents and authentic urban flavor, and the opening of Maize, the Robert Treat Hotel's sleek bistro and cigar lounge, where executives and artists socialized and sipped martinis. Rumors circulated that Shaquille O'Neal, Robert DeNiro, Newark native Queen Latifah, and other high-profile names would soon be putting major money, along with their celebrity cachet, into one or another project in the city.[40]

Sharpe James claimed responsibility for his city's upward trajectory, yet the mayor still received heaps of criticism. For one thing, the apparent success of the new baseball stadium was tempered by the city's costly subsidy of the team. Newark not only put $15 million into the six thousand-seat stadium, it agreed to let the Bears collect all revenues for its first season. The Newark government also paid $70,000 that first season for barely discounted tickets and food in order to give them away to residents.[41]

Even worse, Newarkers didn't seem to care much for the Bears, and the team faced competition due to the 1998 opening of another minor-league stadium a few miles away in suburban Little Falls. Over the years, less than half of the available tickets would sell for each game, on average, and the "official attendance" figures seemed to be higher than what the thousands of empty seats suggested. Stadium backers predicted at least four thousand fans per game, yet the Bears averaged less than three thousand tickets sold. The team lost hundreds of thousands of dollars annually.[42]

The larger gripe about Sharpe James, and city leadership as a whole, was that any successes downtown had almost no impact in the neighborhoods where people actually lived. Hearing about the city's "revival," in fact, often stirred resentment among residents. Baseball stadiums and arts centers—these were gimmicks that failed to improve the life of the average Newarker, critics argued. If the city was doing so well, they wondered, why did a 1999 survey declare Newark the worst city in the United States for raising children? Why was unemployment still double the national average? Why did one out of three Newark kids continue to live in poverty? Why did 123 Newarkers under age nineteen contract a sexually transmitted disease each month, on average?[43]

Mayor James preached patience to constituents seeking quicker improvements. The neighborhoods had gotten better, the mayor argued, though the changes might be difficult to perceive. Around the millennium, homeownership rates stood at 26 percent, the mayor pointed out. It was far below the national rate of 49 percent, but a significant leap from the mid-1980s when only 14 percent of Newark residents owned homes. The number of violent crimes in Newark had plummeted from ten thousand per year in the early 1990s to below five thousand annually by 1999. Also, according to the 2000 census, Newark's population had finally stabilized. Thousands of white and black residents had left the city in the early 1990s, but an influx of newcomers—largely Ecuadorians, Mexicans, and other Latinos—meant Newark's overall population dropped by less than 1 percent over the decade.[44]

As the 2002 election loomed, and the possibility of a fifth term for Mayor Sharpe with it, the question became: Which picture of the city was more accurate? Was the city progressing on the right path? Or was the administration holding the city back due to incompetence or corruption?

The two men embodying these opposing perspectives, Mayor James and Councilman Cory Booker, seemed predestined to face each other in the

2002 election. Despite their well-publicized hug inside Booker's tent, they'd since been needling each other relentlessly at city meetings and community events. "How were the Hamptons?" the mayor asked Booker at one meeting, after hearing the councilman spent the weekend in the ritzy Long Island resort area rather than in his RV. Booker responded by telling the mayor he was going to "put him out to pasture."[45] In another showdown, Booker was the lone council member to vote against giving the mayor a raise. By then, Sharpe James had become a state senator as well as Newark's mayor, and his combined salaries made him the highest-paid official in the state.[46]

Mayor James followed his 2001 state-of-the-city address, which proclaimed Newark a "destination city," by hosting his annual February birthday bash. It was one of his biggest-ever parties, with more than a thousand supporters and colleagues. On his sixty-fifth birthday, more than a year before the 2002 elections, the mayor announced he would seek another term.[47]

The thirty-two-year-old Cory Booker, in turn, declared his candidacy at an outdoor rally on a frigid day in January of 2002. "If there is a renaissance in Newark," Booker said, "then it's time for a renaissance for the rest of us."[48]

At the time, Mayor James's campaign slogan was "Experienced Leadership ... Let's Continue the Progress." The young challenger, standing in front of Brick Towers, the dilapidated housing complex where he lived without heat or hot water, twisted the incumbent's slogan. "This is not progress," Booker said, waving an arm toward the rundown brick behemoths behind him.[49]

———

One week into his governorship, James McGreevey visited Newark to attend a 2002 Martin Luther King Day celebration with one his strongest allies, Mayor Sharpe James. At George Washington Carver School, in the South Ward that James had first represented as a councilman in 1970, McGreevey formally endorsed the mayor seeking a fifth term. The previous fall, a state bill had collapsed that would have funded a proposed $355 million downtown Newark arena to host the Devils and the Nets, which both sought to leave their aging arena in East Rutherford. Yet a few months later, mere days after the Cory Booker–Sharpe James mayoral matchup became official, Governor McGreevey discussed the arena as if it was nearly a done deal. "Newark, you give me Sharpe James," a smiling McGreevey said. Then, pointing his finger to the crowd, McGreevey said, "Devils and Nets," giving the implication that the city would land the new arena.[50]

Promising money or gifts in exchange for votes is illegal, and McGreevey quickly backtracked, dismissing any notion of a quid pro quo arrangement linking James's election and approval for the arena. Nonetheless, the insinuation had been set in the minds of voters.[51]

Jim McGreevey arguably owed his gubernatorial election to Sharpe James. "The governor knows who was there for him, and that's why he's here for me," James said.[52] In 1997, McGreevey had lost the governor's race to the Republican incumbent Christie Whitman. Four years later, Democrats seemed to be lining up behind U.S. Senator Robert Torricelli as their candidate for governor, rather than Woodbridge's mayor, Jim McGreevey—that is, until Sharpe James got involved. McGreevey was an old friend of Calvin West, the former Newark councilman and top advisor to James. McGreevey won over West's and James's support, partly by bringing along several philanthropists willing to write checks for hundreds of thousands of dollars to Newark community groups. With the influential Sharpe James on board, McGreevey's campaign took off, securing endorsements from most of the state's African American leaders.[53]

The newly elected governor, in turn, was doing all he could to repay the favor to James. Before McGreevey moved into the governor's mansion, he offered Cory Booker the position of commissioner of the department of commerce—a move many viewed as a transparent attempt to get Booker out of the 2002 Newark mayoral election. The young councilman turned McGreevey down.[54]

After thirty-two years in which he'd never lost an election, Mayor James easily shored up the support of leading Democrats all over the state. Most notably, Governor McGreevey and U.S. Senator Jon Corzine pushed hard for Sharpe James, no matter his administration's history of scandals.

Allegiances were much harder to come by for Cory Booker. It was widely known that Sharpe James would lash back against his enemies vindictively. A month after State Senator Ronald L. Rice lost the 1998 mayoral election to James, for example, Rice's wife was laid off from her job in the mayor's office of employment. Even so, in 2002, Rice endorsed Sharpe James, supposedly with the idea that James would return the favor by not running in 2006 and essentially ceding that election to Rice.[55]

People who wanted to support Booker were often scared off by James's tactics. City agents suddenly arrived to hand out mysterious code violations to businesses displaying Booker posters or churches hosting speaking engagements with the councilman. Police relentlessly ticketed cars with Booker stickers, and ripped down or painted over Booker signs. Public-housing residents who volunteered for Booker were threatened with eviction. A restaurant was shut down the day before it was scheduled to host a Booker function.[56]

Cory Booker took support where he could get it, generally among the younger generation of reform-minded believers. Ronald C. Rice, the state senator's thirty-four-year-old son, seeing an opportunity to form a coalition of young leaders, broke ranks with his father, and ran for an at-large council position with Booker's 2002 slate. (On the ballot and in campaign literature, the younger Rice was intentionally listed without his middle initial to nab support from voters who would confuse him with his father.) Pablo Fonseca, Newark's former chief code inspector, who'd been a municipal employee for twelve years and who was fired in 1999 shortly after supporting a candidate opposing a James ally, became Booker's campaign manager.[57]

In the course of the 2002 election race, a total of $5 million would be spent, then the highest ever in Newark by far. Naturally, money became a frequently discussed campaign issue. James told his stories of growing up in a cold-water flat without a father. He harped on about Booker's rich upbringing in white suburbia, and how so much of Booker's funding suspiciously came from outside Newark. Booker's people cracked back at the mayor's substantial income through "double dipping" in two government offices, the Rolls Royce he drove, the millions in real estate he owned, and his failure to release his tax returns.[58]

The attacks grew much uglier as the campaign progressed. Governor McGreevey lent Sharpe James his campaign manager, pollsters, and a media consultant who immediately revamped the mayor's slogan to "The Real Deal." The message—that James was authentic, and that Booker was anything but—dominated the mayor's campaign. "He is a smoke-and-mirror poster boy," Mayor James said of Booker. "His living in the camper was a publicity stunt. Everything is a publicity stunt. That was five days of taking pictures." Again and again, James smacked Booker as a fraud. "He is a professional liar," the mayor said. "His whole campaign is a David Copperfield. He is playing the public."[59] Jesse Jackson endorsed his old friend Sharpe James and called Booker a "wolf in sheep's clothing," despite the fact that Cory Booker worked for Jackson during his 1988 presidential campaign.

Though both candidates were black, James managed to bring race into the 2002 campaign, questioning Booker's credentials as an African American. "It takes more to be black than just skin color," James said. "It's your experiences, it's what you've gone through. Booker says he's a Democrat, but he's really a Republican inside. He says he's proud to be black, but he hasn't had any of the experiences we've had."[60] James also called his opponent a "faggot white boy," and accused him of "collaborating with the Jews to take over Newark."[61]

"Sharpe James is running a campaign that uses every attempt possible to distract voters from the issues," Booker countered, attempting to seize the higher ground. "He's making racial allegations; he's appealing to people's worst fears. And if all he can bring to the table is negativity and bigotry, then he's going to lose."[62]

A few weeks before the election, police raided a topless club called Sights and arrested two dozen women, including a sixteen-year-old girl. One of Booker's aides had been waiting outside the club and was detained by police, providing James with fresh ammunition to bombard the moral stance taken by his opponent. Hundreds of flyers were mailed out reporting the incident, and James distorted the facts in speeches. The strip club was "a place of prostitution and narcotics," where "fourteen-year-olds are doing live sex acts," the mayor told crowds.[63]

Unfortunately for Sharpe James, the owner of the strip club grew disgusted by the mayor's hypocrisy. James himself had visited the club on more than one occasion in the past, the owner announced publicly. Several security guards and topless dancers backed up the claims. "He looked like he was having a good time," one dancer said of the mayor.[64]

The intensity of voter intimidation, wild propaganda, and race-baiting hadn't been seen in a Newark election since 1970. The spectacle was too fascinating for the media to resist. The campaign received attention from the likes of *The Economist*, the *Wall Street Journal*, *The Today Show*, and the front page of the *New York Times*. In the matchup of the aging machine kingpin versus the independent, young reformer—a larger, fiercer replay of Booker's 1998 city council campaign, really—journalists tended to fawn over the challenger. They were enamored by Booker's inclusive, post-racial campaign, which drew support from a wide spectrum that included Democrat Bill Bradley and Republican Jack Kemp. Booker's run for office was often compared to the candidacies of Bobby Kennedy, John Lindsay, George McGovern, and other visionary idealists. In an age of cynics, Booker's earnest, perhaps naïve, approach genuinely inspired people. Many of them eagerly volunteered to work in the grim, old industrial factory serving as Booker's campaign headquarters. Booker was their Muhammad Ali to James's Joe Frazier, as one magazine put it.[65] Or, to use a more local metaphor, Booker was their Ken Gibson to Sharpe James's Hugh Addonizio, their principled leader for change targeting the incumbent's tired, corrupt regime.

The *Star-Ledger* and the *New York Times* gave Cory Booker back-to-back endorsements. "What the city needs now is a dynamic new leader unencumbered by Newark's long, corrosive history of machine politics who can take it to the next level," wrote the *Times*. "Cory Booker fits the bill."[66] The *Ledger*, in an extraordinary long, fourteen hundred-word editorial, hammered Sharpe James's so-called renaissance: "The city still has too many vacant lots, too many drug corners, too many fences topped with razor wire and too many derelict, boarded-up buildings." Listing the awful conditions for kids, widespread incompetence at City Hall, city contracts delivered to unqualified political donors, and James's lack of plans to increase jobs or improve schools, the *Ledger* wrote, "Newark deserves better. It is time for a change."[67]

To many Newarkers, however, such endorsements meant nothing. The people writing those editorials were outsiders like Cory Booker who didn't know Newark. Some voters may have been more influenced by the endorsements James received from New Jersey's top Democrats or national African American leaders like Jesse Jackson and Al Sharpton. Late in the campaign, Sharpton visited Newark on James's behalf and drew a crowd to a Pathmark that had opened under the mayor's watch. "He has PRO-duced houses!" Sharpton riffed in front of the supermarket's produce aisle. "He had PRO-duced crime cuts! He's PRO-duced education! He's always in front of the PRO-duce!"[68]

On a spring afternoon, Governor Jim McGreevey rallied a crowd of James supporters beneath a tent in the North Ward. Behind the governor was a carefully chosen backdrop: a handsome new public-housing complex of two-story townhouses, which the James administration had built to replace the old Columbus Homes projects. While awkwardly holding the mayor's raised hand, the thin, pasty-white governor with short black hair led the chant, "SHARP JAMES is the REAL DEAL!" Years afterward, when McGreevey faced a sexual harassment lawsuit from a male subordinate and famously came out to his wife and the world as a "gay American," the "real deal" chant would seem ironic. As McGreevey later wrote in his autobiography, standing by Sharpe James's side, even as James called Booker a "faggot white boy" came down to "self-interest and not ethics."[69]

One week before Newark's 2002 election, Governor McGreevey appeared again in the city, this time at NJPAC. Standing in front of Sharpe James, as well as two former governors, much of Newark's city council, and several state legislators, McGreevey announced a new financing plan for the proposed arena in downtown Newark. A number of details had yet to be finalized—redevelopment plans, coming to agreements with team owners, getting approval of the legislature—but McGreevey said that the Nets and the Devils would soon be playing in Newark. Mayor James, grinning from ear to ear, declared that with the new arena, Newark would be "the comeback city of America."[70]

The arena and the high-profile endorsements may have been good campaign tools, but a certain segment of Newark residents loyally defended their mayor for altogether different reasons. Sharpe James had been with them through the truly rough years. When few people had anything nice to say about Newark, James had been the city's hardest-hitting promoter. Mayor James consistently delivered for Newark, they reasoned, and now it was up to Newark to return the favor via four more years. Older African Americans, in particular, supported the mayor, perhaps because he'd helped them get a job or had unfailingly come through with money for community centers. Or people simply loved Mayor James because they felt they understood him, and he understood them. Newark without Sharpe James was almost unimaginable. At campaign stops, people living in some of the city's worst housing complexes spontaneously burst into song when the mayor arrived. "Sha-ah-arpe James, he's our MAY-yor," they cheered, mimicking the chorus of the campaign song blared all over town for weeks.[71]

"The Real Deal" message hit home with many voters. The suspicion some people held regarding Cory Booker, the uppity, judgmental do-gooder from the suburbs, could not be underestimated. "Come Tuesday," a sixty-five-year-old James volunteer told a reporter in anticipation of the election, "we're going to send this interloper packing." To demonstrate his disgust for everything Booker stood for, the volunteer finished his statement by spitting on the sidewalk.[72] "You can't bring in a bunch of out-of-towners and white lawyers and tell me how to vote," another longtime James supporter said.[73]

On election day, the vote was divided largely along ethnic lines. Booker carried the predominantly Latino and Portuguese neighborhoods. James won 59 percent of the votes in African American areas. The polarizing campaign James ran had successfully resulted in polarized election results. And in the city where blacks were the majority, Sharpe James was again victorious, receiving 53 percent of the total vote.[74]

The day after his ninth consecutive win in political office, the mayor canceled an afternoon press conference and then, surprisingly, appeared on the steps of City Hall amid cameramen, journalists, and dozens of supporters. "We've got a lot more work to do," Sharpe James said, initially discussing in modest terms the need to fight crime and fix the schools. Then, prompted by a question about the arena promised by Governor McGreevey, the flashy old joker in Sharpe James returned. "Everyone's going to get a job!" the mayor shouted to the crowd roaring with excitement. "I might even be selling hot dogs at the arena."[75]

———

By early 2004 it was evident that if Newark actually did land a downtown arena, the facility wouldn't be hosting professional basketball anytime soon.

New York developer Bruce Ratner won a bidding war to purchase the New Jersey Nets and was intent on bringing the team to a new arena planned for Brooklyn. No matter Jim McGreevey's promises, the governor had failed in two years in office to convince the state legislature to get behind the Newark arena. Now New Jersey had lost one of its pro sports franchises.

With or without the Nets, Mayor Sharpe James refused to let his dream die. He quickly introduced plans for a new arena that would host pro hockey, college basketball, concerts, and the like. Under the new arrangement, Newark wouldn't need an OK from the state. All financing would come from the city, the Devils organization, and private developers.[76]

In a rare turn of fortune, Newark was due to receive a windfall of hundreds of millions of dollars from the Port Authority's leasing of the airport. The mayor wanted to use approximately $200 million of that money to build the arena. The Devils were expected to pay another $100 million or so. People with experience constructing arenas said that even $350 million wouldn't be nearly enough to cover all the expenses involved, especially in a state like New Jersey where labor costs were higher than the average. The larger criticism, however, was that funding an arena was a foolish waste of money in a city that had so many other pressing needs. The *Star-Ledger* rounded up more than two dozen experts who concluded as much in the course of offering several other uses for the $210 million. The proposals included: creating a downtown development fund to attract investment and new businesses; dramatically renovating the waterfront; building an arts district; and investing in job-training academies. Each of the proposals cost a fraction of the cost of the arena, so several of them could go forward at the same time. These ideas would arguably bring in more revenues to the city in the long run than a sports facility, and they certainly would create more immediate full-time jobs.[77]

Nonetheless, Sharpe James pushed his agenda through with the help of a majority of the city council. Council members and citizens argued for two hours over James's proposal before the council approved it in a 6–3 vote. Mayor James, accustomed to unanimous support, attributed the rigorous opposition to former councilman Cory Booker and his allies. "They want to see no progress in the city before 2006," said James. "It's a sad day when you have Cory Booker trying to destroy the city."[78]

Two years had passed since the bitter 2002 election, yet Booker and James continued sparring in public. Booker, only thirty-three at the election, had immediately vowed to run again for mayor. Sharpe James remained mum on the possibility of a sixth term, though he took every opportunity to criticize his young nemesis. The night of the election, Booker gave a concession speech before calling to congratulate the mayor—a faux pas. (An election loser traditionally calls before conceding publicly.) When Booker dialed Sharpe James, the mayor refused to come to the phone. Booker called again, and again James rejected him.[79]

While Sharpe James tried to build on his legacy with a new arena, Cory Booker became a partner in a West Orange law firm, founded a nonprofit community group called Newark Now, and worked steadily attracting support for another election run. It didn't take long before observers started getting a sense that the wily old mayor was on his last legs. "Everyone's rising against him," one Democratic insider said of James just half a year after his 2002 election. "He's considered a lame duck."[80] In the spring of 2003, a slate of school-board candidates endorsed by Cory Booker trounced the mayor's establishment ticket. "The election is the first obvious sign" of changes to come, said Booker. "To see this many people going against the machine at their own risk is great."[81]

When Sharpe James presented his new downtown-arena proposal, Booker didn't oppose the mayor, but instead took a stand demanding that the community be involved in the planning. "This decision is far bigger than him or me," said Booker. "No one should be making decisions about this $200 million without the full inclusion of the community. It's too large a piece of the city's resources."[82]

The Booker-James war hadn't ended in May of 2002. The battles may have come less frequently, but the hostility was as intense as it had ever been. At a 2005 city youth basketball tournament, ironically called "Unity in the Community," Mayor James insulted a few men standing by Cory Booker as "paid goons" and "political whores." The mayor directed his comments to Councilman Luis Quintana and a political consultant named Oscar James (no relation to the mayor), both former James allies who had defected to Booker's side. The clash escalated into a pushing and shoving match in which one of the mayor's bodyguards had to be restrained by police. The mayor reportedly threatened to knock Cory Booker out, prompting Booker to get in Sharpe James's face and yell, "You want to hit me? Come on, hit me."[83]

Many observers speculated that the ugly showdown was orchestrated by Booker to send the message that he was not the same man Sharpe James had slapped down in the 2002 election. Now the soft Ivy League boy was literally ready to fight. It remained unclear whether Sharpe James had the energy and desire to meet the challenge in another election.

Even with the criticism of the arena—would fans of the "white" sport of hockey really flock to Newark?—getting approval for the project was a major coup for the forceful mayor. The city also continued to gain national attention for its improved downtown, which obviously boded well for Sharpe

James. *Inc.* magazine named Newark one of the top ten cities in the country for doing business in 2004. A *USA Today* feature story praised the city, citing in particular Newark's range of attractive, affordable housing and greatly improved transit systems.[84]

It seemed that just as often, however, Mayor James attracted bad press. *Street Fight,* an Academy Award–nominated documentary film covering the 2002 mayoral race, was released in 2005 and introduced national audiences to Sharpe James's antics, which came across as paranoid, hateful, and hypocritical. The film shows three busloads of Pennsylvania workers paid by the James campaign who arrive in Newark to canvass streets and bring James voters into the polls. The movie then cuts to a scene of Sharpe James praising his "volunteer army" and criticizing Booker's "paid army."

In late 2005, news surfaced that for years a select few politically connected figures had been given inside lines to purchase vacant city land at fire-sale prices. The land was then developed with multifamily homes or quickly flipped to other buyers. Either way, the profits were enormous. The city had regularly sold lots for $4 a square foot when the going rate was closer to $30 a square foot. Rather than putting the land up for public auction, Newark potentially lost out on millions by quietly steering parcels at dirt-cheap rates to companies such as ATS Development Group. The company's owner had run an East Ward auto shop and had no experience in housing developments when he suddenly got into the business in 2001. A partner of ATS happened to be Jackie Mattison, Sharpe James's disgraced former chief of staff, who'd gone to jail in 1997 on bribery charges and was released in 2000. Between 2001 and 2005, ATS purchased 116 city lots. The properties' total assessed value was $1.4 million, yet ATS bought them for less than $300,000. The company had since built seventy-four homes and stood to reap phenomenal profits. Several longtime James supporters benefited from similarly cozy real estate deals. Jacinto Rodrigues, for instance, who regularly donated to James's campaigns, bought 4.7 acres in the Ironbound in 2000 for just a dollar. He then constructed fifty-two family homes in a development called Sumo Villages and sold them off for more than $17 million.[85]

Jackie Mattison's shady real estate transactions weren't limited to city-owned lots. Not long after he'd been released from prison, Mattison opened a downtown office and was openly welcomed at nearby City Hall. Security guards allowed Sharpe James's old friend and confidante Mattison to bypass the building's metal detectors. Over a seven-week period in early 2005, companies controlled by Mattison banked over $1 million in three quick and easy deals. In each instance, Mattison purchased the property, used his VIP status to secure city approvals or permits, and resold them shortly afterward at huge profits. Mattison bought one home for a mere $26,500, for example, and on the very same day sold it for $299,000.[86]

Sickened by the barrage of negative media attention, Sharpe James and the city council gave a $100,000 no-bid contract to a publishing company whose job it was to print "positive stories" about Newark. The move backfired. *Metro Visions Weekly,* as the publication was known, became a laughingstock. The concept of a city so desperate for positive news coverage it would pay for it was ridiculed by media outlets around the world, including Comedy Central's satire *The Daily Show.*[87]

Sharpe James remained coy regarding the 2006 election well into early 2006. On the night of his twentieth state-of-the-city address, Mayor James delivered a sermon heralding his city's renaissance. A video showed Spring-field Avenue circa the 1967 riots, followed by images of the street today, where a Home Depot had just opened. The speech ended with chants of "four more years, four more years" from a crowd of supporters, but the mayor refused to say whether he was running or not.[88]

While everyone speculated about the likelihood of another James campaign, the mayor executed a maneuver aimed at maintaining his hold on power whether or not he was in office. On Wednesday, March 1, James oversaw the incorporation of two nonprofits. The mayor named himself as a trustee of both organizations with terms that never expired. He was also in charge of recruiting other board members, ensuring he had the dominant voice. On the very same day that the two nonprofits came into existence—before some people were even alerted that they'd been named to the organizations' boards—the city council approved endowments for them totaling $80 million. Mayor James had gotten the council to support his hastily made plans by guaranteeing at least $6 million for each of the city's five wards. What exactly Sharpe James's two organizations might do with the rest of the funds remained vague. "The mayor is setting himself up to give money to his friends," said Councilman Luis Quintana, a Cory Booker ally and one of the few council members to vote against the endowments.[89] A lawsuit filed by Newark residents prompted the state to step in, however, and funding for James's two organizations was put on hold, impeding the mayor at least momentarily.[90]

And then one afternoon, Sharpe James hopped on a mountain bike and pedaled around the third floor of City Hall. On Thursday, March 16, 2006, Mayor James registered what has to be one of the most bizarre performances in the history of New Jersey politics. Half an hour before the filing deadline for mayoral candidates, James borrowed a police bike and dodged reporters and TV cameras on two loops around Newark government headquarters.

He dismounted at the city clerk's office and removed his yellow-and-black Malcolm X Shabazz High School letter jacket. Wearing shorts, gold chains, sunglasses, a straw hat, and a black tank top that revealed the seventy-year-old mayor's thick biceps rippling with veins, James delivered a post-office cart full of paper with five times the number of signatures required for a candidate to run for office.[91]

Still, the mayor didn't state directly that he would actually be running for another term. "I filed the petitions, and that should speak volumes as to what I'm going to do," he said. A reporter asked James how he was going to deal with his well-financed young opponent, and the mayor wisecracked, "Who is Cory Booker?"[92]

The odd scene at City Hall stirred immediate attention for the *Street Fight* rematch. The *New York Times* even assigned a pair of reporters to blog about the campaign. A week and a half after his bike ride, though, Sharpe James addressed a letter to the city clerk. "As an opponent of dual office holding, I will not be a candidate for reelection in the 2006 Newark Municipal Election and hereby request that my name be removed from the ballot," the letter began. Over six pages, James rambled on in a retrospective of his career, mentioning everything from his days as a community activist to his "precious" experience staying in the Lincoln Bedroom at the White House. He rehashed the city's desperate situation when he first came to office, and its startling turnaround from "urban blight to urban bright" with him as mayor. He produced mysterious statistics no one had heard of—a $400 million budget surplus? Polls showing James leading the mayoral race with 60 percent? (Both were news to everyone covering City Hall, and later proved false.) Housing, police, business, and schools had all improved dramatically under his watch, according to James. In thirty-six years in office, "I received and gave heartfelt love to the wonderful citizens of Newark, who became my extended family," James wrote. "No publicity stunts. No false, undeserved, and unwarranted or self-serving media-driven support. In fact, I had no media support whatsoever, even when deserved! And no outsiders controlled us. We were from Newark, for Newark, and loved Newark."[93]

Cory Booker's name was not mentioned once in James's letter, yet the mayor attacked his "closest challenger" directly and by inference throughout. Since the last election, James wrote that his "challenger had been invisible, inactive, a 'no show' at community events and living out of the city." The mayor said that supporters constantly told him, "Sharpe, there is no way you will not be a candidate in 2006. No one simply gives up power. You can't do it. You still have that fight in you. Let's win the sixth term and then retire! Let's drive your opponent out of Newark forever."

Sharpe James claimed there was every indication he could do just that. But, the mayor wrote, his opposition to dual office holding was simply too strong to allow him to continue serving as a mayor and a state senator. Few people bought the mayor's explanation as the true reason he was dropping out of the race. James had held two political offices going on seven years, so the timing of his announced opposition to "double dipping" was more than a little suspect. If dual office holding truly was the issue, it would have been just as easy for James to resign as a state senator, which was the less important of his two posts. Also, for a man who had just ridden a bike in City Hall and flexed his buff arms to reporters, it took plenty of chutzpah to write the words "no publicity stunts."

Rumors immediately spread that Booker had paid James off, or at least promised not to go after him legally for any misdeeds James may have been a part of while in office. Booker denied that any such arrangement occurred. "I think Sharpe did an internal calculus and made a decision for himself," Booker said. "I think he made a rational decision." Cory Booker did confirm that he and James had convened two weeks before the mayor dropped out of the race. People in the Booker campaign said the meeting was mainly about Sharpe James's son John, who was running for the South Ward council seat. Both sides said no deal had been brokered.[94]

Ronald L. Rice faced Cory Booker in the mayoral election, but because Sharpe James dropped out of the contest so late, it was difficult for Rice to muster up much of a challenge. Booker had some $6 million to use in the campaign, while Rice's disorganized team had around $150,000. Booker secured three times as many votes as Rice—72 percent of the total, representing the biggest landslide mayoral victory in Newark history.[95]

A month later, in the council race runoffs, every candidate endorsed by Cory Booker won. With Booker's support, three Latinos (and one member of Portuguese descent) would be on the council, the most ever.[96]

Like African Americans and other ethnic groups before them, Newark's Latinos trickled into the city seeking opportunity and eventually scraped their way to positions of political and economic clout. Immigrants from the Caribbean and South and Central America took hold as the North Ward's majority population in the 1990s, and by 2000, Latinos constituted about one-third of the city as a whole. Along Broadway and other main thoroughfares cutting through the North Ward, an area once dominated by Italian-owned businesses, signs for restaurants, travel agencies, and bodegas were increasingly written in Spanish. Leaflets advertising soccer matches featuring Central and South American national teams filled storefront windows. The group began flexing its political muscles in the mid-1990s, when Luis Quintana, Newark's first at-large Latino councilman, led an assault challenging Steve Adubato Sr.'s longtime stranglehold on power in the North Ward, and around Essex County as a whole. While Adubato couldn't be ousted entirely, Latinos were rapidly emerging as players who demanded respect—and positions of authority and power. In 2000, Mayor Sharpe James appointed Amilkar Velez-Lopez, a North Ward attorney, as a municipal judge. Quintana was joined on the council in 2002 with fellow Latino (and Mayor James's deputy mayor) Hector Corchado, who defeated Anthony Carrino, a twenty-eight-year incumbent and the last of the city's Italian American council members. With the support of Steve Adubato and Cory Booker, Anibal Ramos Jr., an up-and-coming player with a background in education, nonprofits, and county government, in turn beat Corchado in the 2006 election. Carlos Gonzalez, a lawyer, entrepreneur, and native of Puerto Rico, won a seat in 2006 as an at-large councilman, as did the incumbent Luis Quintana.[97]

Besides being a triumph of the Booker slate, the 2006 election was one of the best demonstrations of how Newark politics was and is a family business. Ronald C. Rice, at once a Cory Booker ally and the son of the man Booker faced off against, was elected as West Ward councilman. Ras Baraka, the son of poet and political activist Amiri Baraka, had made peace with Mayor James and was named to a city council seat after one member died. Then, in June of 2006, the short-term incumbent Baraka failed again to get enough votes to hold onto his at-large council seat. John James, Sharpe's son, had been placed on the 2006 ballot as "J. Sharpe James." (The middle name of all three of James's sons was Sharpe, the maiden name of the mayor's mother.) Even with the purposeful name confusion, John James lost the South Ward election to a candidate on the Booker slate, Oscar James II. That James was the son of one of Booker's key consultants, Oscar James Sr., a powerful player who was forbidden from holding political office due to a 1991 guilty plea to mail fraud, but had long been a top advisor to Sharpe James.[98]

In the weeks leading up to Cory Booker's inauguration, Mayor James stayed mostly out of sight, leaving the country at least once. The mayor elect, meanwhile, met regularly with media outlets and steadfastly preached safety as the number-one issue in the new administration. "I have no stomach for, and cannot tolerate, children being shot," said Booker. He announced the city would immediately be hiring fifty to sixty new police officers, and taking another seventy-five or so off of desk duty and putting them out on the streets. At the same time, security efforts for Booker had to be increased due to a handful of death threats, including one from members of the Bloods street gang.[99]

Even after he had won office, Booker had to defend himself against the old criticism that he would jump ship and leave Newark once a plum national post presented itself. "This is not a stepping stone for me," the mayor-elect declared. "This is an end game, to take an American city so many people have given up on, a city full of people who have never given up on the American dream, and work with them to create something that's a better reflection of what this country stands for. That's something I've dreamed of all my life, to be involved in a righteous struggle, a righteous fight. I'm here for at least two terms, and I'll consider running for a third whenever that is. This is where I was meant to be."[100]

CHAPTER 10

STAND UP

A NEW ADMINISTRATION, A NEW ARENA, AND SOME AGE-OLD STRUGGLES

Cory Booker began Monday, July 3, 2006—his first full work day as mayor—with a 6:30 AM tour of the Fifth Precinct, the Newark police department's South Ward headquarters. The building, opened in 1911, hadn't been renovated in at least three decades. Rotting, rusted air conditioners jutted from the windows. Inside, mold climbed walls, ceilings leaked, and foul stenches emanated from bathrooms that were in such poor condition that police officers used the facilities in nearby businesses instead. The detective squad shared a single computer. Regular police officers used "typewriters that belonged in museums," as the mayor put it, like a scene out of the old TV cop show *Barney Miller*. Appalled, Mayor Booker invited reporters to take a look at the building with him. "This looks like a tour of a disaster zone, not a police precinct," the mayor said. He quickly ordered that the new computer on his desk in City Hall be sent to the precinct, where it was needed more.[1]

Mayor Booker next moved on to City Hall, where he greeted city employees, shook hands, asked names, and smiled. Then, with a flashlight in hand, the mayor asked a police officer to bring him to the building's dank, dusty sub-basement, an area known as the "dungeon." Musty mounds of papers and trash filled the low-ceilinged level. "City Hall reflects the city in every aspect, and this is not a good reflection," said Booker.[2]

The morning's performance, watched by the media at every turn, had a bit of stagecraft to it; surely this was not the first time Cory Booker had visited the Fifth Precinct or City Hall's dungeon. Nonetheless, the message hit home: Newark's new leader would immediately confront the dysfunction that permeated the city, if need be by spelunking through the ugly bowels of bureaucracy, mismanagement, and corruption.

Deeper levels of dysfunction grew apparent with each passing day. The mayor noticed a clerk at City Hall's employee entrance assigning workers to different responsibilities as they arrived. Mayor Booker asked the clerk the obvious: didn't people know where they had to go to work? With a surprised look, she replied, "Mayor, I don't know who's going to show up each day." Never sure of who was going to arrive ready for work, she was accustomed to doling out duties on the fly. Long ago, she'd tried to discipline or fire workers, but those efforts had always been quashed by Mayor James. In a similar vein, Booker discovered that workman's compensation claims were never investigated under the James administration. Normally, 30 percent of such claims are proven bogus, but in Newark, checks were quickly issued without question to thousands of employees who said they were somehow injured on the job.[3]

An audit commissioned by Mayor Booker revealed that Newark had lost out on $80 million in tax revenue due to mismanagement and incompetence. Late in the James administration, for example, the city simply stopped trying to collect unpaid water bills, losing out on millions. More than 10 percent of tax and water bills sent to residents were returned to the city as undeliverable, yet there was no system of tracking the bad addresses. As a result, the city wasted more than $100,000 every month on postage for bills that never reached their intended address. In several instances, city contracts for towing and other services had inexplicably gone to the highest bidders, the audit showed.[4]

As for the police department, the physical condition of its buildings was hardly the only problem. Because of perplexing bureaucratic practices and outdated technology, nearly one-third of all officers spent their time answering phones or filling out paperwork, rather than policing the streets. Federal grants were available to purchase new police cars, computers, and other equipment, but no one had bothered to claim the funds. Some 60 percent of police officers worked solely during the daytime, rather than at night when they were needed more. The city had no narcotics unit, and the gang unit worked exclusively during hours when gangs were least likely to be active, 8 AM to 4 PM Monday to Friday.[5]

Inefficiency and disorganization likewise infiltrated Newark's court system. Paying a simple traffic ticket could easily gobble up two hours. Countless people showed up for court dates to discover their names were not listed in the computer. Police officers often never received messages requesting them to testify. Prosecutors were always pleasantly surprised when an officer actually appeared in court on the proper day. Well aware that the system was a mess, citizens accused of violations knew that their cases would likely be dismissed so long as they were willing to line up and wait all day to be called by the court.[6]

From the time Sharpe James dropped out of the 2006 election, speculation arose over who Cory Booker would name as top appointees to help solve the city's troubles. Would Booker, the Ivy Leaguer from the suburbs, choose well-educated outsiders like himself? Would he hold over any of Mayor James's appointees, or otherwise tap homegrown talent? Would he make a point of hiring people of color? The new mayor offered a flat response to all of these questions: "We have a single standard: hire the best. I'm not going to play this insider-outsider game. My standard is not politics." The mayor said he refused to factor race into the equation, even with the frequent promptings of his chief of staff, Pablo Fonseca, who often said: "This is Newark—it matters."[7]

Critics, including several of the mayor's city council allies, said the team assembled by Booker consisted of too many whites, too many outsiders, and too many folks with impressive academic records but not enough experience related to their duties. The two men the mayor appointed as his top police officials particularly worried some Newarkers, and not only because both were white. Anthony Campos, a Newark native of Portuguese ancestry and twenty-year department veteran, was named police chief. Mayor Booker stood by him during a mini-scandal in which photographs surfaced of Campos in uniform with nearly naked women during a 1993 show hosted by radio's Howard Stern. Mayor Booker named Garry McCarthy, a gruff, goateed twenty-five-year veteran of the New York Police Department, as his police director. He, too, was attached to a minor scandal; the previous year, McCarthy and his wife were arrested and fined after interfering with a police officer ticketing their daughter for parking in a handicapped spot. Again, Booker defended his appointee, and stated the color of his appointees' skin was unimportant. "I'm tired of racial politics," Booker said.[8]

Of Mayor Booker's African American appointees, several had no previous ties to Newark. They also tended to be young. Keith Kinard, a thirty-seven-year-old lawyer and director of Pittsburgh's housing authority, was wooed to Newark to take over the Newark Housing Authority, which ranked in the bottom 5 percent of all such U.S. agencies and was threatened with federal takeover. Bo Kemp, also thirty-seven, a graduate of Yale University and Harvard Business School, became Newark's business administrator, even though he'd never been an administrator of a large government or private organization. His background was limited mostly to publishing, investment groups, and Internet startups. More worrisome to Newarkers, however, was that Kemp didn't reside in Newark, or even elsewhere in New Jersey. He lived with his wife and four children in New York's Westchester County.[9]

The presence of so many whites and outsiders in the administration was met with a mix of anger, fear, and insecurity among insular Newarkers. Weren't hardworking, lifelong Newark residents good enough to serve the new mayor? they wondered. They worried the city was drifting out of their control and into the hands of corporations and individuals who had no clue about life in the ghetto. "Some people around the city are beginning to call this place 'Occupied Newark,'" said poet-activist and outspoken Booker critic Amiri Baraka.[10] The new "occupiers" were the kinds of people who could afford Cory Booker's $500-a-head inauguration gala at Bears & Eagles Riverfront Stadium. Old Newarkers resented people coming into their city simply to get in on the real estate market just as it was booming, or to break bread and establish relationships with the hotshot young mayor.

However, the criticisms of Mayor Booker rarely matched the support and adulation thrown his way, from inside and outside Newark. Most people were won over by the young mayor with boundless energy, obvious intelligence, old-fashioned charisma, and a disposition that appropriately shifted from cheerful to thoughtful, determined to angry. Mayor Booker was also renowned as an empathetic listener, with gifts as a speaker that many a preacher would envy. At Booker's inaugural speech at NJPAC, the crowd of two thousand burst into ovation dozens of times, none louder and more frenzied than when the new mayor harped on crime. "We have work to do in America when any child is killed," he cried. "I will now lead the charge to take back our streets."[11]

"This nation has struggled to be a more perfect union. It still has more work to do," Mayor Booker later proclaimed in his inaugural address. "Newark, let us save the dream. Let us reclaim the dream." As a guest speaker at high school graduations and the like, Cory Booker often invoked the idea that people must "stand up"—for righteousness, for one's beliefs, for the sake of humanity, for the people who had proudly stood up for good causes in the past. As his inaugural speech rose to a crescendo, Booker asked the crowd, "Will you stand with me?" "Yes," they cheered, louder and louder each time the mayor repeated the line, at once a question and call to action. "Will you stand with me?"[12]

———

Cory Booker's celebrity status soared once he settled into the mayor's office. Magazines from *Essence* to *Time* featured Newark's handsome new leader, and *Esquire* asked him to pen a story on his experiences in the city. He campaigned with another post-racial, charismatic political superstar, presidential candidate Barack Obama. Gossip columns tied Booker romantically to Oprah Winfrey's high-profile best friend, Gayle King. When Oprah welcomed Booker on her TV show a few months into his term as mayor, she introduced him by saying, "By all accounts, Cory Booker has the makings of a golden boy."[13]

It remained to be seen if the ambitious, forward-thinking Booker administration could live up to the hype amid the daunting, rough-and-tumble atmosphere of Newark politics. To keep himself focused on his reformist ideals, Mayor Booker kept in his pocket a copy of his far-reaching mission statement. The piece of paper listed grand goals in which Newark would "set a standard for urban transformation" and be "America's leading urban city."[14]

From day one, Mayor Booker set a tone of openness and innovation that broke sharply from the old business-as-usual mode of government. He not only shook hands on that first day as mayor at City Hall, he asked city employees what he could do to help them do their jobs better. He also welcomed their suggestions. "I like ideas," he said. "The best ideas come from the front lines." City workers seemed pleasantly shocked that anyone cared what they thought. "No one ever wanted to listen" in the past, one building inspector said.[15]

Changes were instituted on many fronts. Aides began serving fruit in addition to doughnuts at City Hall offices. Parking tickets could be paid online. Gifts to politicians from companies with city contracts were banned. Garbage men picked up trash earlier and more efficiently.[16]

New approaches to battling crime, which Booker himself called the linchpin of his administration, deservedly received the most attention. While with the NYPD, Police Director Garry McCarthy had helped set up Comstat, the crime-tracking program that was credited for the plummeting crime rates during the Giuliani administration and had since been adopted around the country. McCarthy installed the system in Newark and sent out patrols strategically to crime-ridden spots. Residents were surprised to see police officers, who in the past only appeared when there was a complaint, regularly walking neighborhood beats. The police director put hundreds more officers out on the streets and altered shifts so that more cops were on duty at night and on weekends. For generations, Newark's police department had played favorites. There was no written test for promotions, and plum assignments had routinely gone to unqualified yet well-connected Italian officers in the past, and to African Americans more recently. Experienced, highly respected officers, meanwhile, were often transferred to the worst beats if they refused to sell tickets to Sharpe James's birthday parties. McCarthy vowed to establish a meritocracy and remove politics from the department. He also doubled the size of the gang unit, and established squads dedicated to tackling narcotics and tracking down fugitives.[17] With Mayor Booker's support, McCarthy targeted the "quality of life" crimes—graffiti, littering, and so on—which police may have overlooked in the past. "The guys who carry guns in their waistbands are also drinking beer on the corner," McCarthy said, explaining the trickle-down approach to all-encompassing law enforcement. "And if you can stop a guy from carrying a gun in his waistband, you can stop the shootings over parking spaces, or over them bumping into each other and feeling disrespected."[18]

Harkening back to his days as a councilman sleeping outside housing projects to protest against drug dealers and subhuman living conditions, Mayor Booker unveiled the Safe Summer Initiative a few days into his term. The program designated fourteen troubled housing developments as safety zones, and flooded them with police, clergy, and neighborhood volunteers. Residents of places like Seth Boyden Terrace—one of the city's oldest public-housing projects, where kids quickly learned to drop to the floor of their apartment at the crack of gunfire—watched movies, played basketball, and spent nights in sleeping bags under the stars. Job fairs and social-service booths filled project courtyards during the day, and Mayor Booker showed up to lead an occasional game of Simon Says with the kids.[19]

Those kinds of personal touches helped define Cory Booker's administration. Many politicians scheduled special times in which they opened their office so that every day citizens could speak with their municipal leaders one on one. Mayor Booker took the concept a step further, heading out to the people in their neighborhoods every few weeks for "office hours" in a school or other meeting place. Anyone who waited in line was entitled to a few minutes of the mayor's time. The people griped about landlords failing to make apartment repairs. They vented about streets overrun with prostitutes and drug dealers. They occasionally appeared just to shake the mayor's hand and offer compliments for some improvement or other. Most people came asking for help of some sort. Men just out of prison begged for assistance finding employment. The mayor made few promises, but listened and offered advice—to speak clearly or dress better on job interviews, for example, or to bring a request to the proper city agency. He occasionally picked up his cell phone to send police to a problem alley or building inspectors to a housing complex.[20]

Mayor Booker also "adopted" a few teenage boys. Not long after authorities had alerted the mayor to credible threats on his life from Bloods gang members, police arrested three teenage boys for breaking into a school and spray-painting the words "Kill Booker" in the hallway. Upon learning the trio vandalizing the school were not gangbangers but foolish juveniles from broken families, Booker suggested that if prosecutors dropped the charges, he would become the teenagers' mentor. "The streets chew up black men like you," the mayor sternly told the boys, who stared at the floor in the prosecutor's office and quickly agreed to the proposition. Booker arranged weekly tutoring sessions with college students for "the boys," as they became known. He dragged them to church on Sundays, taught them how to tie neckties, played dozens of games of Uno and Risk, and took them to dinners where he relentlessly corrected their English. All the while, Mayor Booker dished out life lessons in the role of wise older brother. "Life is about focus," he said over dinner one night with the boys. "What you focus on, you become. If you focus on nothing, you become nothing."[21]

There was only so much one man could do, however. Taking the boys to the movies once a week or letting them play video games in his apartment wasn't going to miraculously turn their lives around. After the teenagers bristled under the barrage of lectures, Mayor Booker eased up on grammar lessons and the constant pearls of wisdom. Progress occurred, but it was limited. One of the boys started earning better grades in school, but another dropped out and stopped showing up at outings with the mayor.[22]

There was the obvious realization that Mayor Booker could not take every one of Newark's thousands of at-risk teenagers under his wing. He likewise couldn't answer each of the requests for help at office-hour meetings. Also, no technological advances, statistical studies, or innovative approaches to law enforcement seemed capable of swaying many Newarkers out of their ingrained instinct to reach for a gun to settle disputes. The mayor's much-hyped Safe Summer Initiative yielded mixed results. Crime dropped in the designated safe zones, but the number of homicides citywide leapt in the weeks after Mayor Booker took office. As a result, by August 2006, there were seventy-seven homicides in Newark, compared to sixty during the same period the previous year.[23]

The police department's Fifth Precinct, which the mayor toured with the media on his first day in office, received a $410,000 renovation the following spring. The tired, old building was transformed with bright paint, clean, new tiles and toilets in bathrooms, and freshly unboxed computers. Such improvements may have helped police morale, but they failed to slow the killings in Newark. Under Director McCarthy's watch, overall crime dipped by 20 percent, but the murder rate didn't budge. At the end of 2006, the year's homicide count stood at 106, the most since a tally of 114 in 1990. While about half of 1990s killings involved guns, nearly 90 percent of 2006's homicides came as a result of shootings, indicating a growing—and alarmingly casual—culture of gun use.[24]

Mayor Booker always demanded that citizens hold him accountable, particularly in regards to crime. Frustration with the administration's stilted progress—and what sometimes seemed like politics as usual—soon surfaced. To the chagrin of the mayor and businessmen hoping to promote the city's safe, welcoming new image, in early 2007 the Newark Teachers Union paid for a series of billboards that read, "Help Wanted, Stop the Killings Now." Some Booker supporters, upon learning that patronage jobs wouldn't be dispensed in the old Newark tradition, vowed to campaign for Cory Booker's challengers in 2010. A backlash ensued after Mayor Booker fired more than 150 city workers and pressured hundreds more into accepting buyouts under the threat of layoffs—at the same time certain city employees were receiving raises. "The reformer has not reformed," one labor union boss said, claiming that the layoffs and buyouts unfairly targeted workers who'd supported Sharpe James.[25]

In June of 2007, more than three hundred Newarkers—many of them current or former city workers—crowded into city council chambers demanding that Mayor Booker be recalled. Wearing white T-shirts that read "Recall" and "We supported Booker and all we got was this lousy T-shirt," they griped about the murder rate and the continued existence of patronage, but most of all about the impending layoffs. Amiri Baraka, in a vivid, emotional plea, announced at the city council hearing that, "Booker swept in like Hurricane Katrina."[26]

The criticism of Mayor Booker continued that summer when one of his speeches surfaced on YouTube. In it, the mayor spoke of the wisdom bestowed by a beloved, recently deceased Newark community leader. Booker described the woman at length, including the fact that she didn't have teeth. Many Newark residents found the speech offensive, perhaps even racist, especially because it was given in front of an all-white audience. They thought the mayor was mocking the woman, giving validity to the old critique that the kid from the suburbs was out of touch with folks from the inner city. Also, in a widely-panned mistake, the city failed to promptly pay hundreds of young residents employed in that summer's special work program.[27]

Newark then drew national attention for the gruesome, cold-blooded murders of several young residents. The city had witnessed its share of horrendous crimes, but this incident was exceptional. It occurred in the West Ward's Ivy Hill neighborhood, one of Newark's better sections, lined with modest homes and plentiful trees near the border of well-to-do South Orange. Homicides in Newark were typically of the thug-on-thug variety, in which personal grudges or turf battles drove drug dealers, gang members, or foolish wannabes to target each other. The young people attacked on the night of August 4, 2007, on the other hand, were universally regarded as good kids. They'd all played in the high school band. One had dreamed of being a preacher since he was a young child. He was ordained as a minister at age fourteen and sometimes gave sermons at Sunday services. All of them had avoided the pitfalls that trapped so many young Newarkers and were either in college or well on their way.

The evening was supposed to be an end-of-summer Saturday night hurrah among four close friends. Terrance Aeriel, the Bible-quoting preacher, and the youngest of the bunch at eighteen, was wiry and meticulously groomed, sometimes sporting a thin mustache and corn rows. He played the French horn and was due at band camp on Monday at Delaware State University, the historically black college he and two of the others attended. His sister Natasha, a year older than Terrance, was a psychology major at Delaware State, played the saxophone, and was set to head to band camp with her brother. Virtually everyone at Delaware State knew "Shawny," or Dashon Harvey, twenty, who'd been a high school drum major in Newark. A lively cutup with a taste for fashion, Harvey was known for dressing up as rap icon Flavor Flav while campaigning on campus in the previous year's "Mr. Junior" contest, which he won. Harvey planned on a career in social work after college. His outgoing personality helped land him a job in the college's admission office, starting the following Monday. While her friends had been away at college, Iofemi Hightower, twenty, who went by her middle name, Sheena, had been strapped for cash. She worked preparing food at a nursing home and at Newark airport to save up money for college, and expected to join them at Delaware State in a few weeks for her freshman orientation.[28]

To mark the end of the summer together in Newark, the foursome rounded up food, drinks, and music, and went to the Ivy Hill section's Mount Vernon School at around 11 PM. They settled in at the playground's aluminum bleachers, where they noticed two Latino men nearby. When a few more Latinos arrived, the four black friends exchanged text messages on their cell phones, wondering if they should leave. It was too late. The men approached in what initially seemed like a robbery. A resident living nearby heard a female voice coming from the schoolyard screaming, "Don't do that! Don't do that!" over and over. Then he heard gunshots. Natasha was hit first, in the face. Her body slumped to the ground near the bleachers. The men marched the other three down a set of stairs and lined them up in front of the playground wall. At some point, one of the perpetrators slashed Iofemi across the forearms with a machete. The Latinos ordered the trio to kneel down facing the wall and shot each execution-style in the back of the head.[29]

On Monday, the day when the college kids were supposed to have arrived at Delaware State, a mere thirty-six hours after the killings, protestors rallied on the steps of City Hall calling for Mayor Booker's resignation. The mayor had clearly failed on many fronts, protestors cried, most obviously in his number-one priority of making the streets safe. At that point, no arrests had been made, and there appeared to be few leads. Video cameras mounted at the school provided no help; they'd somehow been vandalized and weren't functional on Saturday night—another blunder for Newark. Reporters hounded Booker with questions, few of which the pale-looking, sleep-deprived mayor could answer definitively.[30]

With protestors still gathered at City Hall, James Harvey, father of Dashon, one of the victims, met with Mayor Booker. Many Newarkers expected the family members of the victims to follow the critics' lead and lash out at the mayor. "I just want to say that I don't blame you for what happened," Harvey told the mayor. "I blame the parents in this city for not raising their children right."[31] The two men hugged. "I really admire you for your courage," Booker said. "I could use a little bit of that right now."[32]

Mayor Booker vowed that the perpetrators would be caught, and he called out for people to stop squabbling and come together. "We will either rise as a community or fall apart," he said at a community gathering in the Ivy Hill neighborhood. On Tuesday night, Riverfront Stadium hosted a previously scheduled charity baseball game as a National Night Out Against Crime. "Our city is stronger than these challenges," the mayor told the crowd. "We will come together. I have been shaken but not deterred by this weekend. We can stand up and win this fight against crime."[33]

Natasha Aeriel, the first of the foursome shot, had survived the attack. She sat in a hospital with a bullet still lodged in her head. Though heavily medicated, she began describing to police what had happened.

Days passed without any arrests. "I'm on the verge of telling my guys to suspend civil liberties and start frisking everybody," said a desperate-sounding Armando Fontoura, Essex County sheriff.[34]

Finally, late on Wednesday, August 8, police arrested a fifteen-year-old Latino suspect who lived near Mount Vernon School. The following day, as Mayor Booker announced the boy's arrest to the media, he received an odd message on his cell phone. Another suspect wanted to turn himself in directly to the mayor. Jose Carranza, a twenty-eight-year-old native of Peru and resident of Orange, was cuffed by the police in Mayor Booker's presence as James Harvey, wearing a black T-shirt memorializing his son, watched. Carranza, as it turned out, had been arrested earlier in the year in a bar fight. Just a month before the killings, he'd been charged with raping a girl over a period of four years, starting when she was just five. Despite the run-ins with the law—and his status as an illegal alien—Carranza was free on bail when the so-called Mount Vernon Massacre took place. The involvement of an illegal alien in the killings brought an all-new level of attention to the case. Talk-show hosts, bloggers, and presidential candidates weighed in on the country's immigration policies, often criticizing so-called "sanctuary cities" like Newark which did little to rid their streets of illegal aliens.[35]

Funerals were held on Saturday, a day after another fifteen-year-old suspect was arrested, and one week after the shootings. Some eighty Delaware State classmates of the deceased were bussed in for the services. Thousands packed the churches and overflowed into the streets. Groups of activists wearing buttons that read "Enough is Enough" and "Stop the Killing Now" handed out leaflets and asked people to get involved in their communities. Speaking to the crowds, a humbled Mayor Booker asked forgiveness for his failings as a city leader. He also demanded justice. At the Terrance Aeriel funeral, he said bluntly, "Get this evil out of my city."[36]

"Everybody is ready to fight a righteous fight," Mayor Booker vented that Saturday en route from one funeral to another. "We have no choice. We're being challenged right now. This is a defining moment in the history of this city."[37]

Many observers echoed Booker's sentiments. The universal sense of outrage provoked by the tragedy offered a rare opportunity for the city to break from its divisive ways and unite in "a righteous fight," as the mayor put it. A few months prior to the killings, the *New York Times* had printed a long story on the deeply entrenched reluctance of Newarkers to cooperate with police. In the "no snitching" code of the inner city, residents often refused to press charges, testify, or help law enforcement in any way, even when they themselves had been victimized. Yet in the aftermath of the Mount Vernon killings, everyone seemed to be actively supporting police efforts, starting with Natasha Aeriel, the lone survivor who bravely described the attackers, leading to arrests.[38]

Newarkers turned out in large numbers for prayer vigils, where they cried, sang hymns, and placed hands on Mount Vernon playground's bullet-scarred wall, sometimes while holding babies in their arms. Strangers arrived at the scene to pay their respects and place candles, balloons, photos, and hand-written messages at the makeshift memorial. Community groups raised $150,000 for the victims' families. A meeting scheduled with the goal of raising $100,000 from corporate leaders and philanthropists for new high-tech video and audio surveillance equipment for law enforcement wound up with an outpouring of pledges to the tune of $3.2 million. Even the recall-crazed critics of Mayor Booker quieted down for the sake of the city.[39]

The manhunt for the remaining suspects spread far outside New Jersey. Two weeks after the murders, police tracked down Rudolfo Godinez, a twenty-four-year-old Nicaraguan immigrant believed to be a main player in the slayings, to a Maryland apartment crowded with day laborers. Godinez was in the country legally, but should have already been locked up. He'd been arrested several times for robbery and jumped bail in 2003. Police gave up looking for him in 2005. "How did you catch me? Someone told on me?" Godinez asked the arresting officers, sounding like a junior high kid rounded up for truancy. "You must be very smart."[40]

Godinez's sixteen-year-old half brother, Alexander Alfaro, turned up shortly afterward, also in an apartment near Washington, D.C. The two had planned on escaping to El Salvador. The trail leading to their capture had started with Alfaro's MySpace page. On it, police saw that Alfaro had friends in the D.C. area and concentrated their efforts there. The final suspect, eighteen-year-old Melvin Jovel, was arrested the following day in a hideout in Elizabeth. All of the suspects had lived or hung out in a high-rise near Mount Vernon School. They claimed affiliation with MS-13, the vicious Latino gang born in Los Angeles in the 1970s, but police downplayed the attackers as mere wannabes. Apparently, the August 4 incident at Mount Vernon School was either a botched robbery or a misguided attempt for the group to somehow prove itself.[41]

"Now the process of healing must take center stage, and the prosecution of the case begins," Mayor Booker said upon the arrest of the last perpetrator.[42] The silver lining of the killings, that Newark might truly rally together and emerge out of the tragedy stronger, driven with a sense of mission like never before, was still very alive in the hearts of many citizens. Others weren't so optimistic. "Nothing's going to change," one twenty-year-old resident told a *Star-Ledger* columnist. "People are going to be people, and Newark is going to be Newark."[43]

After Labor Day, the *Ledger* quietly noted on page 18 that the city's sixty-sixth and sixty-seventh homicides of the year had occurred over the weekend. Newark was on track to host fewer killings than the previous year, but the rate was still appallingly high. One of that weekend's homicides was all too typical for Newark. A male was shot multiple times in the parking lot of a public-housing complex. There were no witnesses or promising leads. Meanwhile, across the Hudson River, New York City announced a 15 percent dip in murders over the year's first eight months. The city was on pace to register the fewest homicides since it started tracking such statistics in 1963.[44]

————

In late June of 2006, a week and a half before Cory Booker replaced Sharpe James as mayor, the two held a transition meeting at City Hall to get the new administration up to speed on finances, public safety, the status of the arena, and other issues. Advisors and department directors did most of the talking during the two-hour discussion, which, at least on the surface, was a fairly cordial affair.[45]

Bitterness remained just below the businesslike façade, however. At the time of the meeting, Cory Booker's lawyers were in court arguing for a judge to uphold a restraining order stopping the sales of some seventy real estate transactions involving city land. In the weeks after Sharpe James announced he wouldn't run for a sixth term, there'd been a flurry of politically connected companies scooping up dozens of city lots—typically sold, as before, at the fire-sale rate of just $4 a square foot. After Cory Booker won the May election in a landslide, he successfully petitioned the courts to put a halt to dozens more such transactions. "We saw this as a very crass, blatantly greedy way of hijacking the city's economic well-being for the benefit of a small number of private individuals," explained Booker. "I felt I had the leverage of an imminent mayor, so I acted."[46]

Sharpe James mysteriously disappeared for several days after the transition meeting. He was back in Newark by July 1, but didn't attend Cory Booker's inauguration. James left his South Ward home in the morning, bound for Trenton, he said, to attend to his duties as state senator. People criticized James for skipping out on the historic switchover of power in Newark. Even more folks griped about Booker's obvious failure to mention his predecessor in his forty-minute inaugural speech, which prominently saluted former mayor Ken Gibson, seated on stage.[47]

In the mayor's office, Booker discovered a gift from James: a Bible. There was also a two-page farewell note, in which the former mayor boasted of the city's "Sharpe change" under his decades of guidance "from one of the worst cities in America to a destination city." James ended the letter with the suggestion: "Please turn to Luke 6:31—Do unto others as you would have them do unto you."[48]

Perhaps Sharpe James highlighted the Golden Rule simply to pass on some age-old wisdom. Then again, maybe he was quoting the Bible in an attempt to save his own skin and avoid the scrutiny he must have known was coming.

A few weeks into his term, Mayor Cory Booker stared in puzzlement at bills from Sharpe James's city credit cards. Almost no one had ever known about the existence of one of the cards, a Platinum Plus Visa listed under the police department's account. The bills revealed where James had disappeared after the June transition meeting. With less than a week left as mayor, Sharpe James went to Rio de Janeiro with two bodyguards and an aide, racking up expenses over $6,500 at a four-star resort and top-notch restaurants. The extravagant trip was one of many James took to places like Puerto Rico, Martha's Vineyard, and Key West, all on the city's dime, and all ostensibly to conduct city business. For some of the trips, the city even covered the expense of shipping James's Rolls Royce so the mayor could ride in style at his destination. The bills also showed that James charged taxpayers for Broadway tickets, NJPAC performances, and Toys"R"Us gifts. James had used the cards to pay for everything from White Castle hamburgers to thousands of dollars worth of movie admissions to the airfare for prominent African American politicians visiting Newark to campaign for him. Some of the charges would even cover James's expenses after he left office—a $9,000 advance on a luxury cruise departing in August 2006, a year's rental fee for James's storage unit.[49]

The Golden Rule didn't stop Mayor Booker from alerting federal prosecutors to the curious ways Sharpe James used city funds. The decision wasn't a difficult one for Booker to make. "We had residents out marching against violence, teenagers getting shot with chilling regularity, police trying to do their jobs with tin cans and string," Booker wrote, "and meanwhile, their leadership was leaving town to enjoy the Brazilian nightlife."[50]

Prosecutors opened an investigation and began issuing subpoenas. As the media grabbed hold of the scandal, out trickled more sordid details of James's misuse of power and taxpayer money. Several young females whom investigators referred to as "travel companions"—everyone else called them Sharpe James's girlfriends—had regularly traipsed around the globe with James. Four of the women either had city jobs or contracts with the city, and all enjoyed special treatment from Sharpe James. When one of the "companions" hit a wall with a redevelopment proposal, for example, James intervened and fired members of the city's historic commission so that a landmark building could be razed and the plans could continue.[51]

Tamika Riley, another of James's travel friends, was a publicist in her early thirties with a background in fashion when she entered Newark's real estate market with startling success. Riley, who had no experience in development, purchased four rundown city-owned homes in August of 2001 for a total of $16,000. By the following spring, she'd unloaded them to buyers for over $330,000 altogether. She then bought three more city properties for $18,000 and resold them one month later for $115,000. In February of 2005, the city again offered Riley two properties for $6,000 a piece, whereupon she resold one a month afterward for $100,000, and the other a few months later for $150,000. All told, Riley's $46,000 in real estate purchases yielded her profits of nearly $700,000. Only a judge's restraining order stopped Riley's attempts to buy three more city parcels in the spring of 2006.[52]

As the investigation continued, James seemed to anticipate the inevitable. He issued a press release stating he wouldn't be running for reelection as a state senator because "it is time to spend more time with my family, win a senior national tennis championship and to finish writing the last chapters of my autobiography."[53] He announced his retirement from a short-lived $150,000-per-year stint as an Essex County College administrator, and withdrew $500,000 from his $1.1 million retirement account.[54]

Some information sought by prosecutors had conveniently disappeared by the time Cory Booker became mayor. The hard drives of computers used by the James administration, for example, were long gone. Even so, in mid-July of 2007, when the flags at City Hall flew at half mast to memorialize the fortieth anniversary of the Newark riots, federal prosecutors had enough evidence to indict Sharpe James on thirty-three counts of fraud and depriving the government of honest services. The charges revolved around James's use of city credit cards and real estate transactions involving his close friend Tamika Riley, who was named a codefendant.[55]

The day after being indicted, the brash, old Sharpe James replaced the one who'd lately been keeping a low profile. James strolled through City Hall in shorts and sneakers, joking with security guards and spouting to anyone who would listen, "They got nothing. That's why I'm here. To say 'hi' to my people." One city employee called the performance "pathetic, regardless of whether he's done anything or not. I wish the man would show more dignity."[56]

The indictments landed in Sharpe James's lap as more and more signs demonstrated that the renaissance he'd promoted for so long was indeed legitimate. One population study revealed Newark as the fastest-growing city in the Northeast. After steadily losing residents for half a century, Newark had grown by 3.3 percent since 2000. Over the same period, median income had jumped by 28 percent, nearly double the national rate of increase. The median price of Newark homes skyrocketed by 180 percent between 2000 and 2007, representing the steepest rise in Essex County. Hip new pockets of commercial activity percolated, particularly along Halsey Street, where young entrepreneurs opened upscale restaurants, an art-supply store, and a yoga center. Cogswell Realty, the company that revamped the National Newark Building, was nearing completion on another monumental renovation around the corner: Eleven80, a sleek residential high-rise with unheard-of amenities such as a basement bowling alley, health club, indoor basketball court, on-demand massages and pedicures, and round-the-clock concierge, valet parking, and car pickup services. The first of its kind to open in Newark in decades, the swanky apartment building was designed to compete with rentals in Manhattan, Jersey City, and Brooklyn, at a fraction of the price those locations charged. Cogswell had also gained control of the old Hahne's department store and several other abandoned old buildings in the vicinity of Military Park and was proceeding with plans to develop them.[57]

Sharpe James deserved credit for steering along such improvements, most of which had originated during his administration. After Cory Booker took office, however, a slew of new faces who'd never before seemed interested in Newark came forward with development proposals. Many of the people taking a fresh look at Newark would say, off the record, that in the past they couldn't bring themselves to do business in the city during the James administration. It was too risky, they'd say, what with the city seemingly cloaked in corruption and incompetence. The city's hot condo market demonstrated the effects of Newark's changed reputation under Mayor Booker. In the first five months of 2007, twenty-two condo projects, representing a total of 770 units, got off the ground. By comparison, only 155 condo units had been approved in Newark over the prior five years.[58]

A few months after the James indictment, NJPAC, one of the former mayor's crowning achievements, celebrated its tenth anniversary. The arts center had attracted some five million patrons in its first decade to top-notch performances by the likes of Bob Dylan, Elvis Costello, Lauryn Hill, Yo-Yo Ma, and Sonny Rollins. Though ticket sales failed to generate as much revenue as originally hoped, and the state had to continue paying millions in annual subsidies to keep the center afloat, NJPAC was largely deemed a success. As projected, the arts center had brought the masses into Newark and inspired a resurgent transformation of downtown.[59]

Around the same time, Newark hosted a red-carpet ribbon-cutting ceremony for another of Sharpe James's monumental visions. The downtown arena James had dreamed of for at least two decades opened to much fanfare in the fall of 2007 as the first major new sports facility in the metropolitan area in twenty-six years. It's safe to say that, under the current circumstances, James didn't quite enjoy NJPAC's anniversary or the christening of the Prudential Center arena, as he'd once imagined. By then, the former mayor faced the humiliation of corruption charges and allegations of womanizing. James had also been widely ridiculed after claiming to be too broke to pay his defense lawyers—puzzling in light of his yacht and Rolls Royce, $125,000 annual pension from the city, million-dollar retirement account, and ownership of properties worth in the neighborhood of $3 million.[60]

The guiding force behind the Prudential Center sat in the third row of the ribbon-cutting festivities wearing a black suit, alligator shoes, and a tie and baseball cap emblazoned with the Devils logo. He arrived alone, and joked with reporters that he planned on becoming a backup goalie for the team. Then he shifted in his seat uncomfortably as his former partners in the project, including Governor Jon Corzine and Devils owner Jeff Vanderbeek, thanked dozens of dignitaries and never once uttered the name Sharpe James. Mayor Cory Booker, however, immediately credited his predecessor for the "strength of a South Side bulldog" which had made the arena a reality. "He faced a lot of criticism—from some good-looking critics, I must say—to make sure this vision truly kicked off," Booker said coyly. James folded his arms as others applauded Mayor Booker and didn't comment when asked about Booker's kind words. "I worked more with Jeff Vanderbeek and other people," James said, steering the focus back to the renaissance born under his watch. "It's good to see that we've started things that will change the economic viability of Newark for the next 50 years. And it's even more beautiful than we had imagined."[61]

James wasn't invited to speak at the event and had to awkwardly look on as cameras flashed around the men cutting the ceremonial ribbon with a giant pair of scissors. Tensions dissipated somewhat when Booker and James embraced in a jovial bear hug.[62]

The consensus of opinion declared the Prudential Center, or "The Rock" as it was called in light of Pru's corporate nickname, a fantastic place to catch a sporting event or concert—vastly superior to the older arena still open for business in nearby East Rutherford. Immense video screens and a pair of enormous, glass-enclosed cylindrical entranceways welcomed spectators into Newark's arena. The amenities inside were unparalleled in such a venue: ample luxury suites attended by concierges and wine sommeliers, restaurants with tables overlooking the arena floor, a sleek lounge with a bar made of real ice, flat-screen TVs in every direction (six hundred in total). The steep seating arrangement ensured there wasn't a bad view of the action in the house.[63]

The area outside The Rock didn't receive quite such stellar reviews. Parking facilities weren't built hand in hand with the arena, so the city put together a confusing hodgepodge plan designating nine thousand spaces from fifty-six different lots for arena parking. Most spots sat within a ten-minute walk of the arena, and on event nights the streets were flooded with police officers to ensure the safety of patrons. The Prudential Center had been drawn up as the centerpiece of a major redevelopment with hotels, restaurants, parks, offices, shops, and residences, but on opening night, parking lots and gutted brick buildings dominated the views from the arena's massive picture windows. Two new bars near the arena bustled with activity, and Ironbound restaurants saw a brisk business, but fast food was the only dining option immediately outside the arena. The hotel, community center, and office tower promised by the Devils weren't even designed. Improvements that the city was responsible for, including a triangular park, entrance plaza, and pedestrian bridge over the train line connecting to the Ironbound neighborhood, had likewise failed to materialize. If and when the periphery projects were completed, the total cost of the arena would top $500 million, not even close to the original $300 million estimate.[64]

There was some indication that parts of the development would never come to fruition as planned. A few months before the Prudential Center's opening, a judge declared that the city had failed to prove that a fourteen-acre site starting one block south of the arena was blighted. The James administration had claimed the ramshackle area of old homes, stores, and industrial sites was in such poor condition that it should be razed and transformed into new condominiums.[65]

Newarkers watched the opening of The Rock with mixed emotions. They were certainly happy that more than half the arena's jobs went to locals. Much about the arena, however, gave residents the impression that this place—like other aspects of the downtown renaissance—didn't have them in mind. Many people of color were turned off by the high ticket prices and a roster of events that seemed aimed mostly at white suburbanites, starting with ten nights of rock band Bon Jovi followed mostly by hockey. Street vendors and small businesses in the city's core felt like they'd soon be pushed out due to higher rents and policies designed to appeal to arena patrons. Rather than facing westward into the heart of the city, the arena's main entrance welcomed outsiders coming into Newark from the train station to the east. From the city's main drag of Broad Street, the arena looked like a large, blank, beige wall. Many Newarkers felt snubbed, as if the designers purposefully placed the arena's backside in their direction. "They're saying, 'kiss my butt,' to City Hall—and all of us," said Amiri Baraka.[66]

The news in Newark through the end of 2007 was likewise mixed, with progress begrudgingly occurring in the form of three steps forward, two steps back. The state department of education, after conducting extensive studies and interviews with Newark public-school employees and parents of students, decided that after a dozen years of state supervision, the city had not yet proven itself ready to fully take back control of the school system. The state granted a limited amount of autonomy back to locals, however.[67]

Scandal touched the city council when Keith Reid, Council President Mildred Crump's chief of staff, was snagged with ten other New Jersey public officials for accepting bribes in a federal corruption sting. Crump and the council were also embarrassed by the publication of a coloring book featuring historic Newarkers to be distributed to school kids. The council had approved $10,000 for four thousand copies of the publication, which included crude renderings of all nine council members but left out important Newark natives such as Philip Roth, Whitney Houston, and Sarah Vaughan. The books were rife with misspellings and grammatical and factual mistakes. Then, in a move demonstrating that they were absurdly out of touch with the public, the city council formally announced a boycott of the Prudential Center's opening festivities—not because the Devils hadn't fulfilled their obligations to build a community center, but because Newark's municipal government hadn't been allotted one of the arena's luxury suites free of charge.[68] Comments from citizens regarding the boycott quickly filled the online forum at nj.com: "Waah! Waah! Waah! . . . They really think they are royalty . . . Awwww, no luxury suite . . . Typical politicians."

At the same time, most Newarkers seemed happy with their mayor. Polls showed that more than a year into his term, Cory Booker was well liked by 58 percent of residents, a sensational approval rating for the leader of a big city. While welcoming developers and new businesses, Mayor Booker oversaw the destruction of many of Newark's derelict buildings, including the Lincoln Motel. An eyesore adjacent to Riverfront Stadium, the motel had been a seedy per-hour joint, then a shelter for the homeless before closing its doors in 2000. The Brick Towers complex, where Booker had lived from his days as an upstart councilman until the dilapidated buildings were abandoned in 2006, was also flattened. The mayor continued his crusade to reclaim city land sold on the cheap by the James administration. Booker planned to make better use than his predecessor of the recouped lots and other city properties. Plans went forward to sell them at market rates, or perhaps at mild discounts if development plans served the public through affordable housing or recreation areas.[69]

At year's end, Newark's murder count stood at 99, down slightly from the unusually high mark of 106 in 2006. The overall number of shooting victims had fallen off far more sharply: 383, compared to 493 the previous year. One law-enforcement think tank was impressed enough with Newark's efforts to single it out as one of the most successful cities in the country in terms of decreasing violent crime.[70]

The Devils sold 23 percent more tickets for hockey games at the Prudential Center than they had the previous year at the Meadowlands. Whereas many brand-new arenas regularly packed seats to capacity, however, events at the Prudential Center rarely sold out. Plenty of seats at typical Devils games were empty, and thousands more went unused during Seton Hall University basketball games. The Rock scored an early coup by welcoming one of the country's hottest music acts, teenybopper Hannah Montana, to sold-out performances, but the Meadowlands arena had earlier won the competition to host many of the year's big crowd pleasers, including Bruce Springsteen and Van Halen.[71]

Like so much about modern-day Newark, the arena and the decrease in violent crime were impressive steps in the city's long-fought recovery. But the end results were not quite as good as they could have been.

———

JAMES GUILTY. That was the *Star-Ledger*'s April 17, 2008, large-type front-page headline. After five weeks of testimony and six days of jury deliberations, former mayor Sharpe James and his mistress Tamika Riley were found guilty on all counts of fraud and conspiracy involving the purchase and resale of city land; Riley was also found guilty of housing fraud and tax violations. (The charges James faced involving misuse of city credit cards had earlier been separated into a different trial.) Around Newark and the metropolitan area, reactions to the verdict ranged from surprise to sadness to relief. Even Newarkers who believed that James shouldn't be sent to prison generally agreed that the former mayor wasn't exactly innocent.[72] James's lawyers argued that the city council—not the mayor—had the ultimate power to sell city land. Yet prosecutors convinced the jury that it was indeed James who had played favorites and orchestrated the transactions, steering cheap land and easy profits to his girlfriend, who was unqualified in almost every way to be a real estate developer. The jury heard testimony about how Riley had boasted of "a 24-hour direct contact" with James; how city housing officials were threatened for not cooperating with the mayor's plans to sell Riley land; how one of James's bodyguards, a twenty-one-year veteran of the Newark Police Department, was ordered by the mayor to install an air-conditioner—which the mayor paid for with a city credit card—in Riley's Jersey City apartment while the officer was on duty. Riley's lawyers portrayed their client as a good-intentioned "small-town girl" with "big dreams and small pockets." Jurors instead believed the prosecution's story of a manipulative, deceptive, and ambitious young woman who used her dalliance with a powerful older man to reap large profits. Testimony even showed that at the same time Riley was flipping lots worth hundreds of thousands of dollars and driving a $50,000 Mercedes Benz, she received nearly $30,000 in government housing subsidies due to her poor financial status.

Throughout the trial, Sharpe James rarely spoke to the press but projected an upbeat, confident image. He brashly parked his Cadillac, which noted his status as a former senator and bore the personalized license plate "BIBLE," illegally in a mall near the courthouse, rather than pay for parking. His car was never ticketed or towed. At one point during jury deliberations, James swaggered down Broad Street, joking and taking pictures with folks along the way. He reached for the door to the current mayor's Ford Explorer in jest, as if about to hop inside. Reveling in his celebrity, James hailed a public bus and spoke into the cell phone of a surprised fellow passenger.

After the jury returned its verdict, a *Star-Ledger* editorial correctly pointed out that Sharpe James was not the only official guilty of impropriety, or at least laziness or negligence, when it came to wide-reaching city land giveaways. "City leaders chose to pass discounts on to builders, not to home-buyers willing to bet their future on Newark," the *Ledger* wrote. "They chose to enrich those few at the expense of the residents and business owners who stuck with Newark through the lean times."[73]

"Sharpe James is guilty of betraying Newark's future," the *Ledger* editorial stated. "So are many others." Fortunately, despite the misdeeds and mistakes of the past, Newark circa 2008 still had a future that looked remarkably promising.

The Prudential Center arena was largely living up to its vision as the modern face of the city's renaissance. Critics griped that progress for the arena's entrance plaza and redevelopment in the area was occurring too slowly. Essex County officials and Devils management also began lobbying the state to close the former Brendan Byrne arena in East Rutherford because competition was hurting the Prudential Center's chances for success. "If they're worried about finances," East Rutherford mayor James Cassella responded, "perhaps they should have thought about that before they went ahead with construction of the facility."[74] Regardless, the city's new arena had succeeded in bringing tens of thousands of newcomers into downtown Newark, and those that came almost always left very impressed.

More importantly, the city finally seemed to be shaking off its legacy of violence. Newark experienced a drastic decrease in violent crime in early 2008. A stretch of forty-three consecutive days passed without a murder. It represented the longest such streak since 1961. More efficient policing techniques, as well as a newly vigilant populace, were credited with the downturn in violent crime, which was too dramatic and long-lasting to be categorized as a fluke.

As if to close the door on the city's reputation for murder and crime, eight months after the notorious triple murder of three young Newarkers a memorial garden was dedicated at Mount Vernon School, where the execution-style slayings took place. Amid freshly planted cherry blossoms and walls inscribed with inspirational messages, dozens of children released balloons, and the school choir sang "Let There Be Peace on Earth."[75]

NOTE ON SOURCES

The starting point for my research (and for all research on Newark, really) was a trio of city histories: Joseph Atkinson's *The History of Newark* (1878), Frank Urquhart's densely detailed three-volume *A History of the City of Newark* (1913), and the book most familiar to modern readers, John Cunningham's *Newark* (first edition, 1966). William Shaw's *History of Essex and Hudson Counties* (1884) also proved very helpful, particularly because it often features significant newspaper articles and historic documents reprinted whole in its pages. While all of these histories cover much of the same ground, each has its own strengths—and flaws. Cunningham's book is easily the most readable and comprehensive, but it is also frequently glosses over darker aspects of the city's past. Political rings of the late 1800s, the growth of organized crime during Prohibition, the taint of pervasive corruption during the years Meyer Ellenstein was mayor, and discrimination and the atrocious state of race relations in the postwar years are among the topics given short shrift or ignored entirely in the first edition. Later editions, published after the 1967 riots, address race more fully, but fail to mention unseemly events like the high-profile corruption scandals during the Sharpe James years.

In an attempt to paint a fuller picture of Newark, I consulted the many newspapers published in the city, as well as the *New York Times* and other papers. (The *Times* searchable historical database is a researcher's dream, and time and again the *Times* offered a perspective more trustworthy than the boosterlike coverage often on display in local papers.) The New Jersey Information Center on the third floor of the Newark Public Library has the most comprehensive collection of Newark newspapers on microfilm, as well as the invaluable subject-by-subject collection of articles in the "morgue files" from the *Newark Evening News*. The library also boasts dozens of extremely detailed dissertations focused on various aspects of Newark's history. While the Newark Public Library undoubtedly offers the most resources on the city, figuring out what the library holds and navigating the bureaucracy of how to get books, images, maps, and other materials can be a chore. Many times, staffers met my requests to see one or another item by throwing up their hands and saying they couldn't find it or that it would take several hours (or a couple weeks) to retrieve. Librarians often complained about being understaffed and explained that books and other research materials had a way of inexplicably disappearing. It's unfortunate that such a wonderful collection is not as accessible as it could be. So, on behalf of researchers everywhere (and the librarians themselves, who were often as frustrated as I was), let me be one of many voices to ask that the means be found to improve staffing and organization.

The best bibliography for city research, in my opinion, is not at Newark Public but a few blocks away (and online) at Rutgers-Newark's Dana Library. Natalie Borisovets and her staff have amassed lists of Web links, databases, books, maps, magazine articles, and more, all arranged by subject, in what's called "The Newark Experience." (Finding it through the Rutgers Web site is difficult; it's easier to simply Google "The Newark Experience.") The New Jersey Historical Society's library, on the building's fifth floor, only manages to be open to the public a few afternoons a week. Even so, Maureen O'Rourke and her colleagues were always remarkably efficient, knowledgeable, and ready to help. Among other materials, the library's photo collections and Vertical Files focused on Newark are great resources.

NOTES

ABBREVIATIONS FOR FREQUENTLY USED SOURCES

IT   *Italian Tribune*
NDA   *Newark Daily Advertiser*
NDE   *Newark Daily Eagle*
NDJ   *Newark Daily Journal*
NDM   *Newark Daily Mirror*
NHA   Newark Housing Authority
NJA   New Jersey Archives, Trenton
NJAA   *New Jersey Afro-American*
NJHS   New Jersey Historical Society, Newark
NMR   *Newark Morning Register*
NN   *Newark Evening News, Newark Sunday News*
NPL   Newark Public Library
NSC   *Newark Sunday Call*
NYT   *New York Times*
NYTM   *New York Times Magazine*
NW   *Newsweek*
RON   Records of the Town of Newark, 1666–1836
SL   *Star-Ledger*
VV   *Village Voice*

PROLOGUE — PRIDE IN NEWARK

1. NJHS Vertical File (Topic: Newark 300th Celebration).

2. *NN* 5/1/1966; *SL* 5/18/1966.

3. Adolf Konrad, "An Artist Looks at Newark" (Newark Museum pamphlet from exhibit, April 16, 1966–September 5, 1966).

4. Newark Museum archives, box 98.

5. John T. Cunningham, *Newark* (Newark: New Jersey Historical Society, 1966), 314. Note that Cunningham made dramatic revisions to later editions of the book, stating,

"Newark was a city waiting for an explosion as it reached its 300th anniversary year in 1966."

6. Konrad, "An Artist Looks at Newark."

7. *NN* 5/1/1966.

8. Eugene H. Methvin, *The Riot Makers: The Technology of Social Demolition* (New Rochelle, NY: Arlington House, 1970), 32.

9. Submitted 4/25/1967, found online at nj.com.

10. *Report for Action: Governor's Select Commission on Civil Disorder* (Trenton: State of New Jersey, February 1968), 12; Robert L. Allen, *Black Awakening in Capitalist America: An Analytic History* (New York: Anchor Books, 1969), 129.

11. *SL* 6/5/1966.

12. Council members charged with crimes: Frank Addonizio, Lee Bernstein, James Callaghan, Philip Gordon, Anthony Giuliano, Irvine Turner, Calvin West (1969, allegedly accepted kickbacks with Mayor Addonizio, none convicted); Dennis Westbrooks (1971, disorderly conduct and resisting arrest in New York City, convicted); Louis Turco (1974, pled guilty to failure to pay income taxes); Anthony Carrino (1976, assault and battery against Mayor Gibson's bodyguard, found guilty, stayed on the council until 2002); Earl Harris (1982, conspiracy and misconduct in hiring former councilman to a no-show job, charges thrown out); Michael Bontempo (1982, former councilman accused of accepting no-show job while living in Florida, charges thrown out); George Branch (1988, allegedly accepted $1,500 in bribes to sell city lots at discounts, case dismissed due to a technicality, stayed on the council until 1998); Marie Villani (1993, pled guilty to federal charges of misusing city funds for personal expenses); Ralph Grant Jr. (1995, accepted tens of thousands of dollars in bribes to steer city towing contracts to a company, convicted); Gary Harris (1995, accepted bribes alongside Grant, guilty); Frank Megaro (1995, former councilman who pled guilty to bribing current councilmen Grant and Harris); Dana Rone (2007, interfering with a police officer, guilty, remains on the council).

13. *NYT* 3/18/1969.

14. Michael C. D. MacDonald, *America's Cities: A Report on the Myth of Urban Renaissance* (New York: Simon & Schuster, 1984), 328.

15. *NW* 8/30/1970; *NYTM* 7/25/1971; *Harper's,* January 1975.

16. *NYT* 12/18/1980.

17. Philip Roth, *Zuckerman Bound: A Trilogy and Epilogue* (New York: Farrar, Straus and Giroux, 1985), 335–336.

18. *NYT* 11/28/2004.

19. *Report for Action*, xi.

CHAPTER 1 — CORPORATION

1. The term *Achter Col* was later Anglicized into Arthur Kill, the current name of the narrow, north-south body of water between Staten Island and New Jersey.

2. As quoted in Frank John Urquhart, *A History of the City of Newark, New Jersey: Embracing Nearly Two and a Half Centuries, 1666–1913* (New York: Lewis Historical Publishing Co., 1913), 1:49.

3. Isabel MacBeath Calder, *The New Haven Colony* (Hamden, CT: Archon Books, 1970), 218–219.

4. Edward P. Rindler, "The Migration from the New Haven Colony to Newark, East New Jersey" (PhD diss., University of Pennsylvania, 1977), 218–219.

5. Rindler, *Migration from New Haven Colony*, 334.

6. John Thornton's "New Mapp of East and West New Jersey," in *The Mapping of New Jersey: The Men and the Art*, ed. John P. Snyder (New Brunswick, NJ: Rutgers University Press, 1973), 30.

7. Calder, *New Haven Colony*, 254–256.

8. Alexander MacWhorter "A Century Sermon," given January 1, 1801, NPL.

9. NJA 1st, XXIV 560–561, *The New York Gazette* or *Weekly Post Boy*, 6/27/1765.

10. Quoted in David McCullough, *John Adams* (New York: Simon & Schuster, 2001), 23.

11. NJA 1st, XXV 489, *The New York Mercury*, 11/16/1767; NJA 1st, XXVI 214–215, *The New York Gazette and Weekly Mercury*, 7/11/1768.

12. NJA 1st, XXVI 250–251, *The New York Gazette and Weekly Mercury*, 8/22/1768.

13. Nicholas Cressell, *The Journal of Nicholas Cressell* (New York: Dial Press, 1924), 157.

14. Duc de la Rochefaucault, quoted in Cunningham, *Newark*, 86.

15. To create the picture of post-Revolution Newark, I used a 1796-era street map from John W. Barber, *Historical Collections of New Jersey: Past and Present* (published by subscription, 1868), 181; and complemented it with dozens of other sources, notably Urquhart, *History of the City of Newark*.

16. Joseph Atkinson, *The History of Newark* (Newark: William B. Guild, 1878), 138; Urquhart, *History of the City of Newark*, 377, 421.

17. Paul A. Stellhorn, ed., *The Governors of New Jersey, 1664–1974* (Trenton: New Jersey Historical Commission, 1982), 91.

18. Henry Wansey, quoted in Urquhart, *History of the City of Newark*, 377.

19. Ron Chernow, *Alexander Hamilton* (New York: Penguin Press, 2004), 370–387; June Avignon, ed., *Downtown Paterson* (Charleston, SC: Arcadia, 1999), 11–13.

20. RON 165–166.

21. Henry Wansey, quoted in Urquhart, *History of the City of Newark*, 377.

22. Atkinson, *History of Newark*, 328–329; Joel Schwartz, "The Development of New Jersey Society," *New Jersey History Series*, 10: 29.

23. William H. Shaw, *History of Essex and Hudson Counties, New Jersey* (Philadelphia: Everts & Peck, 1884), 688–689.

24. Cunningham, *Newark*, 83–84; Atkinson, *History of Newark*, 146–149.

25. Howard L. Green, ed., *Words That Make New Jersey History* (New Brunswick, NJ: Rivergate Books, 2006), 88–89.

26. Raymond Michael Ralph, "From Village to Industrial City: The Urbanization of Newark, New Jersey, 1830–1860" (PhD diss., New York University, 1978), 19–20.

27. In addition to histories and encyclopedias, I used a few other sources to characterize Boyden, including "New Jersey Inventors and Their Inventions," *Jersey Journeys*

(New Jersey Historical Society) (Oct. 2000),1:3; G. Clifford Jones, "Seth Boyden: A Forgotten Inventor" (unpublished manuscript, NPL); O. Henry Mace, "Seth Boyden: Unsung Hero of Photography" (New Jersey Historical Commission, 1991); Terry Karschner, comp., *Industrial Newark* (Fourteenth Annual Conference of the Society for Industrial Archaeology, May 1985, available at NJHS), 43–45, 116; Theodore Runyon, "An Address Delivered at the Newark Opera House, May 22, 1872, on the Inauguration of a Popular Movement in that City for an Erection of a Statue to Seth Boyden" (NPL, 1880).

28. Atkinson, *History of Newark*, 160–161; Cunningham, *Newark*, 99; Susan Eleanor Hirsch Bloomberg, "Industrialization and Skilled Workers: Newark, 1826 to 1860" (PhD diss., University of Michigan, 1974), 20–23.

29. Ralph, "From Village," 13.

30. Richard F. Veit, *The Old Canals of New Jersey: A Historical Geography* (Little Falls, NJ: New Jersey Geographical Press, 1963), 19–21.

31. Ibid., 28.

32. Ibid., 32–33, 45.

33. Ibid., 32.

34. Harry Sinclair Drago, *Canal Days in America: The History and Romance of Old Towpaths and Waterways* (New York: Crown Publishers, 1972), 119; Russell Bourne, *Floating West: The Erie and Other American Canals* (New York: W. W. Norton, 1992), 194.

35. "Newark 1836," a NPL pamphlet from 1986 has a map showing the Morris Canal's path and street names from the era.

36. Drago, *Canal Days in America*, 119; Cunningham, *Newark*, 101.

37. Thomas F. Gordon, *Gazetteer of the State of New Jersey* (Trenton: Daniel Fenton, 1834), 24.

38. Alvin R. Harlow, quoted in Drago, *Canal Days in America*, 119–120.

39. Edwin G. Burrows and Mike Wallace, *Gotham: A History of New York City to 1898* (New York: Oxford University Press, 1999), 569.

40. Veit, *The Old Canals*, 45, 53.

41. Kevin Hillstrom and Laurie Collier Hillstrom, eds., *The Industrial Revolution in America* (Santa Barbara, CA: ABC-CLIO, 2007), 9:10–13; Drago, *Canal Days in America*, 111.

42. Cunningham, *Newark*, 106–108; Maxine Lurie and Marc Mappan, eds., *Encyclopedia of New Jersey* (New Brunswick, NJ: Rutgers University Press, 2005), 113, 199, 674–675.

43. Veit, *The Old Canals*, 56–57.

44. Ibid., 53–54.

45. Atkinson, *History of Newark*, 190–191.

46. RON 148, 151, 190, 211–212, 232.

47. Atkinson, *History of Newark*, 191.

48. RON 263.

49. *NDA* 5/5/1834.

50. Frederick Branch and Jean Kuras, *Bloomfield Revisited* (Charleston, SC: Arcadia Publishing, 2006), 8; Henry Whittemore, *History of Montclair Township* (New York: Suburban Publishing Co., 1894), 34.

51. *NDA* 1/5/1836.

52. Atkinson, *History of Newark*, 184–185; Cunningham, *Newark*, 104, 109–110.

53. Bloomberg, "Industrialization and Skilled Workers," 35; Cunningham, *Newark*, 113.

54. Atkinson, *History of Newark*, 193, 233.

55. Cunningham, *Newark*, 114–124; Stuart Galishoff, *Newark: The Nation's Unhealthiest City, 1832–1895* (New Brunswick, NJ: Rutgers University Press, 1975), 11–14; Bloomberg, "Industrialization and Skilled Workers," 28, 55.

56. Richard C. Jenkinson, *Old Broad Street* (Newark: Newark Public Library, 1930), 20–21; Galishoff, *Newark: The Nation's Unhealthiest City*, 34–39; Bloomberg, "Industrialization and Skilled Workers," 35.

57. Galishoff, *Newark: The Nation's Unhealthiest City*, 34–39; Bloomberg, "Industrialization and Skilled Workers," 35.

58. Galishoff, *Newark: The Nation's Unhealthiest City*, 30–34.

59. Cortlandt Parker in *NDM*, 1/7/1851.

60. Galishoff, *Newark: The Nation's Unhealthiest City*, 16–17; Bloomberg, "Industrialization and Skilled Workers," 39.

61. Galishoff, *Newark: The Nation's Unhealthiest City*, 11, 16–17.

62. *NDM* 4/27/1853.

63. *NDM* 1/6/1851.

CHAPTER 2 — POLITICS TO THE DOGS

1. Sources for William Wright include: William W. Morris, "Biographical Sketches of Mayors" (NJHS MG#92); *Biographical and Genealogical History of the City of Newark and Essex County, New Jersey* (New York: Lewis Historical Publishing Co., 1898), 2:15–18; *Cyclopedia of New Jersey Biography* (New York: American Historical Society, 1923), 159–160; William H. Shaw, *History of Essex and Hudson Counties, New Jersey* (Philadelphia: Everts & Peck, 1884), 582–583; Alan A. Siegel, *For the Glory of the Union* (Cranbury, NJ: Associated University Press, 1984), 52; Frederick Theodore Frelinghuysen, "Death of Senator Wright" (NJHS Collections, 1866); Samuel Orcutt, *A History of the Old Town of Stratford and the City of Bridgeport, Connecticut* (New haven: Tuttle, Morehouse & Taylor, 1886), 712–715; Edward F. Folsom, ed., *The Municipalities of Essex County, 1666–1924* (New York: Lewis Historical Publishing Co., 1925), biographical volume 126–127.

2. Austin Dickinson, *The National Preacher* (New York: E. Carpenter, 1853), 17:34–42.

3. Article on Sheldon Smith, *NDA* 9/25/1863.

4. Cunningham, *Newark*, 107; Henry Varnum Poor, *History of the Railroads and Canals of the United States* (New York: J. H. Schultz & Co., 1860), 411; *NDM*, 1/18/1851.

5. There is a photo of the Wright house in NJHS Proceedings 1964, between pages 164–165.

6. NJHS Proceedings, 1964, 81–82, 216.

7. *NYT* 11/21/1855; *The Municipalities of Essex County*, biographical volume 126–127.

8. NJHS Proceedings, 1964, 163.

9. NJHS Proceedings, 1964, 170–171.

10. NJHS Proceedings, 1964, 261–262.

11. Through the mid-1800s, William Kinney (and later his son Thomas) also clashed with William Wright in the media world; the Kinneys edited and managed the mainstream *Newark Daily Advertiser*, while Wright owned the Democrat-slanted *Newark Daily Journal*.

12. "An Appeal to the Whigs of New-Jersey by the Conservative Whigs of the Fifth District" (NJHS manuscript, 1847).

13. NJHS Proceedings, 1964, 99

14. NJHS Proceedings, 1964, 99.

15. *NYT* 1/29/1853, 2/5/1853.

16. *NYT* 1/29/1853, 2/5/1853; *Encyclopedia of New Jersey*, 782.

17. Kenneth C. Davis, *Don't Know Much About the Civil War* (New York: William Morrow, 1996), 136–137.

18. William Gillette, *Jersey Blue: Civil War Politics in New Jersey, 1854–1865* (New Brunswick, NJ: Rutgers University Press, 1995), 103–104.

19. Quoted in Shaw, *History of Essex and Hudson Counties*, 58.

20. NDJ 12/19/1860, 12/20/1860, 6/20/1864, 7/19/1864; Gillette, *Jersey Blue*, 86; Edwin A. Charlton, *New Hampshire As It Is* (Claremont, NH: A. Kenney & Co., 1857), 557.

21. *NDE* 3/1/1854.

22. Printed in Cunningham, *Newark*, 151.

23. NDJ 4/4/1861; *NDA* 4/5/1861, 5/6/1861.

24. Siegel, *For the Glory of the Union*, 52.

25. From Mayor Bigelow's message to the Common Council, January 1861, quoted in Urquhart, *A History of the City of Newark*, 680.

26. Charles Perrin Smith, *New Jersey Political Reminiscences, 1828–1882* (New Brunswick, NJ: Rutgers University Press, 1965), 108.

27. From Bigelow's message to the Common Council, January 1861, quoted in Urquhart, *A History of the City of Newark*, 680.

28. *NDM* 2/22/1861.

29. *Philadelphia Inquirer*, 2/22/1861, quoted in Siegel, *For the Glory of the Union*, 19.

30. The anonymous "R" in *NDA* 4/20/1861.

31. Bradley M. Gottfried, *Kearny's Own: The History of the First New Jersey Brigade in the Civil War* (New Brunswick, NJ: Rutgers University Press, 2005), 6–7.

32. *NDA* 4/23/1861.

33. *NDA* 4/29/1861.

34. *NDA* 4/29/1861; *NDM* 4/30/1861.

35. Quoted in Davis, *Don't Know Much About the Civil War*, 257.

36. Davis, *Don't Know Much About the Civil War*, 257–262.

37. Stephen W. Sears, *George B. McClellan: The Young Napoleon* (New York: Ticknor & Fields, 1988), 326.

38. Quoted in Cunningham, *Newark*, 159.

39. Quoted in Charles Merriam Knapp, "New Jersey Politics during the Period of the Civil War and Reconstruction" (PhD diss., Columbia University, 1924), 71–72.

40. Quoted in William J. Jackson, *New Jerseyans in the Civil War: For Union and Liberty* (New Brunswick, NJ: Rutgers University Press, 2000), 107.

41. NDJ 11/5/1862.

42. Gillette, *Jersey Blue*, 202–203; Knapp, "New Jersey Politics," 74; Jackson, *New Jerseyans in the Civil War*, 109.

43. Gillette, *Jersey Blue*, 147–148; Knapp, "New Jersey Politics," 63–65.

44. *NDA* 1/15/1863.

45. Quoted in Gillette, *Jersey Blue*, 227; William Cook Wright, *Secession and Copperheadism in New Jersey during the American Civil War* (Master's thesis, University of Delaware, 1965), 229–231.

46. *Trenton Gazette,* 2/28/1863.

47. Gillette, *Jersey Blue*, 229–231; Edward F. Folsom, ed., *The Municipalities of Essex County, 1666–1924* (New York: Lewis Historical Publishing Co., 1925), biographical volume, 126–127.

48. Smith, *New Jersey Political Reminiscences*, 138–139.

49. Davis, *Don't Know Much About the Civil War*, 312.

50. Knapp, "New Jersey Politics," 146.

51. Knapp, "New Jersey Politics," 40, 147; Larry A. Greene, "The Emancipation Proclamation in New Jersey and the Paranoid Style," *New Jersey History* (Summer 1973): 118–119.

52. The Eleventh Regiment, quoted in Siegel, *For the Glory of the Union*, 148.

53. NDJ 5/13/1863.

54. Knapp, "New Jersey Politics," 96.

55. Luc Sante, *Low Life: Lures and Snares of Old New York* (New York: Farrar, Straus and Giroux, 1991), 350–353.

56. *NDA* 7/14/1863.

57. Quoted in Wright, *Secession and Copperheadism in New Jersey*, 265–267.

58. Provost-Marshal-General James B. Frey, quoted in Knapp, "New Jersey Politics," footnote 96.

59. NDJ 5/27/1864, 5/30/1864.

60. *Encyclopedia of New Jersey*, 152.

61. NDJ 7/19/1864.

62. Knapp, "New Jersey Politics," 119.

63. NDJ 7/22/1864.

64. NDJ 7/30/1864.

65. Gillette, *Jersey Blue*, 268; Davis, *Don't Know Much About the Civil War*, 374–375.

66. Jennifer L. Weber, *Copperheads: The Rise and Fall of Lincoln's Opponents in the North* (New York: Oxford University Press, 2006), 198–199.

67. Quoted in Jackson, *New Jerseyans in the Civil War*, 201.

68. NDJ 8/5/1864.

69. Gillette, *Jersey Blue*, 223–224; account and quotes from the trial *NDA* 2/16/1865.

70. NDJ 4/15/1865.

71. Quoted in Gillette, *Jersey Blue*, 311.

72. Edgar H. Trelease, "Letter from a Soldier," *Harper's Weekly*, January 1, 1865, 93–94.

73. *The Northern Monthly Magazine*, November 1867, 19; Cunningham, *Newark*, 159.

74. Cunningham, *Newark*, 159–160; Jackson, *New Jerseyans in the Civil War*, 109; Quotes from NJHS MG #28, Ward papers, folder 6.

75. "Copperhead Love for the Soldier" (NJHS manuscript, 1865), 6.

76. "Marcus L. Ward, The Soldier's Friend for Governor of New Jersey," printed in Cunningham, *Newark*, 163.

77. Quoted in Donald A. Sinclair, *A Bibliography: The Civil War and New Jersey* (New Brunswick, NJ: Friends of the Rutgers University Library, 1968), 130.

78. Quoted in Gillette, *Jersey Blue*, 323.

79. Gillette, *Jersey Blue*, 323; Knapp, "New Jersey Politics," 182.

80. Knapp, "New Jersey Politics," 163–165; Gillette, *Jersey Blue*, 325–326.

81. *NYT* 11/4/1866.

82. *Dictionary of American Biography* (New York: Charles Scribner's Sons, 1936), 20:571.

83. *NDA* 5/5/1866, 3/2/1867; *NN* 2/8/1914.

CHAPTER 3 — GREATER NEWARK

1. Details on the exposition come primarily from widespread coverage in Newark and New York newspapers, as well as the pamphlet "Newark Industrial Exhibition: Report and Catalogue of the First Exhibition of Newark Industries, Exclusively 1872" (Holbrook's Steam Printery, 1882).

2. *NDA* 4/3/1872.

3. *The Northern Monthly Magazine*, September 1867, 385.

4. Unless otherwise noted, quotes regarding the exhibition are from excerpts in "Newark Industrial Exhibition," 21–40.

5. *NDA* 8/4/1872; *NMR* 8/22/1872.

6. *NMR* 9/20/1872.

7. *NMR* 9/20/1872.

8. *NYT* 12/30/1872.

9. *NDA* 2/1/1870.

10. Board of Trade Report, 1873, 16, Board of Trade Report, 1880, 14 (both available at NPL).

11. Neil Baldwin, *Edison: Inventing the Century* (New York: Hyperion, 1996), 50–52, 60–72; Reese V. Jenkins, ed., *The Papers of Thomas A. Edison* (Baltimore, MD: Johns Hopkins University Press, 1989), 1:146–149, 301, 385, 642–644.

12. Cunningham, *Newark*, 180–181; *Encyclopedia of New Jersey*, 399.

13. Cunningham, *Newark*, 179–180; *Encyclopedia of New Jersey*, 864

14. William H.A. Carr, *From Three Cents a Week: The Story of the Prudential Insurance Company of America* (Englewood Cliffs, NJ: Prentice-Hall, 1975), 12–24; Cunningham, *Newark*, 186.

15. Carr, *From Three Cents a Week*, 28–30, 62, 169; Cunningham, *Newark*, 186–188.

16. Galishoff, *Newark: The Nation's Unhealthiest City*, 64–65.

17. Martha Lamb, "Sketch of Newark," *Harper's New Monthly Magazine*, October 1876, 675–676.

18. *Industrial Newark*, 71–72.

19. David Steven Cohen, ed., *America, The Dream of My Life: Selections from the Federal Writers' Project's New Jersey Ethnic Survey* (New Brunswick, NJ: Rutgers University Press, 1990), 63–64.

20. Dorothea Adams Pantages, quoted in Angelique Lampros, *Remembering Newark's Greeks: An American Odyssey* (Virginia Beach: Donning Company Publishers, 2006), 27.

21. Stuart Galishoff, *Safeguarding the Public Health: Newark, 1895–1918* (Westport, CT: Greenwood Press, 1975), 135.

22. Galishoff, *Newark: The Nation's Unhealthiest City*, 103–104.

23. Cunningham, *Newark*, 200; "The Eighth Annual Message of Hon. Joseph E. Haynes, Mayor, Prepared January 6th, Presented to the Common Council of the City of Newark, N.J., Feb. 7th, 1891" (Newark: Grover Brothers, Printers, NJHS pamphlet), 5, 71.

24. *NYT* 3/8/1884; Galishoff, *Newark: The Nation's Unhealthiest City*, 137; Cunningham, *Newark*, 200; "The Ninth Annual Message of Hon. Joseph E. Haynes, 1892" (NJHS pamphlet), 66.

25. Lamb, "Sketch of Newark," 677.

26. Cunningham, *Newark*, 224–225; *NYT*, 1/13/1892.

27. "The Ninth Annual Message of Hon. Joseph E. Haynes, 1892," 36.

28. *NYT* 4/3/1893.

29. *NYT* 10/15/1887, 10/12/1891, 10/16/1891.

30. *NYT* 4/13/1894.

31. *Industrial Newark*, 72–73, 92.

32. *NDA* 12/13/1894; *NYT* 6/23/1891; *Cyclopedia of New Jersey Biography* (New York: American Historical Society, 1923), 2:226–227; Frederick W. Ricord, *Biographical and Genealogical History of the City of Newark and Essex County, New Jersey* (New York: Lewis Historical Publishing Co., 1898), 112–114.

33. Cunningham, *Newark*, 226; Galishoff, *Newark: The Nation's Unhealthiest City*, 124.

34. Ricord, *Biographical and Genealogical History*, 112–114; Cunningham, *Newark*, 226.

35. Galishoff, *Safeguarding the Public Health*, 126–129; Glenn R. Modica, "The History of the Newark Sewer System" (Cranbury, NJ: Richard Grubb & Associates, 2001).

36. Galishoff, *Newark: The Nation's Unhealthiest City*, 66.

37. Lamb, "Sketch of Newark," 678.

38. *NYT*, 11/15/1894.

39. Ricord, *Biographical and Genealogical History*, 114; *NN* 2/28/1895; *NYT* 3/17/1894.

40. *NYT* 3/17/1895.

41. *NYT* 3/19/1895, 3/28/1895.

42. *NN* 3/4/1895; *NDA* 3/6/1895.

43. *NYT* 1/14/1896, 11/12/1900; *NDA* 9/17/1898.

44. *NYT* 4/15/1896; Ricord, *Biographical and Genealogical History*, 112–114.

45. *NSC* 12/2/06.

46. Charles Wesley Churchill, *The Italians of Newark: A Community Study* (New York: Arno Press, 1975), 24–27, 38.

47. Ronald L. Becker, "History of the Jewish Community in Newark, New Jersey," part of *Greater Newark's Jewish Legacy*, a 1995 NPL exhibit; Patricia M. Ard and Michael Aaron Rockland, *The Jews of New Jersey: A Pictorial History* (New Brunswick, NJ: Rutgers University Press, 2002), 10, 15; "The Essex Story: A History of the Jewish Community in Essex County, New Jersey" (Jewish Education Association of Essex County, 1955), 46.

48. Samuel H. Popper, "Newark, New Jersey, 1870–1910: Chapters in the Evolution of an American Metropolis" (PhD diss., New York University, 1952), 392.

49. Frank Kingdon, *John Cotton Dana: A Life* (Newark: Newark Public Library and Museum, 1940), 83–84, 94, 97; Cunningham, *Newark*, 218–220.

50. "The Eighth Annual Message of Hon. Joseph E. Haynes, 189" (NJHS document), 94.

51. Cunningham, *Newark*, 227–229; Jean-Rae Turner and Richard T. Koles, *Newark, New Jersey* (Charleston, SC: Arcadia, 2001), 69.

52. *NSC* 4/22/1900.

53. Sample ads in *NDA* 11/26/1906, 12/3/1906, 12/20/1906.

54. Ads from December 1906 in *NN*; *NDA*.

55. *NDA* 12/19/1906.

56. Karl Baedeker, ed., *The United States, with an Excursion into Mexico: A Handbook for Travellers* (1893; rpr. New York: Da Capo Press, 1971), 208; Lamb, "Sketch of Newark."

57. *NSC* 12/9/1906.

58. *NN* 12/20/1906.

59. *NSC* 12/9/1906.

60. *NDA* 12/20/1906; *NN*12/20/1906; *NSC* 12/2/1906.

61. Galishoff, *Newark: The Nation's Unhealthiest City*, 22–23, 66, 100; Theodore Runyon, "An Address Delivered at the Newark Opera House, May 22md, 1872, on the Inauguration of a Popular Movement in that City for the Erection of a Statue to Seth Boyden" (NPL document), 5; the statue Runyon sought was erected in Washington Park in 1890.

62. *NN* 12/20/1906.

63. *NN* 10/17/1907.

64. Popper, "Newark, New Jersey, 1870–1910," 433–435.

65. Alan A. Siegel, *Our Past: A History of Irvington, New Jersey* (Irving Centennial Committee, 1974), 190–194; *NN* 4/12/1903, 4/15/1903.

66. *NN* 10/30/1908.

67. *NN* 11/4/1908; *NYT* 4/16/1935.

68. Kenneth T. Jackson, *Crabgrass Frontier: The Suburbanization of the United States* (New York: Oxford University Press, 1987), 148–150.

CHAPTER 4 — DEAD WEIGHT

1. Bradley Robert Rice, *Progressive Cities: The Commission Government Movement in America, 1901–1920* (Austin: University of Texas Press, 1977), 3–18.

2. *NYT* 6/6/1915; Ryan's book is titled *Municipal Freedom* (New York: Doubleday, 1915).

3. "Report on the Social Evil Conditions of Newark, New Jersey, 1913–1914" (document available at Rutgers-Newark Dana Library).

4. "Report on the Social Evil Conditions of Newark, New Jersey, 1913–1914," 11–13, 61, 71, 126–129, 164–167.

5. "Report on the Social Evil Conditions of Newark, New Jersey, 1913–1914," 11–12.

6. "Report on the Social Evil Conditions of Newark, New Jersey, 1913–1914," 70, 139.

7. Willard D. Price, "The Ironbound District: A Study of a District in Newark, N.J." (Newark: Neighborhood House, 1912), 4–12, 24–25.

8. Andrew Sinclair, *Prohibition: The Era of Excess* (Boston: Little, Brown, 1962), 180–181.

9. "Final Report of the Charter Commission of the City of Newark" (Charter Commission, 1953), 14.

10. Paul Anthony Stellhorn, "Depression and Decline, Newark, New Jersey: 1929–1941" (PhD diss., Rutgers University, 1982), 17–18, 39–40, 54.

11. *NN* 9/17/1917.

12. *NN* 10/10/1917.

13. Stellhorn, "Depression and Decline," 49–50; *NYT* 7/1/56; Cunningham, *Newark*, 262.

14. *NYT* 10/19/1913.

15. Cunningham, *Newark*, 233, 245–249, 264; *NYT* 5/7/1916, 12/21/1917.

16. *NYT* 6/11/1918, 7/13/1918, 7/22/1918, 5/6/1919, 3/21/1920.

17. Stellhorn, "Depression and Decline," 40, 50; *NYT* 5/18/1921.

18. *NN* 5/15/1930; *NYT* 5/15/1930; Stellhorn, "Depression and Decline," 50.

19. William M. Ashby, *Tales without Hate* (Newark: Newark Preservation and Landmarks Committee; Metuchen, NJ: Upland Press, 1996), 109–102.

20. *NN* 4/26/1921.

21. *NN* 5/6/1921.

22. *NN* 5/5/1925.

23. *NN* 11/23/1923.

24. *NN* 4/23/1921.

25. *NYT* 9/10/1922; *NN* 9/28/1928.

26. *NN* 9/19/1921, 9/22/1921.

27. *NN* 2/2/1922.

28. *NN,* 2/7/1922.

29. *NN* 1/23/1923.

30. Mark A. Stuart, *Gangster #2: Longy Zwillman, the Man Who Invented Organized Crime* (Secaucus, NJ: Lyle Stuart, 1985), 19–22.

31. Stuart, *Gangster #2*, 23–27.

32. Carl Sifakis, *The Mafia Encyclopedia*, 3rd ed. (New York: Facts on File, 2005), 412, 488; *NYTM* 2/1/1970.

33. Douglas V. Shaw, *Immigration and Ethnicity in New Jersey History* (Trenton: New Jersey Historical Commission, 1994), 55; Stuart, *Gangster #2*, 31–32.

34. Quoted in Stuart, *Gangster #2*, 33; *NYTM* 2/1/1970.

35. Stuart, *Gangster #2*, 34–35.

36. Stuart, *Gangster #2*, 30–35.

37. Stuart, *Gangster #2*, 40.

38. Stuart, *Gangster #2*, 45–46, 50–53.

39. Stuart, *Gangster #2*, 58; Michael Immerso, *Newark's Little Italy: The Vanished First Ward* (New Brunswick, NJ: Rutgers University Press, 1997), 110–111.

40. *NN* 11/23/1930.

41. Stuart, *Gangster #2*, 58–66.

42. *NN* 10/6/1930, 10/7/1930.

43. *NN* 11/23/1930.

44. *NN* 11/23/1930.

45. *NN* 12/4/1930.

46. *NYT* 3/21/1931.

47. *NN* 8/7/1931; *NYTM* 2/1/1970.

48. *NYT* 3/11/1931, 11/17/1932, 11/18/1932, 11/20/1932, 11/22/1932, 12/13/1932, 12/21/1932; Stuart, *Gangster #2*, 152–153; *NYTM* 2/1/1970.

49. Kenneth T. Jackson, "Gentleman's Agreement: Discrimination in Metropolitan America," in *Reflections on Regionalism*, ed. Bruce Katz (Washington, DC: Brookings Institution Press, 2000), 198; Federal Writers' Project, *New Jersey: A Guide to Its Present and Past* (New York: Hastings House, 1946), 325, 327.

50. Cunningham, *Newark*, 270–272; *NYT*, 12/22/1929; Federal Writers' Project, 107.

51. *NN* 4/28/1923.

52. Stellhorn, "Depression and Decline," 26–33.

53. Stellhorn, "Depression and Decline," 55, 58; *NYT* 5/16/1929.

54. Stellhorn, "Depression and Decline," 67–71, 82; Joseph Gowaskie, "Workers in New Jersey History," *New Jersey History Series* 6 (New Jersey Historical Commission, 1992), 52; T. H. Watkins, *The Great Depression: America in the 1930s* (Boston: Little, Brown, 1993), 55.

55. Gowaskie, "Workers in New Jersey History," 52; Stellhorn, "Depression and Decline," 84.

56. Gowaskie, "Workers in New Jersey History," 51; Kenneth T. Jackson and Barbara B. Jackson, "The Black Experience in Newark: The Growth of the Ghetto, 1870–1970," *New Jersey since 1860*, ed. William C. Wright (Trenton: New Jersey Historical Commission, 1972), 39, 44.

57. Jackson and Jackson, "Black Experience in Newark," 46, 49.

58. Stellhorn, "Depression and Decline," 80–82.

59. Stellhorn, "Depression and Decline," 82–84, 93; Cunningham, *Newark*, 281.

60. *NN* 10/8/1932; Stuart, *Gangster #2*, 132.

61. *NN* 10/8/1932.

62. *NYT* 5/11/1933, 9/24/1933.

63. "Final Report of the Charter Commission of the City of Newark," 24.

64. *NYT* 10/12/1936.

65. *NYT* 3/23/1935.

66. *NY* 10/30/1933, 2/10/1934.

67. *NYT* 10/12/1936.

68. *NYT* 10/12/1936.

69. *NYT* 10/14/1937.

70. *NYT* 12/3/1937; *NN* 7/19/1938, 7/20/1938.

71. *NYT* 3/24/1939.

72. *NYT* 4/22/1939, 4/25/1939.

73. *NYT* 6/13/1939.

74. *NYT* 1/7/1940.

75. *NN* 5/6/1941.

76. *NYT* 5/14/1941, 5/11/1949.

77. *NYT* 10/23/1935, 10/24/1935; Paul Sann, *Kill the Dutchman: The Story of Dutch Schultz* (New Rochelle, NY: Arlington House, 1971), 11–25.

78. *NYT* 10/25/1935.

79. *NYT* 10/24/1935, 10/25/1935.

80. *NYT* 10/25/1935.

81. Sann, *Kill the Dutchman*, 19–20; Stuart, *Gangster #2*, 101–102; *NYT* 10/25/1935.

82. Stuart, *Gangster #2*, 114, 186; Immerso, *Newark's Little Italy*, 111.

83. Immerso, *Newark's Little Italy*, 130–131; Sifakis, *Mafia Encyclopedia*, 47; *NYTM* 2/1/1970; Richard Ben Cramer, *Joe DiMaggio: The Hero's Life* (New York: Simon & Schuster, 2000), 132–133.

84. *Encyclopedia of New Jersey*, 562–563.

85. Edward S. Shapiro, "Ethnicity and Employment: The Early Years of the Jewish Vocational Services of Newark, 1939–1952," *New Jersey History*, no. 1/2 (1988): 23–27.

86. Stuart, *Gangster #2*, 107–111; Immerso, *Newark's Little Italy*, 112; Warren Grover, *Nazis in Newark* (New Brunswick, NJ: Transaction Publishers, 2003) covers in-depth the anti-Nazi riots provoked by Nat Arno's Minutemen; also see Ron Nessen, "Newark's Other Riots," *New Jersey Monthly*, July 2005, 58–75.

87. Stellhorn, "Depression and Decline," 27–28.

88. Jackson, *Crabgrass Frontier*, 275.

89. *NN* 3/25/41, 5/9/1941; *NYT* 4/6/1935.

90. Cunningham, *Newark,* 299; Gowaskie, "Workers in New Jersey History," 48.

91. Cunninghan, *Newark,* 288–296.

92. *NN* 9/5/1939; Stuart, *Gangster #2,* 147.

93. *NN* 5/1/1950.

94. "Official Corruption and Organized Crime: Kefauver Committee," excerpt from Senator Kefauver's *Crime Committee Report,* printed in *Theft of the City: Readings on Corruption in Urban America,* ed. John A. Gardiner and David J. Olsen (Bloomington: Indiana University Press, 1974), 68–72.

95. Stuart, *Gangster #2,* 174–185; Sifakis, *Mafia Encyclopedia,* 240–241; *NN* 6/26/1952.

96. *NYT* 9/20/1949, 5/3/1951; *NN* 7/11/1951, 10/6/1951.

97. *NN* 10/6/1951.

98. *NYT* 5/13/1953.

99. "Final Report of the Charter Commission of the City of Newark," 1.

100. "Final Report of the Charter Commission of the City of Newark," 2–3.

101. "Final Report of the Charter Commission of the City of Newark," 16, 19–22, 25–27.

102. Cunningham, *Newark,* 305–307.

103. "Final Report of the Charter Commission of the City of Newark," 8.

CHAPTER 5 — THE SLUMS OF TEN YEARS FROM NOW

For description of events on Columbus Day 1956, I consulted newspaper coverage (particularly *NN, SL,* and *IT*); I also spoke at length with Monsignor Joseph Granato, of Saint Lucy's Church, who was present on Christopher Columbus Homes' dedication day; for visuals of the First Ward and construction of the Columbus Homes, see "Construction Report" (NHA, 1956).

2. Thanks to Monsignor Granato and the Newark First Ward Heritage and Cultural Society, I was able to interview various former residents and visitors of the First Ward in its heyday; also Immerso, *Newark's Little Italy,* 80–97.

3. *NN* 10/12/1956.

4. *NN* 1/22/1952.

5. *IT* 1/25/1952.

6. *NN* morgue file, see St. Lucy's Church; also, Immerso, *Newark's Little Italy,* 65–79.

7. Per interviews with Monsignor Granato in the spring of 2006.

8. *IT* 10/19/1956 printed Father Ruggiero's entire speech; additional description comes from conversations with Monsignor Granato.

9. For background on Louis Danzig: Harold Kaplan, *Urban Renewal Politics: Slum Clearance in Newark* (New York: Columbia University Press, 1963); David Levitus, "An

Anatomy of Urban Renewal in Newark, N.J., 1933–1967: How Patronage Politics, Planning Policy, and a Powerbroker Shaped a City" (Master's thesis, New York University, 2005) 39–67; *SL* 4/28/1982; *NN* 7/14/1946, 4/15/1948, 1/23/1952.

10. Kaplan, *Urban Renewal Politics*, 40–41.

11. *NN* 4/15/1948.

12. Kaplan, *Urban Renewal Politics*, 40–41.

13. *NN* 7/4/1948.

14. Quoted in Levitus, "Anatomy of Urban Renewal," 42.

15. Jay Rumney and Sara Shuman, "The Cost of Slums in Newark" (Housing Authority of the City of Newark, 1946).

16. Central Planning Board, *The Master Plan for the Physical Development of the City of Newark, N.J.* (Newark: Central Planning Board, 1947), 9, 38, 45–46, 51.

17. Kaplan, *Urban Renewal Politics*, 114–115.

18. Le Corbusier, *The Radiant City* (New York: Orion Press, 1967), 121.

19. Le Corbusier, *The City of To-morrow*, 3rd ed. (Cambridge, MA: MIT Press, 1971), 1, 164; *Radiant City*, 123.

20. Charles V. Craster, "Slum Clearance: The Newark Plan," *American Journal of Public Health and the Nation's Health* (September 1944): 935.

21. "Rebuilding Newark" (NHA, 1952), 14.

22. *NN* 3/31/1950.

23. Kaplan, *Urban Renewal Politics*, 15.

24. Kaplan, *Urban Renewal Politics*, 36, 164.

25. *NN* 6/17/1949.

26. *NN* 6/27/1951.

27. Jackson, *Crabgrass Frontier*, 225–227.

28. "Construction Report," (NHA, 1956) 1.

29. Jackson, *Crabgrass Frontier*, 225.

30. Levitus, "Anatomy of Urban Renewal," 10–11.

31. "Theme Song of Baxter Terrace," by J. M. Johnson, lyrics printed in NHA Quarterly Report, October 1951.

32. Levitus, "Anatomy of Urban Renewal," 12–13; Kaplan, *Urban Renewal Politics*, 151.

33. Kaplan, *Urban Renewal Politics*, 15–16.

34. Kaplan, *Urban Renewal Politics*, 17.

35. *NN* 1/20/1952.

36. *NN* 1/22/1952.

37. *NN* 1/20/1952.

38. *NN* 1/21/1952.

39. "Rebuilding Newark" (NHA pamphlet, 1952), 3.

40. *NN* 7/24/1952.

41. *NN* 1/21/1952.

42. Immerso, *Newark's Little Italy*, 128.

43. *NN* 11/26/1954.

44. Photos in Immerso, *Newark's Little Italy*, 142–143.

45. *NN* 2/5/1952; *IT* 2/8/1952.

46. *SL* 2/4/1952.

47. *NN* 2/5/1952; *SL* 2/5/1952.

48. *IT* 2/17/1952.

49. *IT* 3/7/1952.

50. *IT* 4/18/1952.

51. *NN* 5/2/1952, 5/4/1952.

52. Levitus, "Anatomy of Urban Renewal," 53.

53. *SL* 5/2/1952.

54. *SL* 5/2/1952.

55. *SL* 5/23/1952.

56. *SL* 5/23/1952.

57. Levitus, "Anatomy of Urban Renewal," 54–55.

58. *IT* 1/9/1953.

59. *IT* 7/22/1955.

60. Quoted in Kaplan, *Urban Renewal Politics*, 155.

61. *NN* 6/29/1956.

62. *NN* 6/29/1956.

63. *IT* 7/17/1953, 2/26/1954.

64. *NN* 8/21/1955.

65. Kaplan, *Urban Renewal Politics*, 152–153.

66. "Construction Report" (NHA, 1956) 17–20.

67. "Newark's Children" (NHA pamphlet, 1957); *NN* 4/23/1958, 12/8/1958.

68. Levitus, "Anatomy of Urban Renewal," 47–48.

69. *NN* morgue file (see Housing—North Ward).

70. *NN* 6/2/1957, 8/19/1957; Levitus, "Anatomy of Urban Renewal," 55.

71. *NN* 4/11/1957.

72. *NN* 4/7/1962.

73. Kaplan, *Urban Renewal Politics*, 159.

74. Jane Jacobs, *Death and Life of Great American Cities* (New York: Random House, 1961) 4.

75. Jacobs, *Death and Life*, 8–9.

76. Jacobs, *Death and Life*, 9.

77. Kaplan, *Urban Renewal Politics*, 66.

78. Anonymous, quoted in George Sternlieb, *The Tenement Landlord* (New Brunswick, NJ: Rutgers University Press, 1966), 165.

79. Sternlieb, *Tenement Landlord*, 167.

80. William Grigsby, quoted in Sternlieb, *Tenement Landlord*, 13.

81. Bernard J. Friden and Lynne B. Sagalyn, *Downtown, Inc.: How America Rebuilds Cities* (Cambridge, MA: MIT Press, 1989), 52; Levitus, "Anatomy of Urban Renewal," 66.

82. Levitus, "Anatomy of Urban Renewal," 66; Central Planning Board, "Renew Newark" (Central Planning Board, Final Report 1961), 84, 100, 103; *Report for Action*, 77.

83. Levitus, "Anatomy of Urban Renewal," 66; Central Planning Board, "Renew Newark" (Central Planning Board, Final Report 1961), 84, 100, 103.

84. *NN* 5/1/1966.

85. *NN* 3/6/1966.

86. *NN* 6/30/1966.

87. *NN* 6/30/1966.

CHAPTER 6 — BOUND TO EXPLODE

1. For events of 7/12/1967: *Report for Action: Governor's Select Commission on Civil Disorder* (Trenton: State of New Jersey, February 1968) has a comprehensive chronological sequence, especially 24, 104–111; also *NYT* 7/13/1967; *NN* 7/13/1967; *SL* 7/13/1967; Tom Hayden, *Rebellion in Newark: Official Violence and Ghetto Response* (New York: Vintage Books, 1967), 6–10.

2. *NN* 2/25/1968; Ronald Porambo, *No Cause for Indictment* (Brooklyn, NY: Melville House, 2006), 100–104.

3. Quoted in Hayden, *Rebellion in Newark*, 10.

4. *NN* 7/14/1967.

5. *Report for Action*, 108.

6. *Report for Action*, 110.

7. *Report for Action*, 111.

8. *NN* 4/17/1967.

9. *NYT* 7/15/1967.

10. *NYT* 12/18/1965.

11. *NN* 7/13/1967; *SL* 7/9/2007.

12. Anonymous oral history in *When I Was Comin' Up: An Oral History of Aged Blacks* (Hamden, CT: Archon Books, 1982), 25.

13. Florette Henri, *Black Migration: Movement North, 1900–1920* (New York: Anchor Books, 1976), 51–55.

14. Henri, *Black Migration*, 57, 60.

15. Ashby, *Tales without Hate*, 17–18.

16. *When I Was Comin' Up*, 22, 206.

17. Helen Pendleton, in *Freedom Not Far Distant: A Documentary of Afro-Americans in New Jersey*, ed. Clement A. Price (Newark: New Jersey Historical Society, 1980), 213.

18. Jackson and Jackson, "Black Experience in Newark," 39; Price, *Freedom Not Far Distant*, 194.

19. Giles R. Wright, *New Jersey Ethnic Life Series* 3 (Trenton: New Jersey Historical Commission, 1986), 13.

20. Price, *Freedom Not Far Distant*, 214.

21. Clement A. Price, "The Beleaguered City as Promised Land: Blacks in Newark, 1917–1947," in *Urban New Jersey Since 1870*, ed. William C. Wright (Trenton: New Jersey Historical Commission, 1975), 16–17, 38.

22. Central Planning Board, *The Master Plan for the Physical Development of the City of Newark, N.J.* (Newark: Central Planning Board, 1947), 38.

23. Clement A. Price, "The Struggle to Desegregate Newark: Black Middle Class Militancy in New Jersey, 1932–1947," *New Jersey*, no. 3/4 (1981): 219–220; Jackson and Jackson, "The Black Experience in Newark," 55–56.

24. Barbara J. Kukla, *Swing City: Newark Nightlife, 1925–1950* (New Brunswick, NJ: Rutgers University Press, 1991), 16–17, 23, 53–60, 121–127, 166–170.

25. James Overmyer, *Effa Manley and the Newark Eagles* (Metuchen, NJ: Scarecrow Press, 1993), 62–67; Amiri Baraka, *The Autobiography of LeRoi Jones* (New York: Freundlich Books, 1984), 33–34.

26. Newark Municipal Council, "Soaring Eagles: Newark and the Negro Leagues" (Newark: The Writing Company, 2002), 20–25.

27. Overmyer, *Effa Manley and the Newark Eagles*, 101–107.

28. Edward D. Williams, *The First Black Captain* (New York: Vantage Press, 1974), 2–3.

29. Williams, *First Black Captain*, 4.

30. Ashby, *Tales without Hate*, 121–123.

31. Baraka, *Autobiography of LeRoi Jones*, 7, 30–31.

32. Ashby, *Tales without Hate*, 93–97.

33. Williams, *First Black Captain*, 18.

34. Ashby, *Tales without Hate*, 188.

35. Robert L. Allen, *Black Awakening in Capitalist America: An Analytic History* (New York: Anchor Books, 1969), 26–27; *Report of the National Advisory Commission on Civil Disorders* (New York: Bantam Books, 1968), 69–70

36. *NYT* 6/16/1963.

37. Jackson and Jackson, "Black Experience in Newark," 56.

38 Jackson and Jackson, "Black Experience in Newark," 39–41; Price, *Freedom Not Far Distant*, 194.

39. Larry A. Greene, Leonard Harris, Clement Price, and Lee Hagan, "New Jersey Afro-Americans: From Colonial Times to the Present," in *The New Jersey Ethnic Experience*, ed. Barbara Cunningham (Union City, NJ: Wm. H. Wise & Co., 1977), 82; *Report for Action*, 72, 78.

40. Curtis Lucas, *Third Ward Newark* (Chicago: Ziff-Davis Publishing Co., 1946), 39.

41. *NN* 8/24/1954, 8/25/1954, 10/19/1954, 2/15/1955.

42. Dorothy H. Guyot, "Newark: Crime and Politics in a Declining City," excerpted in *Crime in City Politics*, ed. Anne Heinz, Herbert Jacob, and Robert L. Lineberry (New York: Longman, 1983), 54–55.

43. Baraka, *Autobiography of LeRoi Jones*, 260.

44. *NN* 8/5/1965.

45. *NN* 7/2/1965.

46. Allen, *Black Awakening*, 126.

47. Quoted in Allen, *Black Awakening*, 34.

48. Quoted in Jerry Gafio Watts, *Amiri Baraka: The Politics and Art of a Black Intellectual* (New York: New York University Press, 2001), 332.

49. *NYT* 12/18/1965.

50. *Report for Action*, 12, 14–15; *NYT* 7/13/1967; *SL* 7/9/2007.

51. *Report for Action*, 12, 14–15; *NYT* 6/13/1967, 7/13/1967; *SL* 7/9/2007. As it turned out, the college wound up built on about one-third of the originally proposed acreage; the college has also been marked with scandals and ordered to be overseen by state officials.

52. Williams, *First Black Captain*, 84–86.

53. *NN* 7/2/1965; Kaplan, *Urban Renewal Politics*, 153–156.

54. Baraka, *Autobiography of LeRoi Jones*, 244.

55. *Report for Action*, 111–112; *NN* 7/14/1967.

56. *Report for Action*, 112–113; *NN* 7/14/1967; *SL* 7/9/2007.

57. *NN* 7/14/1967; Hayden, *Rebellion in Newark*, 17.

58. Baraka, *Autobiography of LeRoi Jones*, 259–260.

59. Williams, *First Black Captain*, 90; *NN* 7/14/1967; *NYT* 7/14/1967.

60. *Report for Action*, 113–114; *NYT* 7/14/1967.

61. *Report for Action*, 114–115; *NYT* 7/14/1967.

62. *Report for Action*, 116–117, 128–129.

63. *Report for Action*, 117–118; *NN* 7/14/1967.

64. *NN* 7/14/1967.

65. *NN* 7/14/1967.

66. *Report for Action*, 118, 133.

67. *Report for Action*, 138–139; *SL* 7/9/2007.

68. *NYT* 7/15/1967.

69. *NN* 7/16/1967.

70. *New Yorker*, 7/22/1967.

71. *NW* 7/24/1967; *NN* 7/14/1967, 7/15/1967, 7/16/1967.

72. *NN* 7/16/1967; Williams, *First Black Captain*, 92; *SL* 7/9/2007.

73. *SL* 7/9/2007.

74. *NN* 7/15/1967.

75. *NN* 7/15/1967, 7/16/1967.

76. *NN* 7/15/1967; *SL* 7/9/2007; *Report for Action*, 138–139.

77. *NN* 7/16/1967; *NYT* 7/17/1967; *Report for Action*, 138–139; *SL* 7/9/2007.

78. *NN* 7/14/1967, 7/15/1967; *NYT* 7/16/1967.

79. *SL* 7/16/1967.

80. *Report for Action*, 118, 138–139.

81. *NN* 7/17/1967.

82. *Report for Action*, 120–122.

83. *NN* 7/17/1967.

84. *Report for Action*, 124; *NYT* 7/17/1967.

85. *NN* 7/14/1967, 7/16/1967.

86. *SL* 7/24/1967.

87. Printed in *NW* 7/31/1967.

88. *NN* 7/15/1967.

89. *NN* 7/15/1967.

90. *NYT* 7/16/1967.

91. *Report for Action*, 130–131, 142.

92. *Life*, 7/28/1967.

93. *NW* 7/24/1967; *NN* 7/16/1967.

94. *Report for Action*, 2–3.

95. *Report for Action*, 138–141; police archives available at nj.com, Newark 1967 special section; Porambo, *No Cause for Indictment*, 128–130.

96. *SL* 7/26/1967.

97. *Report for Action*, 143; *SL* 7/9/2007.

98. *NN* 7/17/1967.

99. *SL* 7/26/1967.

100. Quoted in Allen, *Black Awakening*, 135.

CHAPTER 7 — THE WORST AMERICAN CITY

1. *NW* 7/31/1967.

2. Allen, *Black Awakening*, 158; *SL* estimated the number of delegates at nearly a thousand; *NW* gave the figure of "more than 600."

3. *NW* 7/31/1967; *SL* 7/23/1967.

4. *SL* 7/23/1967.

5. Allen, *Black Awakening*, 157.

6. *NW* 7/31/1967.

7. Allen, *Black Awakening*, 12, 159.

8. *SL* 7/24/1967.

9. *NW* 7/31/1967.

10. Allen, *Black Awakening*, 160.

11. *SL* 7/24/1967.

12. *SL* 7/24/1967.

13. *SL* 7/24/1967.

14. Baraka, *Autobiography of LeRoi Jones*, 266.

15. Jerry Gafio Watts, *Amiri Baraka: The Politics and Art of a Black Intellectual* (New York: New York University Press, 2001), 22.

16. Hettie Jones, *How I Became Hettie Jones* (New York: E. P. Dutton, 1990).

17. Watts, *Amiri Baraka*, 44–45.

18. Jones, *How I Became Hettie Jones*, 139, 201, 218.

19. Jones, *How I Became Hettie Jones*, 218.

20. *NYT* 2/28/1966, 3/17/1966, 3/19/1966.

21. Jack Richardson, "Blues for Mr. Jones," *Esquire*, June 1966, 106.

22. *NYT* 3/19/1966.

23. *NYT* 3/19/1966.

24. Baraka, *Autobiography of LeRoi Jones*, 230.

25. Baraka, *Autobiography of LeRoi Jones*, 244, 267; David Llorens, "Ameer (LeRoi Jones) Baraka," *Ebony*, August 1969, 75–83.

26. Quoted as such several times in *Ebony*, August 1969, 75–83 and in an article written by him in *NYT* 11/16/1969; Allen, *Black Awakening*, 165–168.

27. Quoted in Allen, *Black Awakening*, 168–170; Theodore R. Hudson, *From LeRoi Jones to Amiri Baraka: The Literary Works* (Durham, NC: Duke University Press, 1973), 34–36.

28. *Ebony*, August 1969, 80.

29. Baraka, *Autobiography of LeRoi Jones*, 264–267.

30. Baraka, *Autobiography of LeRoi Jones*, 268, 272.

31. *NYT* 3/28/1967.

32. Stanley B. Winters, "Turbulent Decade: Newark since the Riots," in *Newark: An Assessment, 1967–1977*, ed. Stanley B. Winters (Newark: New Jersey Institute of Technology, 1979), 3.

33. Komozi Woodard, *A Nation within a Nation: Amiri Baraka (LeRoi Jones) and Black Power Politics* (Chapel Hill: University of North Carolina Press, 1999), 94–97.

34. *NYT* 6/24/1968.

35. *NYTM* 9/29/1968.

36. Allen, *Black Awakening*, 141, 201; Watts, *Amiri Baraka*, 358–359.

37. Baraka, *Autobiography of LeRoi Jones*, 274.

38. Allen, *Black Awakening*, 135–138; *NYTM* 9/29/1968.

39. Charles Kinney, quoted in Watts, *Amiri Baraka*, 307.

40. *Time*, 4/26/1968; Allen, *Black Awakening*, 137–138.

41. Baraka, *Autobiography of LeRoi Jones*, 274–275; *NYT* 8/15/1968; *NYTM* 9/29/1968.

42. *NYT* 7/26/1968, 8/26/1968.

43. Woodard, *A Nation within a Nation*, 97, 112; Watts, *Amiri Baraka*, 358–359.

44. Williams, *First Black Captain*, 95–97.

45. *NYT* 3/2/1968, 2/14/1968; Williams, *First Black Captain*, 95–97.

46. Porambo, *No Cause for Indictment,* 76–77.

47. *NYT* 4/16/1968.

48. Porambo, *No Cause for Indictment,* 77.

49. *NYT* 7/26/1968.

50. *NYT* 11/5/1968, 11/8/1968.

51. *NYT* 12/18/1968, 12/20/1968.

52. *NYT* 12/17/1968.

53. *NYT* 12/21/1969.

54. *NYT* 12/10/1969, 12/18/1969.

55. *NYT* 12/17/1968, 12/18/1968, 4/23/1978.

56. *Report for Action,* 55.

57. *NN* 4/22/1969.

58. *NN* 6/19/1969.

59. *NN* 6/21/1969.

60. *NYT* 12/20/1969; *Time,*12/26/1969.

61. *SL* 7/23/1970 stated the maximum prison sentence for Addonizio as 1,280 years.

62. Nikki Giovanni, "Black Poems, Poseurs and Power," *Negro Digest,* June 1969, 30–31.

63. *NYT* 11/16/1969.

64. Amiri Baraka, *Raise Race Rays Raze: Essays since 1965* (New York: Random House, 1971), 98.

65. *Negro Digest,* January 1969, 4–9, 77–79.

66. *Negro Digest,* January 1969, 4–9, 77–79.

67. Watts, *Amiri Baraka,* 367; Woodard, *Nation within a Nation,* 118.

68. Allen, *Black Awakening,* 176; Harry J. Elam, Jr., *Taking It to the Streets: The Social Protest Theater of Luis Valdez and Amiri Baraka* (Ann Arbor: University of Michigan Press, 1997), 116.

69. *Los Angeles Times,* 5/14/1971; *NYT* 10/7/1970; Paul Mulshine, "Happy Kwanzaa," *Front Page Magazine,* 12/26/2002; Baraka, *Autobiography of LeRoi Jones,* 275–276; Watts, *Amiri Baraka,* 367.

70. Fred Barbaro, "Political Brokers," *Society,* September-October 1972, 42–55; *SL* 11/19/1969.

71. *SL* 11/6/1969; *NJAA* 11/8/1969.

72. *NYT* 11/15/1969, 11/16/1969; *SL* 11/9/1969–11/16/1969.

73. *SL* 11/16/1969.

74. *SL* 11/17/1969.

75. *SL* 11/9/1969, 11/19/1969.

76. Quoted in Woodard, *Nation within a Nation,* 147.

77. *Atlantic Monthly,* August 1969.

78. *SL* 11/17/1969.

79. By the UPI, in *NJAA* 5/9/1970, among other newspapers.

80. *NJAA* 5/2/1970.

81. *NJAA* 5/2/1970.

82. L. H. Whittemore, *Together: A Reporter's Journey into the New Black Politics* (New York: William Morrow, 1971), 99.

83. *NJAA* 5/9/1970.

84. Baraka, *Autobiography of LeRoi Jones*, 284.

85. *NJAA* 4/11/1970; Woodard, *A Nation within a Nation*, 144–148.

86. *VV* 4/16/1970, 4/30/1970.

87. Fred Barbaro, "Political Brokers," *Society*, September-October 1972, 50.

88. Ads in *NJAA* 4/25/1970, 5/9/1970.

89. *NJAA* 5/9/1970.

90. Whittemore, *Together*, 106, 109; *NJAA* 6/20/1970.

91. *NJAA* 6/6/1970.

92. *SL* 5/3/1970, 6/14/1970.

93. Whittemore, *Together*, 198.

94. Whittemore, *Together*, 106–107; *NJAA* 6/6/1970.

95. Whittemore, *Together*, 198.

96. *NYT* 6/14/1970.

97. *NJAA* 6/20/1970.

98. *NJAA* 6/20/1970; Woodard, *A Nation within a Nation*, 153.

99. Baraka, *Autobiography of LeRoi Jones*, 287.

100. *New York* 7/20/1970; *NJAA* 6/20/1970; Baraka, *Autobiography of LeRoi Jones*, 287.

101. *New York* 7/20/1970.

102. *NYT* 7/7/1970, 7/23/1970, 4/23/1978; Michael Dorman, *Payoff: The Role of Organized Crime in American Politics* (New York: David McKay, 1972), 52–67.

103. Dorman, *Payoff*, 55–63.

104. *SL* 9/23/1970.

105. Anonymous worker, quoted in Robert Curvin, "Black Power in City Hall," *Society*, September-October 1972, 57.

106. *New York*, 7/20/1970; *SL* 11/13/1970, 7/11/1971.

107. *NYT* 9/20/1970.

108. *NW* 8/3/1970.

109. *NYT* 9/20/1970; *SL* 12/12/1970.

110. *SL* 12/12/1970.

111. *SL* 12/12/1970.

112. *SL* 4/2/1971; *NN* 4/4/1971.

113. *NN* 4/2/197, 4/4/1971; *SL* 4/2/197, 4/3/1971, 4/6/1971.

114. *NN* 4/2/197, 4/4/1971; *SL* 4/2/197, 4/3/1971, 4/6/1971.

115. *SL* 4/6/1971.

116. *NN* 4/4/1971.

117. *NN* 4/2/1971, 4/5/1971.

118. *SL* 4/6/1971.

119. *SL* 4/1/1971, 4/3/1971, 4/4/1971; *NN* 4/2/1971.

120. *NN* 4/2/1971, 4/4/1971; Steve Golin, *The Newark Teacher Strikes: Hopes on the Line* (New Brunswick, NJ: Rutgers University Press, 2002).

121. Quoted in Golin, *Newark Teacher Strikes*, 124.

122. Golin, *Newark Teacher Strikes*, 124–126.

123. Frank A. Fiorito, *The Anatomy of a Strike* (Newark: Teachers Union, 1970), 92–96; Golin, *Newark Teacher Strikes*, 80–81, 110–114.

124. Golin, *Newark Teacher Strikes*, 154–155; *NYT* 8/15/1971.

125. Golin, *Newark Teacher Strikes*, 156–166.

126. Golin, *Newark Teacher Strikes*, 146–147; *NN* 4/6/1971.

127. *SL* 4/7/1971; *NN* 4/7/1971.

128. *SL* 4/7/1971; *NN* 4/7/1971.

129. *SL* 4/7/1971; *NN* 4/7/1971.

130. Golin, *Newark Teacher Strikes*, 174.

131. *SL* 4/7/1971, 4/8/1971; *NN* 4/7/1971

132. *SL* 4/8/1971; *NN* 4/8/1971.

133. *SL* 4/8/1971; Golin, *Newark Teacher Strikes*, 173.

134. *NN* 4/8/1971; *NYT* 4/11/1971.

135. *NN* 4/8/1971.

136. *SL* 4/9/1971.

137. *NYT* 7/15/1970, 9/20/1970; *NYTM* 7/25/1971; *SL* 8/27/2000.

138. *SL* 4/9/1971.

139. *SL* 4/11/1971.

140. *NN* 4/12/1971.

141. *NN* 4/11/1971.

142. *NN* 4/12/1971; Heninberg in *NN* 4/6/1971; James in *NN* 4/7/1971; Redden's entire statement at *NYT* 4/13/1971.

143. *NYT* 4/19/1971; Golin, *Newark Teacher Strikes*, 176–178.

144. Woodard, *A Nation within a Nation*, 230–231; Watts, *Amiri Baraka*, 371.

145. *NYT* 11/22/1972, 11/28/1972; Woodard, *A Nation within a Nation*, 232–239.

146. *NYT* 11/29/1972.

147. *NYT* 12/1/1972.

148. Watts, *Amiri Baraka*, 372.

149. *NYT* 5/15/1974.

150. *NYT* 10/17/1973, 10/23/1973, 3/7/1974; 4/26/1974, 7/6/1974.

151. *NYT* 7/6/1974.

152. *NYT* 4/12/1971.

153. Quoted in Robert Curvin, "The Persistent Minority: The Black Political Experience in Newark" (PhD diss., Princeton University, 1975), 1.

154. *NYT* 9/4/1974; Michael Fernandez, "The Puerto Ricans in New Jersey," in *New Jersey Ethnic Experience*, 372.

155. Arthur M. Louis, "The Worst American City," *Harper's*, January 1975, 67–71.

CHAPTER 8 — SHARPE CHANGE

1. *NYT* 10/31/1981.

2. Wilbur C. Rich, *Black Mayors and School Politics: The Failure of Reform in Detroit, Gary, and Newark* (New York: Garland Publishing, 1996), 101.

3. *NYT* 10/31/1981; *NYT* 10/2/1983; Winters, *Newark: An Assessment*, 47–48; Willa Johnson, "Illusions of Power: Gibson's Impact upon Unemployment Conditions in Newark, 1970–1974" (PhD. diss., Rutgers University, 1978), 137–138.

4. *SL* 11/11/1973; *NYT* 11/12/1973.

5. Winters, *Newark: An Assessment*, 3–6, 363; St. Lucy's Community Relations Committee, "Columbus Homes: The Case for the People" (pamphlet in NPL files, 1973).

6. Winters, *Newark: An Assessment*, 3–6, 363.

7. Golin, *Newark Teacher Strikes*, 223–224.

8. *NYT* 1/29/1971.

9. Winters, *Newark: An Assessment*, 6–11.

10. Winters, *Newark: An Assessment*, 6–11.

11. *New Jersey Monthly*, January 1979, 52, 81.

12. *NYT* 2/22/1976.

13. Guyot, "Newark: Crime and Politics in a Declining City," 78.

14. Guyot, "Newark: Crime and Politics in a Declining City," 88–90.

15. *New Jersey Monthly*, January 1979, 91.

16. Johnson, "Illusions of Power," 149–150; *NYT* 5/3/1978, 5/10/1978.

17. *NYTM* 10/2/1983; *NYT* 8/21/1983, 1/20/1985.

18. *NYT* 10/31/1981.

19. *NYT* 3/7/1981, 3/13/1981.

20. *NYT* 10/31/1981, 5/9/1982.

21. Unity Movement's William Smith, quoted in Johnson, "Illusions of Power," 146.

22. Quoted in Johnson, "Illusions of Power," 148.

23. *NYT* 3/14/1982.

24. *NYT* 10/31/1981.

25. *NYT* 10/31/1981.

26. *NYT* 5/9/1982.

27. *NYT* 6/11/1982.

28. *NN* morgue file, see Sharpe James.

29. *NYTM* 10/2/1983.

30. Rich, *Black Mayors and School Politics*, 122.

31. Rich, *Black Mayors and School Politics*, 114–122; *SL* 8/18/1985.

32. *NYT* 6/23/1985.

33. All quotes from *NYTM* 10/2/1983.

34. *NYT* 3/1/1989, 2/18/1996.

35. *NYT* 7/22/1984.

36. *NYT* 4/26/1986.

37. *NYT* 5/15/1986; *NJAA* 5/24/1986.

38. *NYT* 5/9/1986.

39. *NYT* 5/15/1986, 5/18/1986; *NJAA* 5/24/1986.

40. *NJAA* 5/24/1986.

41. *NYT* 5/18/1986; *NJAA* 5/24/1986.

42. *SL* 7/2/1986.

43. *SL* 7/2/1986; *NJAA* 7/12/1986.

44. *NJAA* 7/12/1986; *NYT* 7/2/1986.

45. Tom Dunkel, "Sharpe James's Possible Dream," *New Jersey Monthly*, February 1987, 46–49, 130–131.

46. Dunkel, "Sharpe James's Possible Dream," 50.

47. Dunkel, "Sharpe James's Possible Dream," 46.

48. *NYT* 9/20/1986.

49. *NYT* 10/6/1986.

50. *NYT* 8/17/1986, 9/21/1986; *SL* 12/17/2004; Marc Holzer, Elizabeth Strom, Lois Redman-Simmons, and Tony Carrizales, *Reinventing Newark: Visions of the City from the Twentieth Century* (Newark: National Center for Public Productivity, 2005), 90–91.

51. *NYT* 8/17/1986, 9/21/1986; *SL* 12/17/2004; Holzer et al., *Reinventing Newark*, 90–91.

52. *NYT* 8/17/1986.

53. *NYT* 8/17/1986, 9/29/1989.

54. *NYT* 8/17/1986.

55. *SL* 12/17/2004.

56. Gordon Bishop, *Greater Newark: A Microcosm of America* (Chatsworth, CA: Windsor Publications, 1989), 187.

57. Dunkel, "Sharpe James's Possible Dream," 46–49; *NYT* 5/18/1986, 12/28/1986, 12/28/1988, 5/4/1990.

58. *NYT* 12/28/1986, 1/21/1987, 12/28/1988, 5/4/1990, 1/19/1991; Rich, *Black Mayors and School Politics*, 121.

59. Robert Brown, quoted in *NYT* 11/13/1992.

60. *NYT* 3/19/1989, 1/18/1990, 11/13/1992; *USA Today,* 9/9/1992.

61. *NYT* 8/31/1992.

62. Helen M. Stummer, "Ordinary Miseries," *Society*, March-April 1987, 83; United Community Corporation, "Brick City Blues: Demographic Changes in Newark, 1970 to 1990" (UCC, 1997).

63. *NYT* 4/8/1991.

64. *The Record*, 10/29/1989; *SL* 12/27/2004.

65. *NYT* 9/29/1989, *The Record*, 10/29/1989; *SL* 12/27/2004.

66. *The Record*, 6/1/1990, 6/30/1990, 7/3/1990; *SL* 12/27/2004.

67. *NYT* 11/19/1995, 5/28/2000; *SL* 12/27/2004.

68. Warren Craig, "The Council Cashes In," *New Jersey Reporter*, July-August 1987, 8–13.

69. *SL* 5/11/1994; *NYT* 3/29/1995.

70. *The Record*, 2/24/1994.

71. *NYT* 5/15/1986, 5/8/1994; *Time*, 7/10/1995.

72. *SL* 5/7/1994–5/11/1994; *NYT* 5/8/1994, 5/11/1994.

73. *NYT* 4/8/1991, 6/18/1991, 3/7/1994.

74. *SL* 12/22/1992; *NYT* 4/4/1993.

75. *NYT* 5/8/1994, 5/11/1994; *SL* 5/11/1994.

76. *SL* 5/11/1994.

77. *NN* 5/11/1966; *NYT* 9/28/1995.

78. *The Record*, 7/16/2000; *SL* 2/4/2007.

79. *SL* 4/7/1971; *NN* 4/7/1971.

80. *The Record*, 8/20/1986; *NYT* 4/9/1987.

81· *The Record*, 9/9/1994, 9/29/1994.

82. Garrett was never charged with a crime. In 1999, he was elected to the Newark Athletic Hall of Fame, and West Side High School named its gym after Garrett, an alumni.

83. *NYT* 2/22/1995, 6/2/1995; *Time*, 7/10/1995; *The Record*, 2/22/1995; *SL* 4/27/1997.

84. *The Record*, 3/29/1995.

85. *NYT* 2/17/1995, 3/29/1995; *The Record*, 2/22/1995–2/24/1995, 3/29/1995.

86. *NYT* 2/17/1995, 3/29/1995; *The Record*, 2/22/1995–2/24/1995, 3/29/1995.

87. *NYT* 3/29/1995, 11/11/1995; *The Record*, 3/29/1995.

88. *NYT* 3/29/1995; *The Record*, 2/24/1995, 3/29/1995.

89. *The Record*, 7/10/1994, 4/18/1995.

90. *NYT* 5/8/1994; *The Record*, 7/10/1994, 4/18/1995.

91. Quoted in Rich, *Black Mayors and School Politics*, 123.

92. *NYT* 11/10/1995–11/12/1995, 1/27/1996; *The Record*, 1/26/1996.

93. *NYT* 11/12/1995.

94. *The Record*, 11/14/1995; *NYT* 11/12/1995.

95. *The Record*, 1/26/1996.

96. *The Record*, 1/26/1996; *NYT* 1/27/1996.

97. *SL* 2/1/1996; *NYT* 11/29/1995; *Time*, 7/10/1995.

98. *NYT* 6/21/1996, 7/26/1996, 8/13/1996.

99. *NYT* 8/13/1996, 12/3/1996.

100. *SL* 1/29/1997.

101. *SL* 2/7/1997–2/9/1997, 3/25/1997; *NYT* 3/22/1997, 7/15/1997.

102. *SL* 7/13/1997.

103. *SL* 7/13/1997.

104. *NYT* 7/14/1997.

105. *NYT* 12/16/1993.

106. *NYT* 10/14/1997, 10/15/1997.

107. *NYT* 10/14/1997, 10/15/1997.

108. *NYT* 10/15/1997.

109. *The New Yorker*, 4/1/2002.

110. *NYT* 10/15/1997, 1/25/1998.

111. *NYT* 1/25/1998.

112. *SL* 7/2/1986.

113. *SL* 4/27/1997.

114. Donald Tucker, *SL* 4/27/1997.

115. *SL* 4/27/1997; 5/13/1998.

116. *SL* 5/3/1998.

117. *SL* 5/7/1998.

118. *SL* 5/13/1998.

CHAPTER 9 — A RENAISSANCE FOR THE REST OF US

1. *SL* 5/17/1998.

2. *SL* 5/17/1998.

3. *SL* 5/17/1998.

4. *SL* 12/29/1996, 1/23/1997.

5. *SL* 5/17/1998.

6. *NYT* 5/3/1998; *SL* 10/3/2000.

7. *SL* 10/3/2000.

8. *SL* 10/3/2000.

9. *NYT* 4/9/1973; *SL* 5/7/1998; *The Record*, 6/8/1998.

10. *NYT* 5/18/1988.

11. *The Record*, 8/31/1988.

12. *The Record*, 3/19/1989, 3/21/1989.

13. *NYT* 5/3/1998; *SL* 10/3/2000.

14. *SL* 10/3/2000.

15. *SL* 6/7/1998.

16. *The Record*, 6/8/1998.

17. *NYT* 5/3/1998.

18. *The Record*, 6/8/1998.

19. *SL* 5/17/1998.

20. *New Jersey Monthly*, January 1979; *SL* 5/17/1998.

21. *SL* 5/17/1998.

22. *SL* 6/10/1998, 10/3/2000.

23. *SL* 5/20/2998, 5/21/1998, 6/7/1998, 6/10/9998.

24. *SL* 6/11/1998.

25. *SL* 6/17/1998, 6/19/1998.

26. *SL* 10/3/2000.

27. *SL* 8/13/1999, 8/17/1999, 10/3/2000.

28. *SL* 8/17/1999.

29. *SL* 8/17/1999, 8/23/1999/ 8/26/1999; *New York*, 4/22/2002.

30. *SL* 10/3/2000.

31. *Time*, 5/22/2000.

32. *SL* 10/3/2000.

33. *SL* 10/3/2000.

34. Unless otherwise noted, the quotes and account of this day come from an interview with Arthur Stern, summer of 2007.

35. Per Stern interview; also *NYT* 1/21/2001.

36. *SL* 4/8/1998; *NYT* 7/5/1998.

37. *NYT* 1/21/2001.

38. *NYT* 7/5/1998, 1/21/2001.

39. *SL* 12/4/2001.

40. *NYT* 5/4/2000.

41. *SL* 9/2/1999.

42. *SL* 9/23/2007.

43. *SL* 4/25/1999; *NYT* 5/13/2001; Navdeep Mathu, "Revitalization: Newark's Tale of Two Cities," *New Jersey Reporter*, April-May 2002.

44. *NYT* 5/13/2001.

45. *SL* 10/3/2000.

46. *SL* 2/22/2001.

47. *SL* 1/9/2001, 4/18/2002.

48. *SL* 1/9/2002.

49. *SL* 1/9/2002.

50. *SL* 1/22/2002.

51. *SL* 1/23/2002; *NYT* 1/23/2002.

52. Shakti Bhatt and Mark J. Magyar, "The Battle for Newark," *New Jersey Reporter*, April-May 2002, 20.

53. James E. McGreevey, *The Confession* (New York: Regan, 2006), 166–168.

54. *SL* 1/22/2002.

55. *SL* 5/8/2002.

56. Marshall Curry, *Street Fight* (Marshall Curry Productions, 2005).

57. *SL* 6/15/1999, 5/8/2002.

58. *SL* 4/18/2002.

59. Bhatt and Magyar, "Battle for Newark," 21.

60. Bhatt and Magyar, "Battle for Newark," 22.

61. *New York*, 4/22/2002.

62. *New York*, 4/22/2002.

63. *NYT* 4/17/2002.

64. *NYT* 4/17/2002.

65. Bhatt and Magyar, "The Battle for Newark," in *New Jersey Reporter*, 19.

66. *NYT* 5/6/2002.

67. *SL* 5/5/2002.

68. *SL* 5/16/2002.

69. McGreevey, *Confession*, 211.

70. *NYT* 5/9/2002.

71. *SL* 5/16/2002.

72. *NYT* 5/12/2002.

73. *NYT* 5/16/2002.

74. *SL* 5/16/2002.

75. *NYT* 5/16/2002.

76. *SL* 1/23/2004.

77. *SL* 2/25/2004, 5/9/2004.

78. *SL* 5/6/2004.

79. *SL* 5/19/2002.

80. *SL* 2/23/2003.

81. *SL* 4/17/2003, 5/6/2004.

82. *SL* 5/6/2004.

83. *SL* 7/16/2005.

84. *Inc.*, March 2004; *USA Today*, 6/24/2004.

85. *SL* 12/4/2005.

86. *SL* 7/31/2005.

87. *SL* 12/18/2006.

88. *NYT* 2/10/2006.

89. *SL* 3/3/2006.

90. *SL* 3/3/2006, 3/8/2006, 3/10/2006, 4/30/2006.

91. *NYT* 3/17/2006; *SL* 3/17/2006.

92. *SL* 3/17/2006.

93. Sharpe James press release, 3/27/2006.

94. *SL* 4/7/2006.

95. *SL* 5/10/2006.

96. *SL* 6/14/2006.

97. *SL* 4/21/1996, 5/7/2000, 5/8/2002, 5/16/2002.

98. *SL* 6/14/2006, 7/3/2006.

99. *SL* 6/3/2006, 6/11/2006.

100. *SL* 6/11/2006.

CHAPTER 10 — STAND UP

1. *SL* 7/4/2006, 4/10/2007; *Esquire*, October 2006.

2. *SL* 7/4/2006.

3. Per interviews with Cory Booker, *New Jersey Monthly*, February 2007; NewYorker.com, May 7, 2007.

4. *NYT* 2/8/2007.

5. *SL* 8/29/2007; *New Jersey Monthly*, February 2007.

6. *SL* 10/15/2006; NewYorker.com, May 7, 2007.

7. *NYT* 6/15/2006, 10/19/2006.

8. *SL* 7/1/2006; *NYT* 9/7/2006, 10/8/2006.

9. *SL* 6/18/2006, 7/23/2006.

10. *SL* 6/21/2007.

11. *SL* 7/2/2006; *NYT* 7/2/2006.

12. *SL* 7/2/2006; *NYT* 7/2/2006.

13. *SL* 11/26/2006; *Esquire*, October 2006; *Daily News*, 8/21/2007.

14. *SL* 7/4/2006.

15. *SL* 7/4/2006.

16. *SL* 7/4/2006, 2/8/2007.

17. *SL* 10/8/2006; *NYT* 9/7/2006, 5/27/2007.

18. *SL* 8/29/2007.

19. *SL* 9/10/2006, 10/8/2006.

20. *NYT* 2/25/2007, 3/8/2007.

21. *NYT* 10/3/2007; *SL* 1/2/2007.

22. *NYT* 10/3/2007.

23. *NYT* 9/7/2006.

24. *SL* 12/31/2007, 4/10/2007, 8/29/2007.

25. *SL* 7/7/2007; *NYT* 3/8/2007.

26. *SL* 6/21/2007.

27. *NYT* 8/14/2007.

28. *SL* 8/6/2007–8/8/2007, 8/9/2007.

29. *SL* 8/7/2007–8/9/2007; *NYT* 8/6/2007.

30. *NYT* 8/7/2007, 8/14/2007; *SL* 8/8/2007, 8/9/2007.

31. *NYT* 8/7/2007.

32. *NYT* 8/7/2007.

33. *SL* 8/8/2007.

34. *SL* 8/8/2007.

35. *SL* 8/10/2007, 8/22/2007; *NYT* 8/21/2007.

36. *NYT* 8/12/2007; *SL* 8/12/2007.

37. *SL* 8/12/2007.

38. *NYT* 5/27/2007, 8/14/2007.

39. *NYT* 8/14/2007; *SL* 8/8/2007, 8/11/2007.

40. *SL* 8/19/2007.

41. *SL* 8/19/2007, 8/20/2007.

42. *SL* 8/20/2007.

43. Hector Mendez, quoted in Mark DiIonno's column, *SL* 8/21/2007.

44. *SL* 9/3/2007; *Daily News*, 9/4/2007; the projections held up, and a lowest-ever 494 homicides were committed in New York City in 2007.

45. *SL* 6/21/2006.

46. *SL* 12/4/2006.

47. *SL* 7/2/2006; *NYT* 7/2/2006.

48. *SL* 7/2/2006.

49. *SL* 8/20/2006, 7/15/2007.

50. *Esquire*, October 2006.

51. *SL* 6/9/2007.

52. *SL* 1/14/2007.

53. *SL* 4/10/2007.

54. *SL* 6/18/2007, 7/11/2007.

55. *SL* 7/14/2007, 7/15/2007; *NYT* 7/14/2007, 7/15/2007.

56. *SL* 7/14/2007.

57. *SL* 8/29/2007, 11/4/2007; *NYT* 6/28/2007.

58. *SL* 5/6/2007; *NYT* 5/6/2007.

59. *SL* 9/16/2007.

60. *SL* 7/11/2007, 8/22/2007, 8/23/2007; *NYT* 7/30/2006.

61. *The Record*, 10/26/2007; *NYT* 10/26/2007.

62. *SL* 10/26/2007.

63. *SL* 10/26/2007.

64. *SL* 10/15/2007, 10/24/2007, 11/21/2007; *NYT* 10/25/2007.

65. *SL* 7/20/2007.

66 .*SL* 10/24/2007—10/26/2007; Baraka quote overheard by author at event in June 2007 for fortieth anniversary of the Black and Puerto Rican Political Convention.

67. *SL* 9/2/2007.

68. *SL* 9/12/2007–9/14/2007, 9/23/2007–9/28/2007.

69. *SL* 7/11/2007, 9/28/2007, 10/4/2007, 12/8/2007, 12/13/2007, 12/19/2007.

70. *SL* 12/31/2007, 1/3/2008.

71. *The Record*, 11/21/2007; *SL* 12/29/2007.

72. The James trial received widespread news coverage, particularly from *SL*; the paper posted all of its James trial articles online at *http://blog.nj.com/ledgerarchives/sharpe_james*. I also consulted *NYT* and *The Record*.

73. *SL* 4/17/2008.

74. *SL* 2/16/2008.

75. *SL* 4/8/2008.

SELECTED BIBLIOGRAPHY

Allen, Robert L. *Black Awakening in Capitalist America: An Analytic History*. New York: Anchor Books, 1969.

Ard, Patricia M., and Michael Aaron Rockland. *The Jews of New Jersey: A Pictorial History*. New Brunswick, NJ: Rutgers University Press, 2002.

Ashby, William M. *Tales without Hate*. Newark: Newark Preservation and Landmarks Committee; Metuchen, NJ: Upland Press, 1996.

Atkinson, Joseph. *The History of Newark*. Newark: William B. Guild, 1878.

Baraka, Amiri. *The Autobiography of LeRoi Jones*. New York: Freundlich Books, 1984.

Barber, John W. *Historical Collections of New Jersey: Past and Present*. New York: Published by Subscription, 1868.

Becker, Ronald L. "History of the Jewish Community in Newark, New Jersey," part of *Greater Newark's Jewish Legacy*, a 1995 Newark Public Library exhibit.

Bloomberg, Susan Eleanor Hirsch. "Industrialization and Skilled Workers: Newark, 1826 to 1860." PhD diss., University of Michigan, 1974.

Calder, Isabel MacBeath. *The New Haven Colony*. Hamden, CT: Archon Books, 1970.

Carr, William H.A. *From Three Cents a Week: The Story of the Prudential Insurance Company of America*. Englewood Cliffs, NJ: Prentice-Hall, 1975.

Central Planning Board. *The Master Plan for the Physical Development of the City of Newark, N.J.* Newark: Central Planning Board, 1947.

Cohen, David Steven, ed. *America, The Dream of My Life: Selections from the Federal Writers' Project's New Jersey Ethnic Survey*. New Brunswick, NJ: Rutgers University Press, 1990.

Craster, Charles V. "Slum Clearance: The Newark Plan." *American Journal of Public Health and the Nation's Health* (September 1944).

Churchill, Charles Wesley. *The Italians of Newark: A Community Study*. New York: Arno Press, 1975.

Cunningham, John T. *Newark*. Newark: New Jersey Historical Society, 1966.

Curvin, Robert. "The Persistent Minority: The Black Political Experience in Newark." PhD diss., Princeton University, 1975.

Dorman, Michael. *Payoff: The Role of Organized Crime in American Politics*. New York: David McKay, 1972.

Dunkel, Tom. "Sharpe James's Possible Dream." *New Jersey Monthly* (February 1987).

Faulkner, Audrey Olsen, comp. *When I Was Comin' Up: An Oral History of Aged Blacks*. Hamden, CT: Archon Books, 1982.

"Final Report of the Charter Commission of the City of Newark." Newark: Charter Commission, 1953.

Folsom, Edward F., ed. *The Municipalities of Essex County, 1666–1924*. New York: Lewis Historical Publishing Co., 1925.

Galishoff, Stuart. *Newark: The Nation's Unhealthiest City, 1832–1895*. New Brunswick, NJ: Rutgers University Press, 1975.

———. *Safeguarding the Public Health: Newark, 1895–1918*. Westport, CT: Greenwood Press, 1975.

Gillette, William. *Jersey Blue: Civil War Politics in New Jersey, 1854–1865*. New Brunswick, NJ: Rutgers University Press, 1995.

Golin, Steve. *The Newark Teacher Strikes: Hopes on the Line*. New Brunswick, NJ: Rutgers University Press, 2002.

Green, Howard L., ed. *Words That Make New Jersey History*. New Brunswick, NJ: Rivergate Books, 2006.

Guyot, Dorothy H. "Newark: Crime and Politics in a Declining City." In *Crime in City Politics*, ed. Anne Heinz, Herbert Jacob, and Robert L. Lineberry. New York: Longman, 1983.

Hayden, Tom. *Rebellion in Newark: Official Violence and Ghetto Response*. New York: Vintage Books, 1967.

Henri, Florette. *Black Migration: Movement North, 1900–1920*. New York: Anchor Books, 1976.

Holzer, Marc. *Reinventing Newark: Visions of the City from the Twentieth Century*. Newark: National Center for Public Productivity, 2005.

Immerso, Michael. *Newark's Little Italy: The Vanished First Ward*. New Brunswick, NJ: Rutgers University Press, 1997.

Jackson, Kenneth T. *Crabgrass Frontier: The Suburbanization of the United States*. New York: Oxford University Press, 1987.

Jackson, Kenneth T., and Barbara B. Jackson. "The Black Experience in Newark: The Growth of the Ghetto, 1870–1970." In *New Jersey since 1860*, ed. William C. Wright. Trenton: New Jersey Historical Commission, 1972.

Kaplan, Harold. *Urban Renewal Politics: Slum Clearance in Newark*. New York: Columbia University Press, 1963.

Karschner, Terry, comp. *Industrial Newark*. Trenton: Fourteenth Annual Conference of the Society for Industrial Archaeology, 1985.

Kingdon, Frank. *John Cotton Dana: A Life*. Newark: Newark Public Library and Museum, 1940.

Knapp, Charles Merriam. "New Jersey Politics during the Period of the Civil War and Reconstruction." PhD diss., Columbia University, 1924.

Kukla, Barbara J. *Swing City: Newark Nightlife, 1925–1950*. New Brunswick, NJ: Rutgers University Press, 1991.

Lamb, Martha. "Sketch of Newark." *Harper's New Monthly Magazine* (October 1876).

Lampros, Angelique. *Remembering Newark's Greeks: An American Odyssey*. Virginia Beach: Donning Company Publishers, 2006.

Levitus, David. "An Anatomy of Urban Renewal in Newark, N.J., 1933–1967: How Patronage Politics, Planning Policy, and a Powerbroker Shaped a City." Master's thesis, New York University, 2005.

Louis, Arthur M. "The Worst American City." *Harper's* (January 1975).

Lucas, Curtis. *Third Ward Newark*. Chicago: Ziff-Davis Publishing Co., 1946.

"Newark Industrial Exhibition: Report and Catalogue of the First Exhibition of Newark Industries, Exclusively 1872." Newark: Holbrook's Steam Printery, 1882.

Overmyer, James. *Effa Manley and the Newark Eagles*. Metuchen, NJ: Scarecrow Press, 1993.

Popper, Samuel H. "Newark, New Jersey, 1870–1910: Chapters in the Evolution of an American Metropolis." PhD diss., New York University, 1952.

Porambo, Ronald. *No Cause for Indictment*. Brooklyn, NY: Melville House, 2006.

Price, Clement A. "The Beleaguered City as Promised Land: Blacks in Newark, 1917–1947." In *Urban New Jersey since 1870*, edited by William C. Wright. Trenton: New Jersey Historical Commission, 1975.

———. "The Struggle to Desegregate Newark: Black Middle Class Militancy in New Jersey, 1932–1947." *New Jersey History* 3/4 (1981).

———, ed. *Freedom Not Far Distant: A Documentary of Afro-Americans in New Jersey*. Newark: New Jersey Historical Society, 1980.

Price, Willard D. "The Ironbound District: A Study of a District in Newark, N.J." Newark: Neighborhood House, 1912.

Ralph, Raymond Michael. "From Village to Industrial City: The Urbanization of Newark, New Jersey, 1830–1860." PhD diss., New York University, 1978.

Report for Action: Governor's Select Commission on Civil Disorder. State of New Jersey, 1968.

Report of the National Advisory Commission on Civil Disorders. New York: Bantam Books, 1968.

"Report on the Social Evil Conditions of Newark, New Jersey, 1913–1914." Document available at Rutgers-Newark Dana Library.

Rich, Wilbur C. *Black Mayors and School Politics: The Failure of Reform in Detroit, Gary, and Newark.* New York: Garland Publishing, 1996.

Ricord, Frederick W. *Biographical and Genealogical History of the City of Newark and Essex County, New Jersey.* New York: Lewis Publishing Co., 1898.

Rindler, Edward P. "The Migration from the New Haven Colony to Newark, East New Jersey." PhD diss., University of Pennsylvania, 1977.

Shaw, William H. *History of Essex and Hudson Counties, New Jersey.* Philadelphia: Everts & Peck, 1884.

Siegel, Alan A. *For the Glory of the Union.* Cranbury, NJ: Fairleigh Dickinson University Press/Associated University Presses, 1984.

Sinclair, Donald A. *A Bibliography: The Civil War and New Jersey.* New Brunswick, NJ: Friends of Rutgers University Library, 1968.

Smith, Charles Perrin. *New Jersey Political Reminiscences, 1828–1882.* New Brunswick, NJ: Rutgers University Press, 1965.

Stellhorn, Paul Anthony. "Depression and Decline, Newark, New Jersey: 1929–1941." PhD diss., Rutgers University, 1982.

Sternlieb, George. *The Tenement Landlord.* New Brunswick, NJ: Rutgers University Press, 1966.

Stuart, Mark A. *Gangster #2: Longy Zwillman, the Man Who Invented Organized Crime.* Secaucus, NJ: Lyle Stuart, 1985.

Urquhart, Frank J. *A History of the City of Newark, New Jersey: Embracing Nearly Two and a Half Centuries, 1666–1913.* New York: Lewis Historical Publishing Co., 1913.

Veit, Richard F. *The Old Canals of New Jersey: A Historical Geography.* Little Falls, NJ: New Jersey Geographical Press, 1963.

Watts, Jerry Gafio. *Amiri Baraka: The Politics and Art of a Black Intellectual.* New York: New York University Press, 2001.

Whittemore, L. H. *Together: A Reporter's Journey into the New Black Politics.* New York: William Morrow, 1971.

Williams, Edward D. *The First Black Captain.* New York: Vantage Press, 1974.

Winters, Stanley B., ed. *Newark: An Assessment, 1967–1977.* Newark: New Jersey Institute of Technology, 1979.

Woodard, Komozi. *A Nation within a Nation: Amiri Baraka (LeRoi Jones) and Black Power Politics.* Chapel Hill: University of North Carolina Press, 1999.

Wright, William Cook. "Secession and Copperheadism in New Jersey during the American Civil War." Master's thesis, University of Delaware, 1965.

INDEX

Abbett, Leon, 74
abolitionist movement, 24, 45, 50
Abyssinian Baptist Church, 178
Academy Street, 20
Achter Col, 15
"An Act to Prevent Immigration of Negroes and Mullatoes" (1863), 53
Adams, John, 17, 19
Addonizio, Frank, 184
Addonizio, Hugh, 8, 88, 115, 122, 123, 132, 133, 138, 181–194; appointment of African Americans to administration, 158; attempts to downplay racial tensions, 145, 146; attempts to quell riots, 161; and building of New Jersey College of Medicine and Dentistry, 157, 158; community opinion of crookedness of, 158; control of welfare money and patronage positions, 192; creation/disbanding of gambling unit, 182; criminal trial, 192; early success, 146; ethnic support for, 4, 5, 146; extortion and, 184; fails to appoint qualified black candidate to Board of Education, 157; fighting subpoenas for financial records, 183, 184; graft and, 159; guilty verdict against, 193, 195; indicted for tax evasion, 184; indictment of, 7; invokes Fifth Amendment, 184; kickbacks and, 7, 112, 159, 184, 194; military service, 146; opposition to civilian review board, 156; and organized crime leaders, 159; refusal to accept Spina resignation, 183; refusal to resign, 185; requests state help in riots, 161; support from African Americans, 192
Adubato, Steve, 206, 219, 244, 245, 263
Aeriel, Natasha, 273, 274
Aeriel, Terrance, 273, 275
African American(s): Black Power Conference, 171–173; difficulties in gaining footholds in industry, 105; first appointments to government, 4, 5; glass ceilings in employment, 151; and Great Depression, 105; influx of, 128, 147, 148; lack of consensus on city's direction among, 212; lack of trust in police, 156; lynchings, 54; migration to Newark, 4, 147, 148; neighborhoods, 80, 135, 136, 149; prostitution and, 91; in public housing, 129; racism and, 149, 151, 152; replacement of white residents by, 154; school population, 140; segregated public services and, 149, 151, 152; singled out for unfair treatment, 155, 156; social life, 149, 150; support for mayors, 4, 5; in teachers union, 199; transition to city life for, 148, 149; voting registration, 188; in workforce, 105, 148
Alfaro, Alexander, 276
Ali, Muhammad, 173
Allen, Jesse, 207
Amador, Augusto, 240, 245, 246
American Civil Liberties Union (ACLU), 156
Aneses, Ramon, 190
Angelou, Maya, 245
Anheuser-Busch Company, 116

Meadowlands parcels, 108, 109; in relief
work, 107; rivalry with La Guardia, 107
Emancipation Proclamation (1863), 50, 52
employment: for African Americans, 154;
blue-collar, 114; colonial, 24, 25, 28, 29,
30; factory, 33 (*see also* manufacturing);
and Great Depression, 104, 105; in retail,
83; white-collar, 154
Englewood (New Jersey), 168
Essex County, 34, 76; election returns in,
57; secession votes in, 10, 47; taxes, 10
Essex County Courthouse, 85, 162
Essex County Parks Commission, 76, 128
Essex House, 115
Essex Trades Council, 94
Ewing, Leon, 165

Faiella, Alfred, 219, 232
Fairmount Avenue, 163
Fair Street, 41
Farley Avenue, 197
Farragut, David, 56
Feast of Saint Gerard, 120
Federation of Italian-American Societies
of Newark, 133
Felix Fuld Court homes, 129, 141
Ferguson, Nancy, 165
Ferry Street, 80
Fifteenth Avenue, 166
Fillmore, Millard, 43
Fireman's Insurance Company, 93
First Ward, 80, 99, 101, 112, 119, 120, 121, 123,
130, 131, 132, 134, 138, 139
Fitch, John, 25
Flegenheimer, Arthur. *See* Schultz, Dutch
Florio, Jim, 229
Fonseca, Pablo, 253, 267
Fontoura, Armando, 274
Ford, Gerald, 208
Forest Hill Terrace, 231
Fourteenth Avenue, 80
Fourteenth Ward Building & Loan
Association, 75
Franklin Savings Institution, 75
Frelinghuysen, Frederick, 61
Friendly Sisters, 81
Fuller, Edward, 45, 46, 47, 52, 53, 55, 56, 57,
58
Fulton, Robert, 25
Furr, William, 167, 168

Gallo, Mario, 184
gambling, 91, 98, 99, 111, 182, 207

Garden Spires, 246
Garrett, E. Wyman, 201, 203, 230–231
Garside Street, 120
Gateway Buildings, 215, 236, 249
Gazeteer of the State of New Jersey
(Gordon), 31
General Motors, 114
George Washington Carver School, 251
German immigrants, 36, 70, 71, 75; after
1848 revolutions, 35; neighborhoods, 79,
80; and Prohibition, 92
Geyer, Charles, 232
Gibson, Harold, 183, 197
Gibson, Kenneth, 6, 8, 88, 178, 189,
190–208; candidacy a national cause,
191; challenges to by Italian-majority
council, 196; dependence on federal
funding, 213, 214; erosion of voter
support for, 217; goal of bringing
efficiency to government, 195;
improvements made by, 215; loses
control of school board appointments,
219; patronage scandal, 216; qualified
support from citizens, 215; in runoff
election, 192; viewed as political
lightweight, 196
Gibson, Willie, 197, 198
Gillen, Charles, 93, 94
Ginsberg, Allen, 174, 175
Giuliano, Anthony, 180, 207
Giuseppe Verdi Society, 131
Glenn, Joseph, 133
Glen Ridge (New Jersey), 34, 77
Godinez, Rudolfo, 275, 276
Goldberg, Herbert, 131
Golden Gibson Girls, 190
Goldman, Lawrence, 238
Gonzalez, Carlos, 263
Gordon, Joe, 113
Gordon, Thomas, 31
governance: bloated agencies of, 7;
commission model, 89, 90, 92, 93, 94,
95, 96, 104, 106, 116, 117; corporation
model, 35; corruption in, 7; duplication
of services in, 10, 117; fiscal insolvency
in, 11; mayor-council system, 8, 117;
mismanagement in, 7; misuse of power
and, 8; oversight lacking, 117; patronage
jobs in, 7, 8; power of wealthy in, 7, 8;
"reciprocal noninterference" in, 107;
recommendation for changes in, 117;
reforms in, 90, 92, 116; town meeting
form of, 34. *See also* politics

Stockton, Richard, 44

Stockton, Robert, 44

Street Fight (documentary film), 259

Streisand, Barbra, 244

Students for a Democratic Society (SDS), 6, 179

Stuyvesant, Peter, 15, 16

Submarine Boat Corporation, 114

Summer Avenue, 121

Summit (New Jersey), 78

Sunday Call (newspaper), 67

Symphony Hall, 191, 202, 221

taxes: collection rates, 224; disappearance of base for, 34, 87, 104, 114; in pre-Revolutionary years, 16; property, 6; rates, 7, 37, 76, 114; reluctance of citizens to use for health reforms, 72; rising rates, 4; spending on public services, 37

Taylor, Edward, 155

teachers: move to suburbs, 213; salary issues, 219; strength of union, 219; strike by, 198–205, 230; unqualified, 213, 232

temperance societies, 90, 91

Temple B'nai Abraham, 80

Tepper, Jules, 109

Tetrault, Francis J., 78

theaters, 83, 108, 236; Blaney's Theatre, 83; Mosque Theater, 86; Newark Theatre, 83; opened on Sunday, 95; Orpheum Theater, 149; Proctor's Theatre, 83; Savoy Theater, 151; Waldmann's Opera House, 83

Third Ward, 97, 98, 101, 102, 103, 106, 135, 149, 151

Third Ward Political Club, 101

Thirteenth Amendment, 60

This Is Newark, 1966 (documentary film), 4

Thomas J. Walsh Homes, 137

Torricelli, Robert, 252

Tory Party, 60

Toto, Fred, 164

transportation, 68; air, 103, 107; auto, 82; canal, 29, 30, 31, 32; ferry, 13, 17, 19, 20; and flight to suburbs, 104; hub, 13; monopolies, 44; public, 82; railroad, 28, 31, 32, 41, 93; roads, 14, 17, 20, 29; subway, 106; trolley, 81, 82

treason, 52

Treat, Robert, 15, 16, 193, 212

Trelease, Edgar, 58

Trenton (New Jersey), 21, 32

Trenton State Prison, 102

Trinity Church, 20

tuberculosis, 72, 125

Tub of Blood tavern, 96, 97

Tucker, Donald, 245

Tuggolo, Vincent, 135

Turco, Louis, 198, 201, 207

Turner, Irvine, 117, 181, 191, 193, 229, 230; claims credit for keeping racial calm, 158; indictment of, 184; questionable motivations of, 158

Turner, J.M.W., 65

typhoid, 72, 73

Union City (New Jersey), 113

Union Democratic Club, 52

Union National Bank, 75

United Afro-American Association, 189

United Brothers, 178, 179, 180, 181, 186

United Community Corporation (UCC), 144, 145, 225

University Avenue, 31

Urban Brothers, 189

Urban Coalition, 205

Urban League, 95, 147, 152, 156, 172

urban renewal projects, 4, 119–141, 142–170; celebration of street life and, 138; citizen protests over, 131, 132, 133, 134; citizen rehabilitation in, 138, 139; contributes to suburban flight, 134; federal funding, 7; housing repair needed, 125; lack of private investment for, 126, 129, 130; and limited open space, 127; Model Cities program, 7; as "Negro removal," 136; pushed through by politicians, 132, 133; and shifting racial makeup of neighborhoods, 140; slum clearance, 126; street elimination/widening, 125, 126

U.S. Council of Mayors, 215

Vailsburg (New Jersey), 77, 85, 86, 146

Valentine Electric Company, 184, 193

Vallandigham, Clement, 52, 53, 56

Van Buren, Thomas B., 66

Vanderbeek, Jeff, 281

Vaughan, Sarah, 150

Velez-Lopez, Amilkar, 263

Verona (New Jersey), 10, 77

Vesuvius (restaurant), 131

Villani, Allen, 227

Villani, Marie, 227

Villani, Ralph, 115, 116, 122, 123, 132; appointment of Danzig by, 123, 124; and public housing projects, 130

Vittorio Castle (restaurant), 131

Volstead Act (1920), 92, 97

Voluntary Association of the People of Newark to Observe the Sabbath, 22